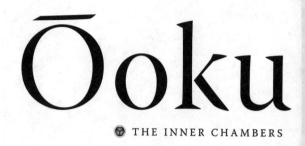

Ōoku

THE INNER CHAMBERS

by **Fumi Yoshinaga**

VOL. **18**

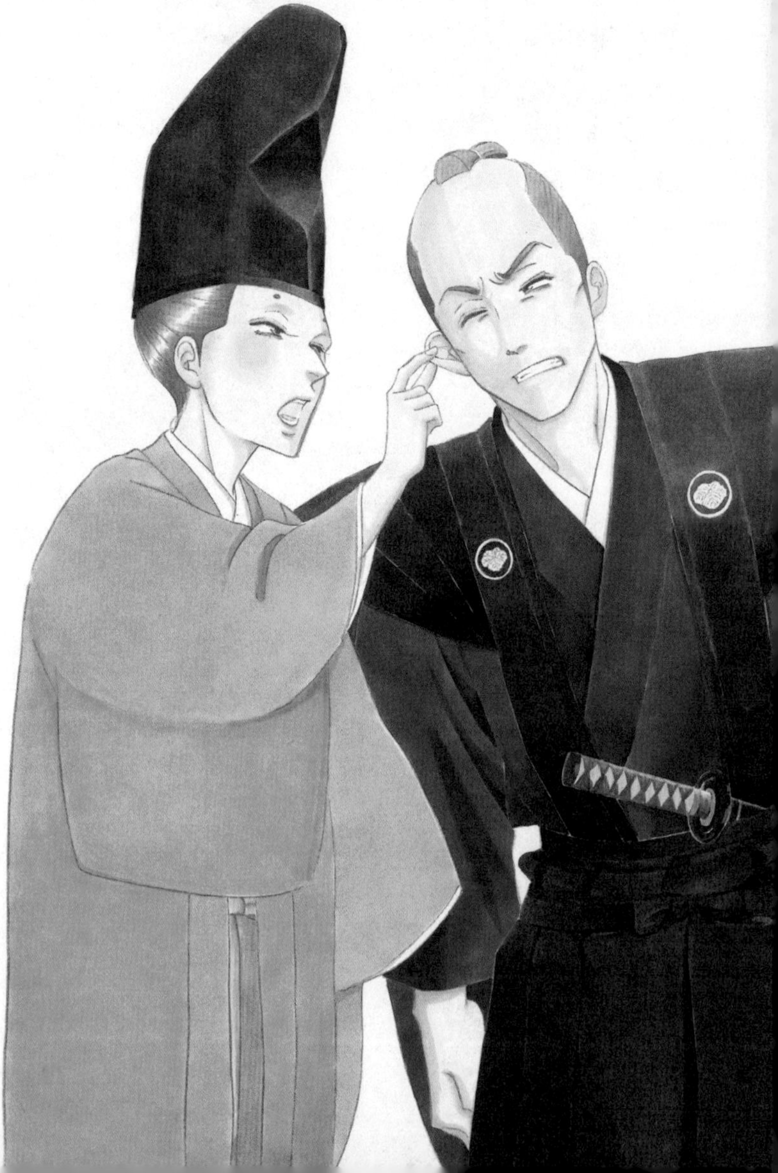

TABLE *of* CONTENTS

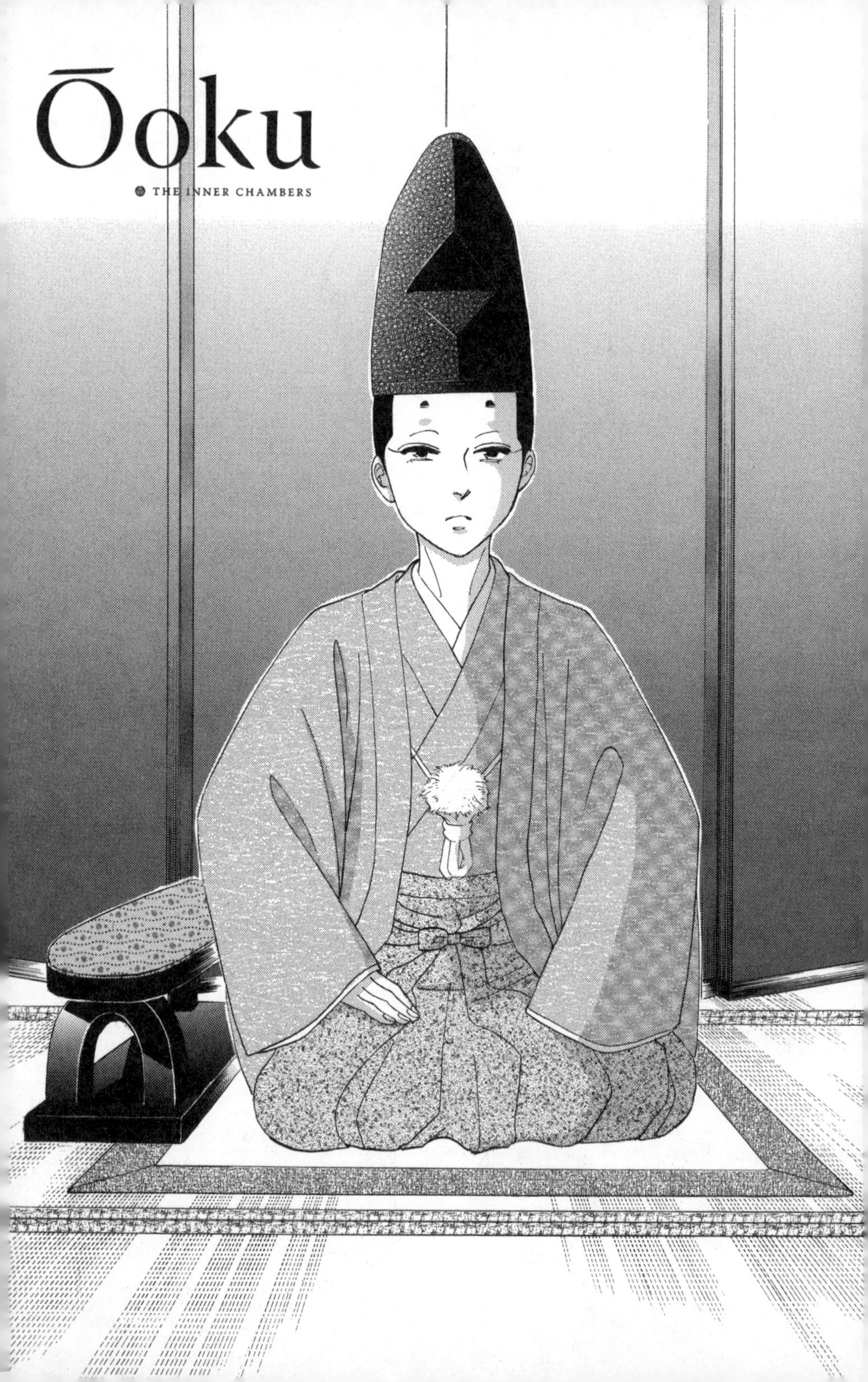
Ōoku
THE INNER CHAMBERS

THE INNER CHAMBERS

CAST *of* CHARACTERS

From the birth of the "inverse Inner Chambers" to its zenith, to eradicating the Redface Pox, and now to the end of Tokugawa rule...?

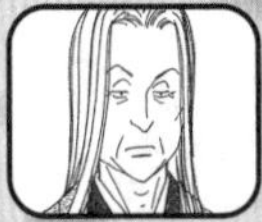

SENIOR CHAMBERLAIN

LADY KASUGA

↓

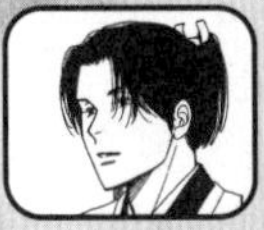

MADE-NOKOJI ARIKOTO (SIR O-MAN)

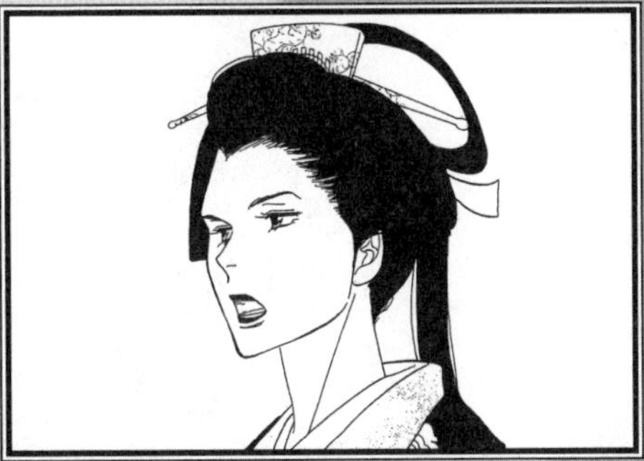

TOKUGAWA IEMITSU (III)

Impersonated her father, Iemitsu, at Lady Kasuga's urging after he died of the Redface Pox. Later became the first female shogun.

TOKUGAWA IETSUNA (IV)

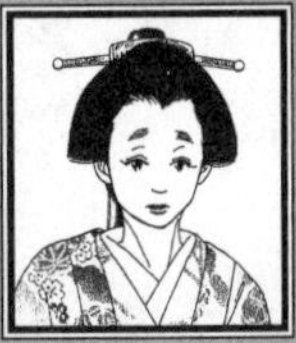

TOKUGAWA TSUNAYOSHI (V)

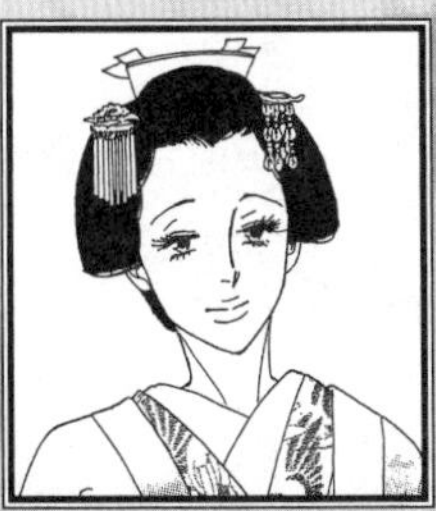

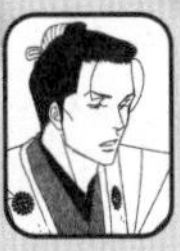

SENIOR CHAMBERLAIN

EMONNOSUKE

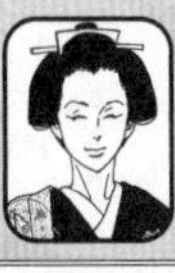

PRIVY COUNCILLOR

YANAGISAWA YOSHIYASU

TOKUGAWA TSUNASHIGE

TOKUGAWA IENOBU (VI)

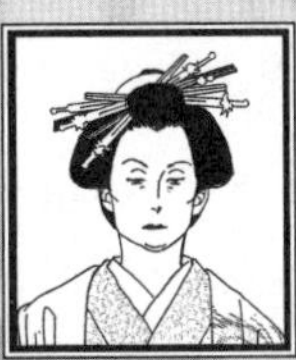

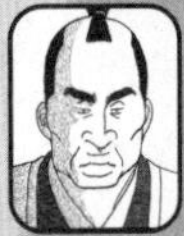

SENIOR CHAMBERLAIN

EJIMA

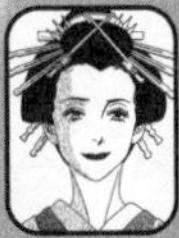

PRIVY COUNCILLOR

MANABE AKIFUSA

TOKUGAWA IETSUGU (VII)

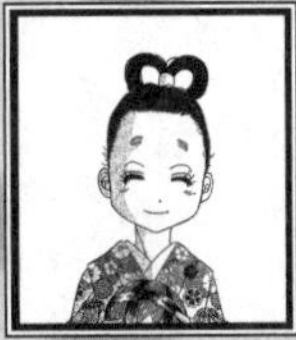

PRIVY COUNCILLOR

KANO HISAMICHI

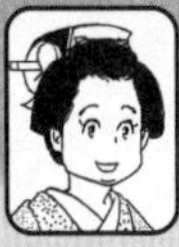

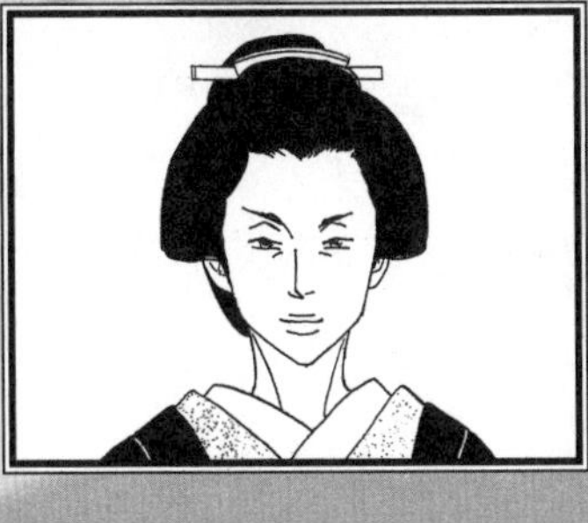

TOKUGAWA YOSHIMUNE (VIII)

Third daughter of Mitsusada, the second head of the Kii branch of the Tokugawa family. Acceded to domain lord and then, upon the death of Ietsugu, to shogun. Imposed and lived by a strict policy of austerity, dismissing large numbers of Inner Chambers courtiers and pursuing policies designed to increase income to the treasury.

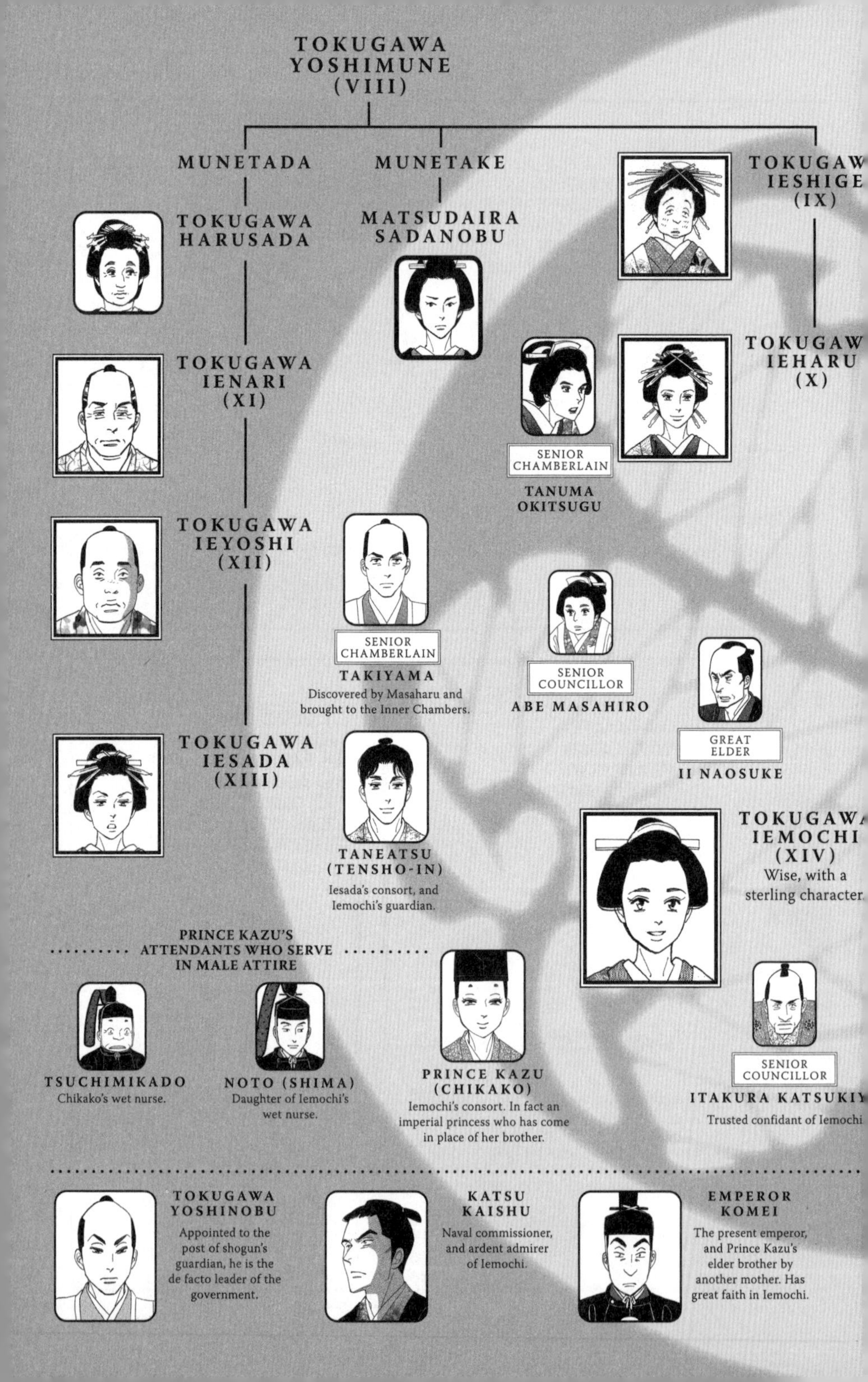
TOKUGAWA YOSHIMUNE (VIII)
MUNETADA
MUNETAKE
TOKUGAWA IESHIGE (IX)
TOKUGAWA HARUSADA
MATSUDAIRA SADANOBU
TOKUGAWA IEHARU (X)
TOKUGAWA IENARI (XI)
SENIOR CHAMBERLAIN
TANUMA OKITSUGU
TOKUGAWA IEYOSHI (XII)
SENIOR CHAMBERLAIN
TAKIYAMA
Discovered by Masaharu and brought to the Inner Chambers.
SENIOR COUNCILLOR
ABE MASAHIRO
GREAT ELDER
II NAOSUKE
TOKUGAWA IESADA (XIII)
TANEATSU (TENSHO-IN)
Iesada's consort, and Iemochi's guardian.
TOKUGAWA IEMOCHI (XIV)
Wise, with a sterling character.
PRINCE KAZU'S ATTENDANTS WHO SERVE IN MALE ATTIRE
TSUCHIMIKADO
Chikako's wet nurse.
NOTO (SHIMA)
Daughter of Iemochi's wet nurse.
PRINCE KAZU (CHIKAKO)
Iemochi's consort. In fact an imperial princess who has come in place of her brother.
SENIOR COUNCILLOR
ITAKURA KATSUKIY
Trusted confidant of Iemochi
TOKUGAWA YOSHINOBU
Appointed to the post of shogun's guardian, he is the de facto leader of the government.
KATSU KAISHU
Naval commissioner, and ardent admirer of Iemochi.
EMPEROR KOMEI
The present emperor, and Prince Kazu's elder brother by another mother. Has great faith in Iemochi.

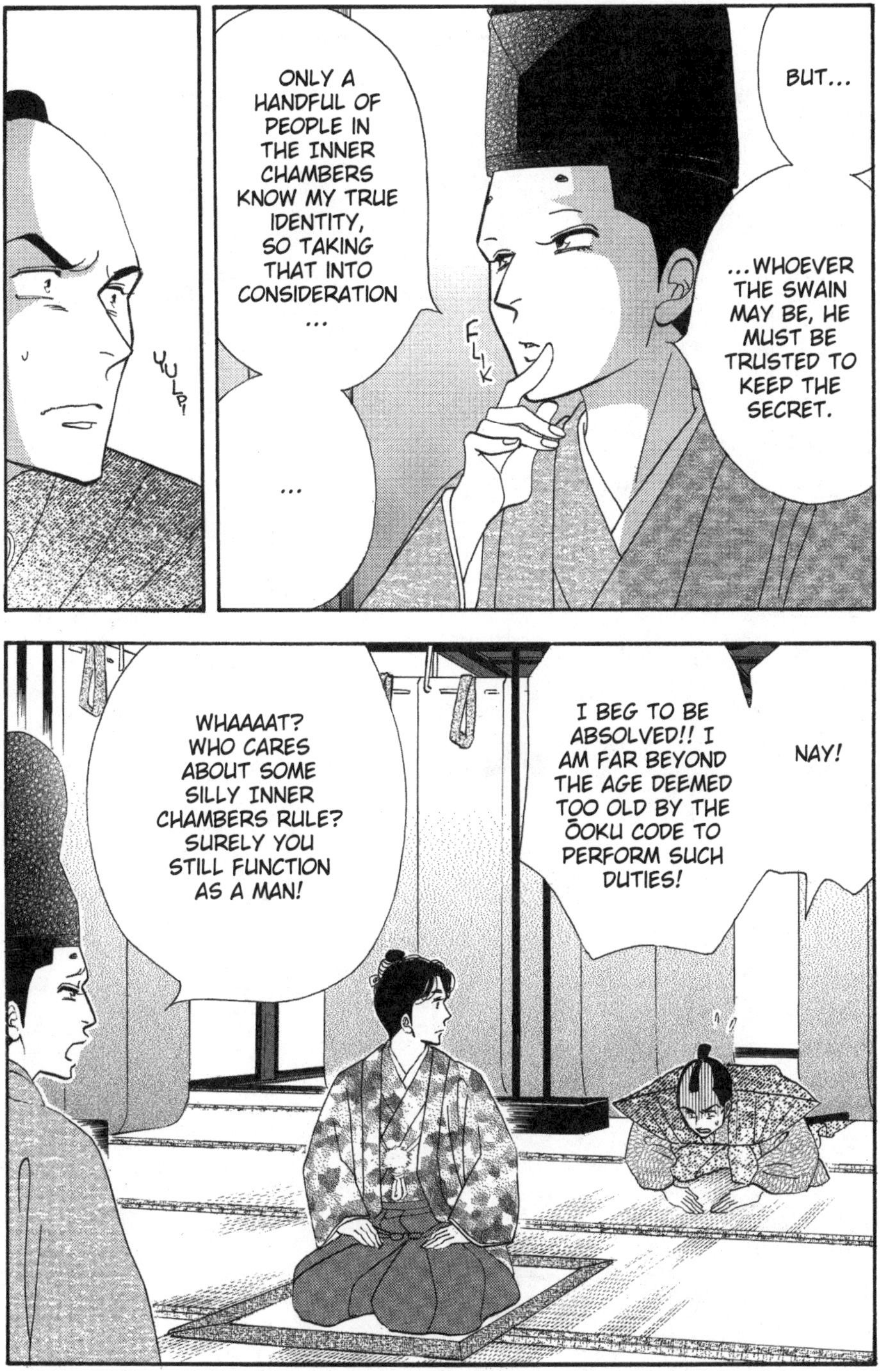

BUT...
...WHOEVER THE SWAIN MAY BE, HE MUST BE TRUSTED TO KEEP THE SECRET.
ONLY A HANDFUL OF PEOPLE IN THE INNER CHAMBERS KNOW MY TRUE IDENTITY, SO TAKING THAT INTO CONSIDERATION...
FLIK
...
YULP!
NAY!
I BEG TO BE ABSOLVED!! I AM FAR BEYOND THE AGE DEEMED TOO OLD BY THE ŌOKU CODE TO PERFORM SUCH DUTIES!
WHAAAAT? WHO CARES ABOUT SOME SILLY INNER CHAMBERS RULE? SURELY YOU STILL FUNCTION AS A MAN!

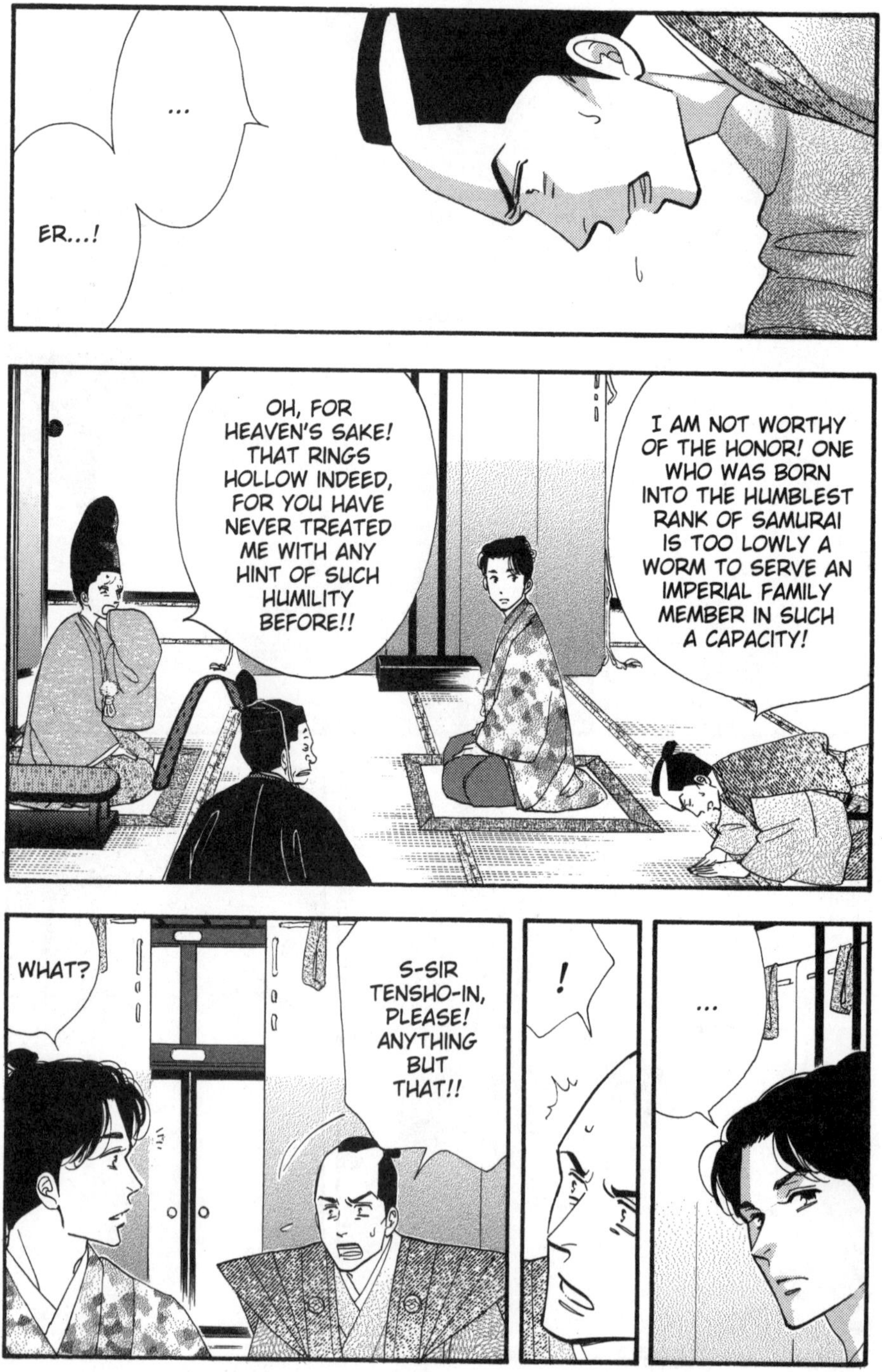
...
ER...!
I AM NOT WORTHY OF THE HONOR! ONE WHO WAS BORN INTO THE HUMBLEST RANK OF SAMURAI IS TOO LOWLY A WORM TO SERVE AN IMPERIAL FAMILY MEMBER IN SUCH A CAPACITY!
OH, FOR HEAVEN'S SAKE! THAT RINGS HOLLOW INDEED, FOR YOU HAVE NEVER TREATED ME WITH ANY HINT OF SUCH HUMILITY BEFORE!!
...
!
S-SIR TENSHO-IN, PLEASE! ANYTHING BUT THAT!!
WHAT?

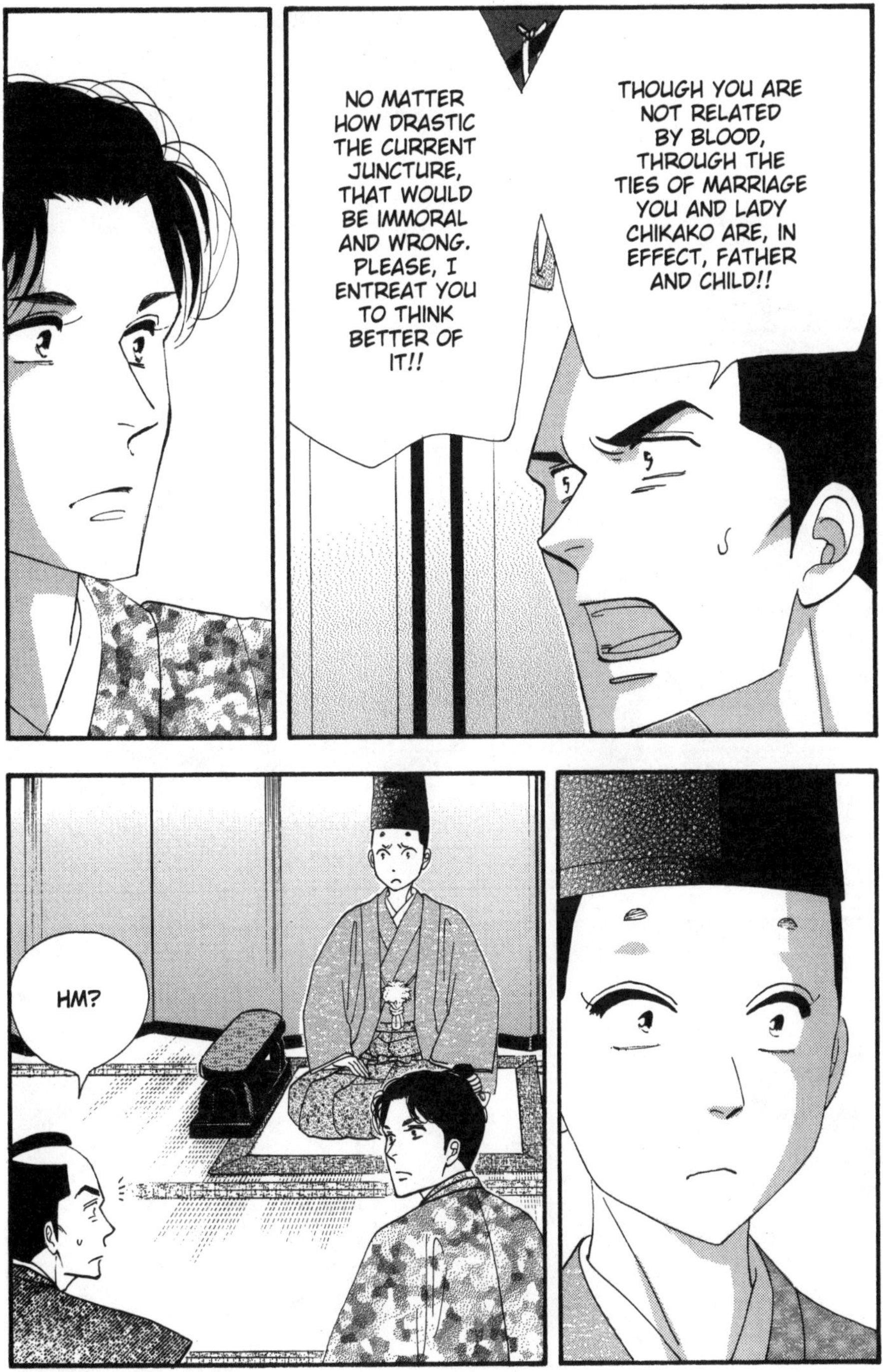
THOUGH YOU ARE NOT RELATED BY BLOOD, THROUGH THE TIES OF MARRIAGE YOU AND LADY CHIKAKO ARE, IN EFFECT, FATHER AND CHILD!!
NO MATTER HOW DRASTIC THE CURRENT JUNCTURE, THAT WOULD BE IMMORAL AND WRONG. PLEASE, I ENTREAT YOU TO THINK BETTER OF IT!!
HM?

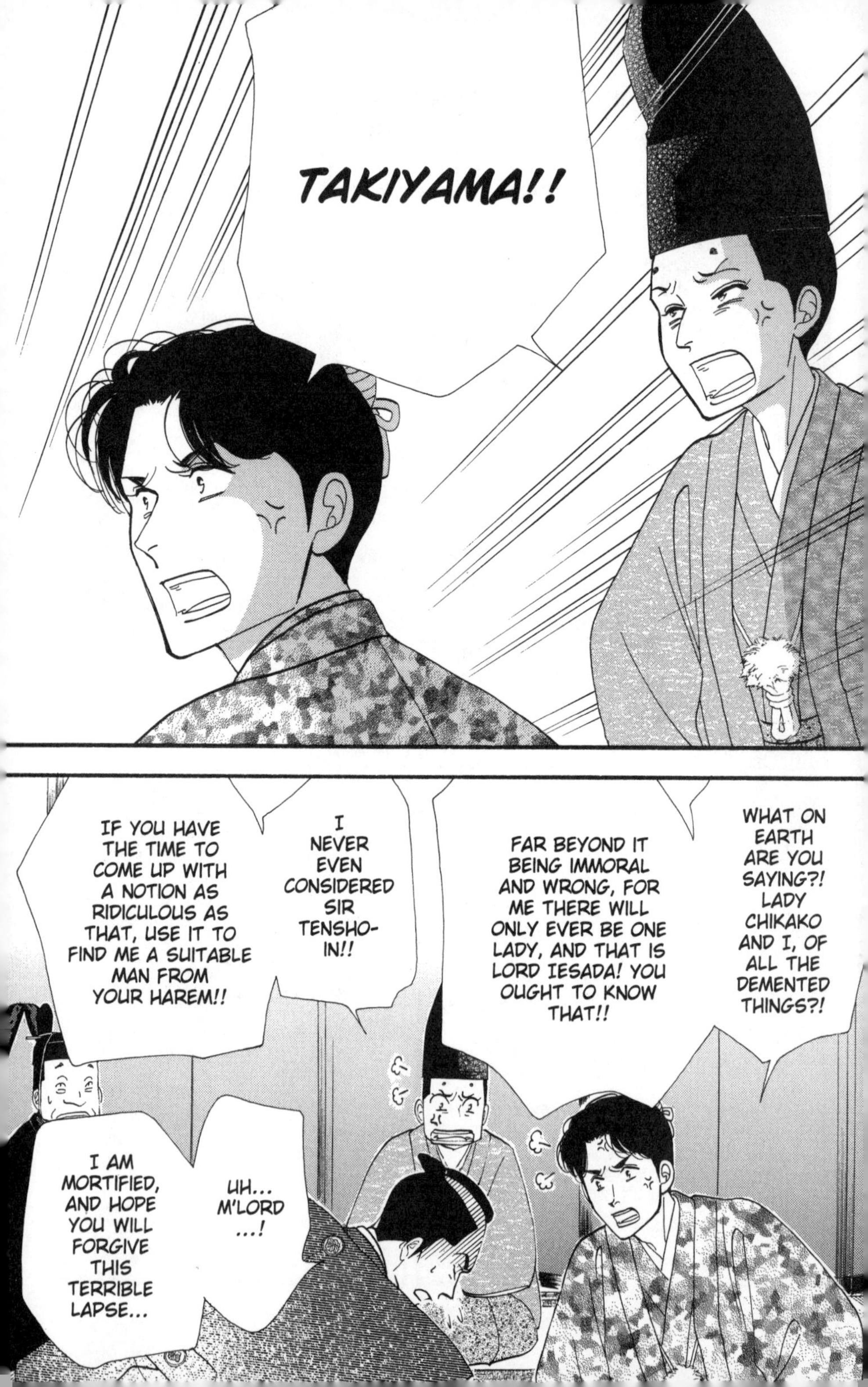
TAKIYAMA!!
WHAT ON EARTH ARE YOU SAYING?! LADY CHIKAKO AND I, OF ALL THE DEMENTED THINGS?!
FAR BEYOND IT BEING IMMORAL AND WRONG, FOR ME THERE WILL ONLY EVER BE ONE LADY, AND THAT IS LORD IESADA! YOU OUGHT TO KNOW THAT!!
I NEVER EVEN CONSIDERED SIR TENSHO-IN!!
IF YOU HAVE THE TIME TO COME UP WITH A NOTION AS RIDICULOUS AS THAT, USE IT TO FIND ME A SUITABLE MAN FROM YOUR HAREM!!
UH... M'LORD ...!
I AM MORTIFIED, AND HOPE YOU WILL FORGIVE THIS TERRIBLE LAPSE...

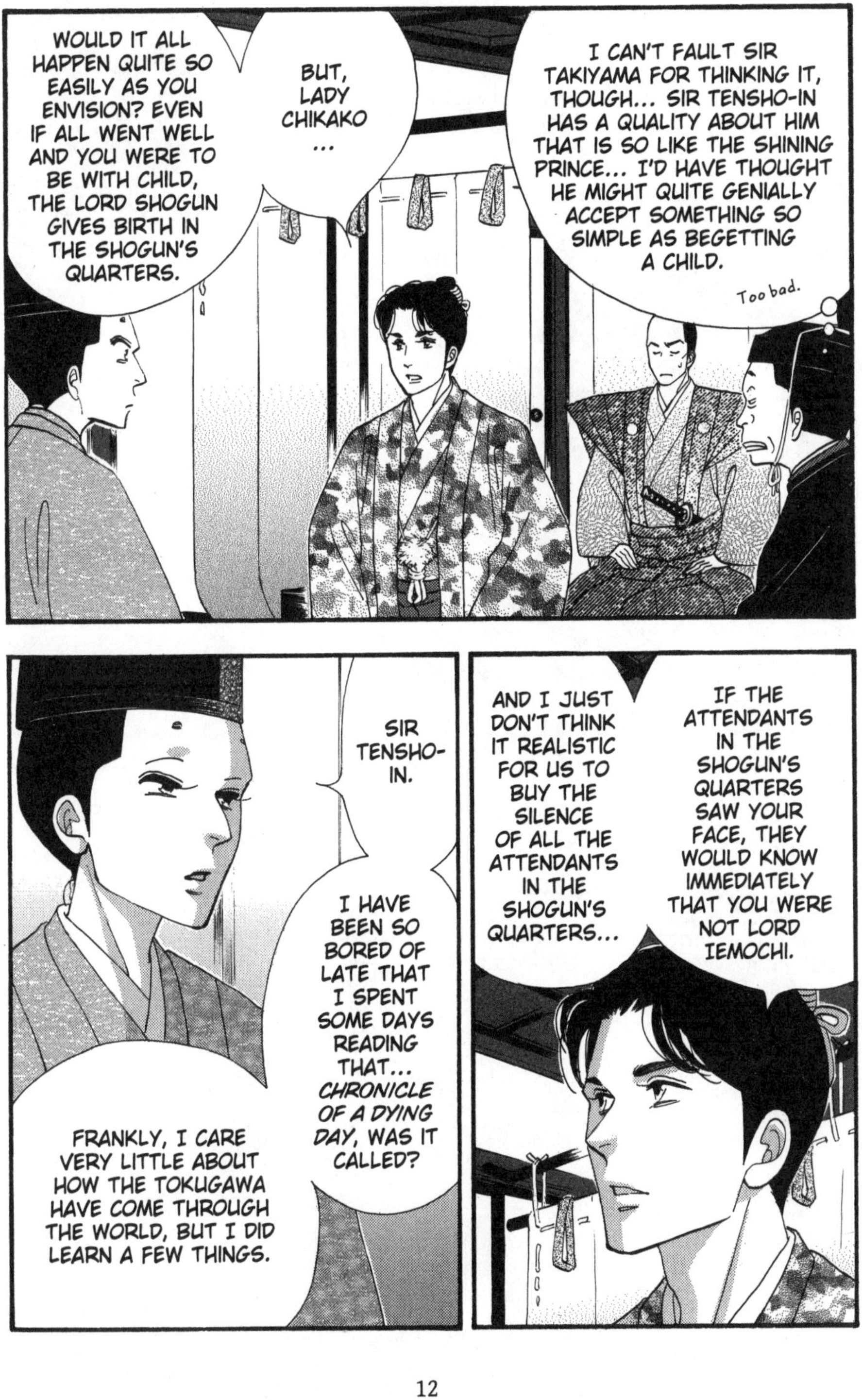
I CAN'T FAULT SIR TAKIYAMA FOR THINKING IT, THOUGH... SIR TENSHO-IN HAS A QUALITY ABOUT HIM THAT IS SO LIKE THE SHINING PRINCE... I'D HAVE THOUGHT HE MIGHT QUITE GENIALLY ACCEPT SOMETHING SO SIMPLE AS BEGETTING A CHILD.
Too bad.
BUT, LADY CHIKAKO ...
WOULD IT ALL HAPPEN QUITE SO EASILY AS YOU ENVISION? EVEN IF ALL WENT WELL AND YOU WERE TO BE WITH CHILD, THE LORD SHOGUN GIVES BIRTH IN THE SHOGUN'S QUARTERS.
IF THE ATTENDANTS IN THE SHOGUN'S QUARTERS SAW YOUR FACE, THEY WOULD KNOW IMMEDIATELY THAT YOU WERE NOT LORD IEMOCHI.
AND I JUST DON'T THINK IT REALISTIC FOR US TO BUY THE SILENCE OF ALL THE ATTENDANTS IN THE SHOGUN'S QUARTERS...
SIR TENSHO-IN.
I HAVE BEEN SO BORED OF LATE THAT I SPENT SOME DAYS READING THAT... *CHRONICLE OF A DYING DAY*, WAS IT CALLED?
FRANKLY, I CARE VERY LITTLE ABOUT HOW THE TOKUGAWA HAVE COME THROUGH THE WORLD, BUT I DID LEARN A FEW THINGS.

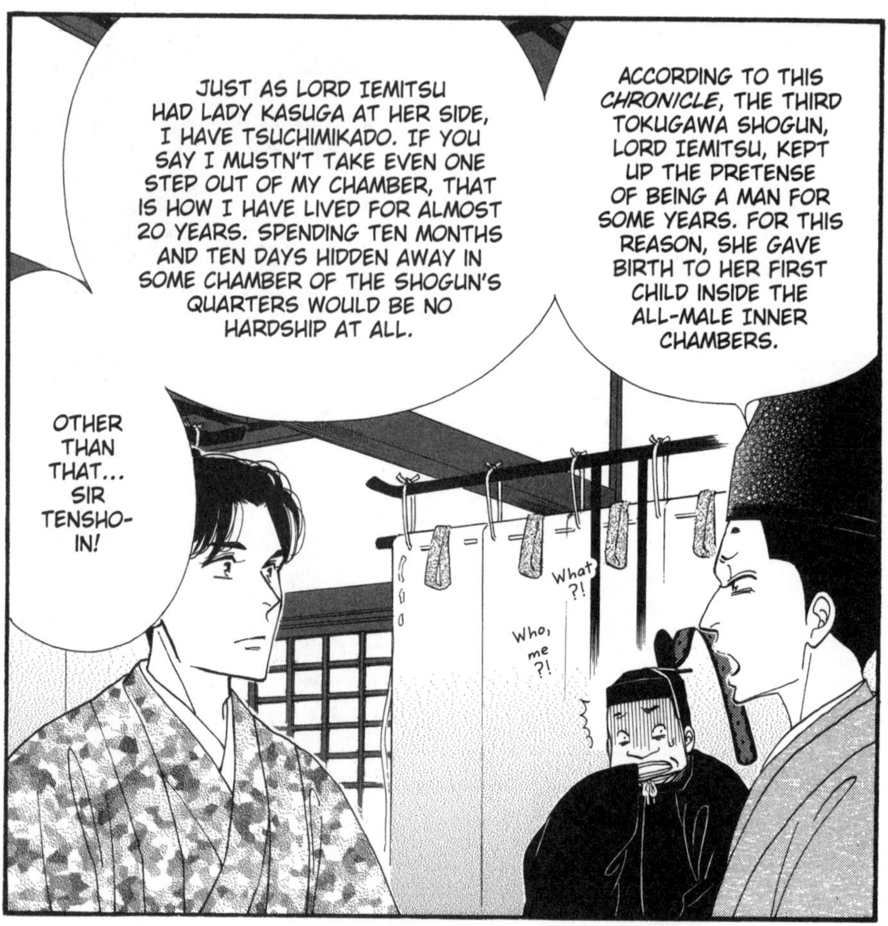
ACCORDING TO THIS CHRONICLE, THE THIRD TOKUGAWA SHOGUN, LORD IEMITSU, KEPT UP THE PRETENSE OF BEING A MAN FOR SOME YEARS. FOR THIS REASON, SHE GAVE BIRTH TO HER FIRST CHILD INSIDE THE ALL-MALE INNER CHAMBERS.
JUST AS LORD IEMITSU HAD LADY KASUGA AT HER SIDE, I HAVE TSUCHIMIKADO. IF YOU SAY I MUSTN'T TAKE EVEN ONE STEP OUT OF MY CHAMBER, THAT IS HOW I HAVE LIVED FOR ALMOST 20 YEARS. SPENDING TEN MONTHS AND TEN DAYS HIDDEN AWAY IN SOME CHAMBER OF THE SHOGUN'S QUARTERS WOULD BE NO HARDSHIP AT ALL.
What?!
Who, me?!
OTHER THAN THAT... SIR TENSHO-IN!
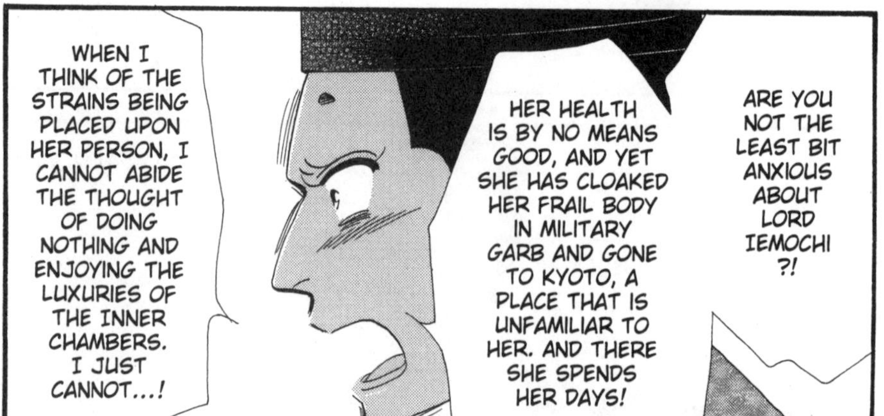
ARE YOU NOT THE LEAST BIT ANXIOUS ABOUT LORD IEMOCHI?!
HER HEALTH IS BY NO MEANS GOOD, AND YET SHE HAS CLOAKED HER FRAIL BODY IN MILITARY GARB AND GONE TO KYOTO, A PLACE THAT IS UNFAMILIAR TO HER. AND THERE SHE SPENDS HER DAYS!
WHEN I THINK OF THE STRAINS BEING PLACED UPON HER PERSON, I CANNOT ABIDE THE THOUGHT OF DOING NOTHING AND ENJOYING THE LUXURIES OF THE INNER CHAMBERS. I JUST CANNOT...!

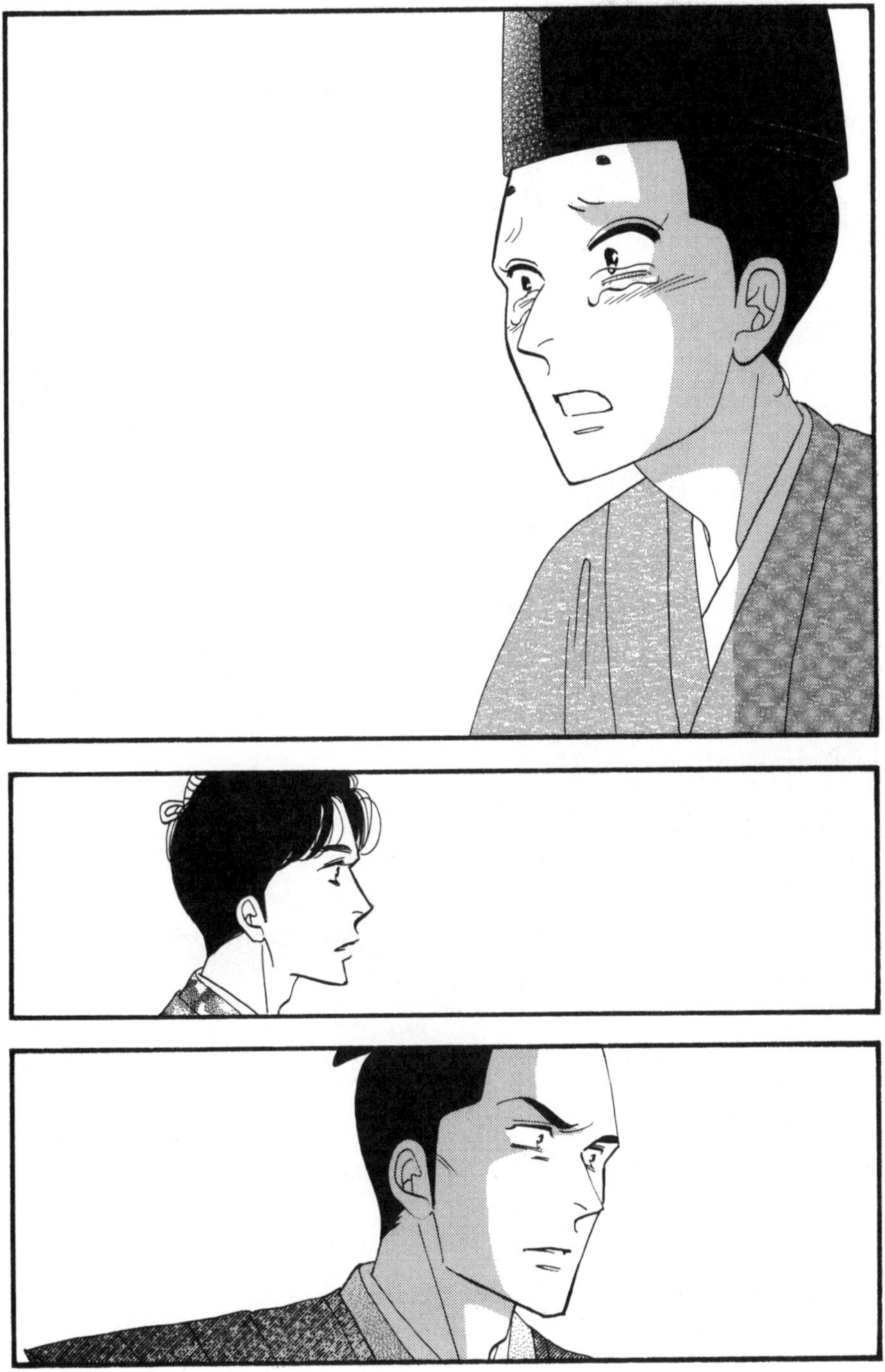

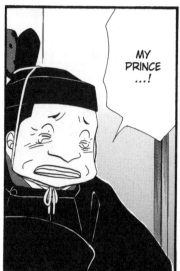

MY
PRINCE
...!

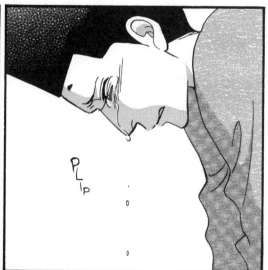

PLIP

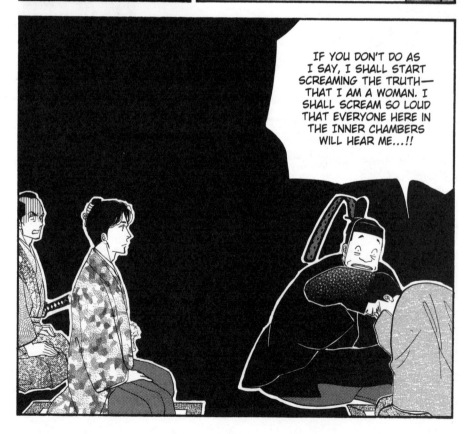

IF YOU DON'T DO AS
I SAY, I SHALL START
SCREAMING THE TRUTH—
THAT I AM A WOMAN. I
SHALL SCREAM SO LOUD
THAT EVERYONE HERE IN
THE INNER CHAMBERS
WILL HEAR ME...!!

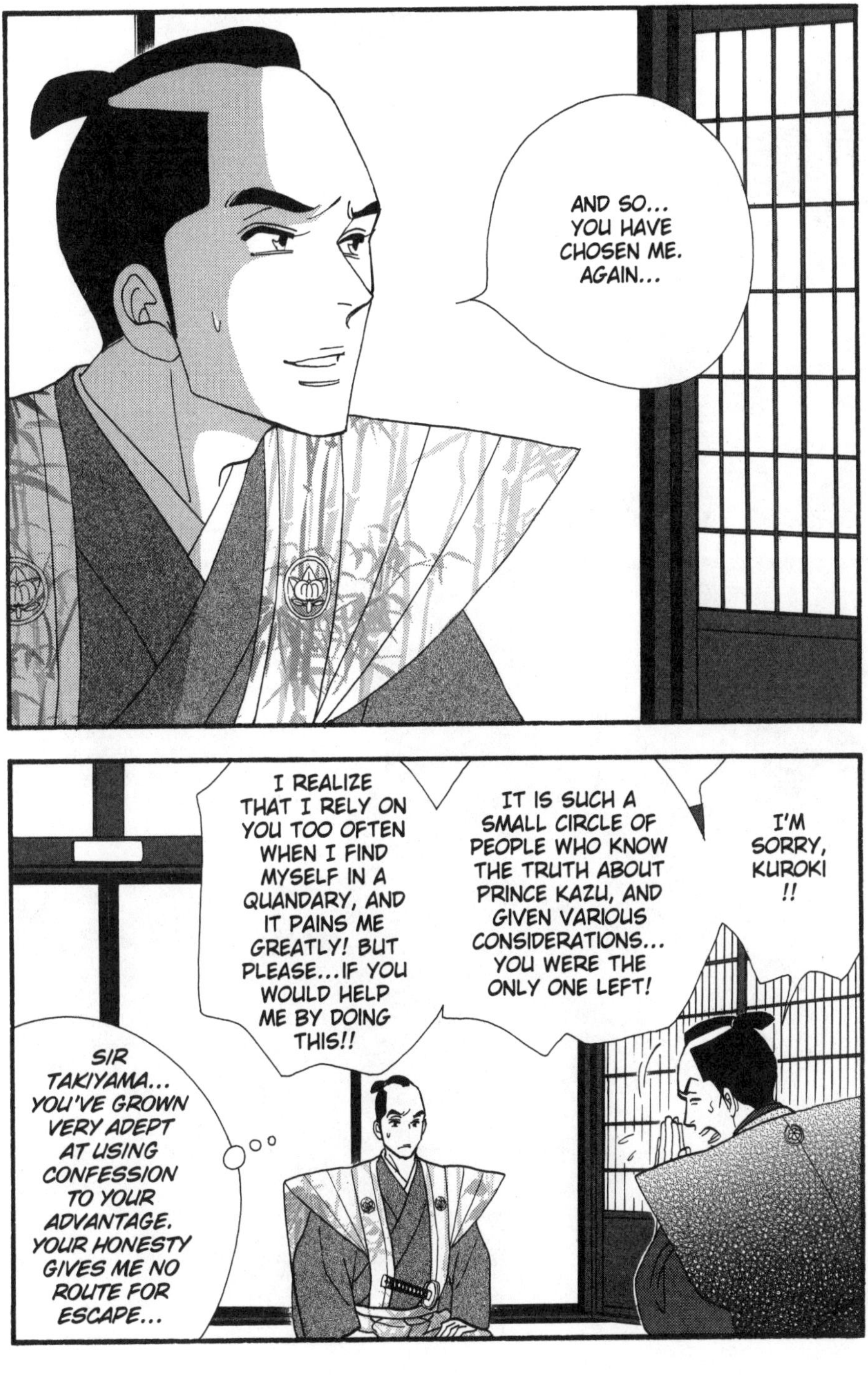
AND SO... YOU HAVE CHOSEN ME. AGAIN...
I'M SORRY, KUROKI!!
IT IS SUCH A SMALL CIRCLE OF PEOPLE WHO KNOW THE TRUTH ABOUT PRINCE KAZU, AND GIVEN VARIOUS CONSIDERATIONS... YOU WERE THE ONLY ONE LEFT!
I REALIZE THAT I RELY ON YOU TOO OFTEN WHEN I FIND MYSELF IN A QUANDARY, AND IT PAINS ME GREATLY! BUT PLEASE... IF YOU WOULD HELP ME BY DOING THIS!!
SIR TAKIYAMA... YOU'VE GROWN VERY ADEPT AT USING CONFESSION TO YOUR ADVANTAGE. YOUR HONESTY GIVES ME NO ROUTE FOR ESCAPE...

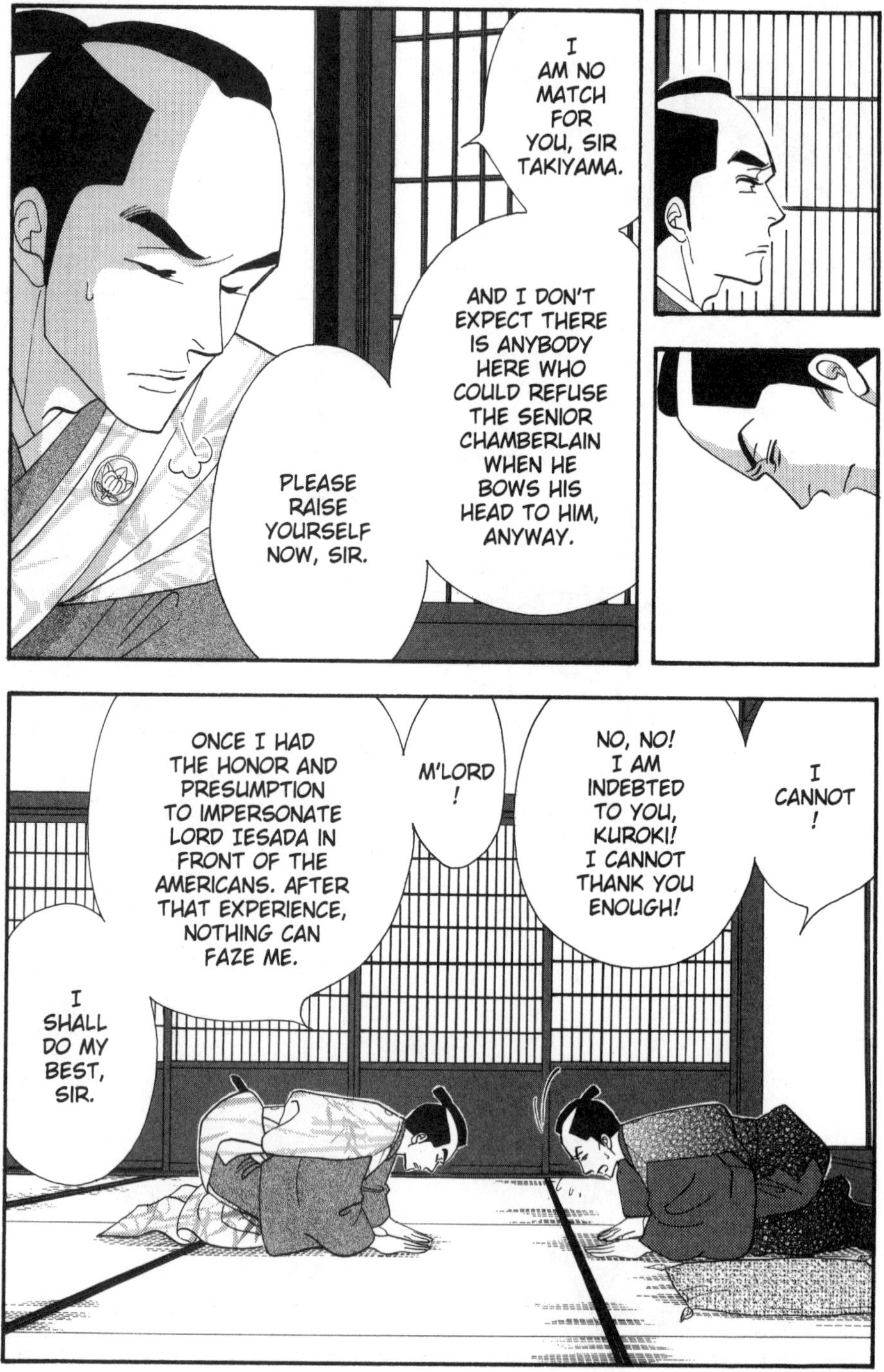
I AM NO MATCH FOR YOU, SIR TAKIYAMA.
AND I DON'T EXPECT THERE IS ANYBODY HERE WHO COULD REFUSE THE SENIOR CHAMBERLAIN WHEN HE BOWS HIS HEAD TO HIM, ANYWAY.
PLEASE RAISE YOURSELF NOW, SIR.
I CANNOT!
NO, NO! I AM INDEBTED TO YOU, KUROKI! I CANNOT THANK YOU ENOUGH!
M'LORD!
ONCE I HAD THE HONOR AND PRESUMPTION TO IMPERSONATE LORD IESADA IN FRONT OF THE AMERICANS. AFTER THAT EXPERIENCE, NOTHING CAN FAZE ME.
I SHALL DO MY BEST, SIR.

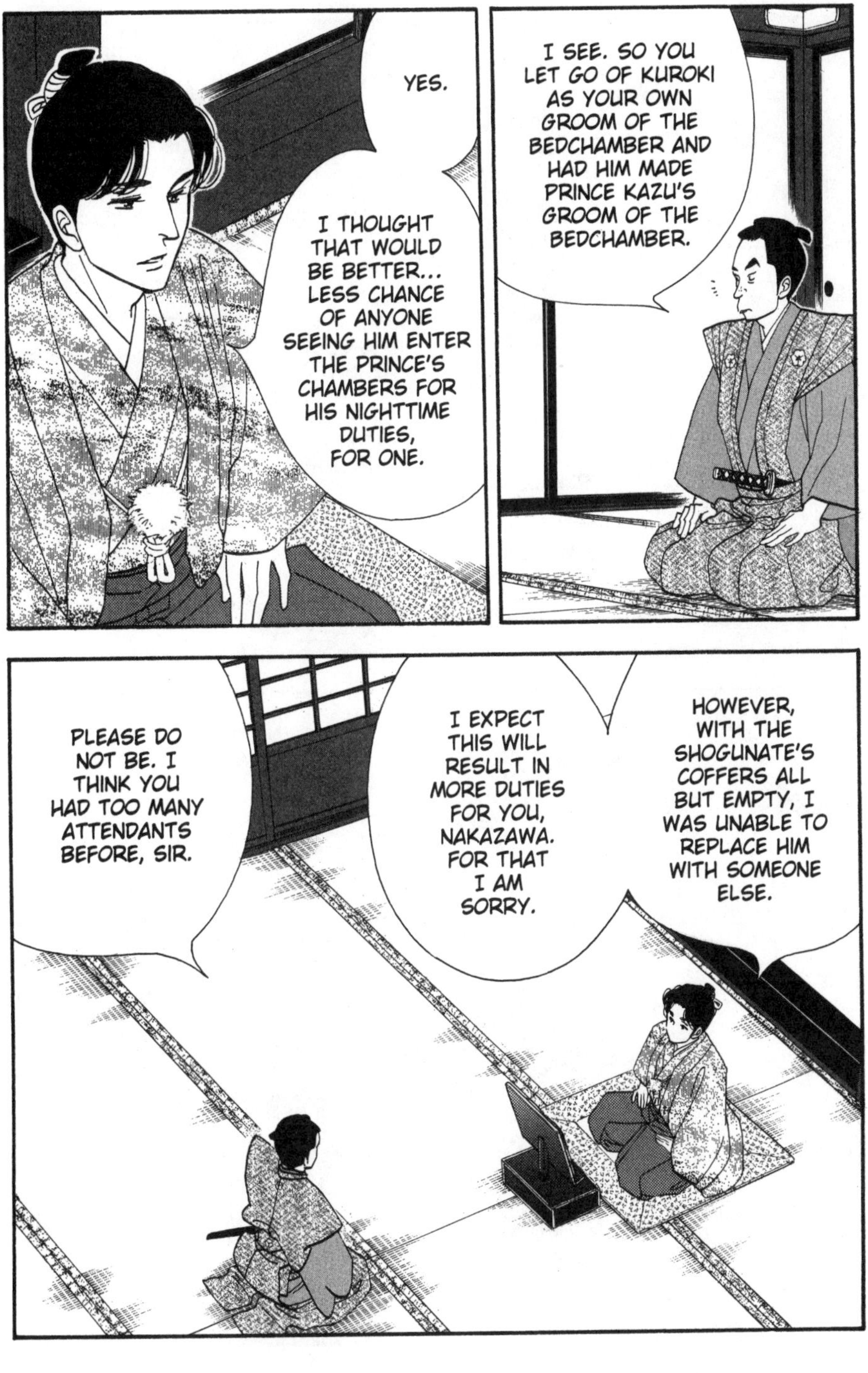
I SEE. SO YOU LET GO OF KUROKI AS YOUR OWN GROOM OF THE BEDCHAMBER AND HAD HIM MADE PRINCE KAZU'S GROOM OF THE BEDCHAMBER.
YES.
I THOUGHT THAT WOULD BE BETTER... LESS CHANCE OF ANYONE SEEING HIM ENTER THE PRINCE'S CHAMBERS FOR HIS NIGHTTIME DUTIES, FOR ONE.
HOWEVER, WITH THE SHOGUNATE'S COFFERS ALL BUT EMPTY, I WAS UNABLE TO REPLACE HIM WITH SOMEONE ELSE.
I EXPECT THIS WILL RESULT IN MORE DUTIES FOR YOU, NAKAZAWA. FOR THAT I AM SORRY.
PLEASE DO NOT BE. I THINK YOU HAD TOO MANY ATTENDANTS BEFORE, SIR.

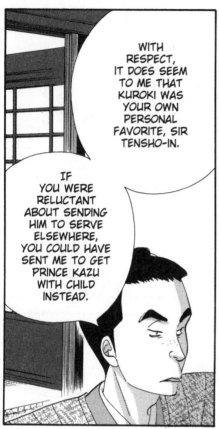

BUT OF ALL MY GROOMS OF THE BEDCHAMBER, KUROKI WAS THE MOST THOUGHTFUL AND ATTENTIVE EVEN OF THE SMALLEST DETAILS. AND HE HAS AN AMIABLE QUALITY THAT SETS PEOPLE AT EASE.
I HOPE PRINCE KAZU TOO WILL FIND HIM AGREEABLE...
WITH RESPECT, IT DOES SEEM TO ME THAT KUROKI WAS YOUR OWN PERSONAL FAVORITE, SIR TENSHO-IN.
IF YOU WERE RELUCTANT ABOUT SENDING HIM TO SERVE ELSEWHERE, YOU COULD HAVE SENT ME TO GET PRINCE KAZU WITH CHILD INSTEAD.
OH.
YES.
I rather like willful wenches like her, actually.

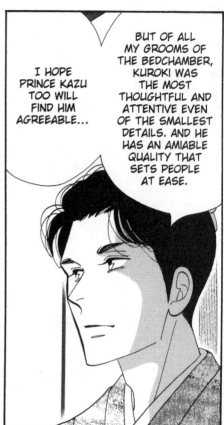

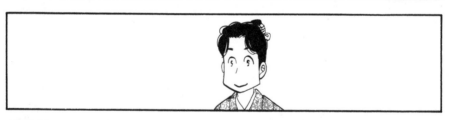

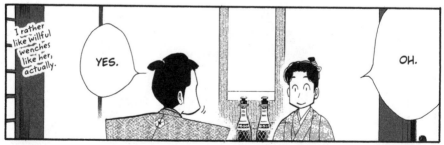

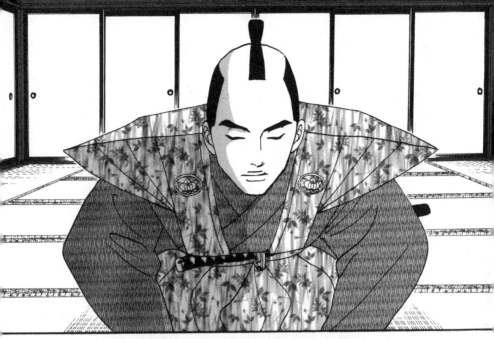

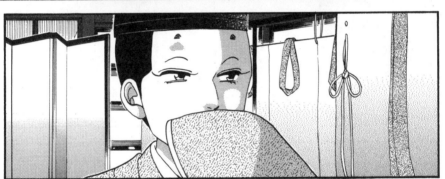

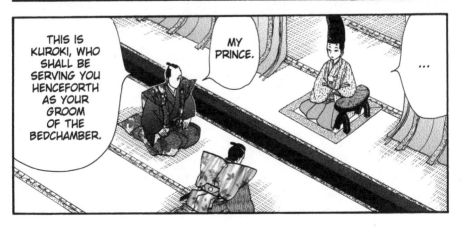

THIS IS KUROKI, WHO SHALL BE SERVING YOU HENCEFORTH AS YOUR GROOM OF THE BEDCHAMBER.

MY PRINCE.

...

20

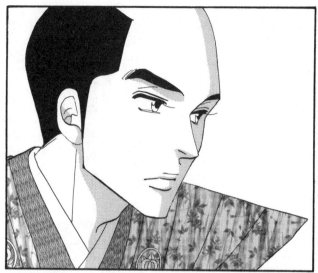

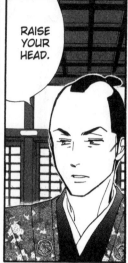

RAISE YOUR HEAD.

YOU'RE THE ONE WHO TRIED TO GRAB MY HAND ON MY VERY FIRST DAY IN THIS PLACE.

OH, YES...

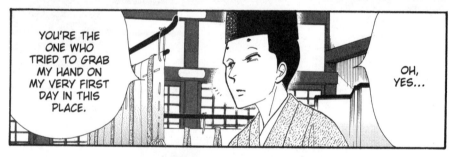

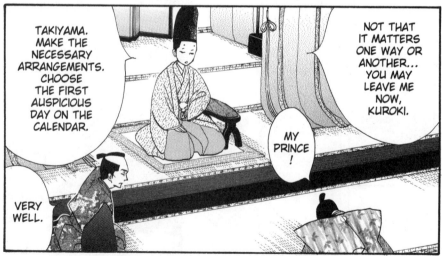

TAKIYAMA. MAKE THE NECESSARY ARRANGEMENTS. CHOOSE THE FIRST AUSPICIOUS DAY ON THE CALENDAR.

NOT THAT IT MATTERS ONE WAY OR ANOTHER... YOU MAY LEAVE ME NOW, KUROKI.

MY PRINCE!

VERY WELL.

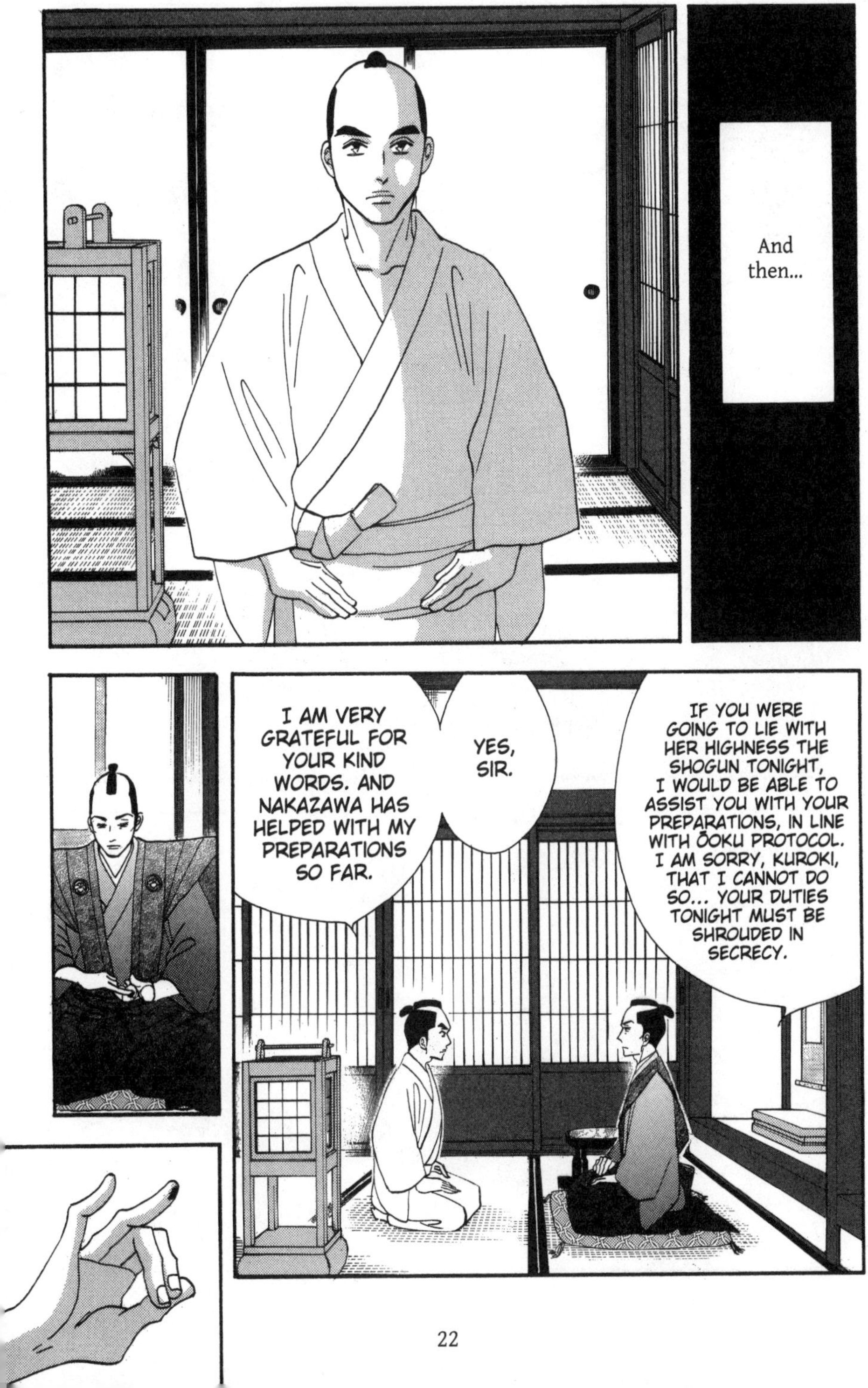
And then...
IF YOU WERE GOING TO LIE WITH HER HIGHNESS THE SHOGUN TONIGHT, I WOULD BE ABLE TO ASSIST YOU WITH YOUR PREPARATIONS, IN LINE WITH ŌOKU PROTOCOL. I AM SORRY, KUROKI, THAT I CANNOT DO SO... YOUR DUTIES TONIGHT MUST BE SHROUDED IN SECRECY.
YES, SIR.
I AM VERY GRATEFUL FOR YOUR KIND WORDS. AND NAKAZAWA HAS HELPED WITH MY PREPARATIONS SO FAR.

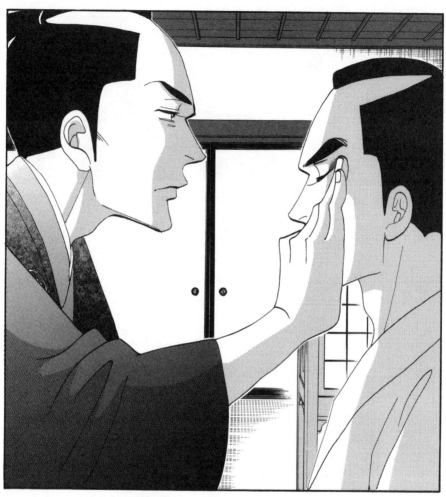

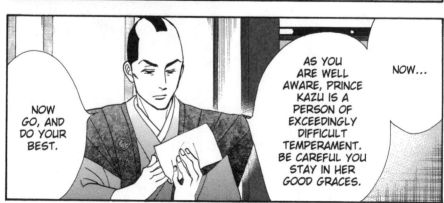

NOW
GO, AND
DO YOUR
BEST.

AS YOU
ARE WELL
AWARE, PRINCE
KAZU IS A
PERSON OF
EXCEEDINGLY
DIFFICULT
TEMPERAMENT.
BE CAREFUL YOU
STAY IN HER
GOOD GRACES.

NOW...

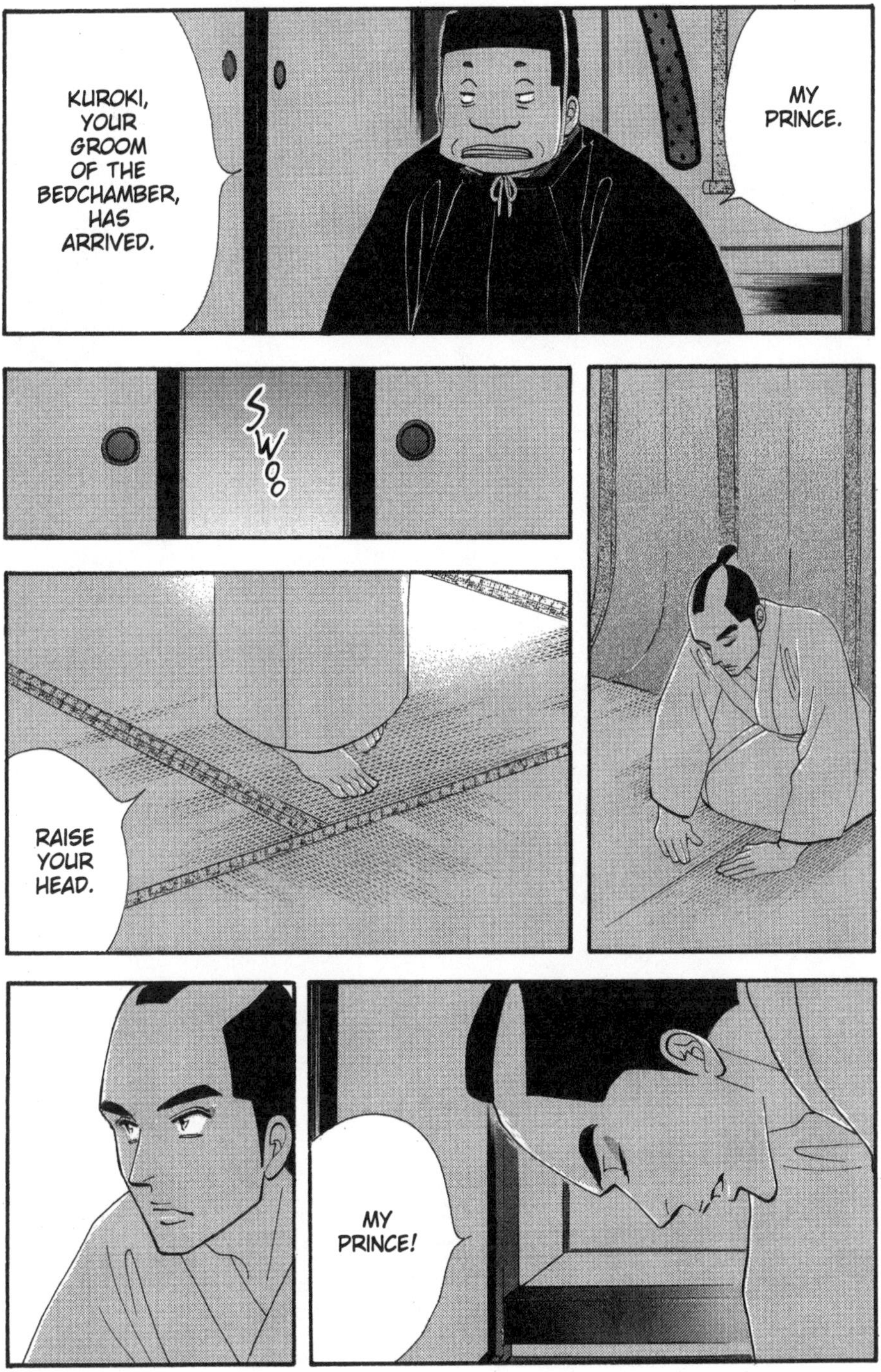
MY PRINCE.
KUROKI, YOUR GROOM OF THE BEDCHAMBER, HAS ARRIVED.
SWOO
RAISE YOUR HEAD.
MY PRINCE!

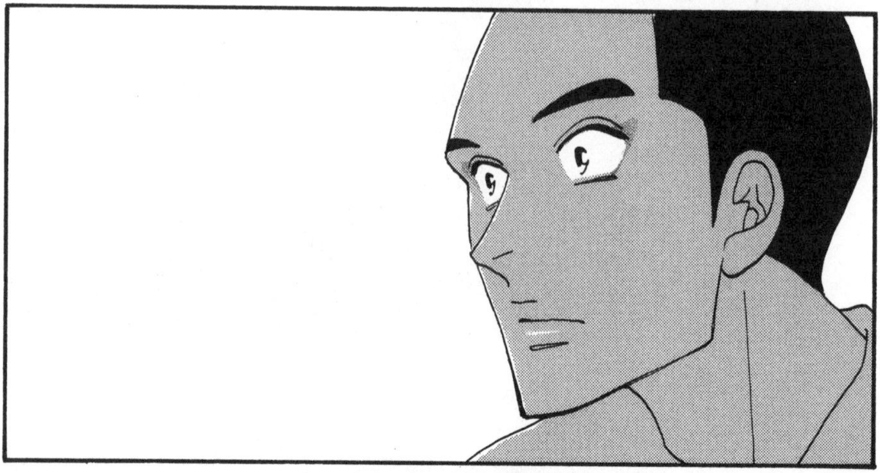
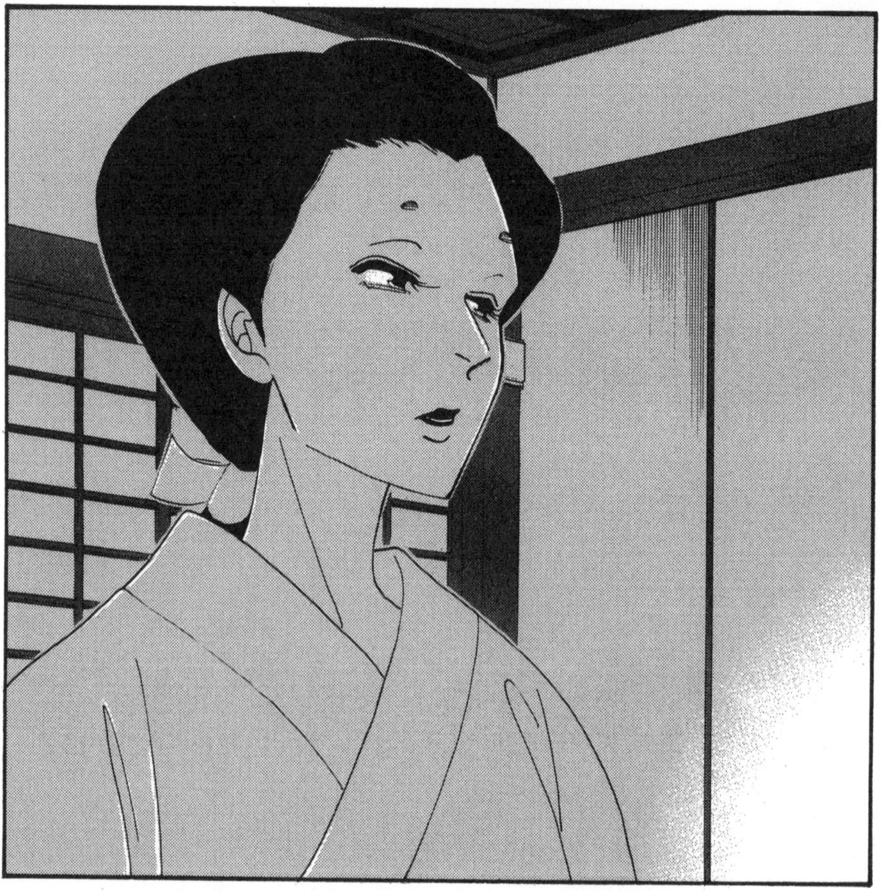

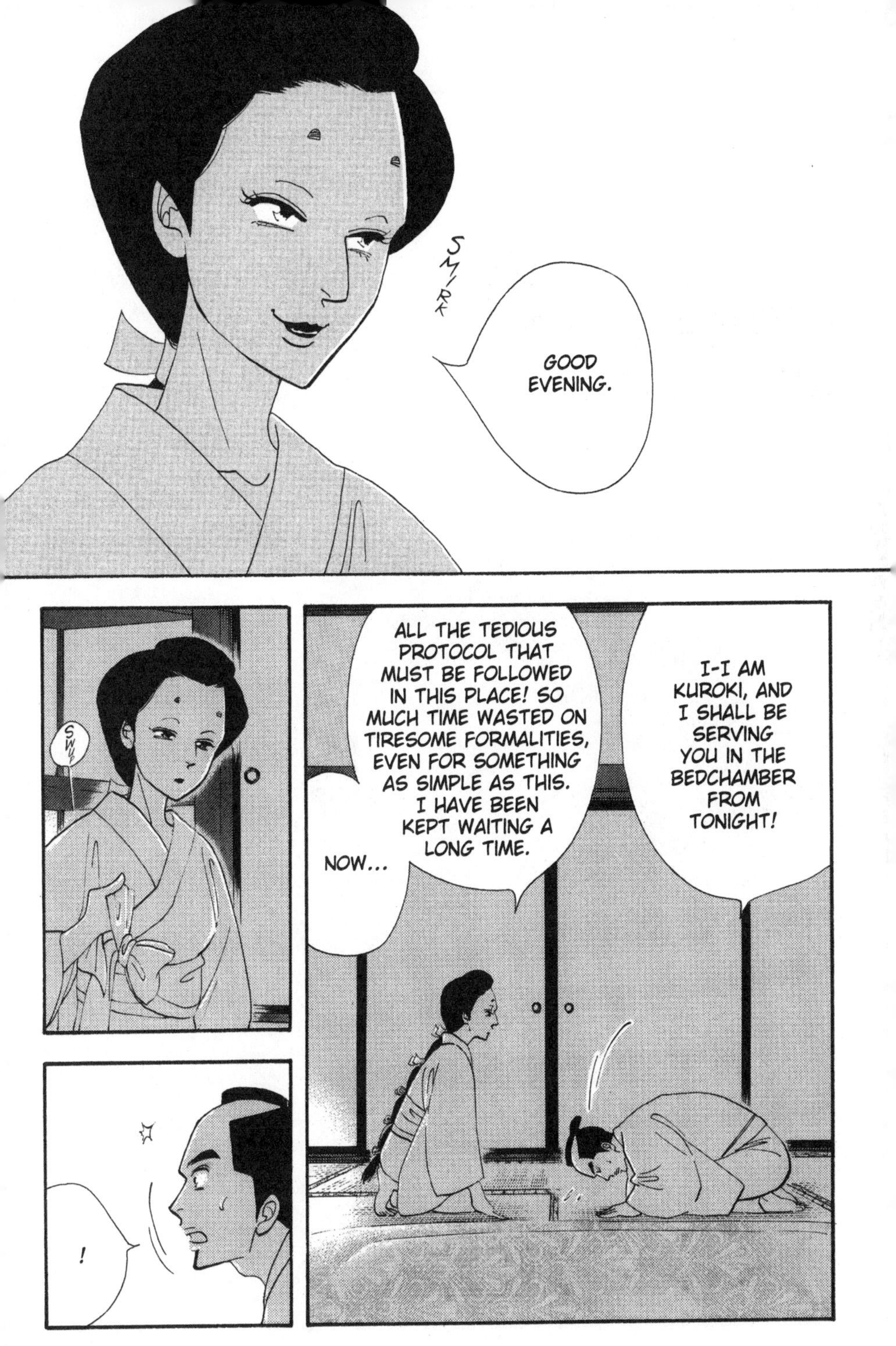
SMIRK
GOOD EVENING.
I-I AM KUROKI, AND I SHALL BE SERVING YOU IN THE BEDCHAMBER FROM TONIGHT!
ALL THE TEDIOUS PROTOCOL THAT MUST BE FOLLOWED IN THIS PLACE! SO MUCH TIME WASTED ON TIRESOME FORMALITIES, EVEN FOR SOMETHING AS SIMPLE AS THIS. I HAVE BEEN KEPT WAITING A LONG TIME.
NOW...
SWUP
!

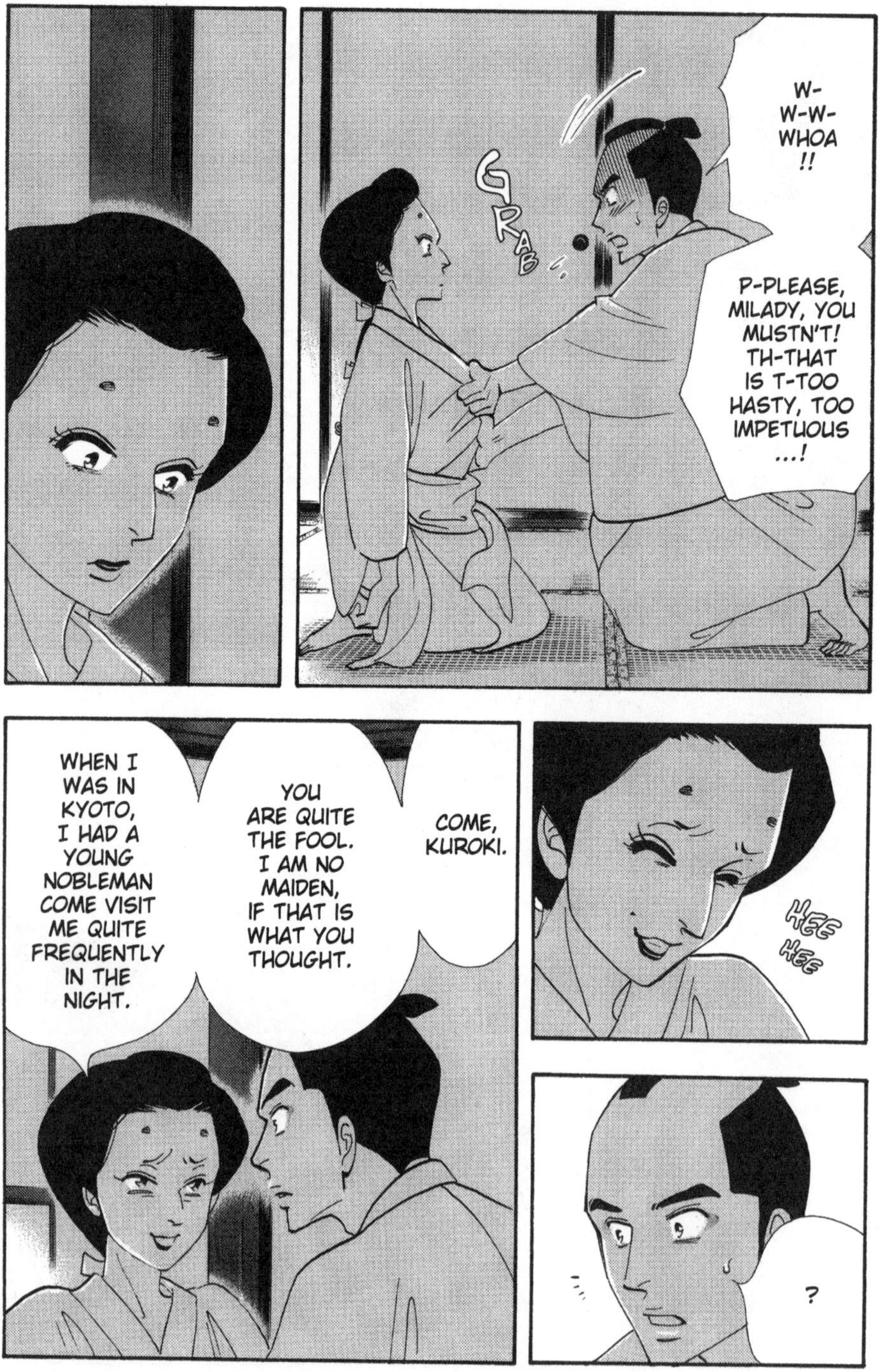
W-W-W-WHOA!!
GRAB
P-PLEASE, MILADY, YOU MUSTN'T! TH-THAT IS T-TOO HASTY, TOO IMPETUOUS...!
HEE HEE
?
COME, KUROKI.
YOU ARE QUITE THE FOOL. I AM NO MAIDEN, IF THAT IS WHAT YOU THOUGHT.
WHEN I WAS IN KYOTO, I HAD A YOUNG NOBLEMAN COME VISIT ME QUITE FREQUENTLY IN THE NIGHT.

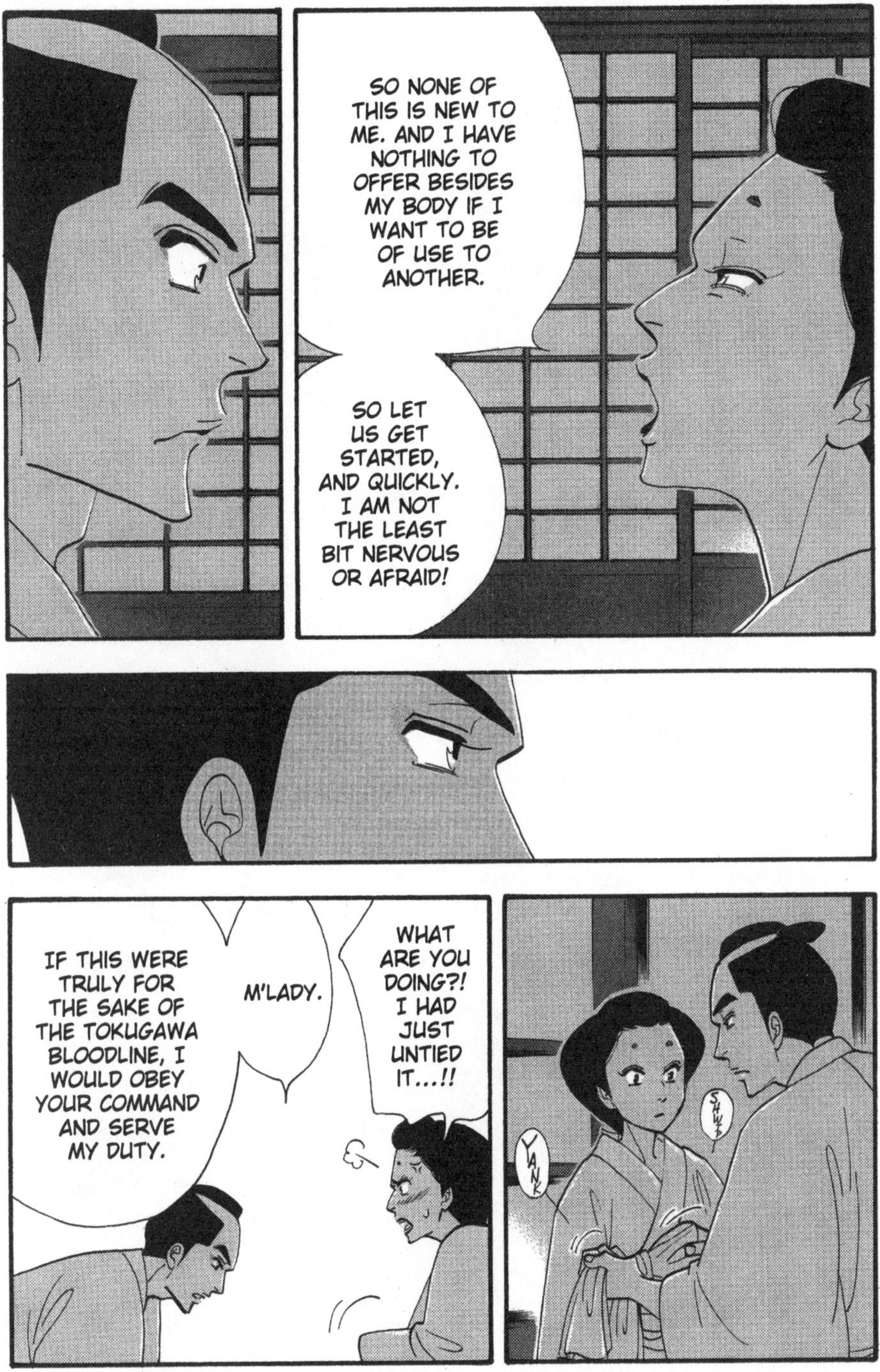
SO NONE OF THIS IS NEW TO ME. AND I HAVE NOTHING TO OFFER BESIDES MY BODY IF I WANT TO BE OF USE TO ANOTHER.
SO LET US GET STARTED, AND QUICKLY. I AM NOT THE LEAST BIT NERVOUS OR AFRAID!
SHWIP
YANK
WHAT ARE YOU DOING?! I HAD JUST UNTIED IT...!!
M'LADY.
IF THIS WERE TRULY FOR THE SAKE OF THE TOKUGAWA BLOODLINE, I WOULD OBEY YOUR COMMAND AND SERVE MY DUTY.

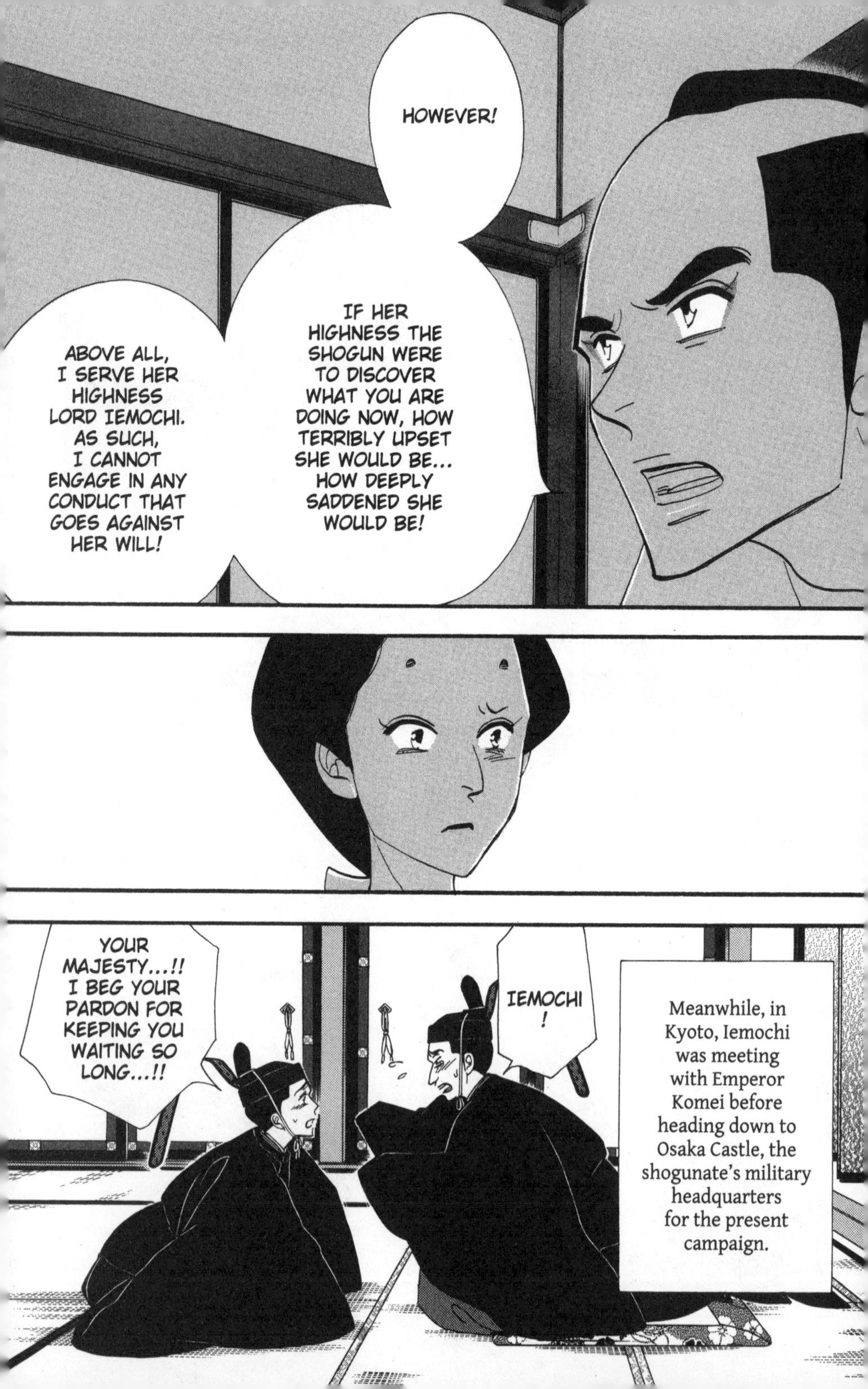
HOWEVER!
IF HER HIGHNESS THE SHOGUN WERE TO DISCOVER WHAT YOU ARE DOING NOW, HOW TERRIBLY UPSET SHE WOULD BE… HOW DEEPLY SADDENED SHE WOULD BE!
ABOVE ALL, I SERVE HER HIGHNESS LORD IEMOCHI. AS SUCH, I CANNOT ENGAGE IN ANY CONDUCT THAT GOES AGAINST HER WILL!
Meanwhile, in Kyoto, Iemochi was meeting with Emperor Komei before heading down to Osaka Castle, the shogunate's military headquarters for the present campaign.
IEMOCHI!
YOUR MAJESTY…!! I BEG YOUR PARDON FOR KEEPING YOU WAITING SO LONG…!!

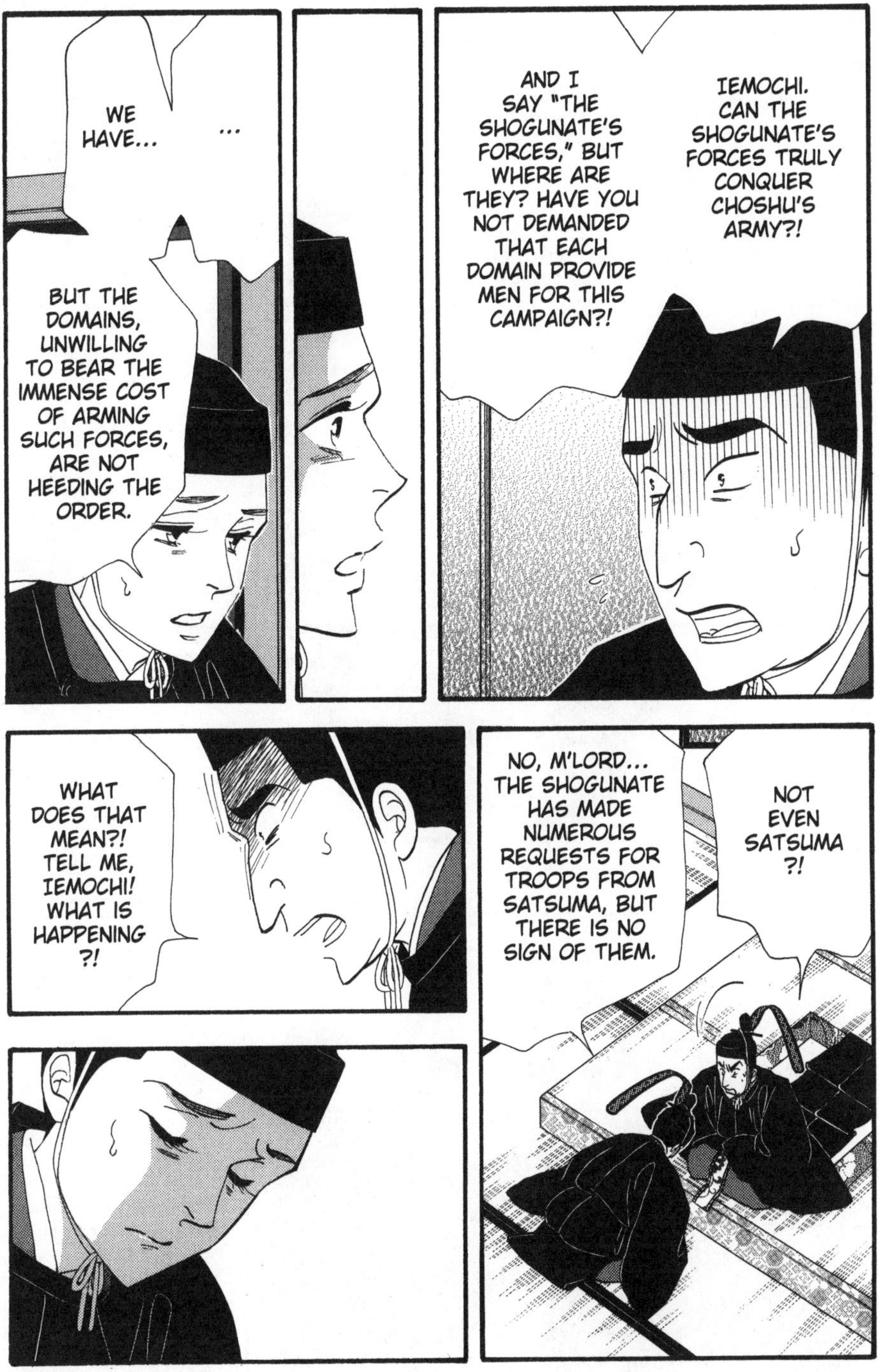
IEMOCHI. CAN THE SHOGUNATE'S FORCES TRULY CONQUER CHOSHU'S ARMY?!
AND I SAY "THE SHOGUNATE'S FORCES," BUT WHERE ARE THEY? HAVE YOU NOT DEMANDED THAT EACH DOMAIN PROVIDE MEN FOR THIS CAMPAIGN?!
...
WE HAVE...
BUT THE DOMAINS, UNWILLING TO BEAR THE IMMENSE COST OF ARMING SUCH FORCES, ARE NOT HEEDING THE ORDER.
NOT EVEN SATSUMA ?!
NO, M'LORD... THE SHOGUNATE HAS MADE NUMEROUS REQUESTS FOR TROOPS FROM SATSUMA, BUT THERE IS NO SIGN OF THEM.
WHAT DOES THAT MEAN?! TELL ME, IEMOCHI! WHAT IS HAPPENING ?!

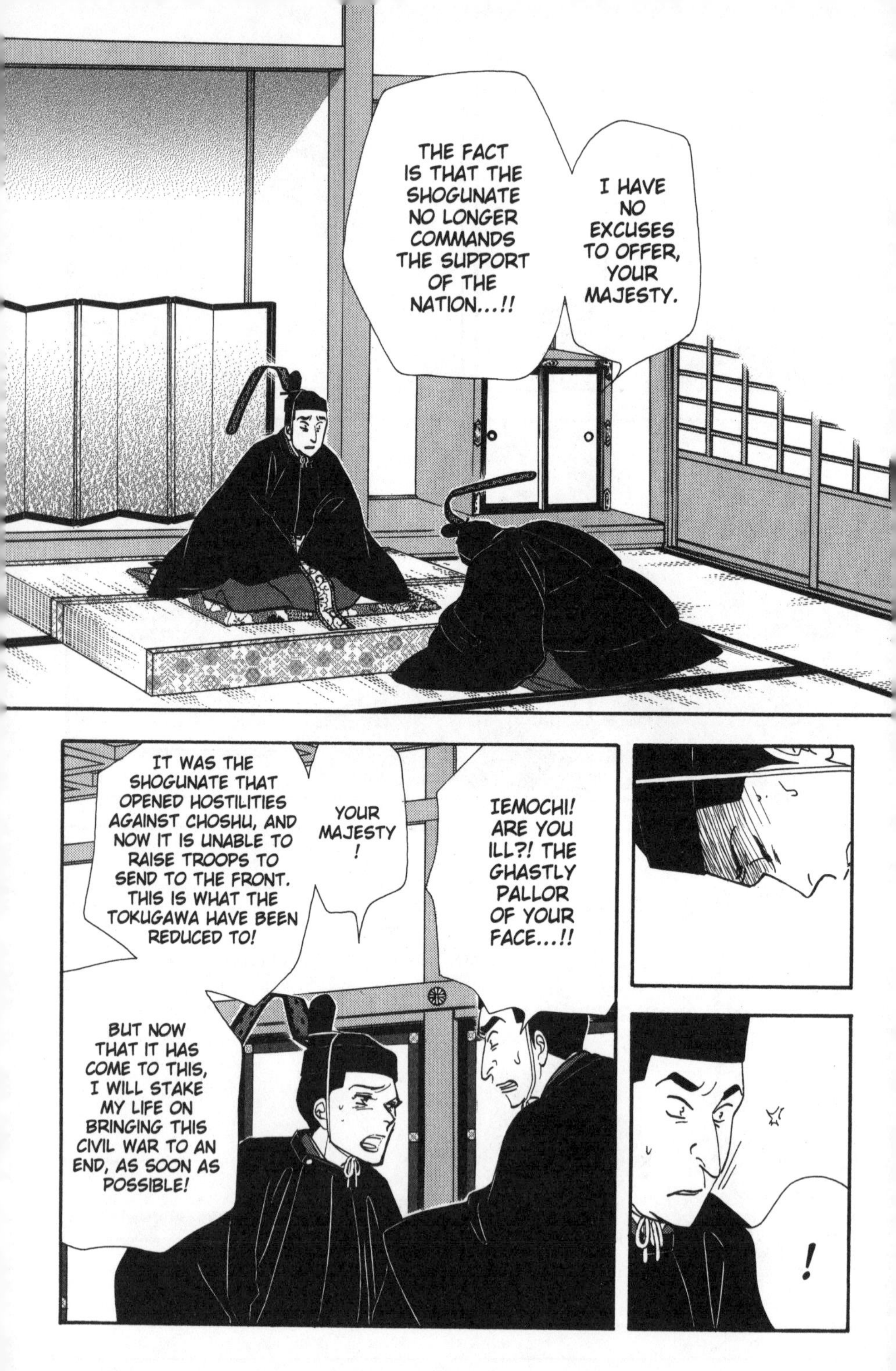
I HAVE NO EXCUSES TO OFFER, YOUR MAJESTY.
THE FACT IS THAT THE SHOGUNATE NO LONGER COMMANDS THE SUPPORT OF THE NATION...!!
!
IEMOCHI! ARE YOU ILL?! THE GHASTLY PALLOR OF YOUR FACE...!!
YOUR MAJESTY!
IT WAS THE SHOGUNATE THAT OPENED HOSTILITIES AGAINST CHOSHU, AND NOW IT IS UNABLE TO RAISE TROOPS TO SEND TO THE FRONT. THIS IS WHAT THE TOKUGAWA HAVE BEEN REDUCED TO!
BUT NOW THAT IT HAS COME TO THIS, I WILL STAKE MY LIFE ON BRINGING THIS CIVIL WAR TO AN END, AS SOON AS POSSIBLE!

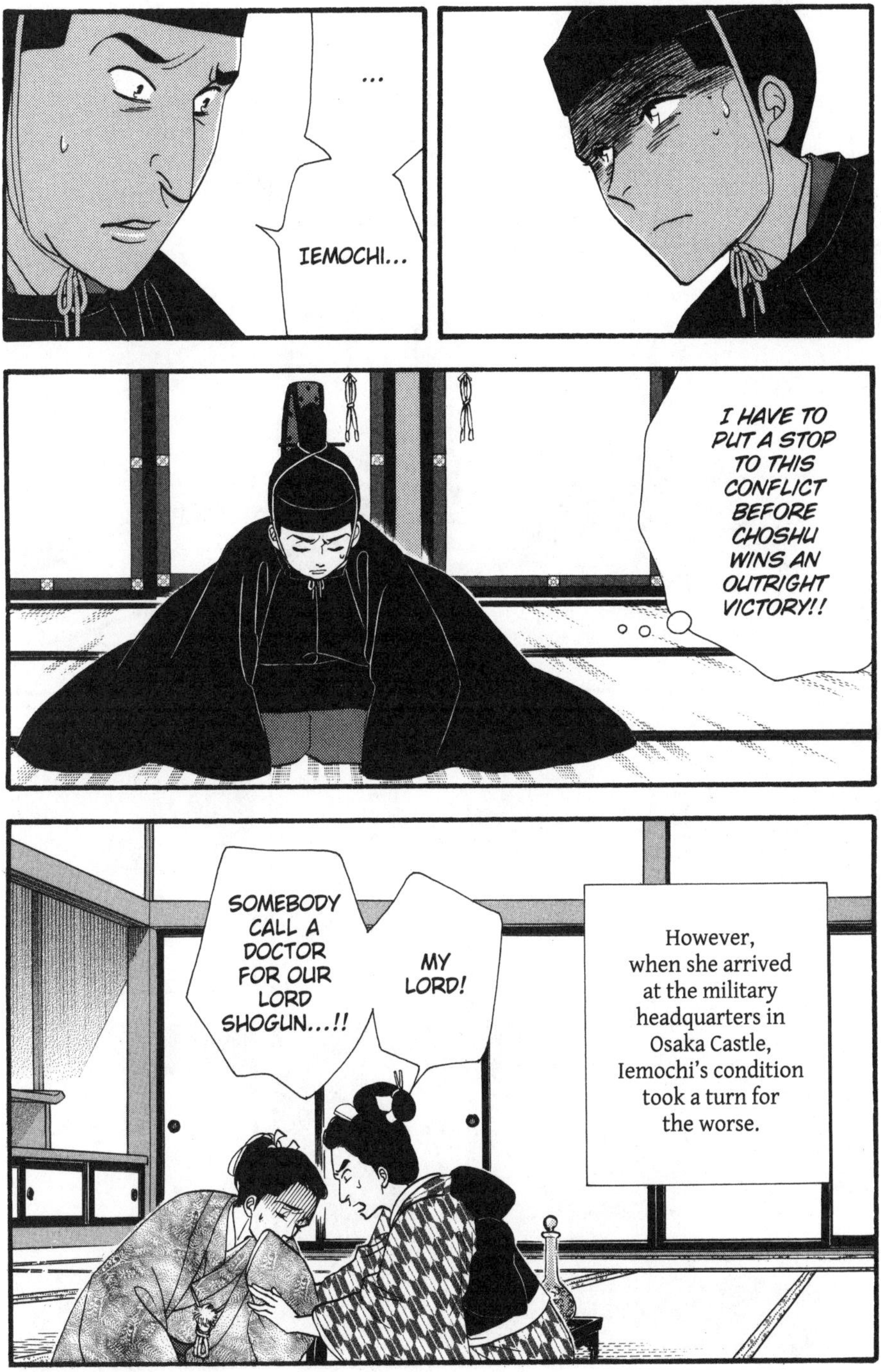
...
IEMOCHI...
I HAVE TO PUT A STOP TO THIS CONFLICT BEFORE CHOSHU WINS AN OUTRIGHT VICTORY!!
However, when she arrived at the military headquarters in Osaka Castle, Iemochi's condition took a turn for the worse.
MY LORD!
SOMEBODY CALL A DOCTOR FOR OUR LORD SHOGUN...!!

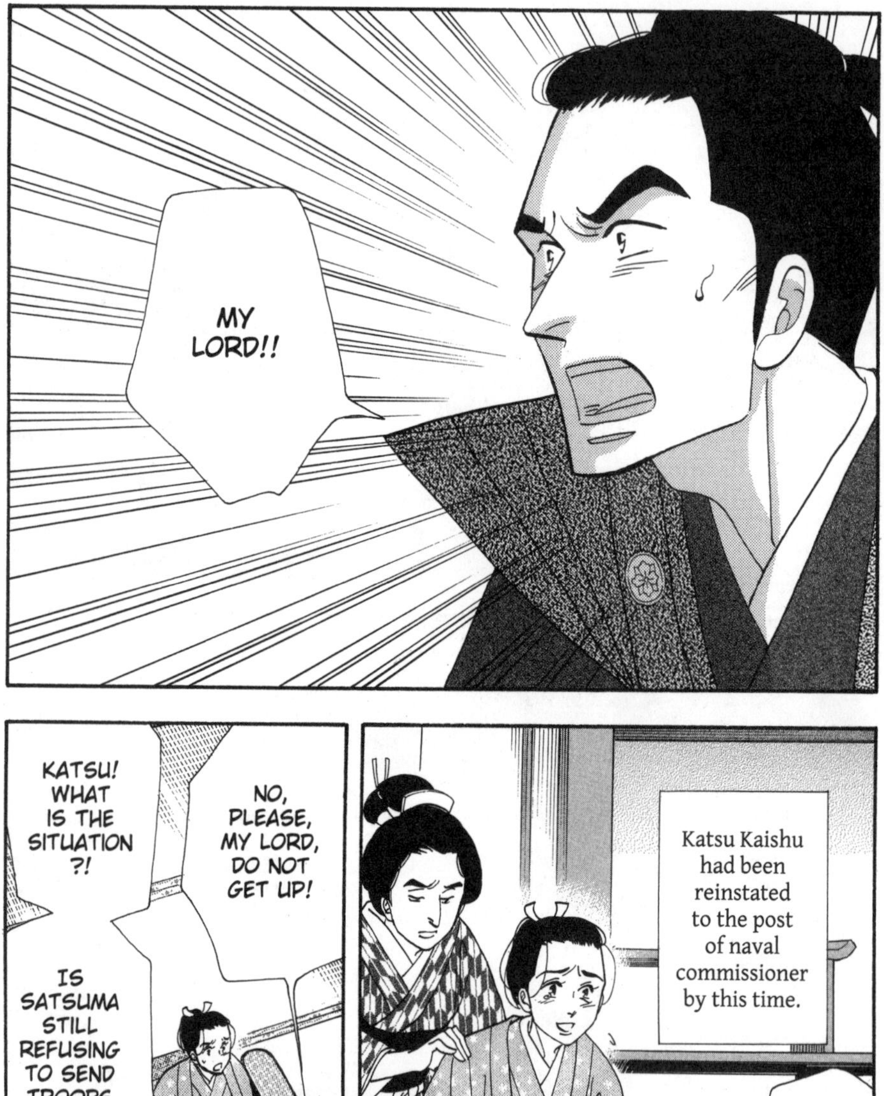
MY LORD!!
Katsu Kaishu had been reinstated to the post of naval commissioner by this time.
...
KATSU ...!!
NO, PLEASE, MY LORD, DO NOT GET UP!
KATSU! WHAT IS THE SITUATION?!
IS SATSUMA STILL REFUSING TO SEND TROOPS TO THE TOKUGAWA ARMY?!

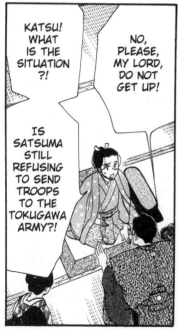

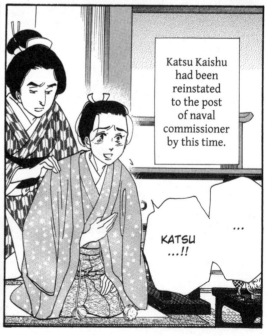

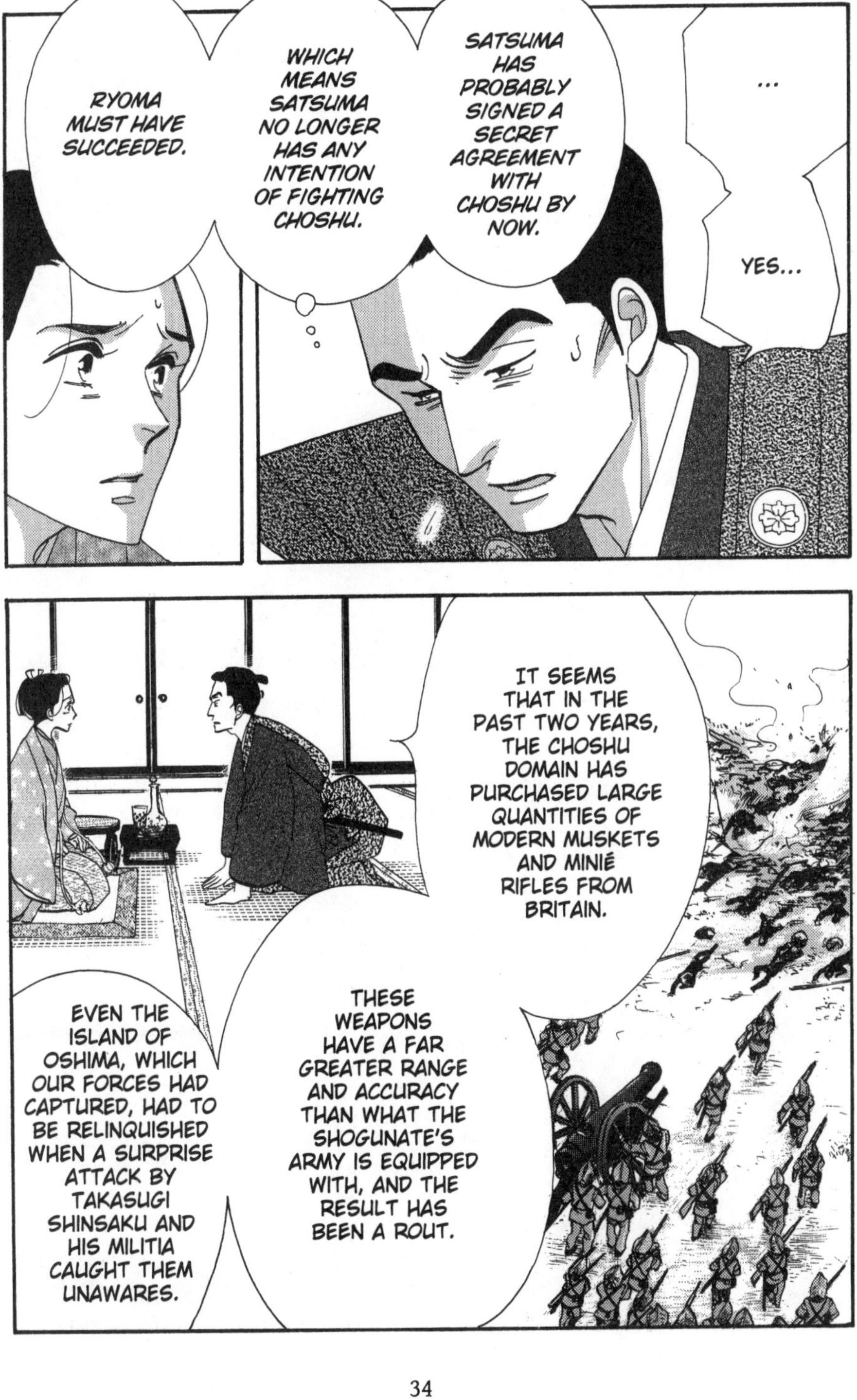
...
YES...
SATSUMA HAS PROBABLY SIGNED A SECRET AGREEMENT WITH CHOSHU BY NOW.
WHICH MEANS SATSUMA NO LONGER HAS ANY INTENTION OF FIGHTING CHOSHU.
RYOMA MUST HAVE SUCCEEDED.
IT SEEMS THAT IN THE PAST TWO YEARS, THE CHOSHU DOMAIN HAS PURCHASED LARGE QUANTITIES OF MODERN MUSKETS AND MINIÉ RIFLES FROM BRITAIN.
THESE WEAPONS HAVE A FAR GREATER RANGE AND ACCURACY THAN WHAT THE SHOGUNATE'S ARMY IS EQUIPPED WITH, AND THE RESULT HAS BEEN A ROUT.
EVEN THE ISLAND OF OSHIMA, WHICH OUR FORCES HAD CAPTURED, HAD TO BE RELINQUISHED WHEN A SURPRISE ATTACK BY TAKASUGI SHINSAKU AND HIS MILITIA CAUGHT THEM UNAWARES.

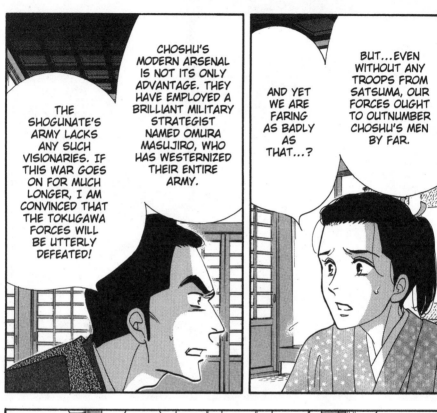

BUT...EVEN WITHOUT ANY TROOPS FROM SATSUMA, OUR FORCES OUGHT TO OUTNUMBER CHOSHU'S MEN BY FAR.
AND YET WE ARE FARING AS BADLY AS THAT...?
CHOSHU'S MODERN ARSENAL IS NOT ITS ONLY ADVANTAGE. THEY HAVE EMPLOYED A BRILLIANT MILITARY STRATEGIST NAMED OMURA MASUJIRO, WHO HAS WESTERNIZED THEIR ENTIRE ARMY.
THE SHOGUNATE'S ARMY LACKS ANY SUCH VISIONARIES. IF THIS WAR GOES ON FOR MUCH LONGER, I AM CONVINCED THAT THE TOKUGAWA FORCES WILL BE UTTERLY DEFEATED!
IF THAT BE SO, THEY MUST RETREAT!!
IS THERE NO WAY OF NEGOTIATING A CEASE-FIRE WITH CHOSHU?! WHAT DOES LORD TOKUGAWA YOSHINOBU HAVE TO SAY ABOUT THIS? LORD YOSHINOBU HAS BEEN APPRISED OF THE SITUATION, HASN'T HE?!
MY LORD.
YES, OF COURSE HE HAS.

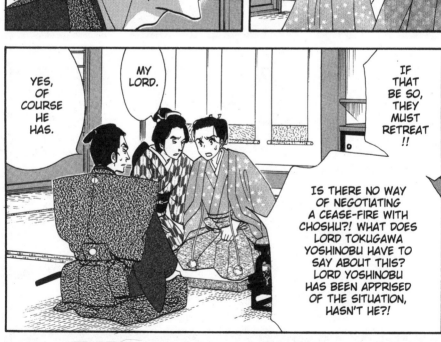

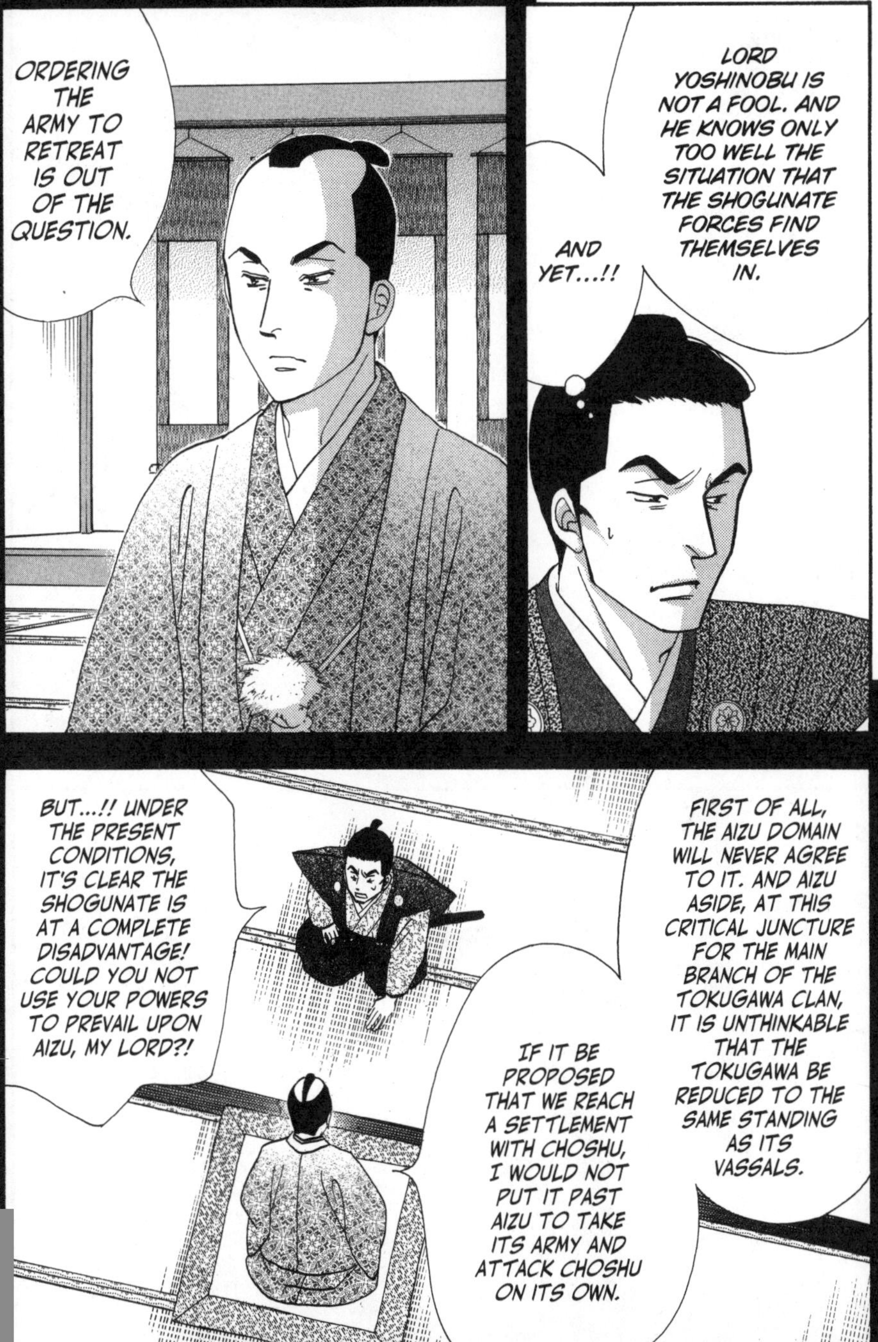
LORD YOSHINOBU IS NOT A FOOL. AND HE KNOWS ONLY TOO WELL THE SITUATION THAT THE SHOGUNATE FORCES FIND THEMSELVES IN.
AND YET...!!
ORDERING THE ARMY TO RETREAT IS OUT OF THE QUESTION.
BUT...!! UNDER THE PRESENT CONDITIONS, IT'S CLEAR THE SHOGUNATE IS AT A COMPLETE DISADVANTAGE! COULD YOU NOT USE YOUR POWERS TO PREVAIL UPON AIZU, MY LORD?!
FIRST OF ALL, THE AIZU DOMAIN WILL NEVER AGREE TO IT. AND AIZU ASIDE, AT THIS CRITICAL JUNCTURE FOR THE MAIN BRANCH OF THE TOKUGAWA CLAN, IT IS UNTHINKABLE THAT THE TOKUGAWA BE REDUCED TO THE SAME STANDING AS ITS VASSALS.
IF IT BE PROPOSED THAT WE REACH A SETTLEMENT WITH CHOSHU, I WOULD NOT PUT IT PAST AIZU TO TAKE ITS ARMY AND ATTACK CHOSHU ON ITS OWN.

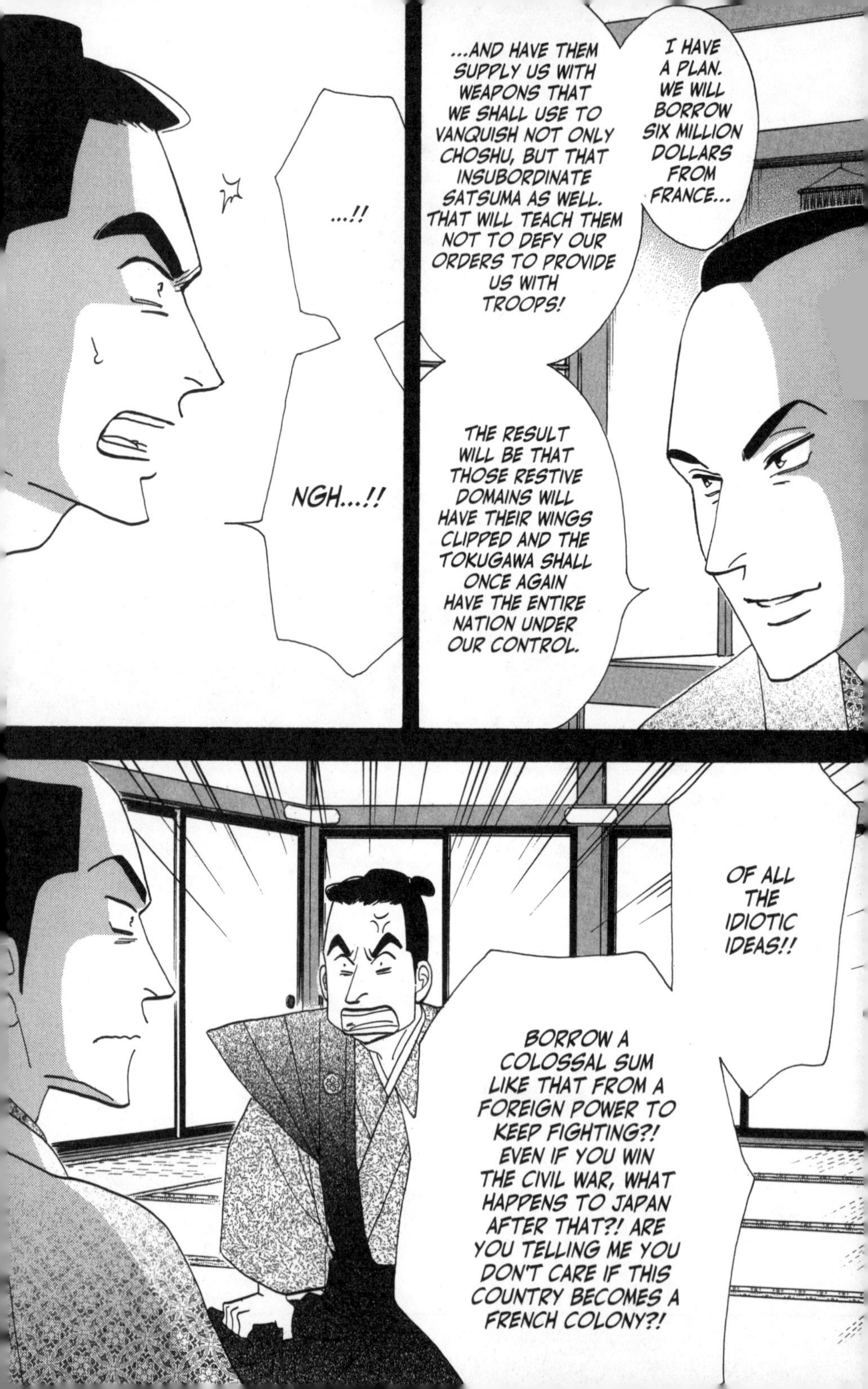
I HAVE A PLAN. WE WILL BORROW SIX MILLION DOLLARS FROM FRANCE...
...AND HAVE THEM SUPPLY US WITH WEAPONS THAT WE SHALL USE TO VANQUISH NOT ONLY CHOSHU, BUT THAT INSUBORDINATE SATSUMA AS WELL. THAT WILL TEACH THEM NOT TO DEFY OUR ORDERS TO PROVIDE US WITH TROOPS!
THE RESULT WILL BE THAT THOSE RESTIVE DOMAINS WILL HAVE THEIR WINGS CLIPPED AND THE TOKUGAWA SHALL ONCE AGAIN HAVE THE ENTIRE NATION UNDER OUR CONTROL.
...!!
NGH...!!
OF ALL THE IDIOTIC IDEAS!!
BORROW A COLOSSAL SUM LIKE THAT FROM A FOREIGN POWER TO KEEP FIGHTING?! EVEN IF YOU WIN THE CIVIL WAR, WHAT HAPPENS TO JAPAN AFTER THAT?! ARE YOU TELLING ME YOU DON'T CARE IF THIS COUNTRY BECOMES A FRENCH COLONY?!

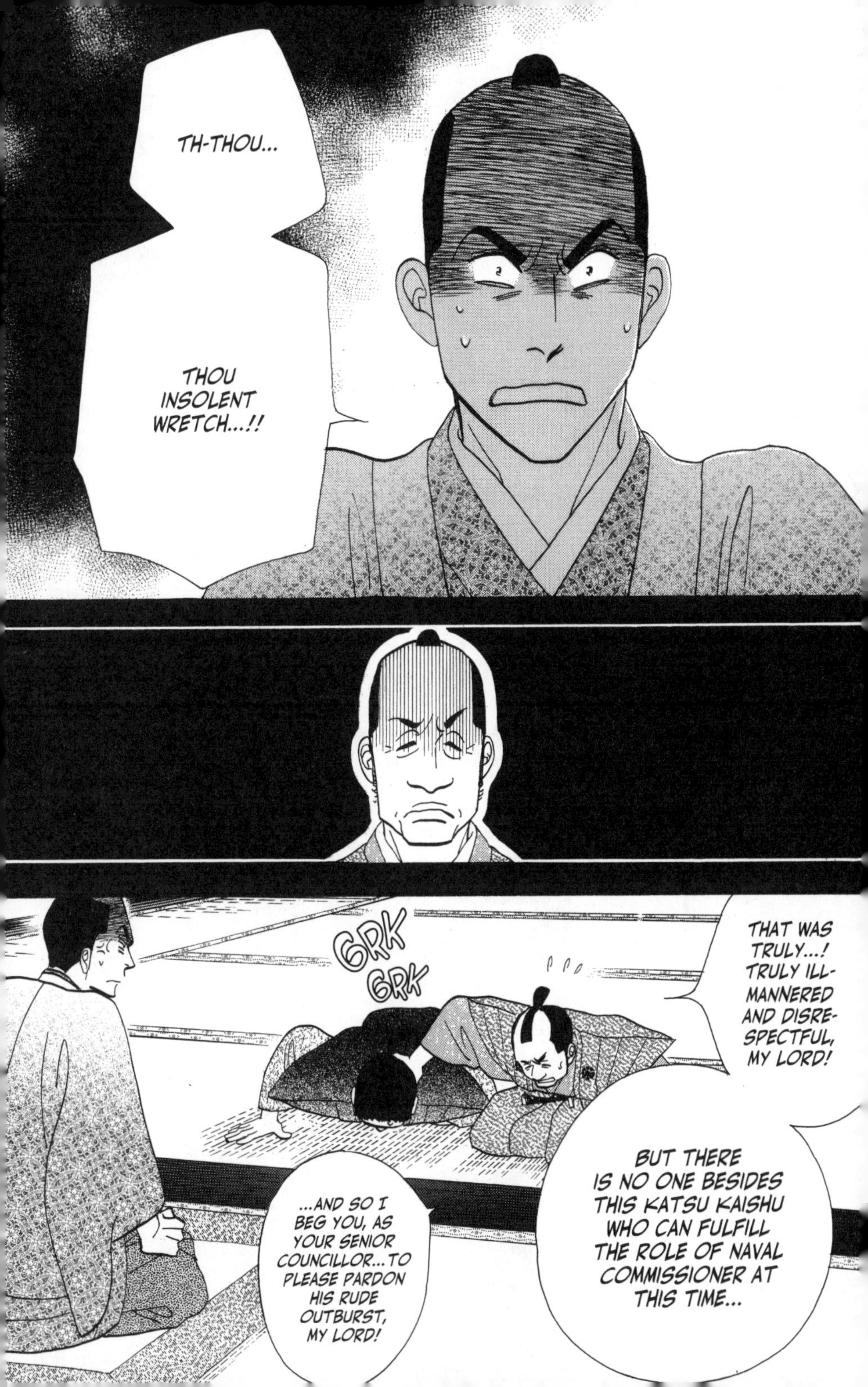
TH-THOU...
THOU INSOLENT WRETCH...!!
THAT WAS TRULY...! TRULY ILL-MANNERED AND DISRE-SPECTFUL, MY LORD!
GRK GRK
BUT THERE IS NO ONE BESIDES THIS KATSU KAISHU WHO CAN FULFILL THE ROLE OF NAVAL COMMISSIONER AT THIS TIME...
...AND SO I BEG YOU, AS YOUR SENIOR COUNCILLOR...TO PLEASE PARDON HIS RUDE OUTBURST, MY LORD!

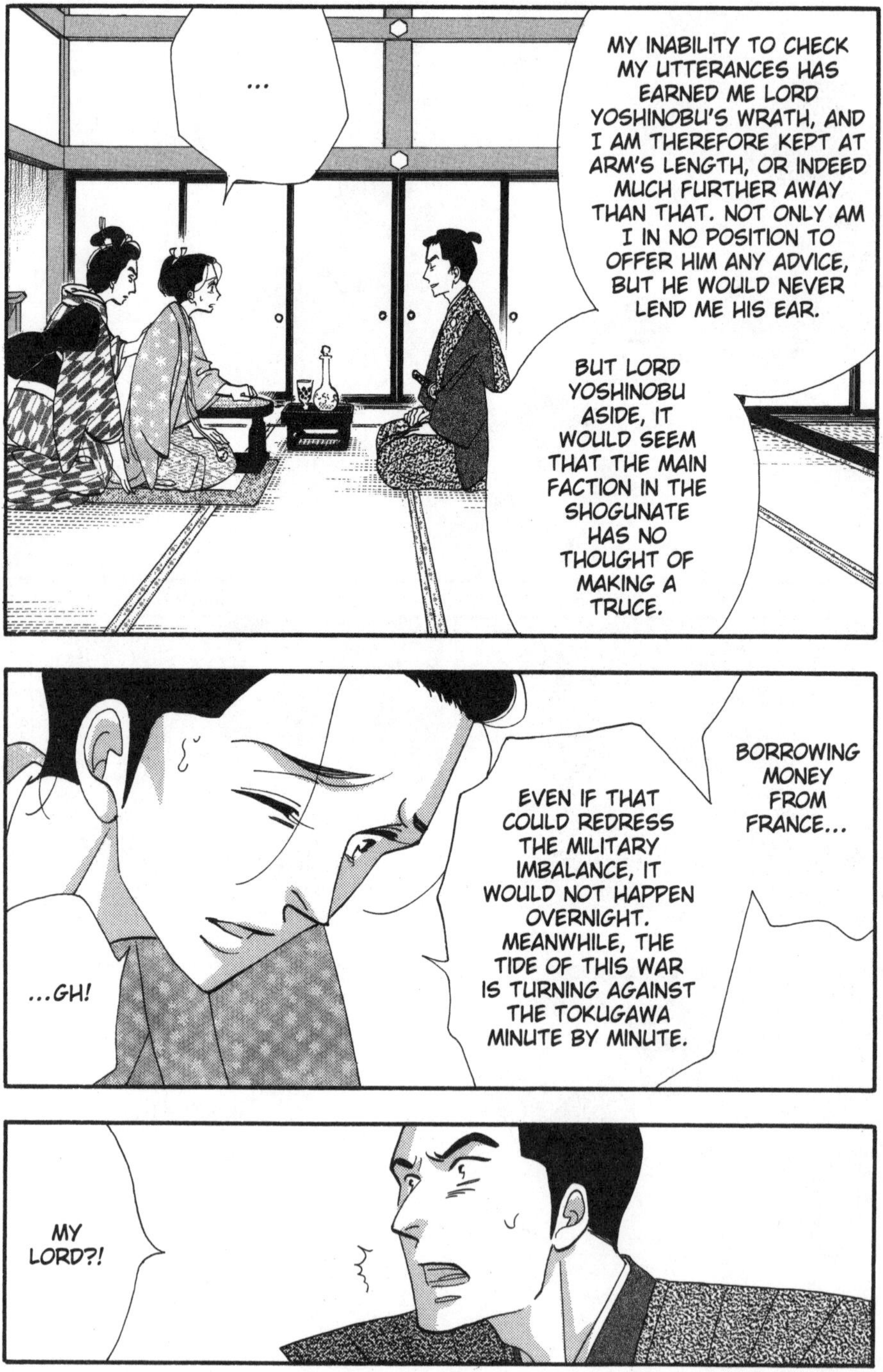
MY INABILITY TO CHECK MY UTTERANCES HAS EARNED ME LORD YOSHINOBU'S WRATH, AND I AM THEREFORE KEPT AT ARM'S LENGTH, OR INDEED MUCH FURTHER AWAY THAN THAT. NOT ONLY AM I IN NO POSITION TO OFFER HIM ANY ADVICE, BUT HE WOULD NEVER LEND ME HIS EAR.
...
BUT LORD YOSHINOBU ASIDE, IT WOULD SEEM THAT THE MAIN FACTION IN THE SHOGUNATE HAS NO THOUGHT OF MAKING A TRUCE.
BORROWING MONEY FROM FRANCE...
EVEN IF THAT COULD REDRESS THE MILITARY IMBALANCE, IT WOULD NOT HAPPEN OVERNIGHT. MEANWHILE, THE TIDE OF THIS WAR IS TURNING AGAINST THE TOKUGAWA MINUTE BY MINUTE.
...GH!
MY LORD?!

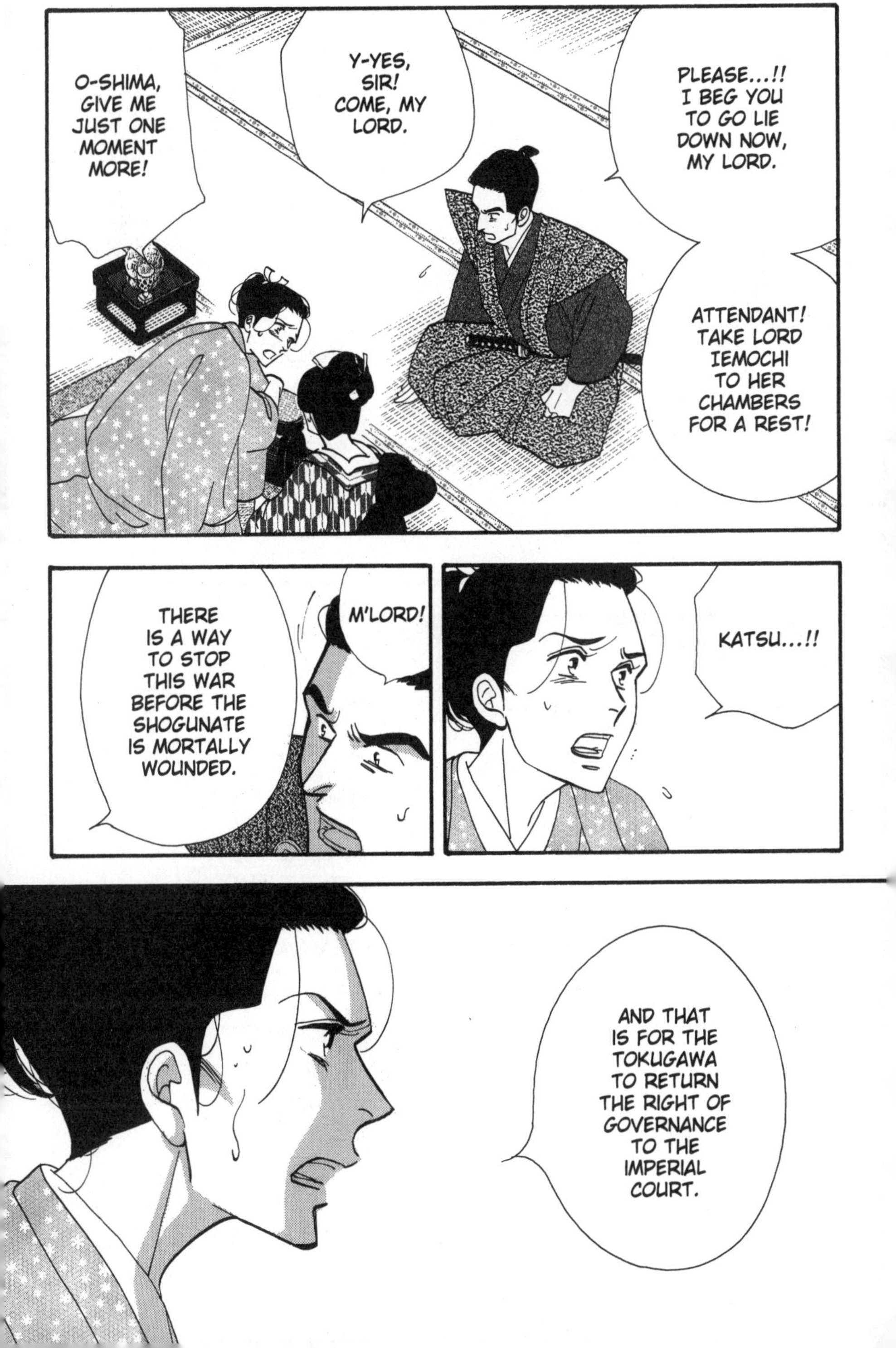
PLEASE...!! I BEG YOU TO GO LIE DOWN NOW, MY LORD.
ATTENDANT! TAKE LORD IEMOCHI TO HER CHAMBERS FOR A REST!
Y-YES, SIR! COME, MY LORD.
O-SHIMA, GIVE ME JUST ONE MOMENT MORE!
KATSU...!!
M'LORD!
THERE IS A WAY TO STOP THIS WAR BEFORE THE SHOGUNATE IS MORTALLY WOUNDED.
AND THAT IS FOR THE TOKUGAWA TO RETURN THE RIGHT OF GOVERNANCE TO THE IMPERIAL COURT.

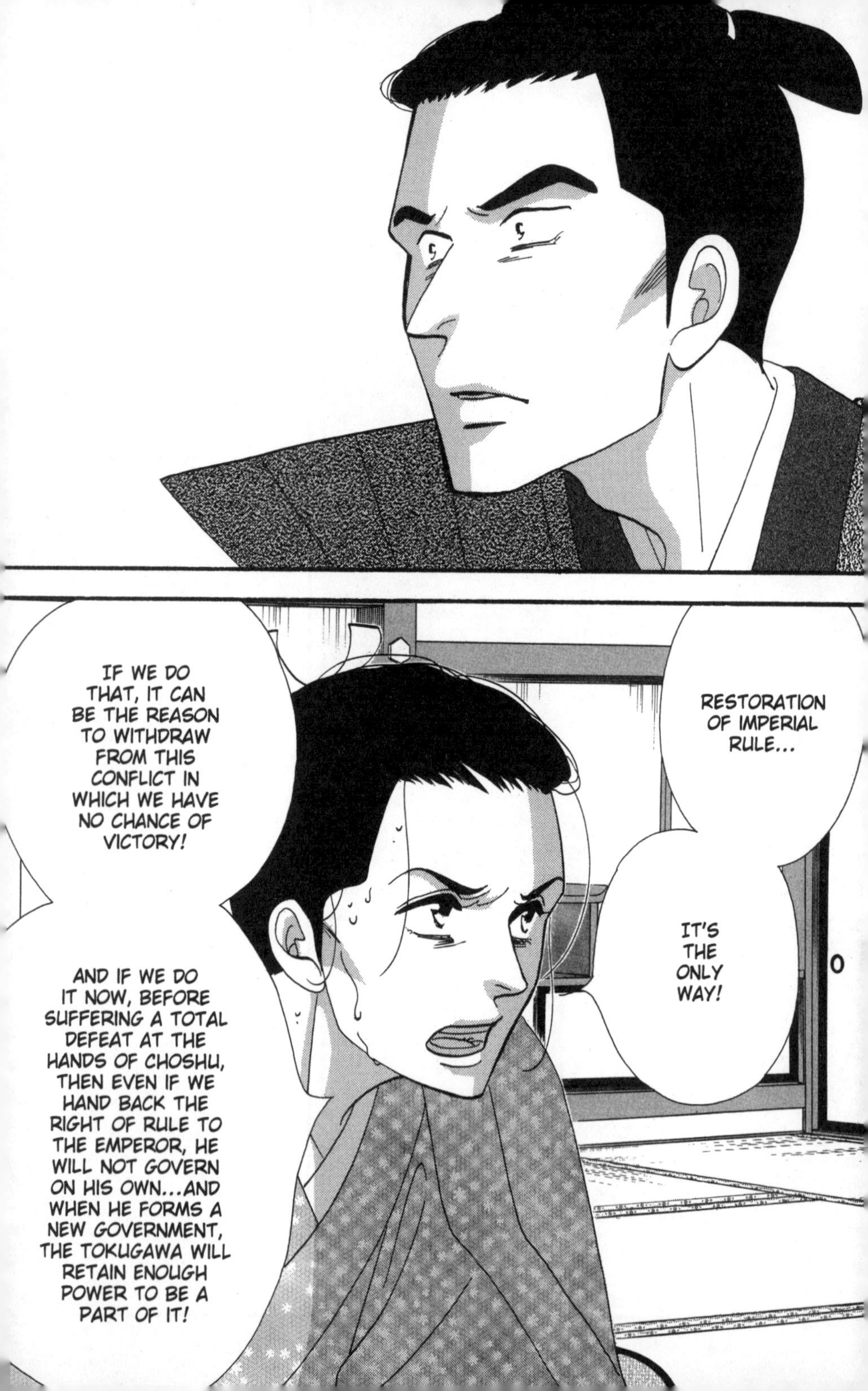
RESTORATION OF IMPERIAL RULE...
IT'S THE ONLY WAY!
IF WE DO THAT, IT CAN BE THE REASON TO WITHDRAW FROM THIS CONFLICT IN WHICH WE HAVE NO CHANCE OF VICTORY!
AND IF WE DO IT NOW, BEFORE SUFFERING A TOTAL DEFEAT AT THE HANDS OF CHOSHU, THEN EVEN IF WE HAND BACK THE RIGHT OF RULE TO THE EMPEROR, HE WILL NOT GOVERN ON HIS OWN...AND WHEN HE FORMS A NEW GOVERNMENT, THE TOKUGAWA WILL RETAIN ENOUGH POWER TO BE A PART OF IT!

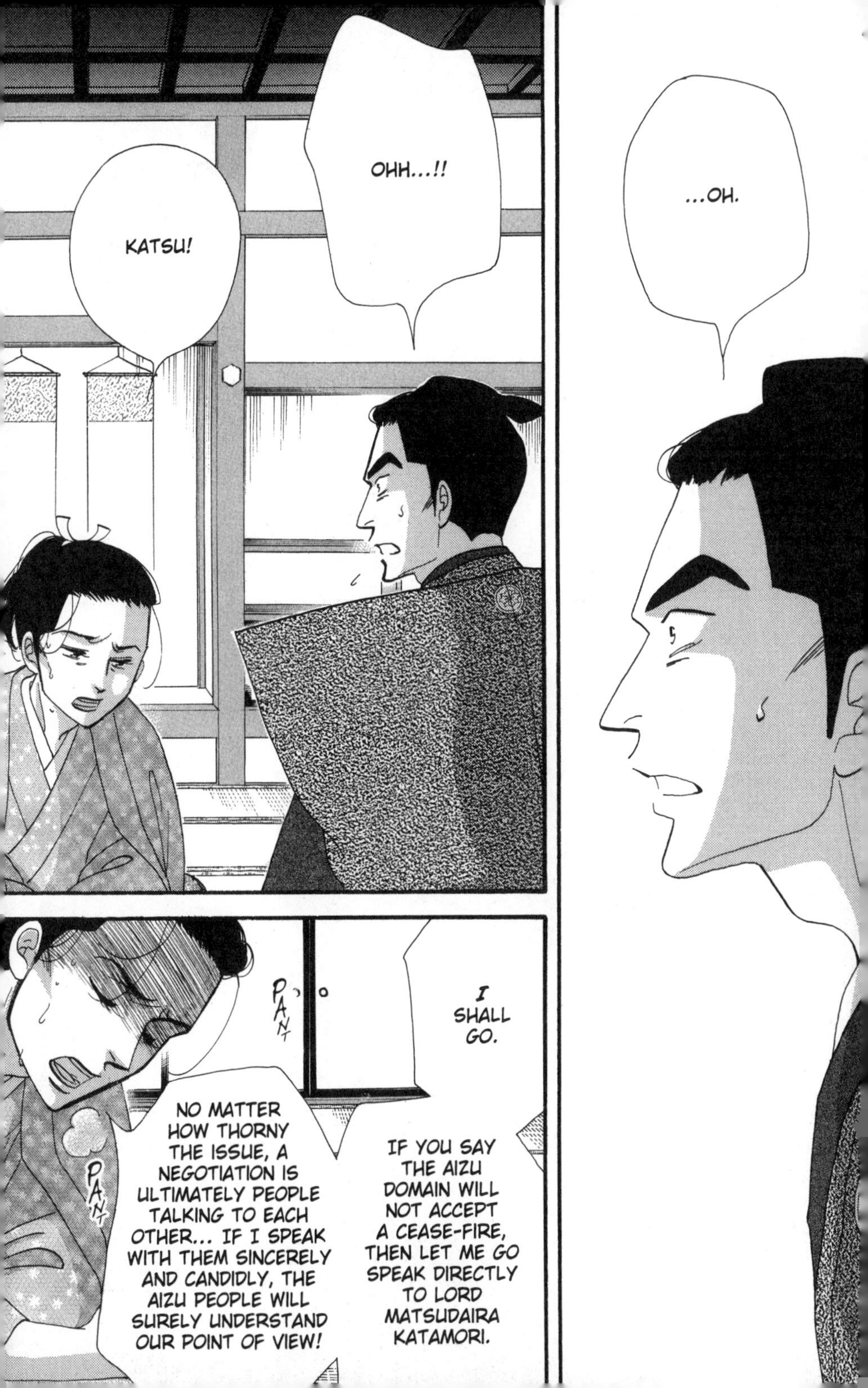
...OH.
OHH...!!
KATSU!
I SHALL GO.
PANT
IF YOU SAY THE AIZU DOMAIN WILL NOT ACCEPT A CEASE-FIRE, THEN LET ME GO SPEAK DIRECTLY TO LORD MATSUDAIRA KATAMORI.
NO MATTER HOW THORNY THE ISSUE, A NEGOTIATION IS ULTIMATELY PEOPLE TALKING TO EACH OTHER... IF I SPEAK WITH THEM SINCERELY AND CANDIDLY, THE AIZU PEOPLE WILL SURELY UNDERSTAND OUR POINT OF VIEW!
PANT

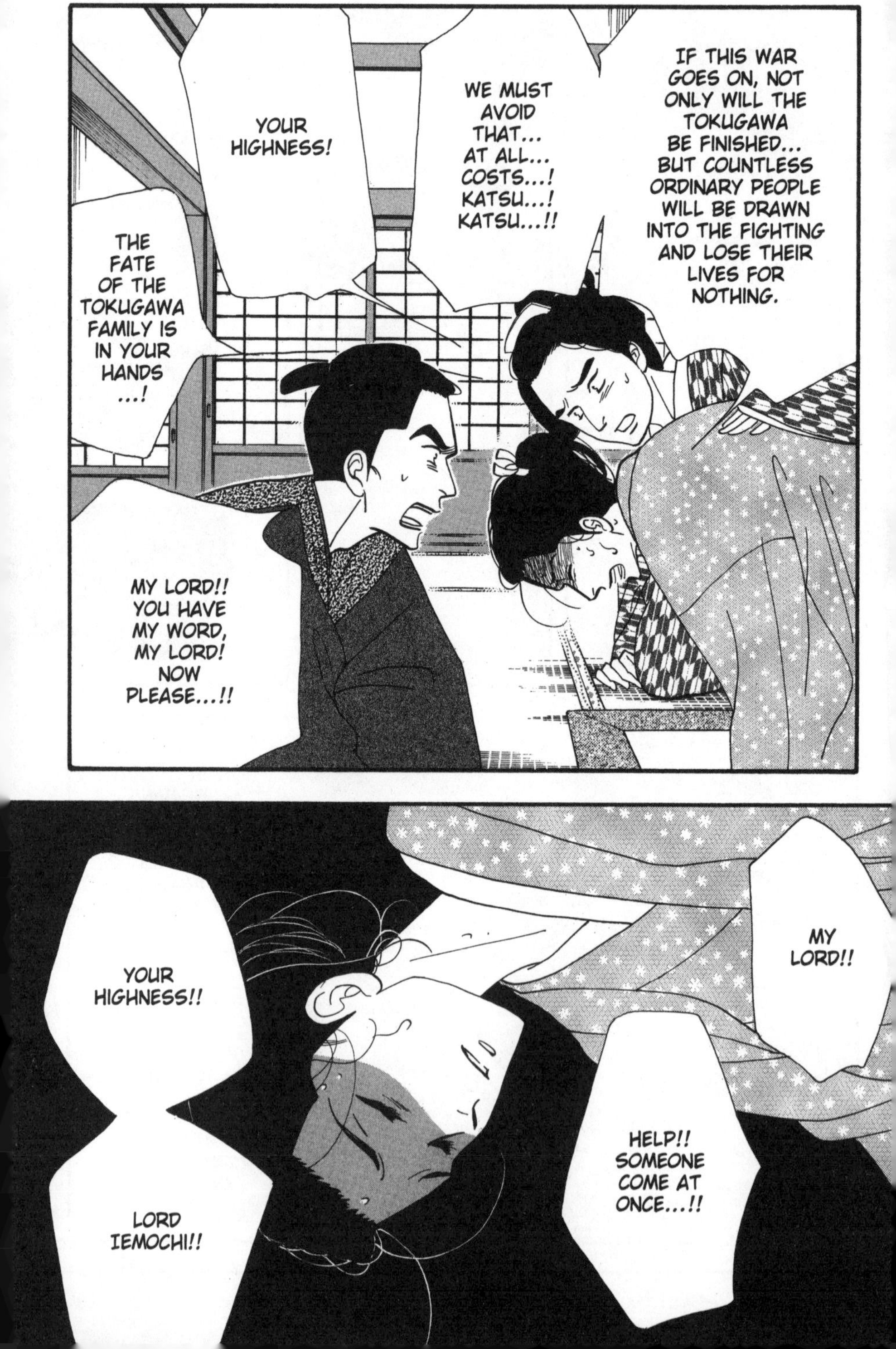
IF THIS WAR GOES ON, NOT ONLY WILL THE TOKUGAWA BE FINISHED... BUT COUNTLESS ORDINARY PEOPLE WILL BE DRAWN INTO THE FIGHTING AND LOSE THEIR LIVES FOR NOTHING.
WE MUST AVOID THAT... AT ALL... COSTS...! KATSU...! KATSU...!!
YOUR HIGHNESS!
THE FATE OF THE TOKUGAWA FAMILY IS IN YOUR HANDS ...!
MY LORD!! YOU HAVE MY WORD, MY LORD! NOW PLEASE...!!
MY LORD!!
HELP!! SOMEONE COME AT ONCE...!!
YOUR HIGHNESS!!
LORD IEMOCHI!!

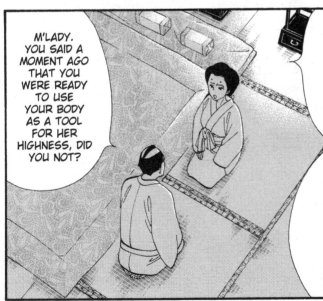

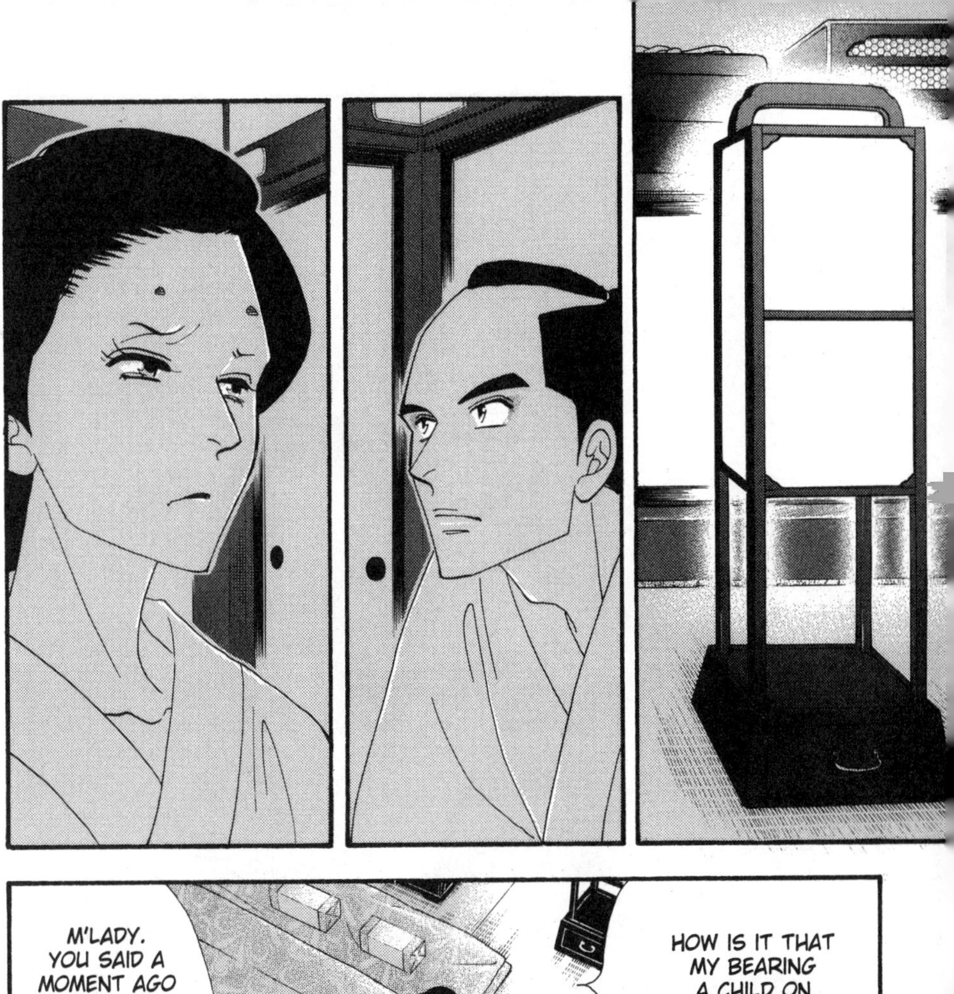
HOW IS IT THAT MY BEARING A CHILD ON BEHALF OF LORD IEMOCHI WOULD GO AGAINST HER WISHES?
IF I GAVE BIRTH TO A CHILD, SHE WOULD LOVE THAT CHILD AS THOUGH IT WERE HER OWN. I JUST KNOW IT!
M'LADY. YOU SAID A MOMENT AGO THAT YOU WERE READY TO USE YOUR BODY AS A TOOL FOR HER HIGHNESS, DID YOU NOT?

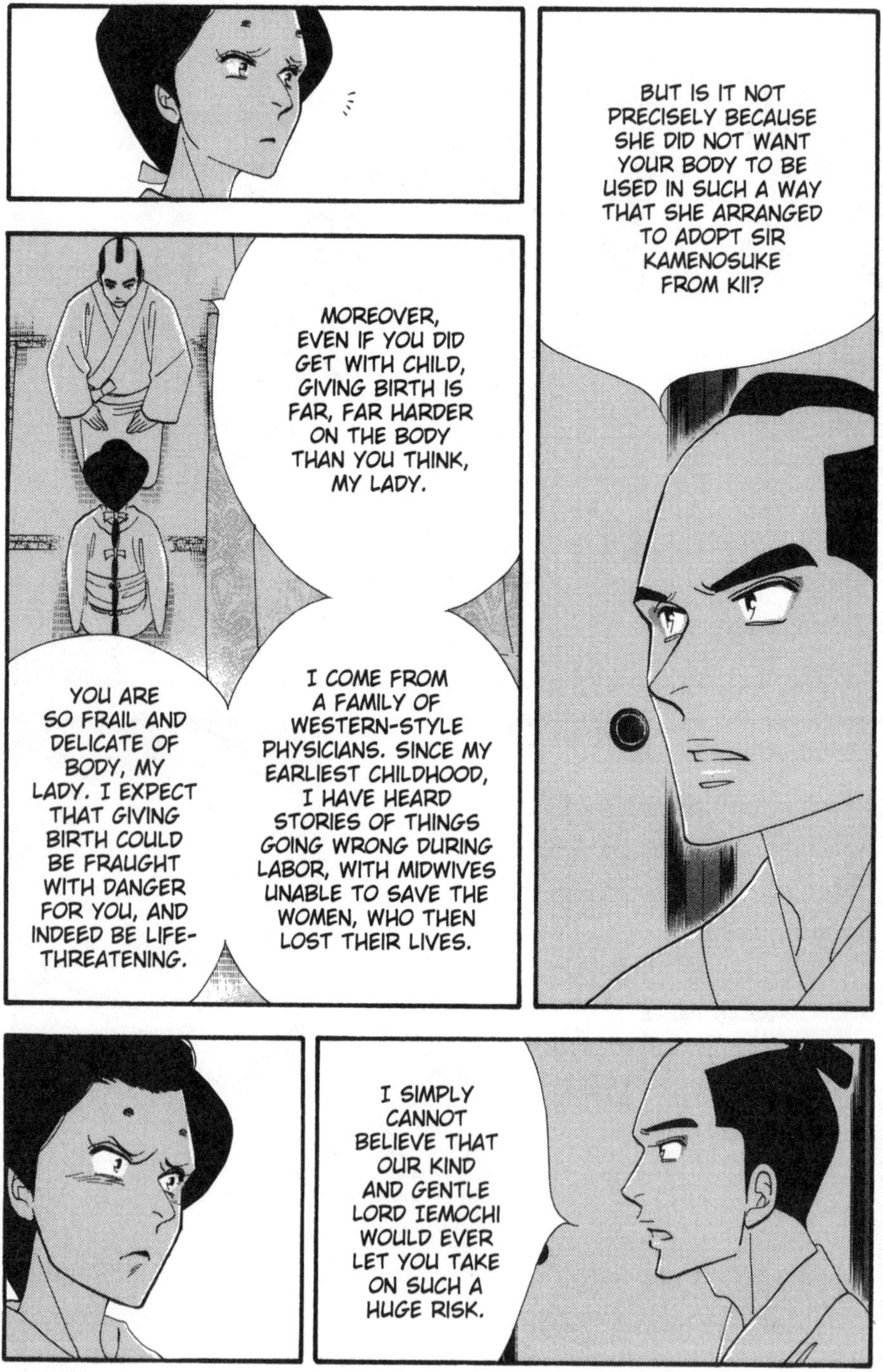
BUT IS IT NOT PRECISELY BECAUSE SHE DID NOT WANT YOUR BODY TO BE USED IN SUCH A WAY THAT SHE ARRANGED TO ADOPT SIR KAMENOSUKE FROM KII?
MOREOVER, EVEN IF YOU DID GET WITH CHILD, GIVING BIRTH IS FAR, FAR HARDER ON THE BODY THAN YOU THINK, MY LADY.
I COME FROM A FAMILY OF WESTERN-STYLE PHYSICIANS. SINCE MY EARLIEST CHILDHOOD, I HAVE HEARD STORIES OF THINGS GOING WRONG DURING LABOR, WITH MIDWIVES UNABLE TO SAVE THE WOMEN, WHO THEN LOST THEIR LIVES.
YOU ARE SO FRAIL AND DELICATE OF BODY, MY LADY. I EXPECT THAT GIVING BIRTH COULD BE FRAUGHT WITH DANGER FOR YOU, AND INDEED BE LIFE-THREATENING.
I SIMPLY CANNOT BELIEVE THAT OUR KIND AND GENTLE LORD IEMOCHI WOULD EVER LET YOU TAKE ON SUCH A HUGE RISK.

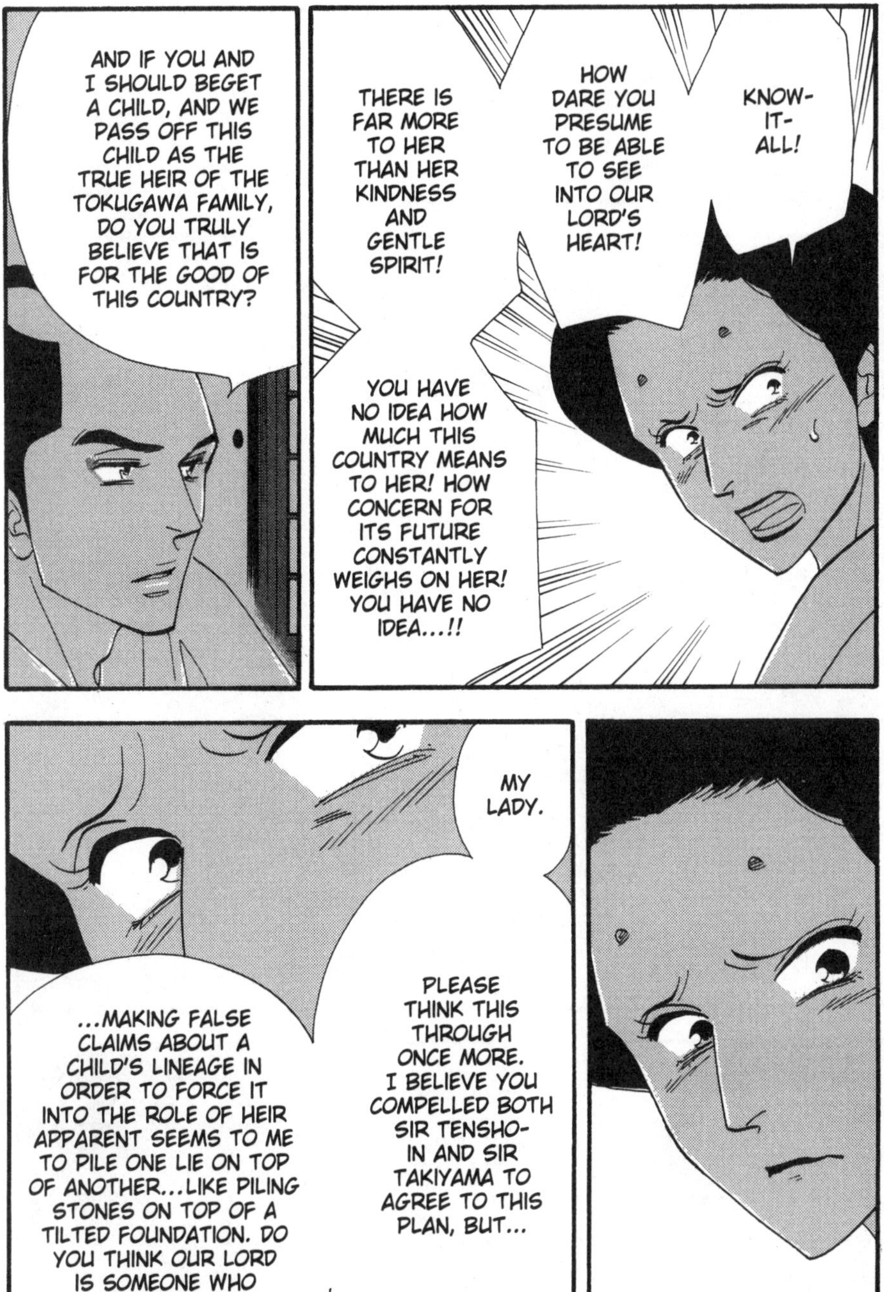
KNOW-IT-ALL!
HOW DARE YOU PRESUME TO BE ABLE TO SEE INTO OUR LORD'S HEART!
THERE IS FAR MORE TO HER THAN HER KINDNESS AND GENTLE SPIRIT!
YOU HAVE NO IDEA HOW MUCH THIS COUNTRY MEANS TO HER! HOW CONCERN FOR ITS FUTURE CONSTANTLY WEIGHS ON HER! YOU HAVE NO IDEA...!!
AND IF YOU AND I SHOULD BEGET A CHILD, AND WE PASS OFF THIS CHILD AS THE TRUE HEIR OF THE TOKUGAWA FAMILY, DO YOU TRULY BELIEVE THAT IS FOR THE GOOD OF THIS COUNTRY?
MY LADY.
PLEASE THINK THIS THROUGH ONCE MORE. I BELIEVE YOU COMPELLED BOTH SIR TENSHO-IN AND SIR TAKIYAMA TO AGREE TO THIS PLAN, BUT...
...MAKING FALSE CLAIMS ABOUT A CHILD'S LINEAGE IN ORDER TO FORCE IT INTO THE ROLE OF HEIR APPARENT SEEMS TO ME TO PILE ONE LIE ON TOP OF ANOTHER...LIKE PILING STONES ON TOP OF A TILTED FOUNDATION. DO YOU THINK OUR LORD IS SOMEONE WHO WOULD APPROVE OF SUCH A PLAN?

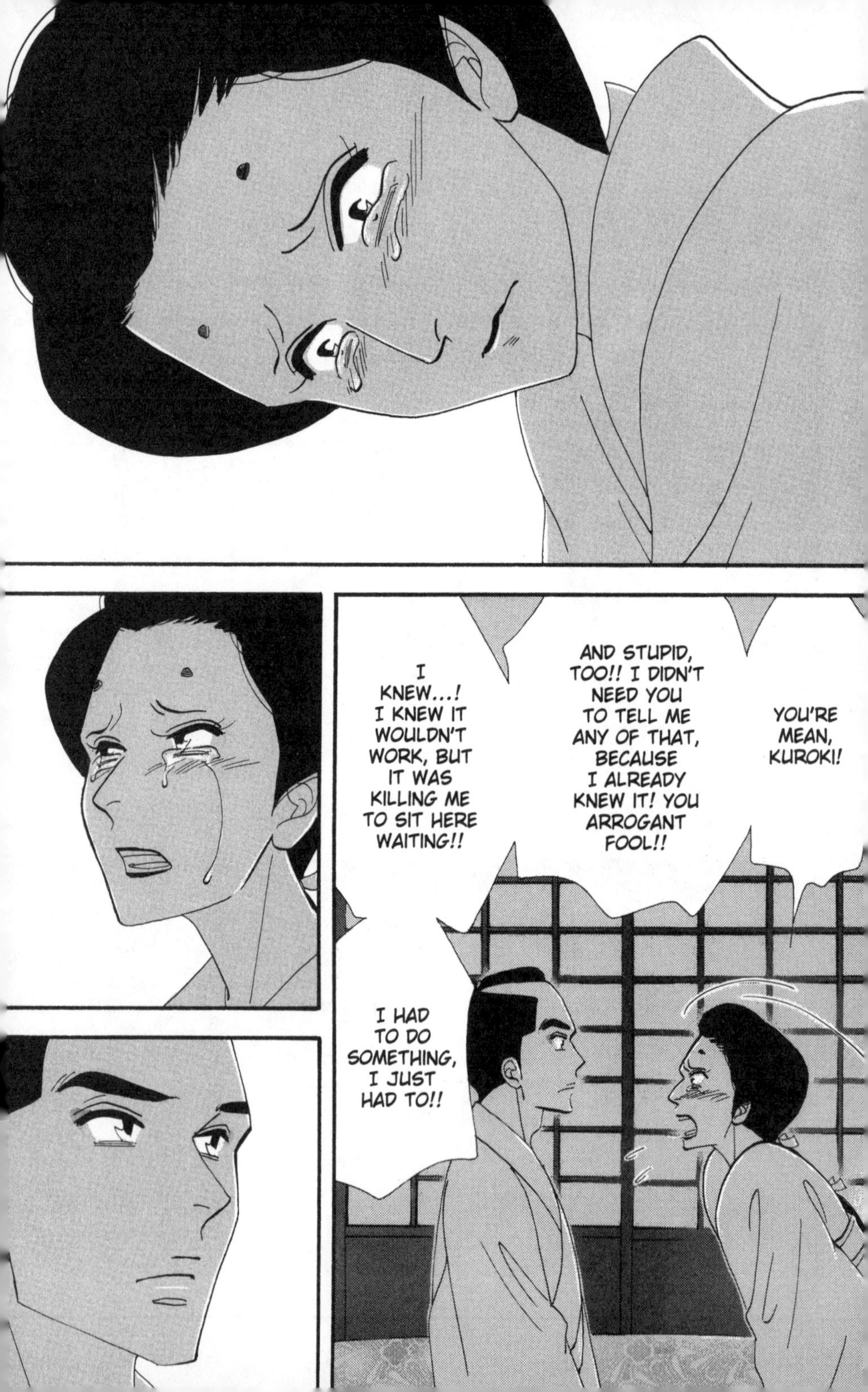
YOU'RE MEAN, KUROKI!
AND STUPID, TOO!! I DIDN'T NEED YOU TO TELL ME ANY OF THAT, BECAUSE I ALREADY KNEW IT! YOU ARROGANT FOOL!!
I KNEW...! I KNEW IT WOULDN'T WORK, BUT IT WAS KILLING ME TO SIT HERE WAITING!!
I HAD TO DO SOMETHING, I JUST HAD TO!!

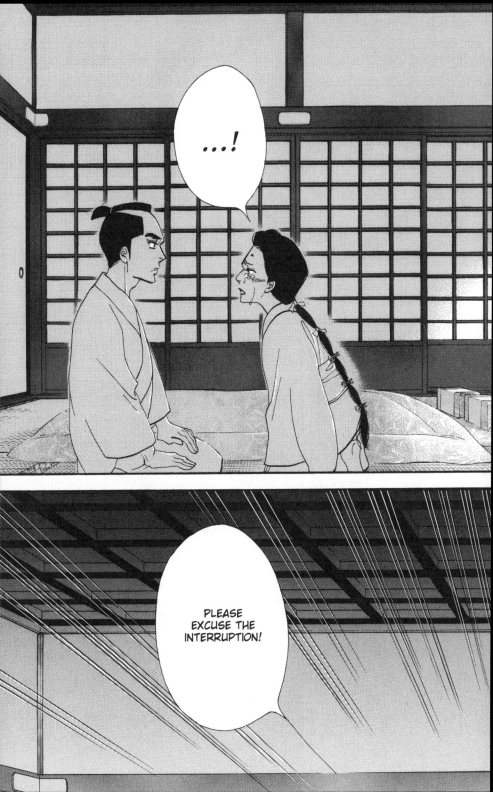

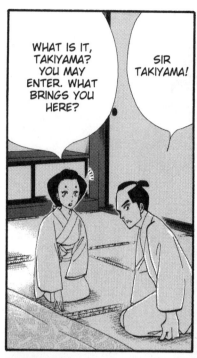

WHAT IS IT, TAKIYAMA? YOU MAY ENTER. WHAT BRINGS YOU HERE?

SIR TAKIYAMA!

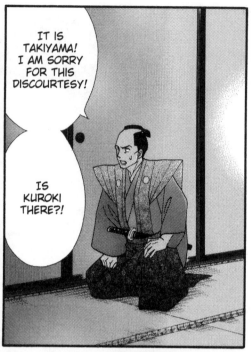

IT IS TAKIYAMA! I AM SORRY FOR THIS DISCOURTESY!

IS KUROKI THERE?!

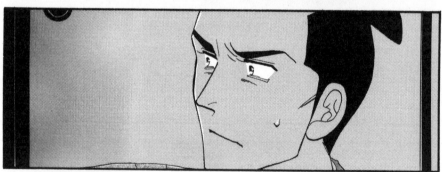

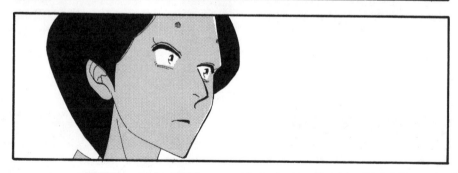

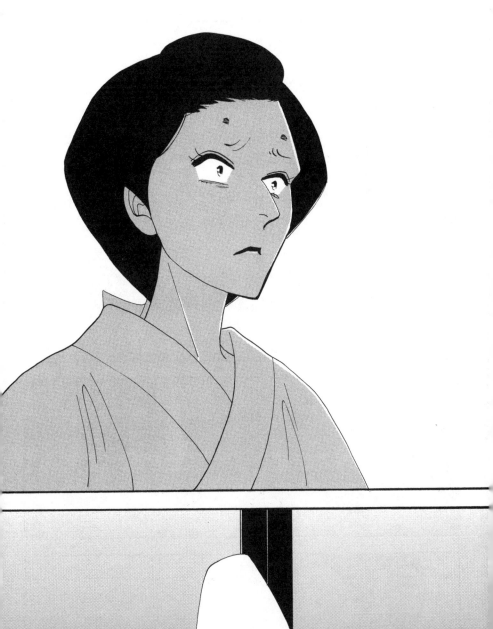

ENTER.

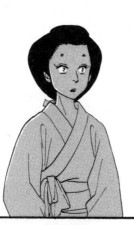

LOOK ME
IN THE
FACE AND
SAY IT.

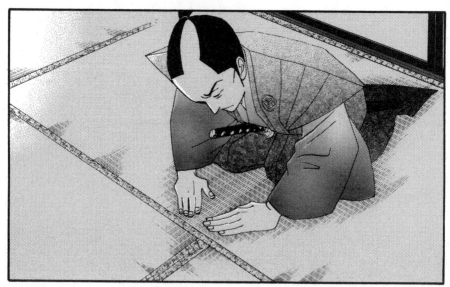

51

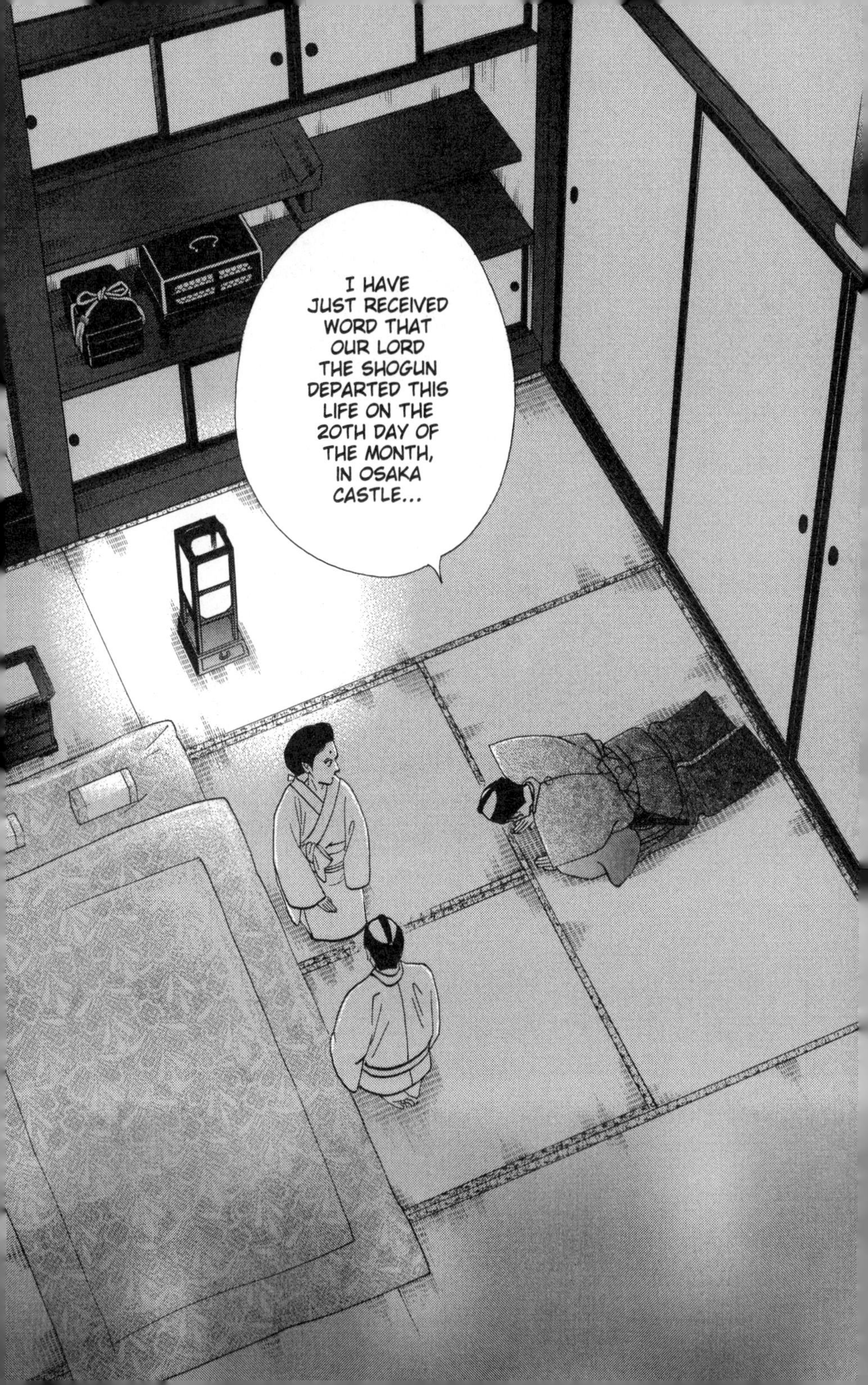
I HAVE JUST RECEIVED WORD THAT OUR LORD THE SHOGUN DEPARTED THIS LIFE ON THE 20TH DAY OF THE MONTH, IN OSAKA CASTLE...

Ōoku

THE INNER CHAMBERS

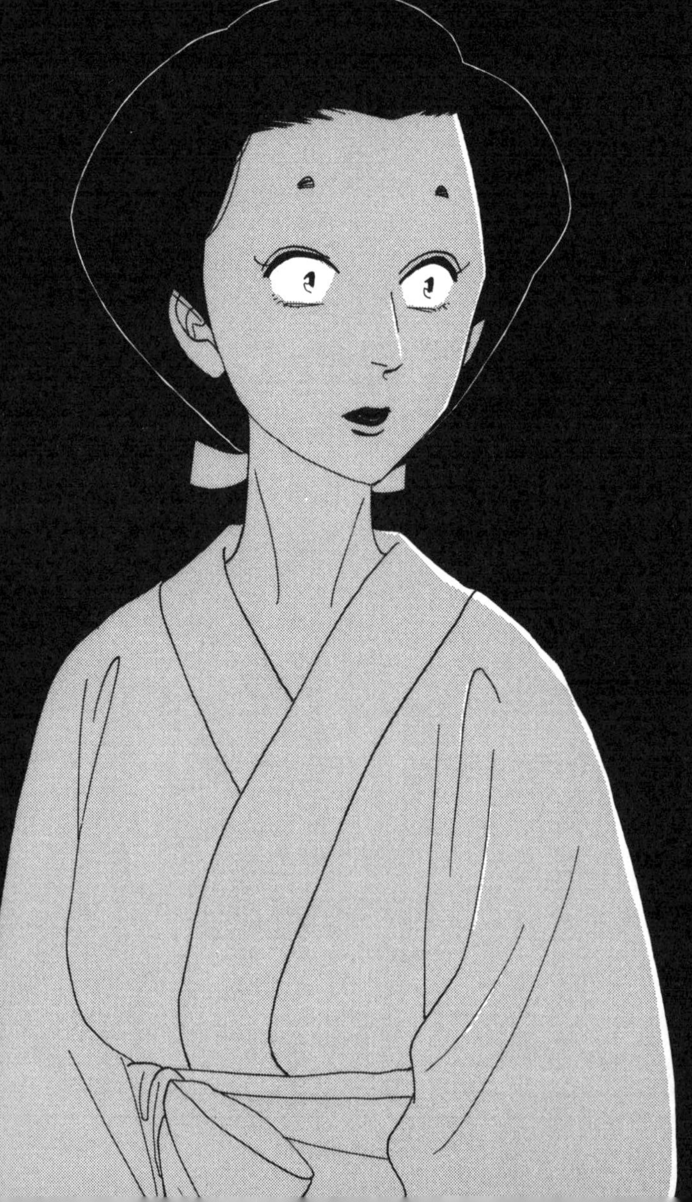

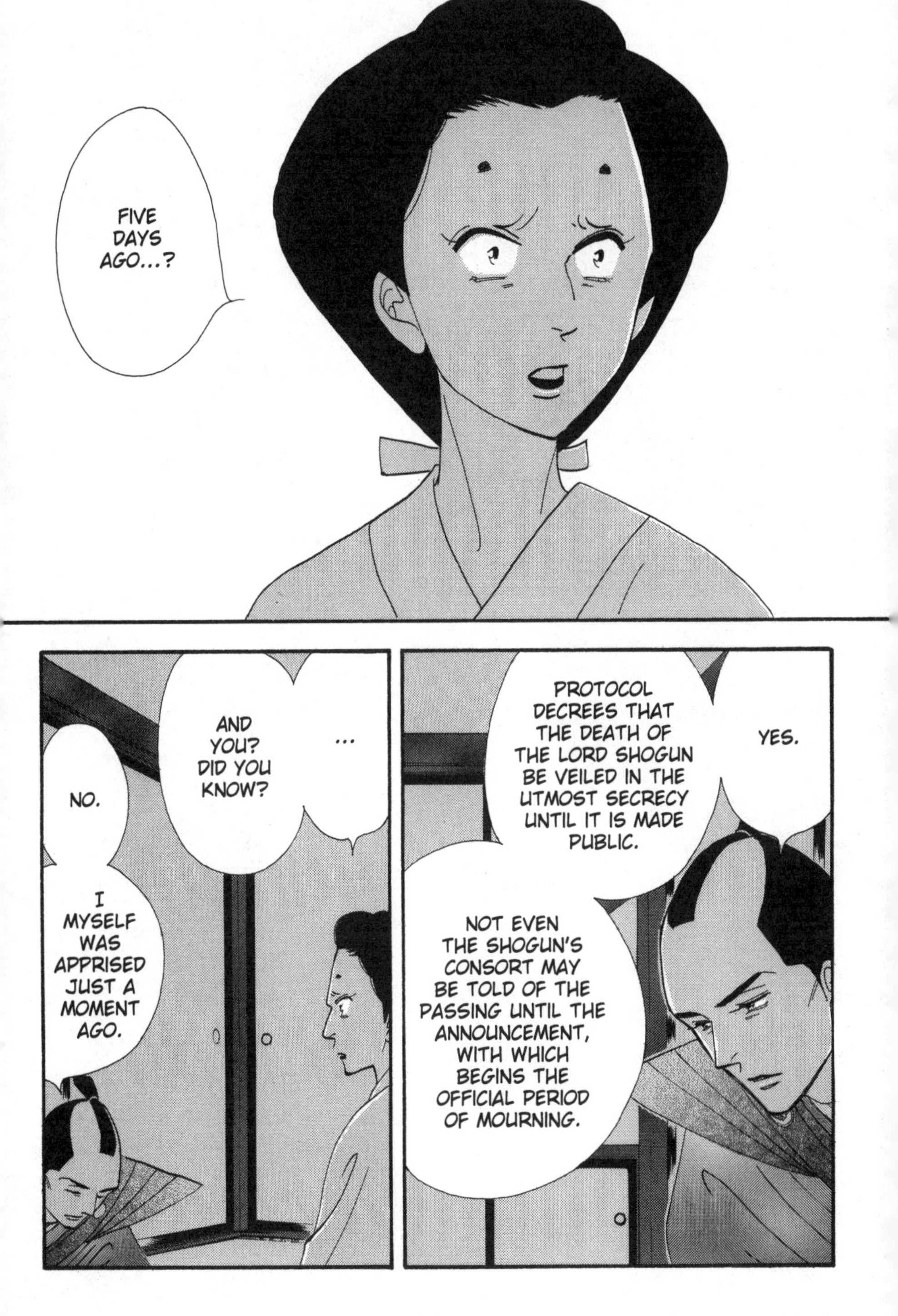
FIVE DAYS AGO...?
YES.
PROTOCOL DECREES THAT THE DEATH OF THE LORD SHOGUN BE VEILED IN THE UTMOST SECRECY UNTIL IT IS MADE PUBLIC.
NOT EVEN THE SHOGUN'S CONSORT MAY BE TOLD OF THE PASSING UNTIL THE ANNOUNCEMENT, WITH WHICH BEGINS THE OFFICIAL PERIOD OF MOURNING.
...
AND YOU? DID YOU KNOW?
NO.
I MYSELF WAS APPRISED JUST A MOMENT AGO.

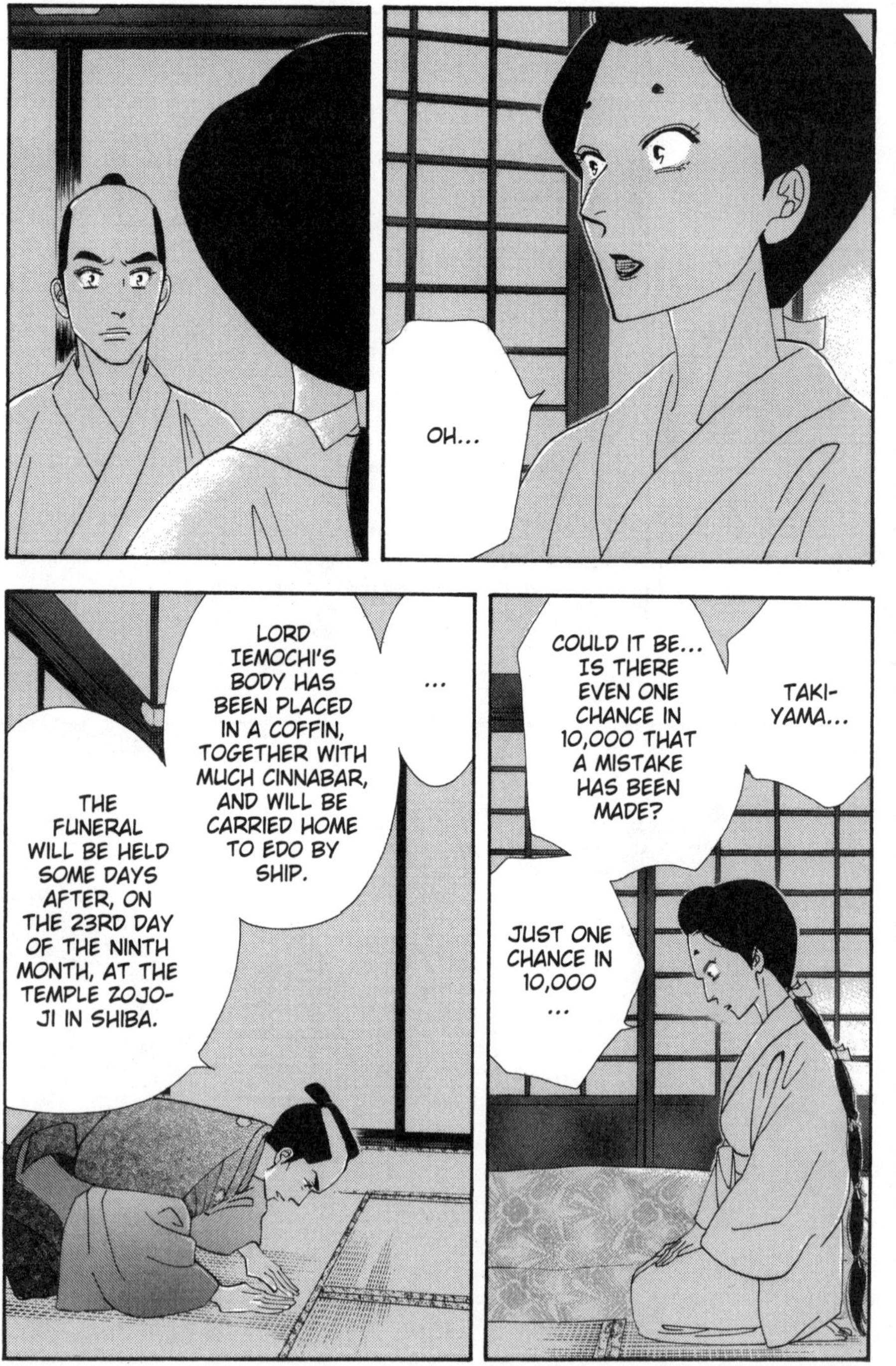
OH...
TAKI-YAMA...
COULD IT BE... IS THERE EVEN ONE CHANCE IN 10,000 THAT A MISTAKE HAS BEEN MADE?
JUST ONE CHANCE IN 10,000 ...
...
LORD IEMOCHI'S BODY HAS BEEN PLACED IN A COFFIN, TOGETHER WITH MUCH CINNABAR, AND WILL BE CARRIED HOME TO EDO BY SHIP.
THE FUNERAL WILL BE HELD SOME DAYS AFTER, ON THE 23RD DAY OF THE NINTH MONTH, AT THE TEMPLE ZOJO-JI IN SHIBA.

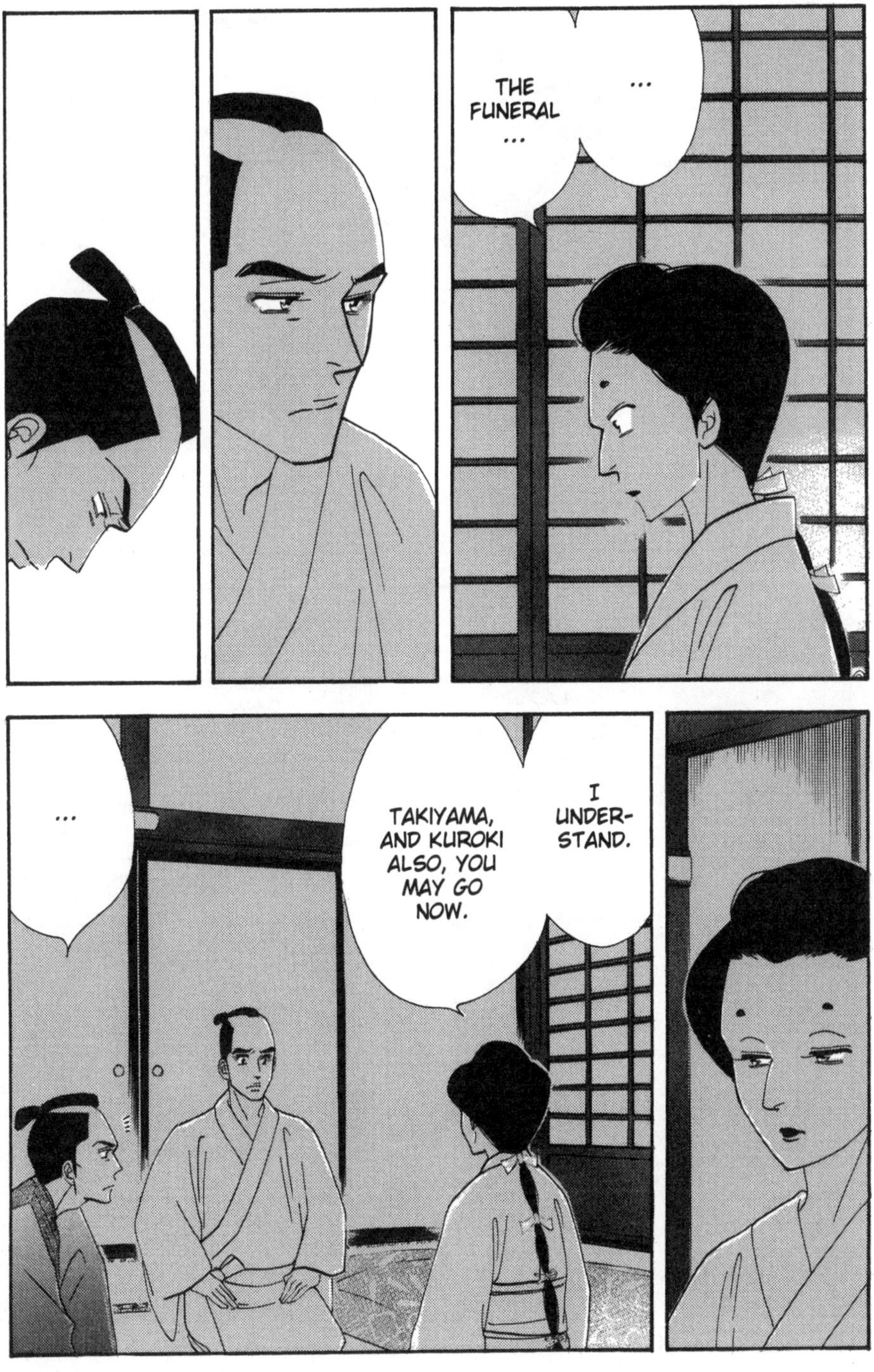
...
THE FUNERAL ...
I UNDER-STAND.
TAKIYAMA, AND KUROKI ALSO, YOU MAY GO NOW.
...

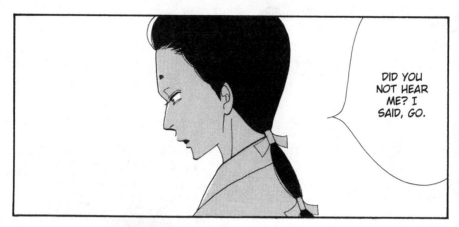

DID YOU NOT HEAR ME? I SAID, GO.

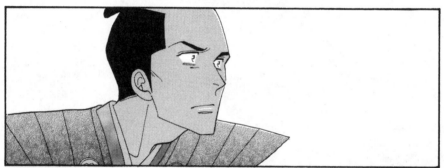

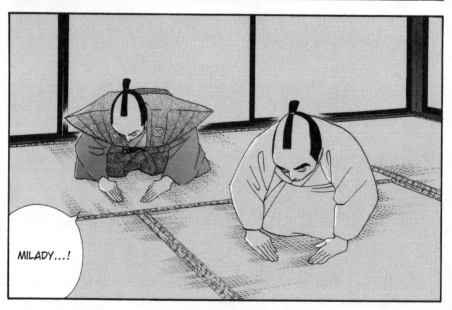

MILADY...!

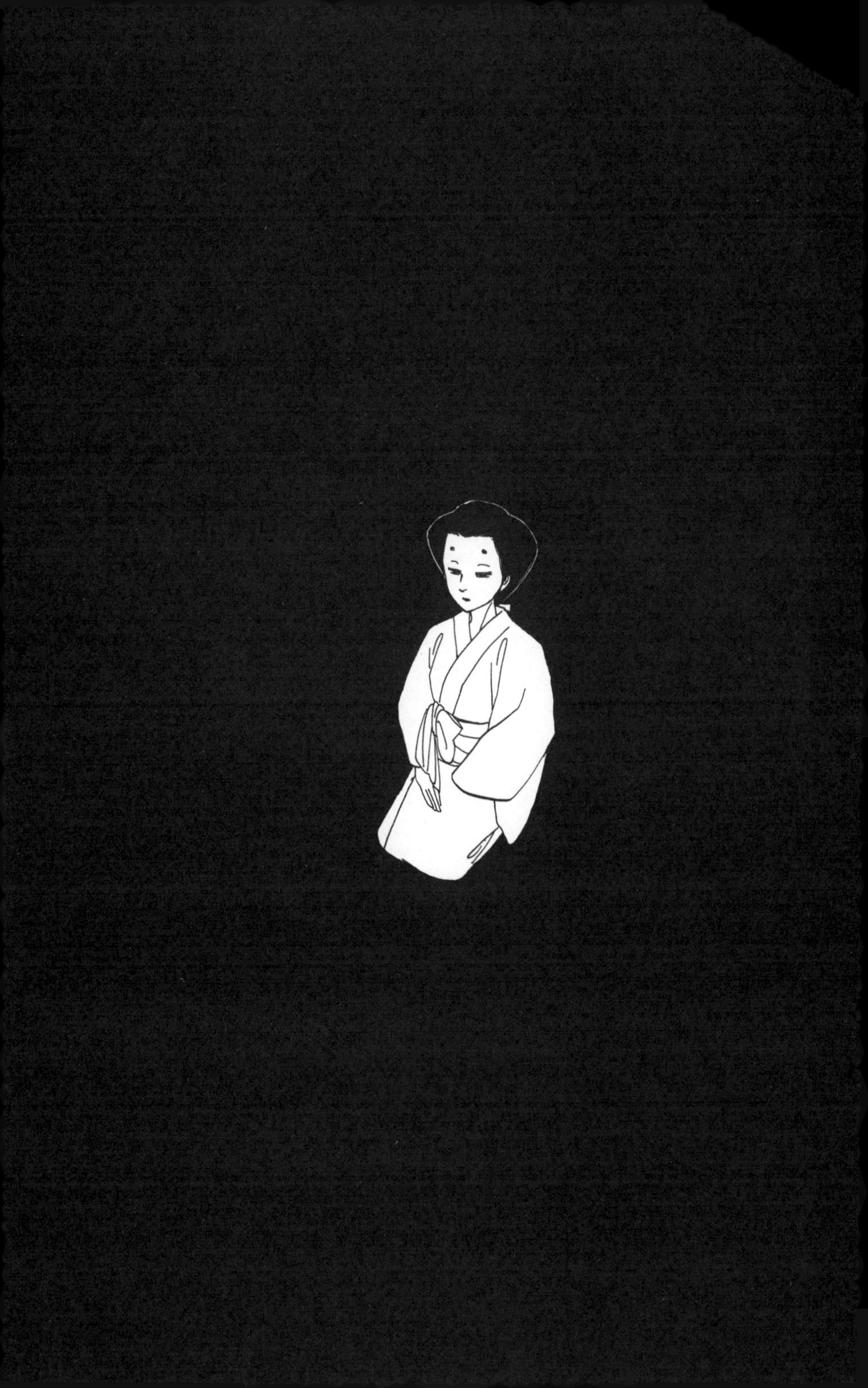

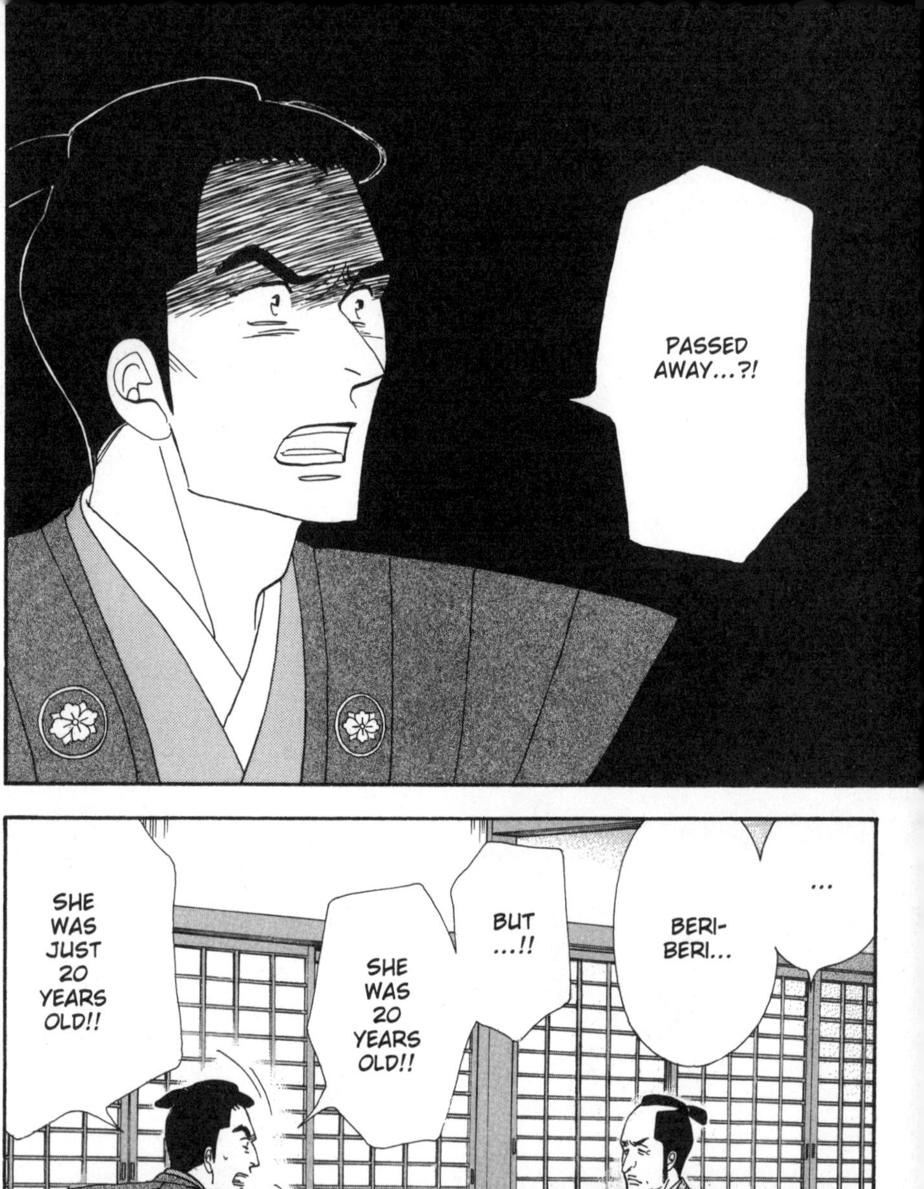
PASSED AWAY...?!
...
BERI-BERI...
BUT ...!!
SHE WAS 20 YEARS OLD!!
SHE WAS JUST 20 YEARS OLD!!

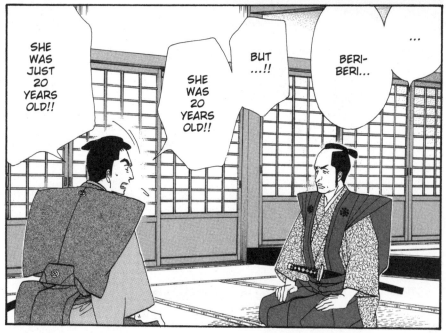

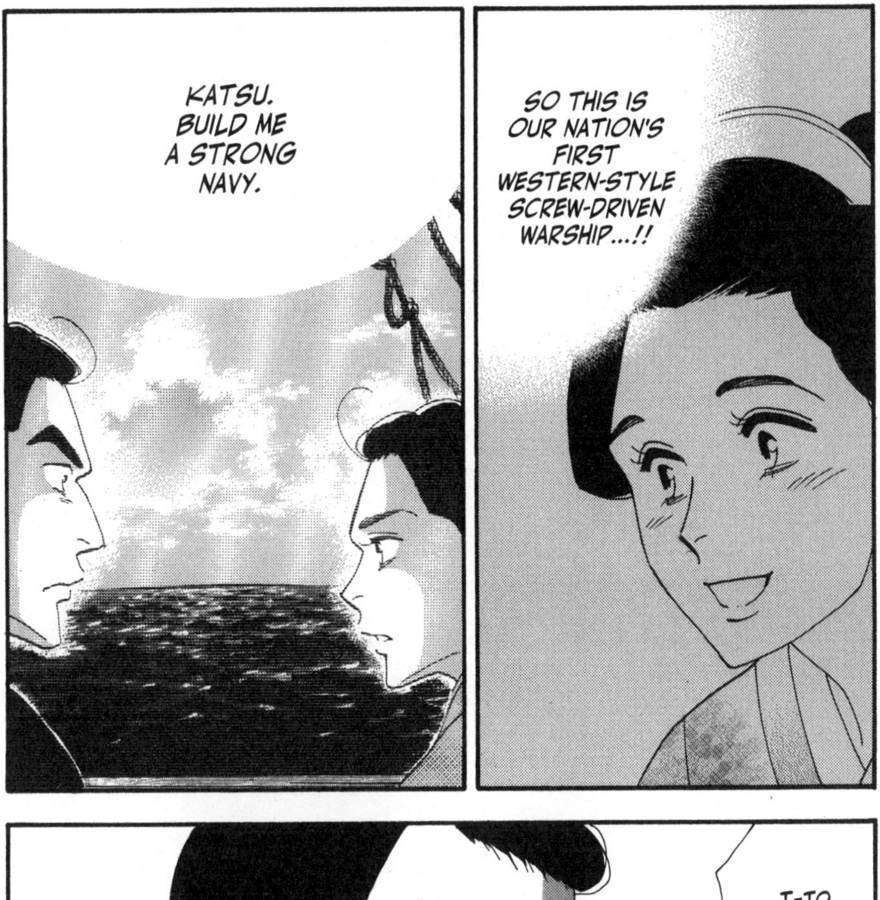
SO THIS IS OUR NATION'S FIRST WESTERN-STYLE SCREW-DRIVEN WARSHIP...!!
KATSU. BUILD ME A STRONG NAVY.
T-TO THINK... TH-THAT...
THAT SOMEONE WHO SPOKE OF JAPAN'S FUTURE WITH SUCH BRIGHT, SHINING EYES IS NO MORE...
AND FOR HER, IT WAS NEVER ABOUT KEEPING THE TOKUGAWA IN POWER. ALL SHE EVER CARED ABOUT WAS THE PEACE AND SECURITY OF THE PEOPLE OF THIS COUNTRY...

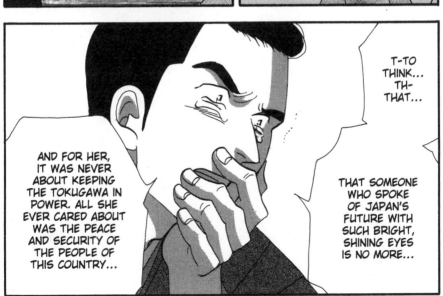

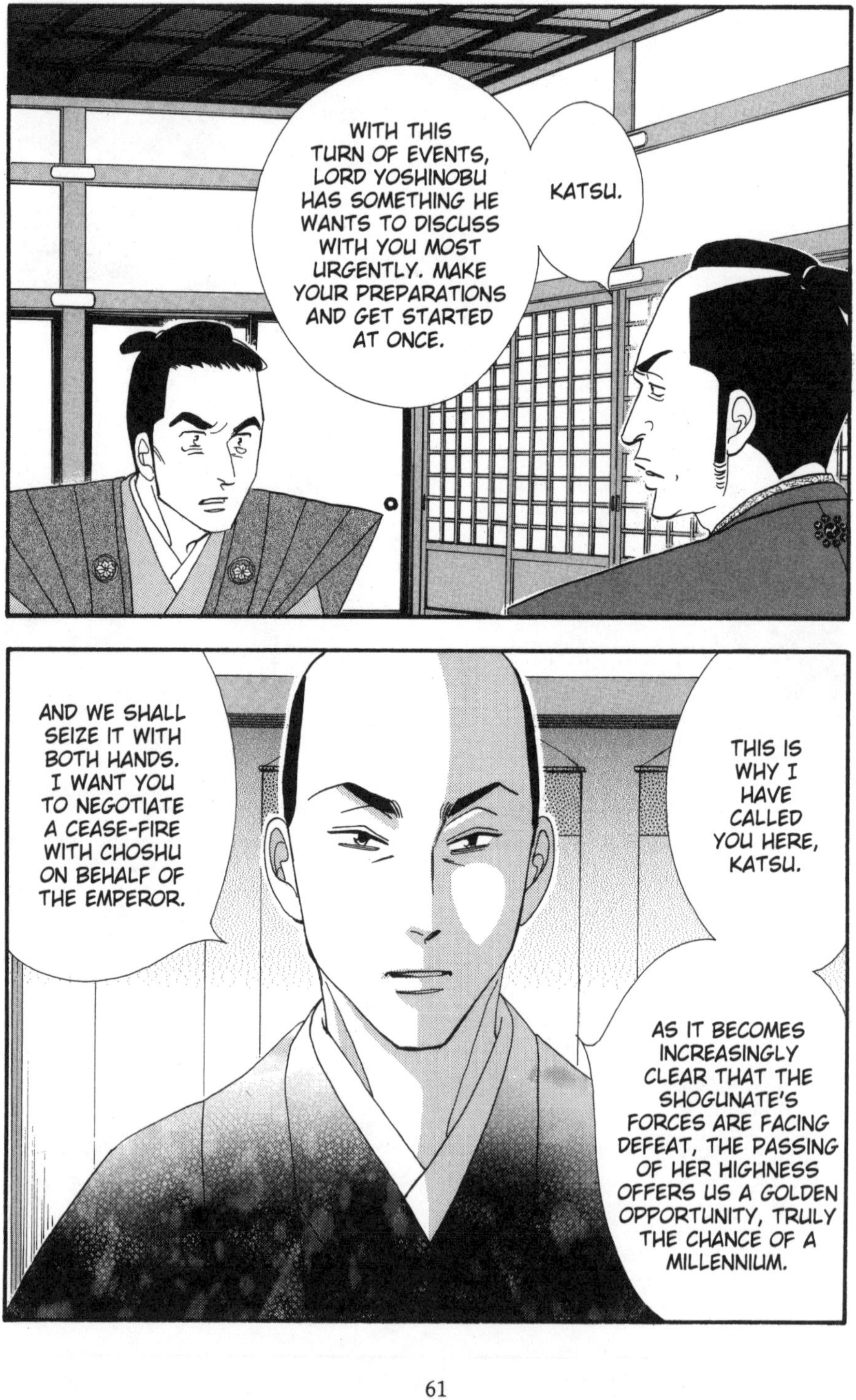
KATSU.
WITH THIS TURN OF EVENTS, LORD YOSHINOBU HAS SOMETHING HE WANTS TO DISCUSS WITH YOU MOST URGENTLY. MAKE YOUR PREPARATIONS AND GET STARTED AT ONCE.
THIS IS WHY I HAVE CALLED YOU HERE, KATSU.
AS IT BECOMES INCREASINGLY CLEAR THAT THE SHOGUNATE'S FORCES ARE FACING DEFEAT, THE PASSING OF HER HIGHNESS OFFERS US A GOLDEN OPPORTUNITY, TRULY THE CHANCE OF A MILLENNIUM.
AND WE SHALL SEIZE IT WITH BOTH HANDS. I WANT YOU TO NEGOTIATE A CEASE-FIRE WITH CHOSHU ON BEHALF OF THE EMPEROR.

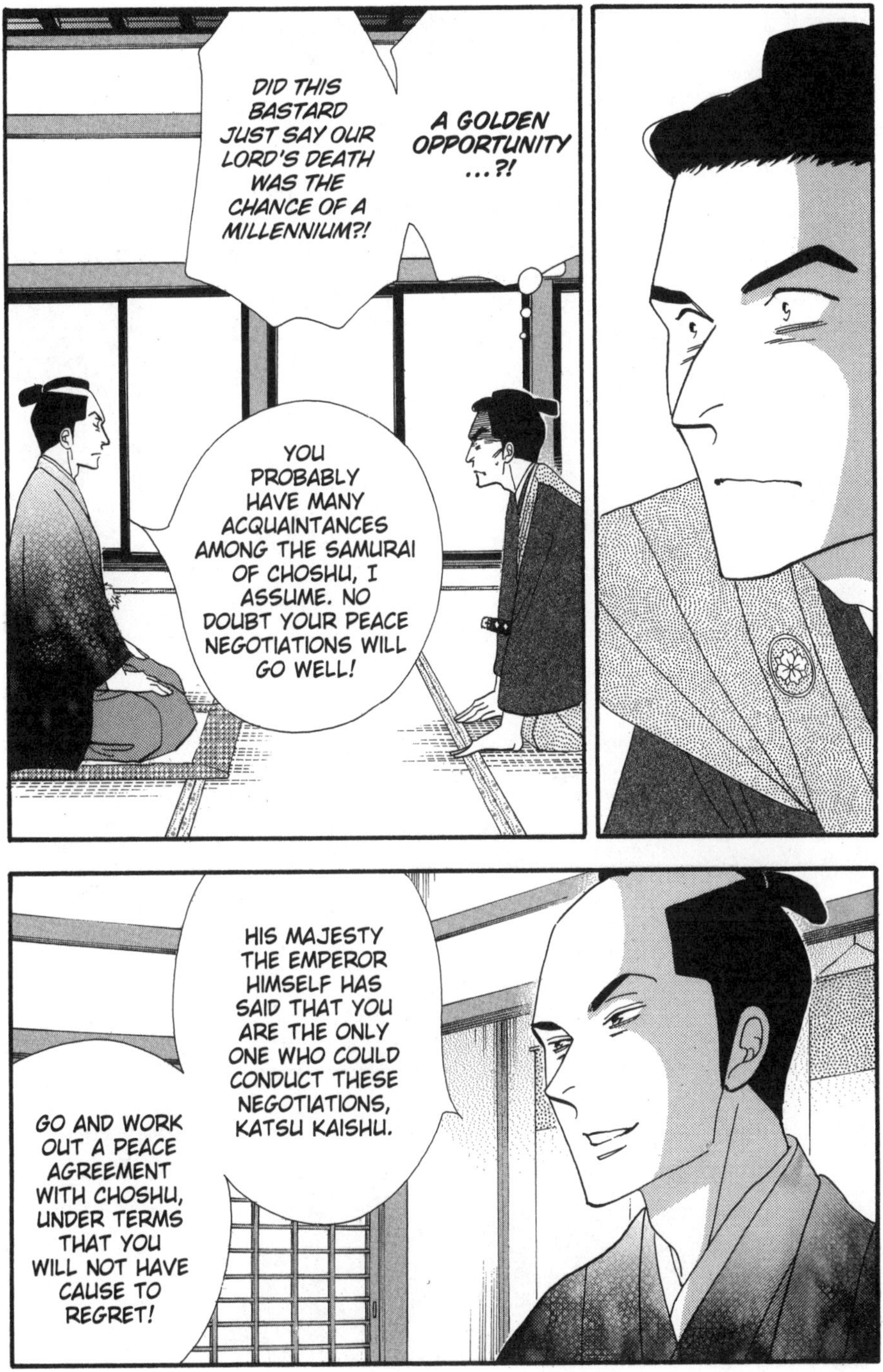
A GOLDEN OPPORTUNITY ...?!
DID THIS BASTARD JUST SAY OUR LORD'S DEATH WAS THE CHANCE OF A MILLENNIUM?!
YOU PROBABLY HAVE MANY ACQUAINTANCES AMONG THE SAMURAI OF CHOSHU, I ASSUME. NO DOUBT YOUR PEACE NEGOTIATIONS WILL GO WELL!
HIS MAJESTY THE EMPEROR HIMSELF HAS SAID THAT YOU ARE THE ONLY ONE WHO COULD CONDUCT THESE NEGOTIATIONS, KATSU KAISHU.
GO AND WORK OUT A PEACE AGREEMENT WITH CHOSHU, UNDER TERMS THAT YOU WILL NOT HAVE CAUSE TO REGRET!

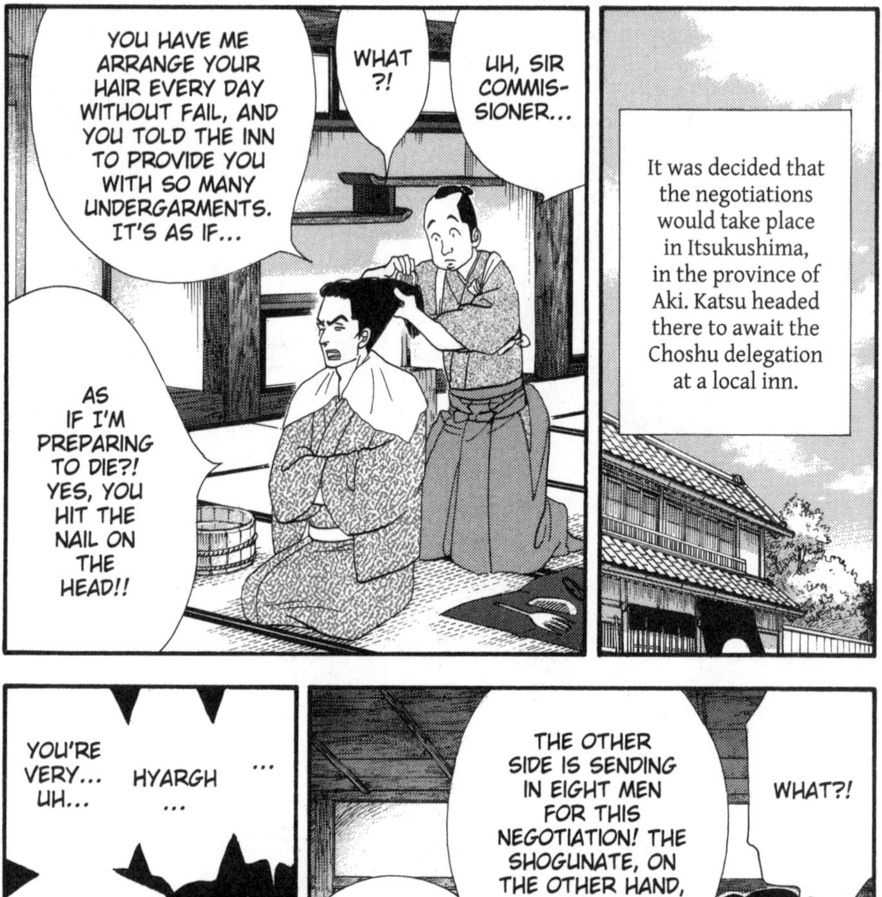
It was decided that the negotiations would take place in Itsukushima, in the province of Aki. Katsu headed there to await the Choshu delegation at a local inn.
UH, SIR COMMISSIONER...
WHAT?!
YOU HAVE ME ARRANGE YOUR HAIR EVERY DAY WITHOUT FAIL, AND YOU TOLD THE INN TO PROVIDE YOU WITH SO MANY UNDERGARMENTS. IT'S AS IF...
AS IF I'M PREPARING TO DIE?! YES, YOU HIT THE NAIL ON THE HEAD!!
WHAT?!
THE OTHER SIDE IS SENDING IN EIGHT MEN FOR THIS NEGOTIATION! THE SHOGUNATE, ON THE OTHER HAND, HAS SENT JUST ONE—ME!
WELL, THAT PUTS ME AT A BIT OF A DISADVANTAGE, DOESN'T IT?! I'M A SITTING DUCK IF THEY CHOOSE TO SLAY ME DURING THE TALKS! WELL, I'LL BE DAMNED IF I GO TO MY DEATH WITH UNKEMPT HAIR OR GRIMY UNDERCLOTHING!!
...
HYARGH...
YOU'RE VERY... UH...
...LOYAL TO THE SHOGUNATE...
HMPH!

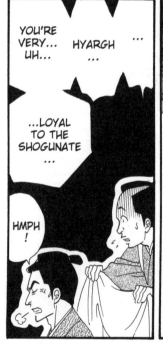

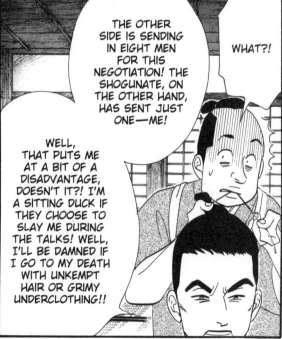

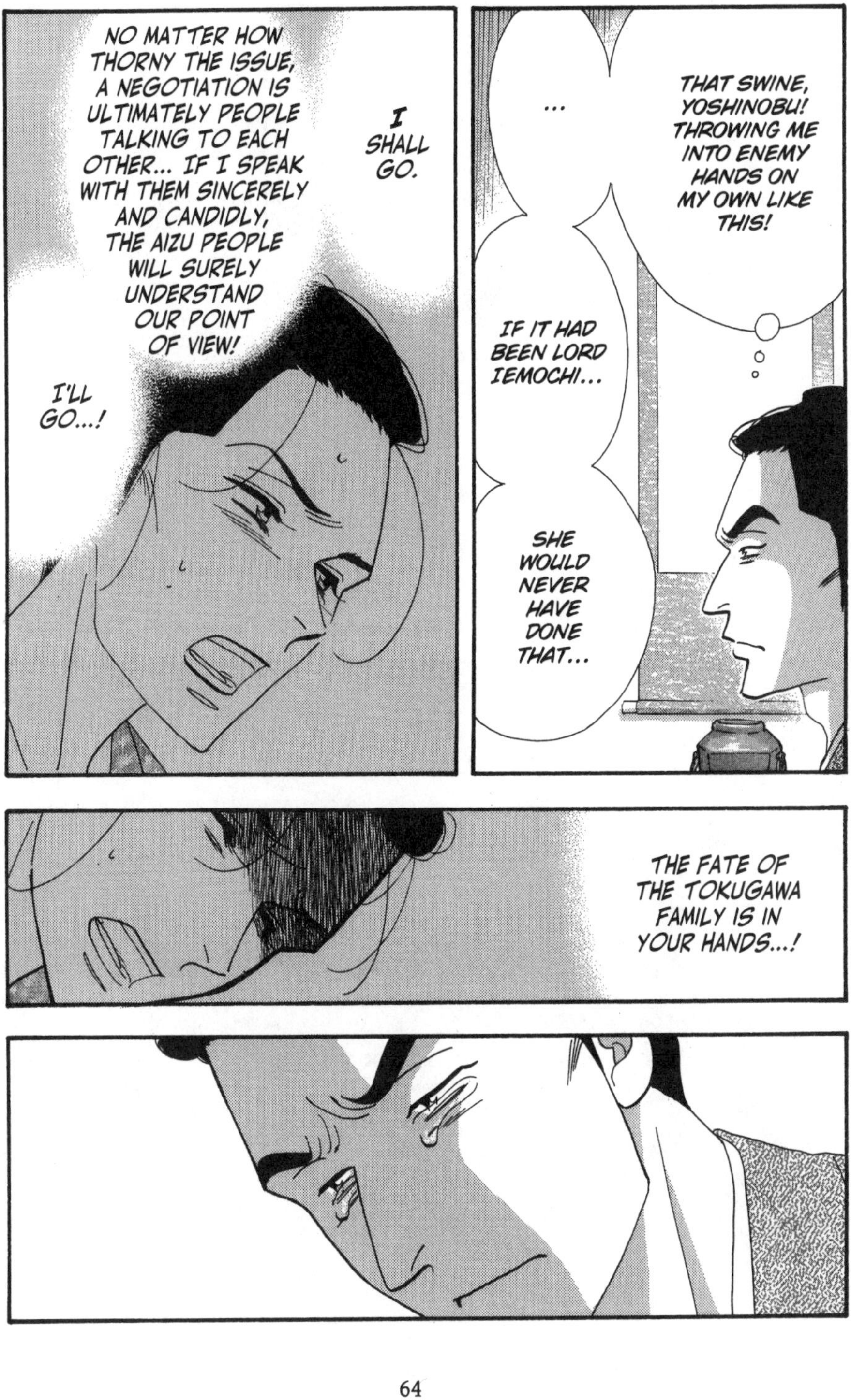
THAT SWINE, YOSHINOBU! THROWING ME INTO ENEMY HANDS ON MY OWN LIKE THIS!
...
IF IT HAD BEEN LORD IEMOCHI...
SHE WOULD NEVER HAVE DONE THAT...
I SHALL GO.
NO MATTER HOW THORNY THE ISSUE, A NEGOTIATION IS ULTIMATELY PEOPLE TALKING TO EACH OTHER... IF I SPEAK WITH THEM SINCERELY AND CANDIDLY, THE AIZU PEOPLE WILL SURELY UNDERSTAND OUR POINT OF VIEW!
I'LL GO...!
THE FATE OF THE TOKUGAWA FAMILY IS IN YOUR HANDS...!

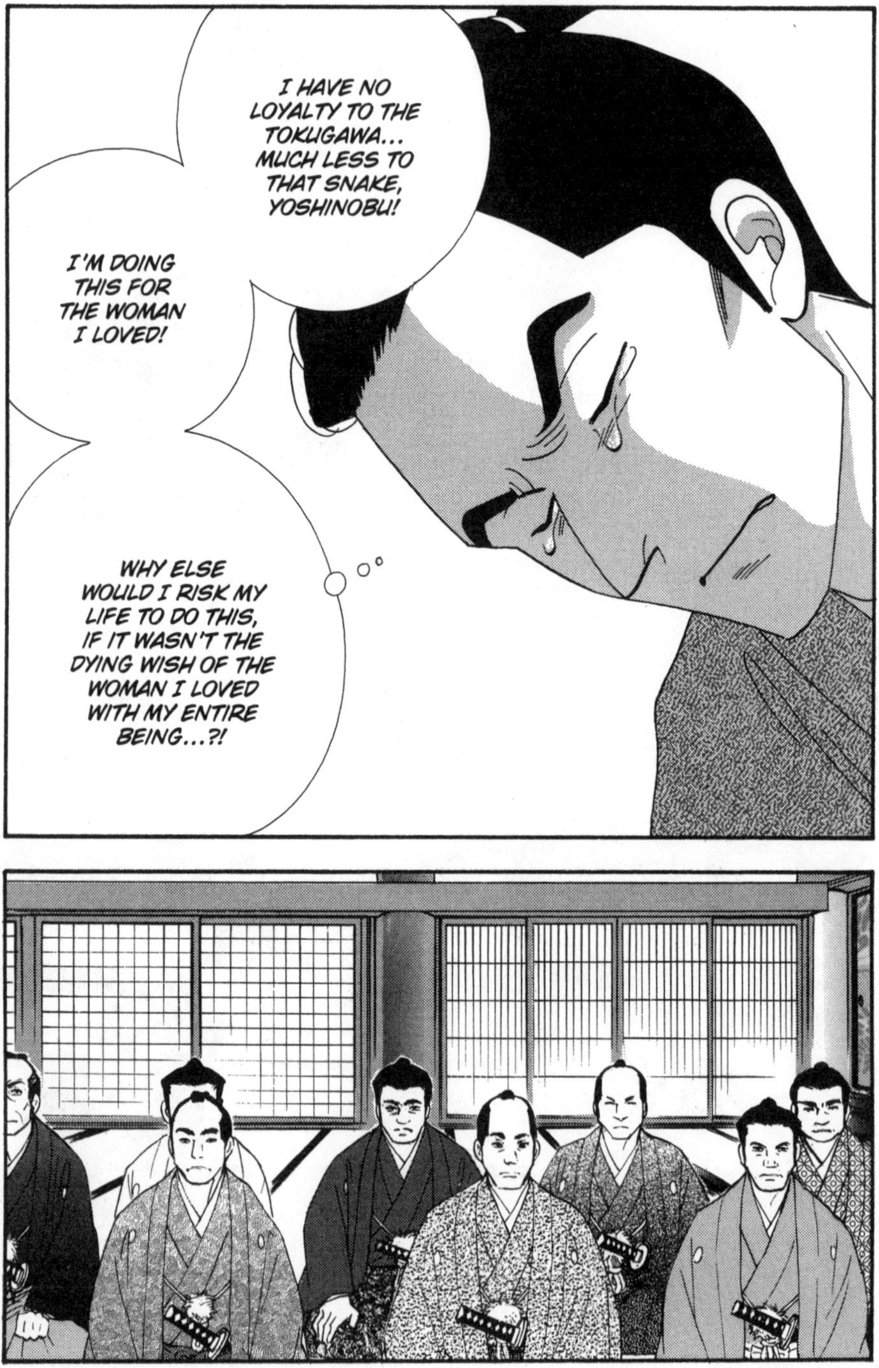
I HAVE NO LOYALTY TO THE TOKUGAWA... MUCH LESS TO THAT SNAKE, YOSHINOBU!
I'M DOING THIS FOR THE WOMAN I LOVED!
WHY ELSE WOULD I RISK MY LIFE TO DO THIS, IF IT WASN'T THE DYING WISH OF THE WOMAN I LOVED WITH MY ENTIRE BEING...?!

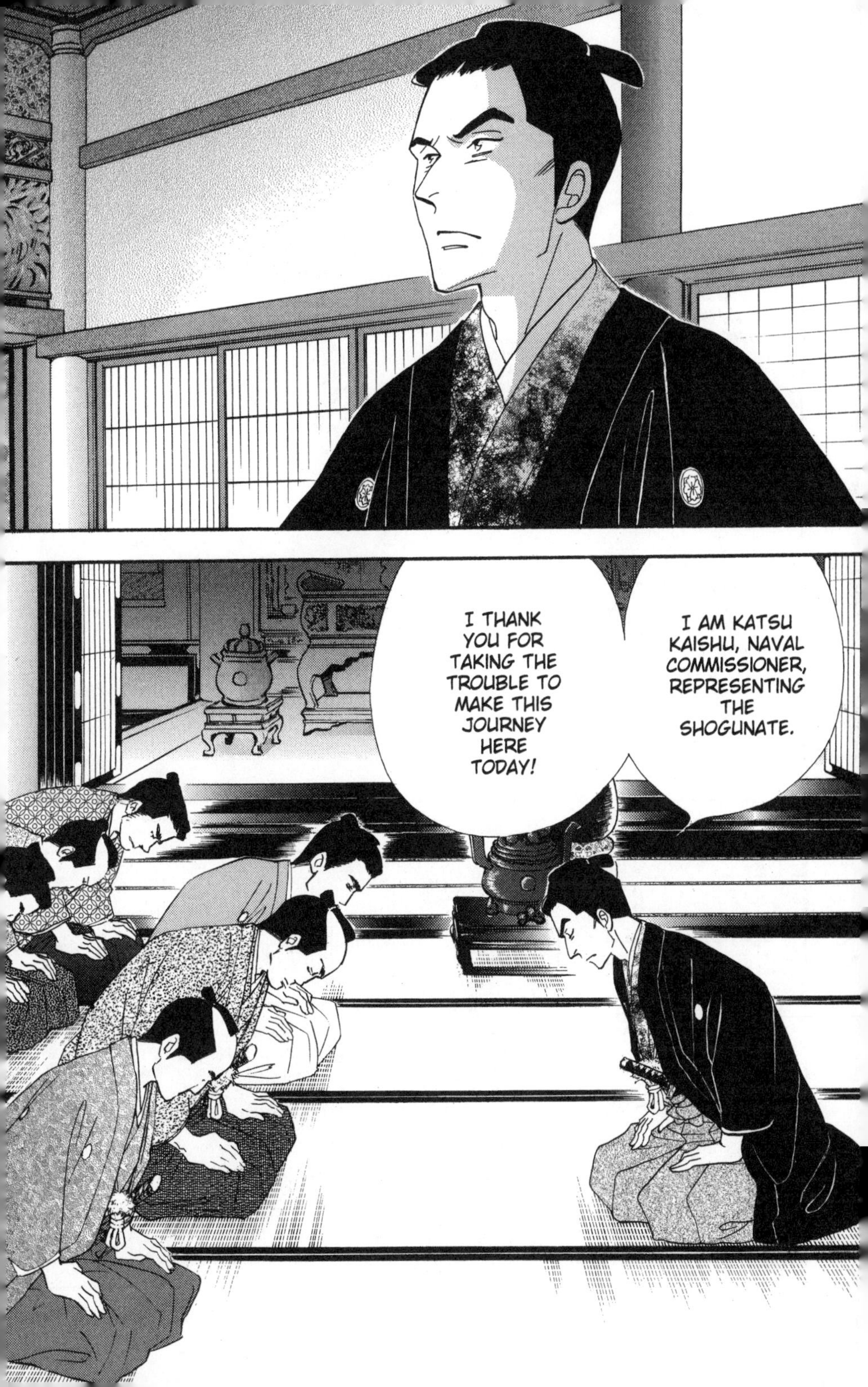
I AM KATSU KAISHU, NAVAL COMMISSIONER, REPRESENTING THE SHOGUNATE.
I THANK YOU FOR TAKING THE TROUBLE TO MAKE THIS JOURNEY HERE TODAY!

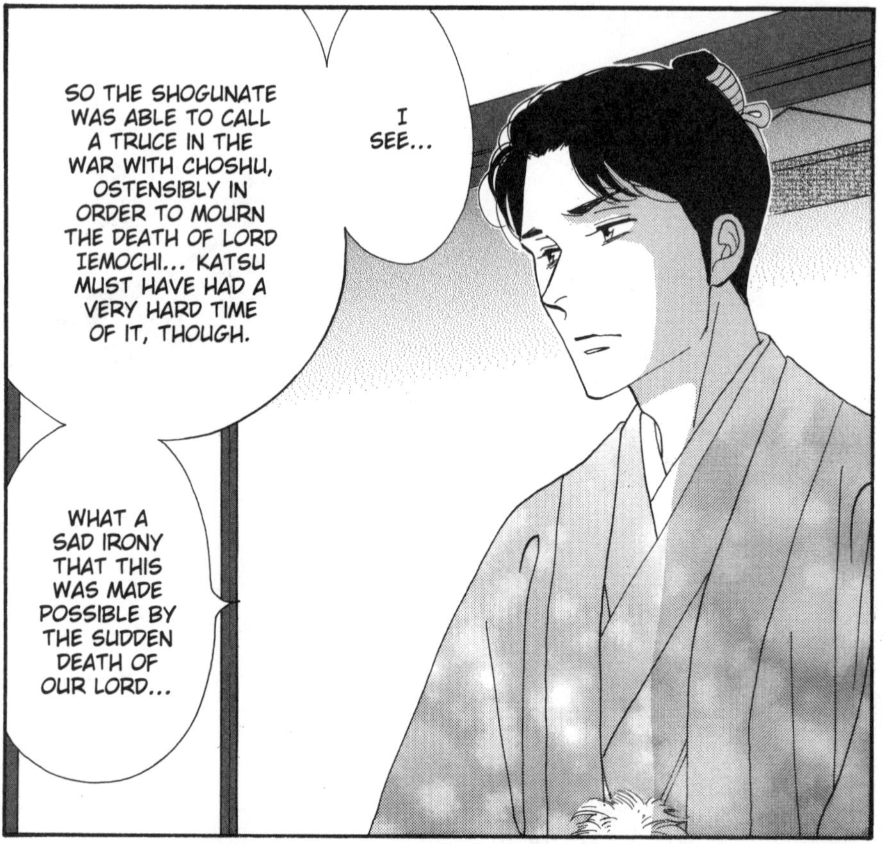
I SEE...
SO THE SHOGUNATE WAS ABLE TO CALL A TRUCE IN THE WAR WITH CHOSHU, OSTENSIBLY IN ORDER TO MOURN THE DEATH OF LORD IEMOCHI... KATSU MUST HAVE HAD A VERY HARD TIME OF IT, THOUGH.
WHAT A SAD IRONY THAT THIS WAS MADE POSSIBLE BY THE SUDDEN DEATH OF OUR LORD...
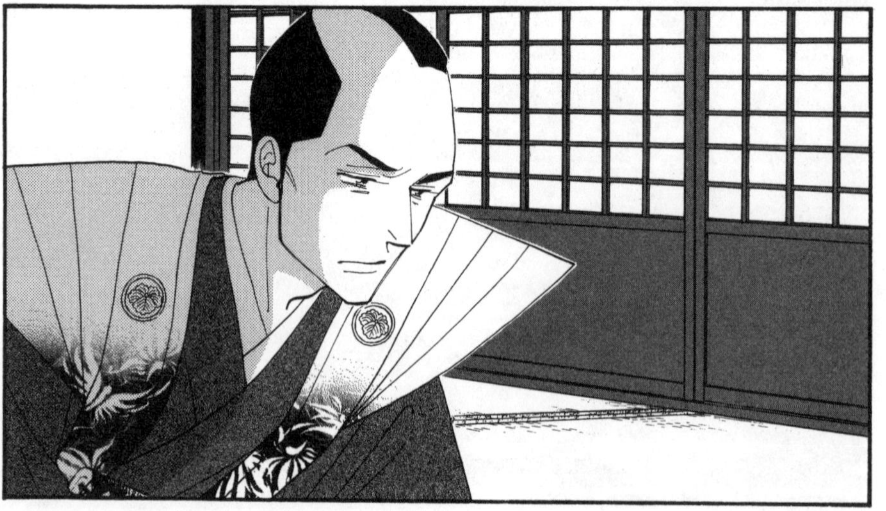

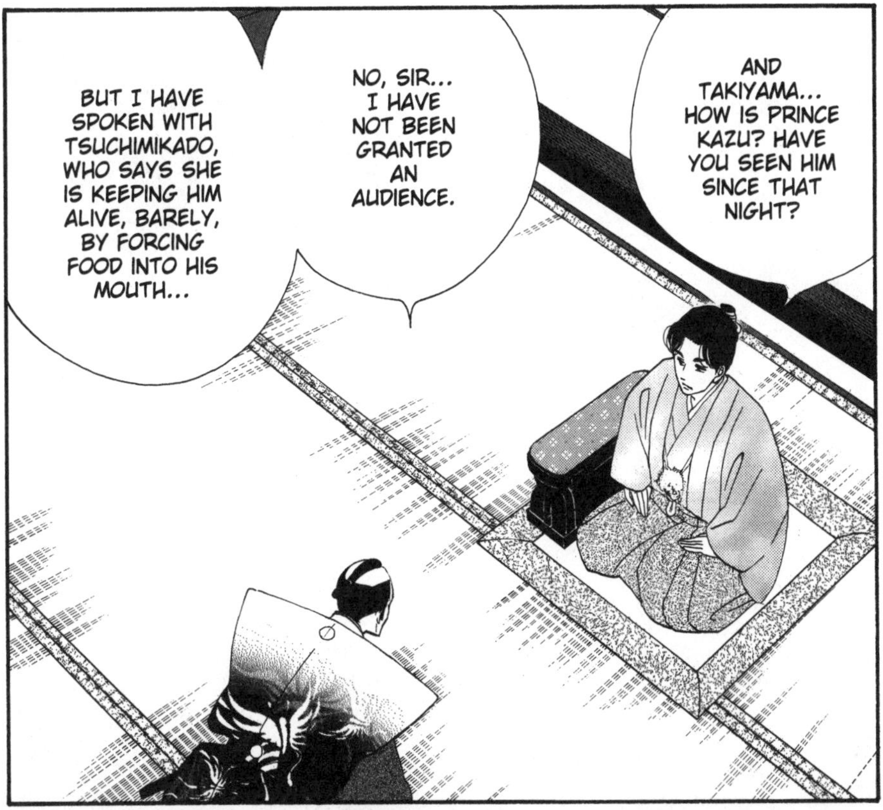
AND TAKIYAMA... HOW IS PRINCE KAZU? HAVE YOU SEEN HIM SINCE THAT NIGHT?
NO, SIR... I HAVE NOT BEEN GRANTED AN AUDIENCE.
BUT I HAVE SPOKEN WITH TSUCHIMIKADO, WHO SAYS SHE IS KEEPING HIM ALIVE, BARELY, BY FORCING FOOD INTO HIS MOUTH...
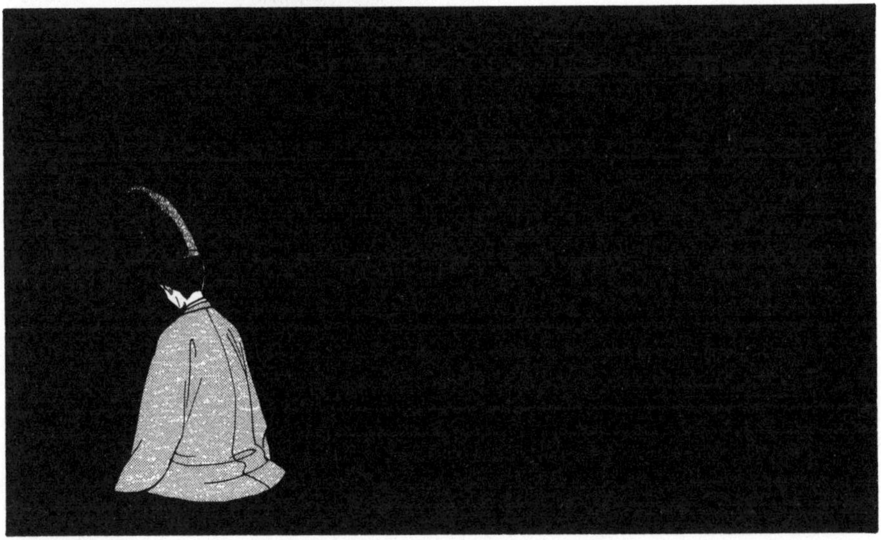

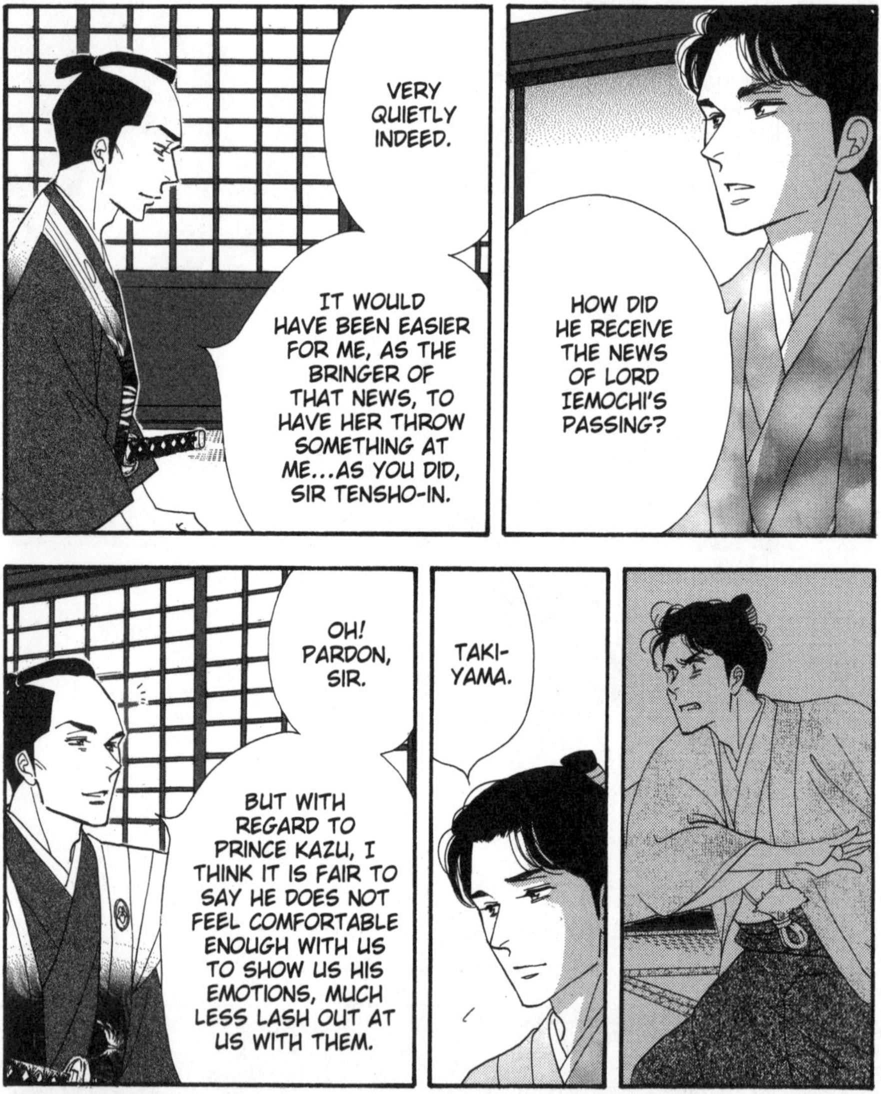
HOW DID HE RECEIVE THE NEWS OF LORD IEMOCHI'S PASSING?
VERY QUIETLY INDEED.
IT WOULD HAVE BEEN EASIER FOR ME, AS THE BRINGER OF THAT NEWS, TO HAVE HER THROW SOMETHING AT ME...AS YOU DID, SIR TENSHO-IN.
TAKI-YAMA.
OH! PARDON, SIR.
BUT WITH REGARD TO PRINCE KAZU, I THINK IT IS FAIR TO SAY HE DOES NOT FEEL COMFORTABLE ENOUGH WITH US TO SHOW US HIS EMOTIONS, MUCH LESS LASH OUT AT US WITH THEM.
TRULY...
OUR LORD IEMOCHI WAS THE ONE AND ONLY PERSON HERE IN THE INNER CHAMBERS WITH WHOM THE PRINCE FELT ABLE TO CONFIDE AND BE ENTIRELY HIMSELF.

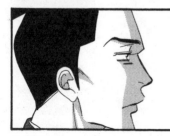

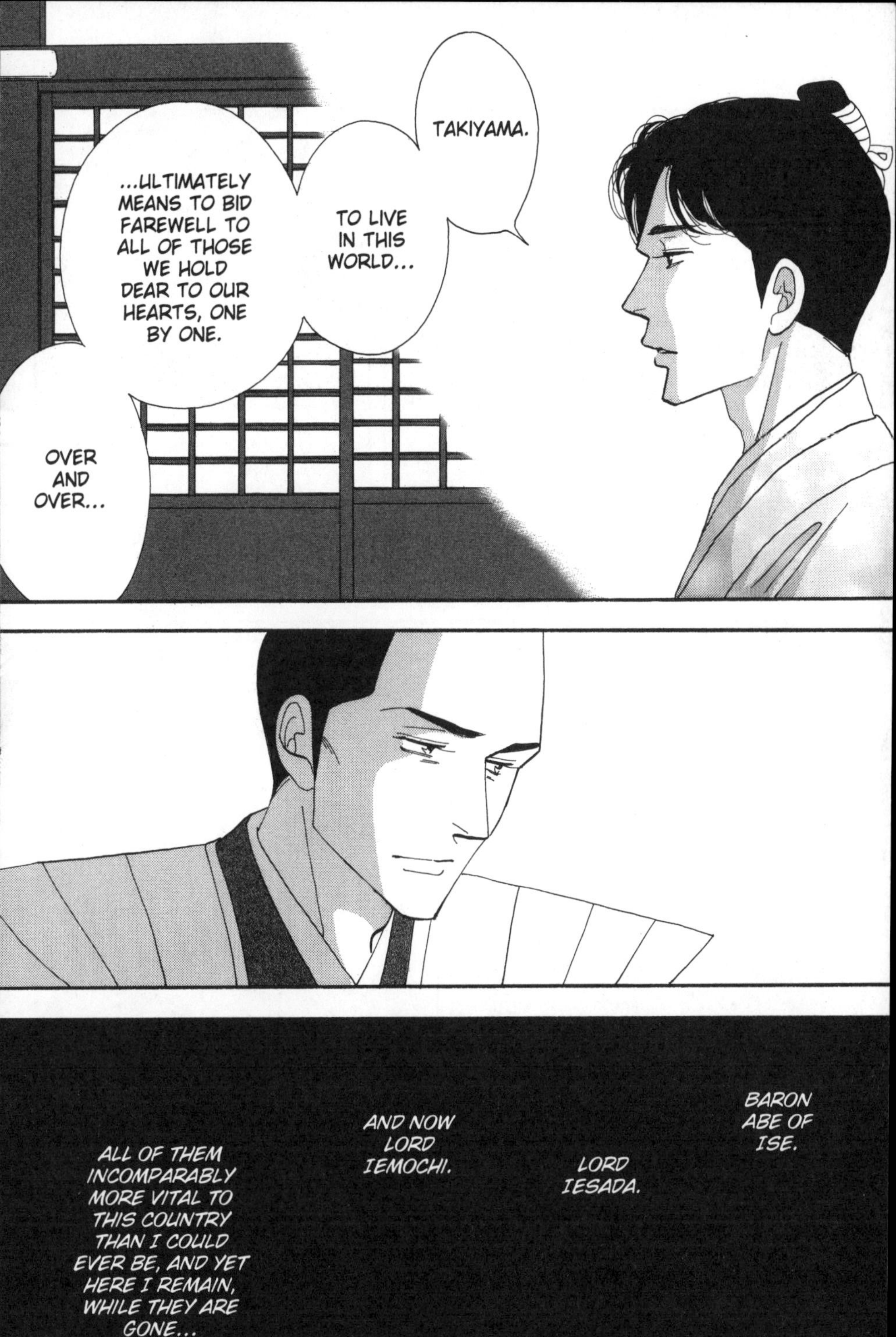
TAKIYAMA.
TO LIVE IN THIS WORLD...
...ULTIMATELY MEANS TO BID FAREWELL TO ALL OF THOSE WE HOLD DEAR TO OUR HEARTS, ONE BY ONE.
OVER AND OVER...
BARON ABE OF ISE.
LORD IESADA.
AND NOW LORD IEMOCHI.
ALL OF THEM INCOMPARABLY MORE VITAL TO THIS COUNTRY THAN I COULD EVER BE, AND YET HERE I REMAIN, WHILE THEY ARE GONE...

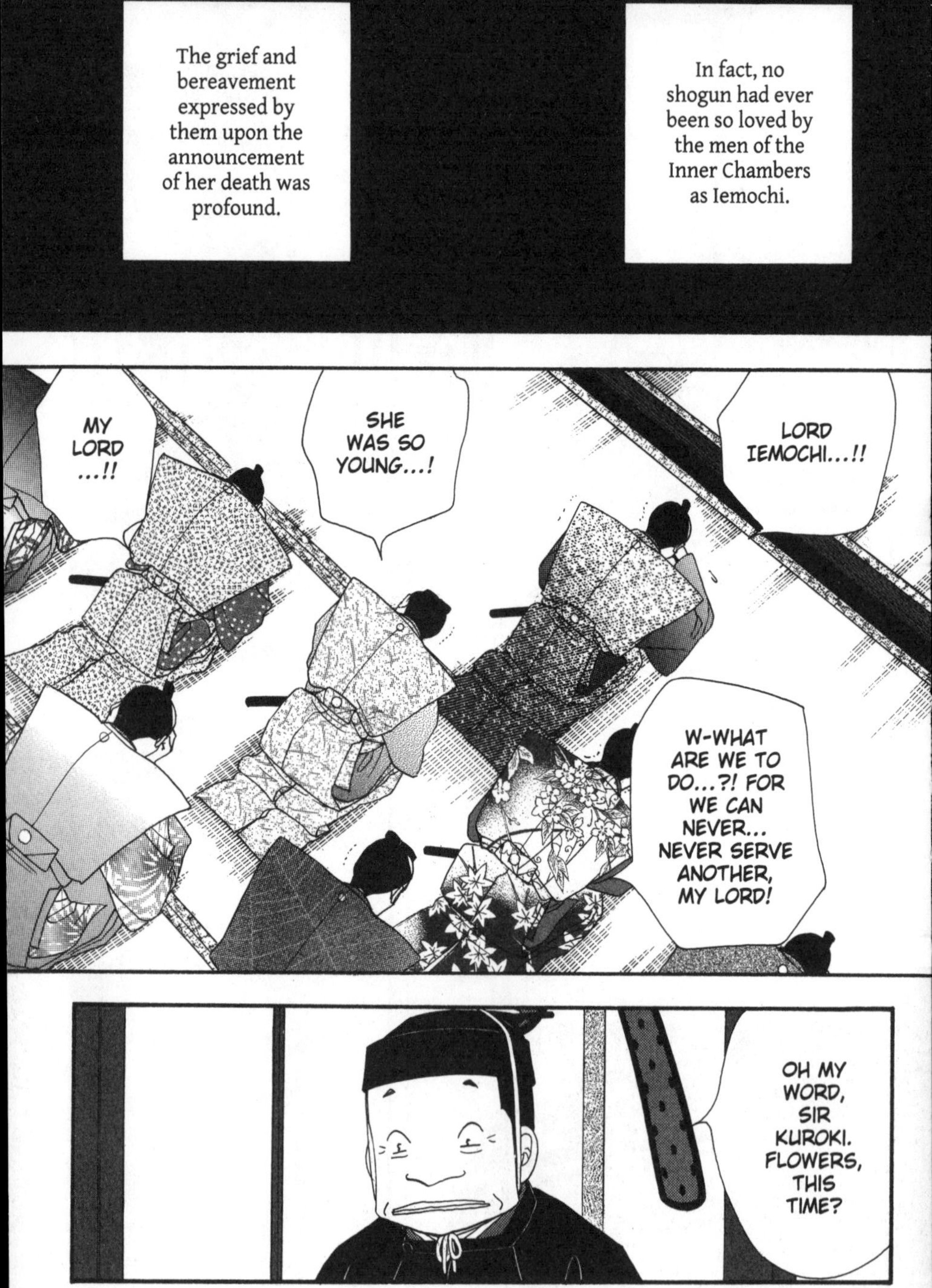
In fact, no shogun had ever been so loved by the men of the Inner Chambers as Iemochi.
The grief and bereavement expressed by them upon the announcement of her death was profound.
LORD IEMOCHI...!!
SHE WAS SO YOUNG...!
MY LORD ...!!
W-WHAT ARE WE TO DO...?! FOR WE CAN NEVER... NEVER SERVE ANOTHER, MY LORD!
OH MY WORD, SIR KUROKI. FLOWERS, THIS TIME?

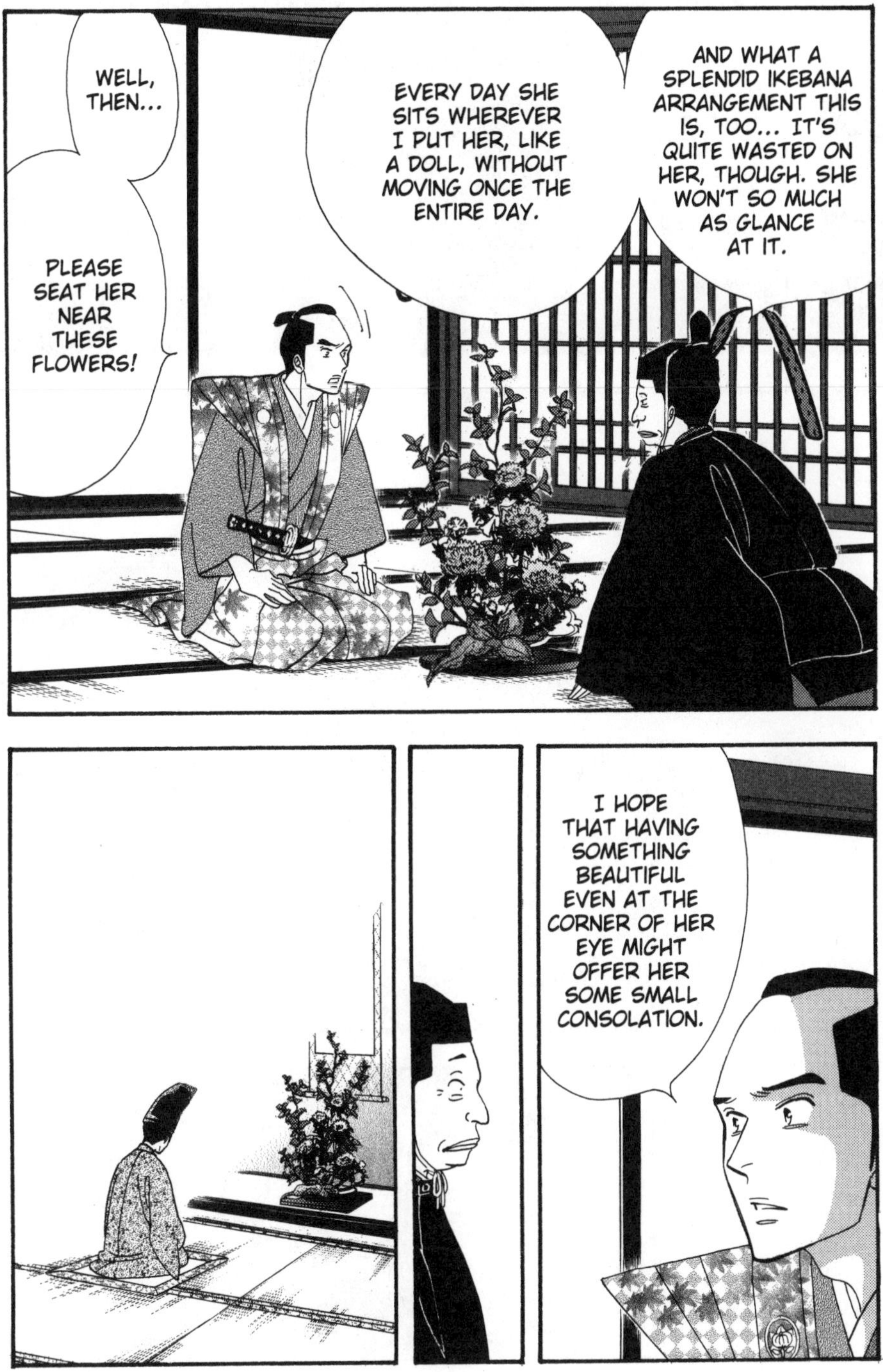
AND WHAT A SPLENDID IKEBANA ARRANGEMENT THIS IS, TOO... IT'S QUITE WASTED ON HER, THOUGH. SHE WON'T SO MUCH AS GLANCE AT IT.
EVERY DAY SHE SITS WHEREVER I PUT HER, LIKE A DOLL, WITHOUT MOVING ONCE THE ENTIRE DAY.
WELL, THEN...
PLEASE SEAT HER NEAR THESE FLOWERS!
I HOPE THAT HAVING SOMETHING BEAUTIFUL EVEN AT THE CORNER OF HER EYE MIGHT OFFER HER SOME SMALL CONSOLATION.

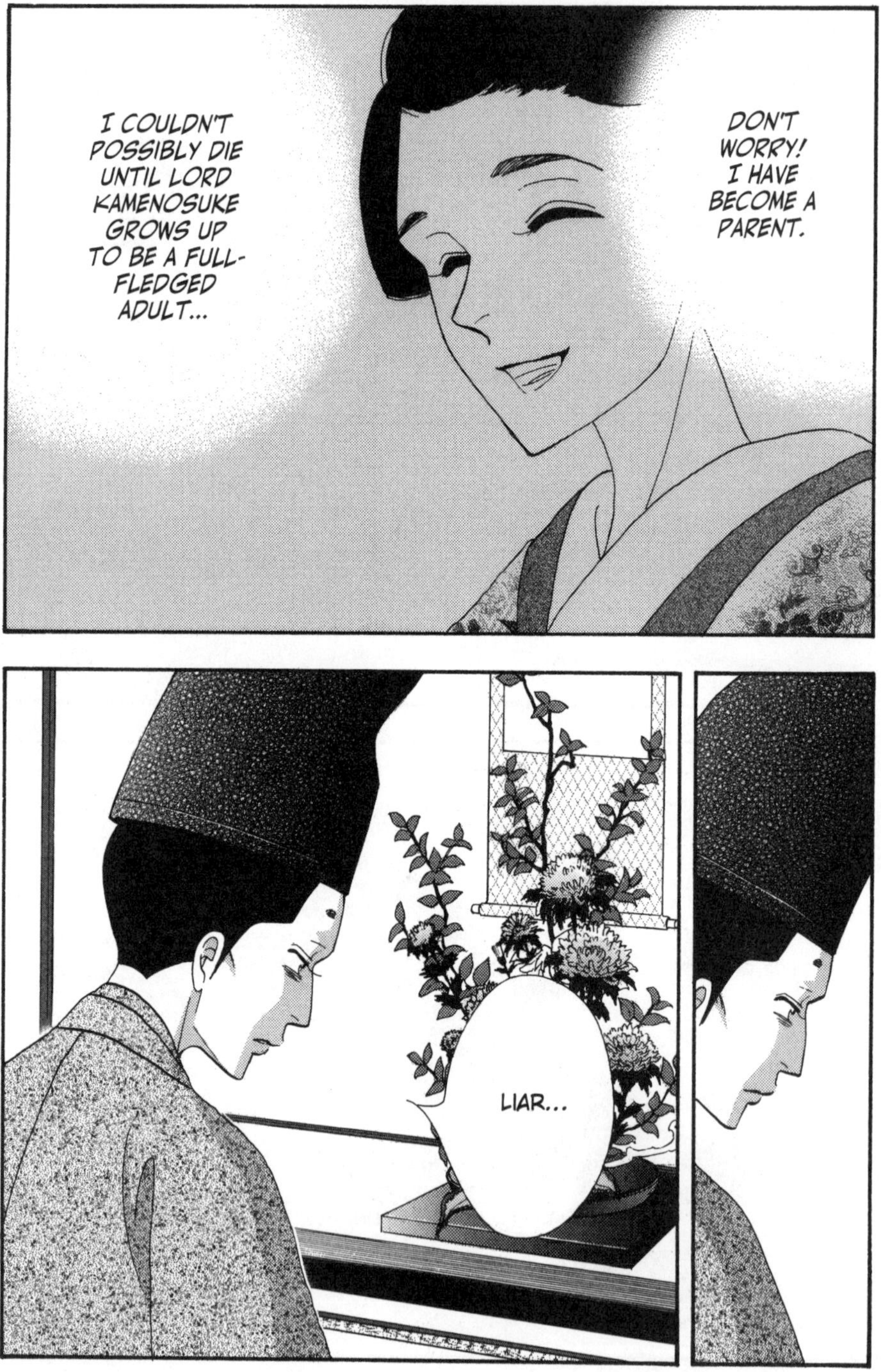
DON'T WORRY! I HAVE BECOME A PARENT.
I COULDN'T POSSIBLY DIE UNTIL LORD KAMENOSUKE GROWS UP TO BE A FULL-FLEDGED ADULT...
LIAR...

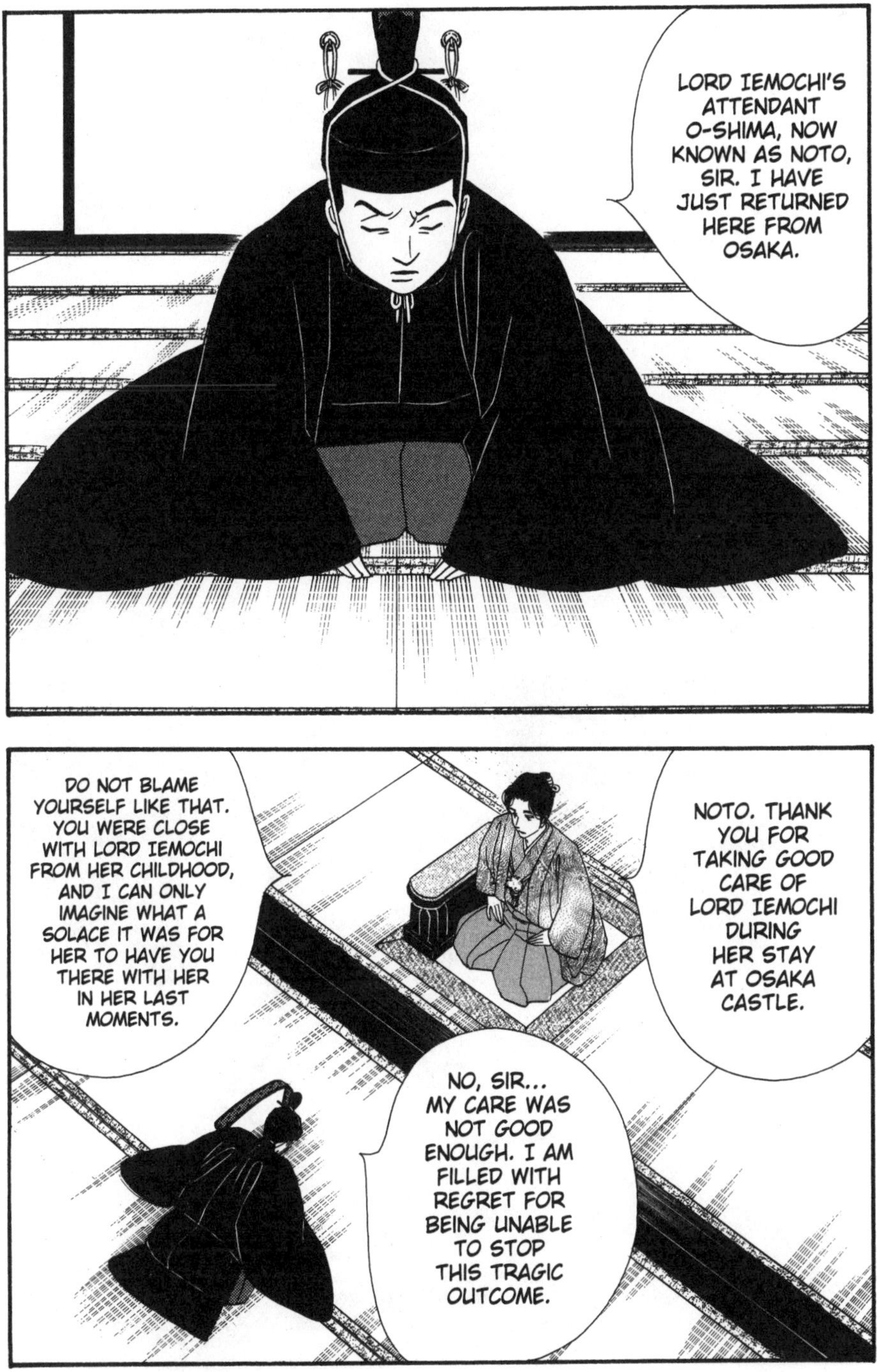
LORD IEMOCHI'S ATTENDANT O-SHIMA, NOW KNOWN AS NOTO, SIR. I HAVE JUST RETURNED HERE FROM OSAKA.
NOTO. THANK YOU FOR TAKING GOOD CARE OF LORD IEMOCHI DURING HER STAY AT OSAKA CASTLE.
NO, SIR... MY CARE WAS NOT GOOD ENOUGH. I AM FILLED WITH REGRET FOR BEING UNABLE TO STOP THIS TRAGIC OUTCOME.
DO NOT BLAME YOURSELF LIKE THAT. YOU WERE CLOSE WITH LORD IEMOCHI FROM HER CHILDHOOD, AND I CAN ONLY IMAGINE WHAT A SOLACE IT WAS FOR HER TO HAVE YOU THERE WITH HER IN HER LAST MOMENTS.

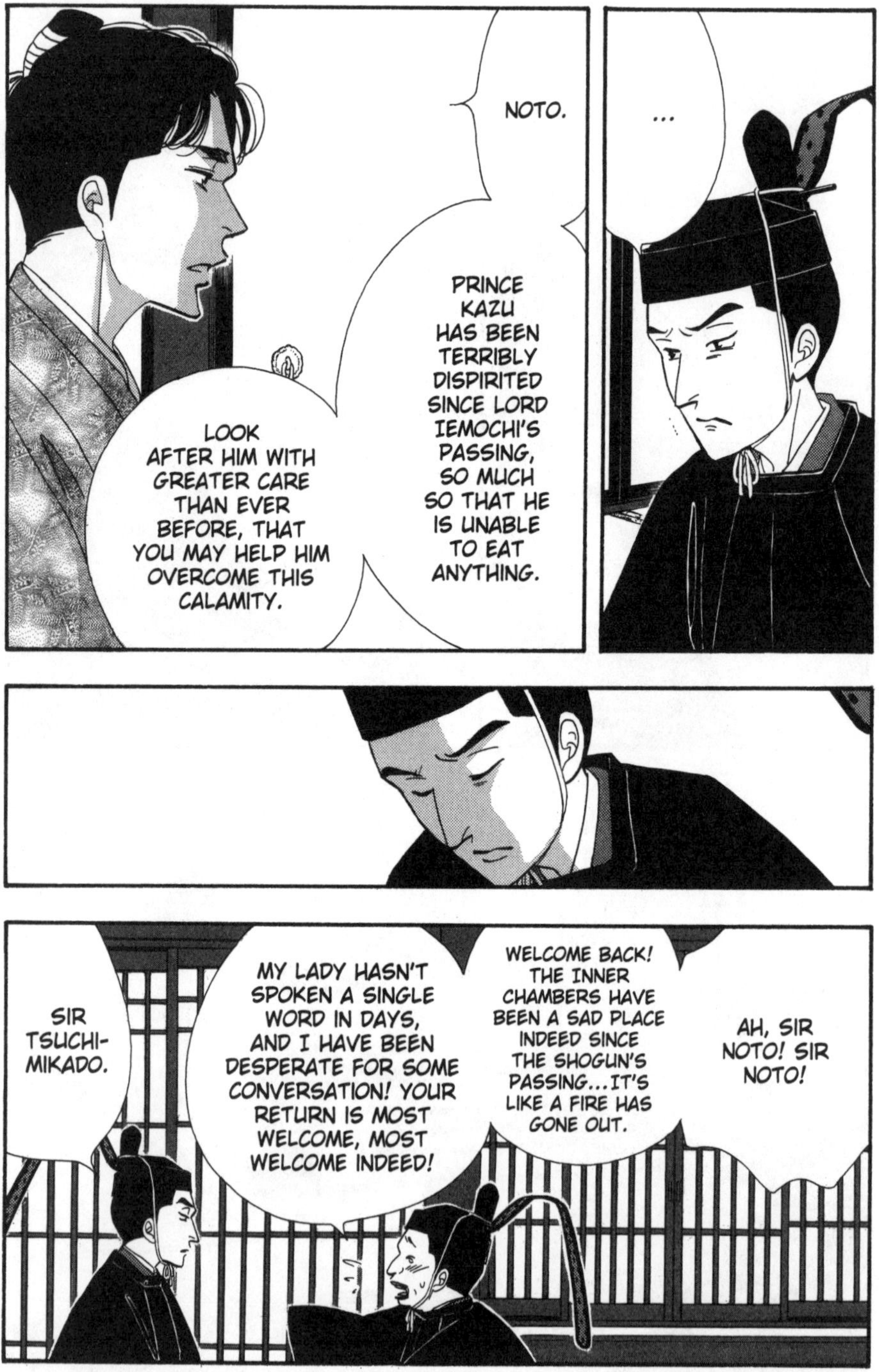
...
NOTO.
PRINCE KAZU HAS BEEN TERRIBLY DISPIRITED SINCE LORD IEMOCHI'S PASSING, SO MUCH SO THAT HE IS UNABLE TO EAT ANYTHING.
LOOK AFTER HIM WITH GREATER CARE THAN EVER BEFORE, THAT YOU MAY HELP HIM OVERCOME THIS CALAMITY.
AH, SIR NOTO! SIR NOTO!
WELCOME BACK! THE INNER CHAMBERS HAVE BEEN A SAD PLACE INDEED SINCE THE SHOGUN'S PASSING...IT'S LIKE A FIRE HAS GONE OUT.
MY LADY HASN'T SPOKEN A SINGLE WORD IN DAYS, AND I HAVE BEEN DESPERATE FOR SOME CONVERSATION! YOUR RETURN IS MOST WELCOME, MOST WELCOME INDEED!
SIR TSUCHI-MIKADO.

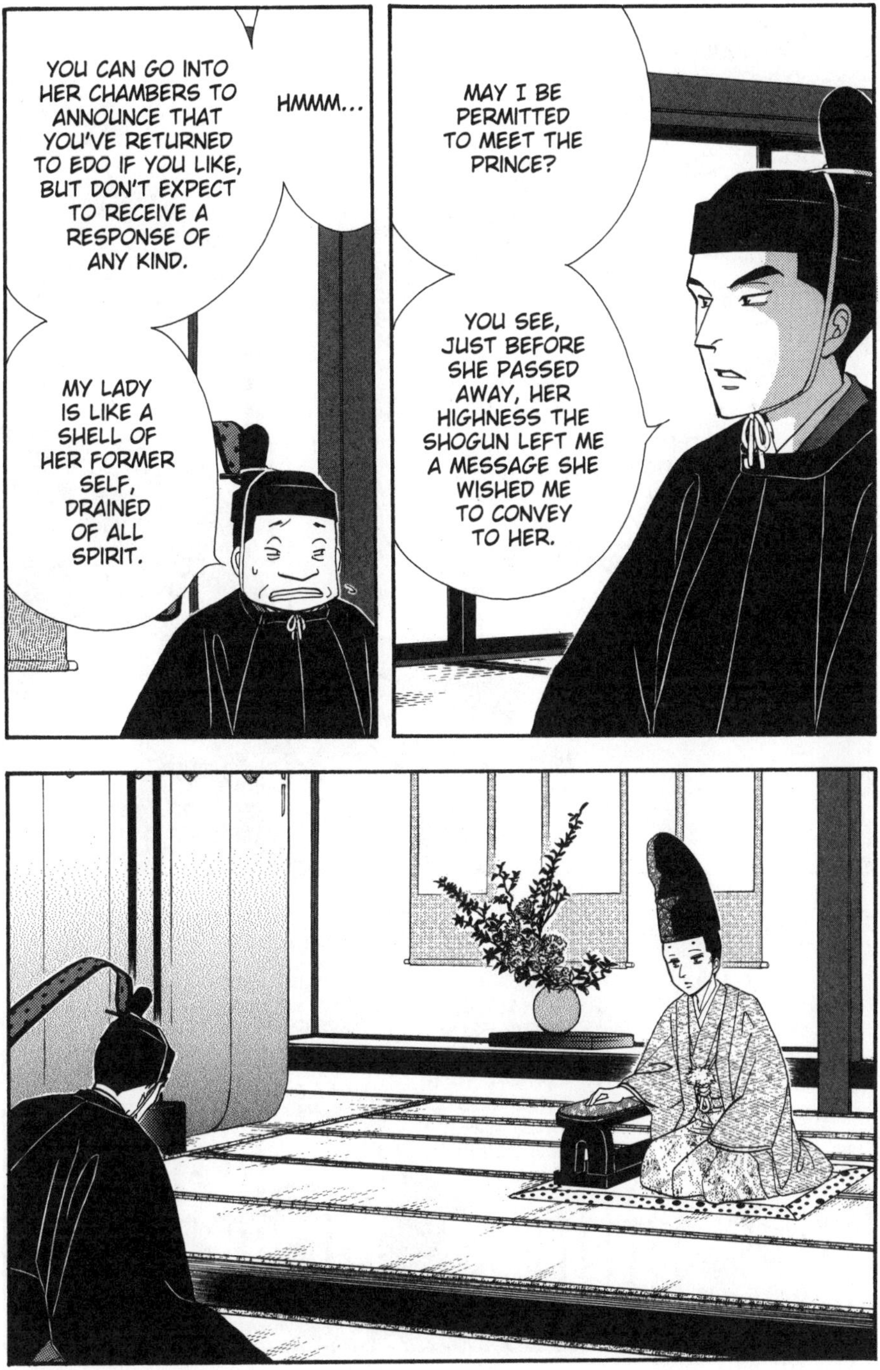

MAY I BE PERMITTED TO MEET THE PRINCE?
YOU SEE, JUST BEFORE SHE PASSED AWAY, HER HIGHNESS THE SHOGUN LEFT ME A MESSAGE SHE WISHED ME TO CONVEY TO HER.
HMMM...
YOU CAN GO INTO HER CHAMBERS TO ANNOUNCE THAT YOU'VE RETURNED TO EDO IF YOU LIKE, BUT DON'T EXPECT TO RECEIVE A RESPONSE OF ANY KIND.
MY LADY IS LIKE A SHELL OF HER FORMER SELF, DRAINED OF ALL SPIRIT.

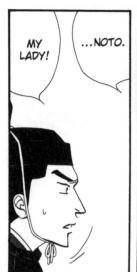

MY LADY!

...NOTO.

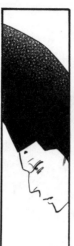

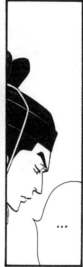

...

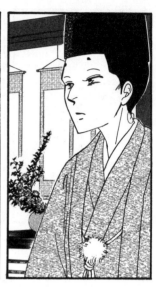

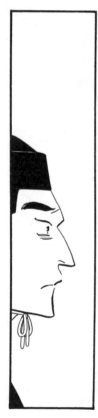

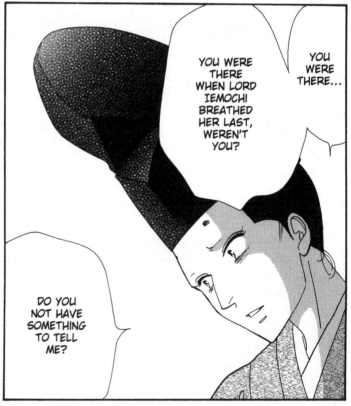

YOU WERE THERE WHEN LORD IEMOCHI BREATHED HER LAST, WEREN'T YOU?

YOU WERE THERE...

DO YOU NOT HAVE SOMETHING TO TELL ME?

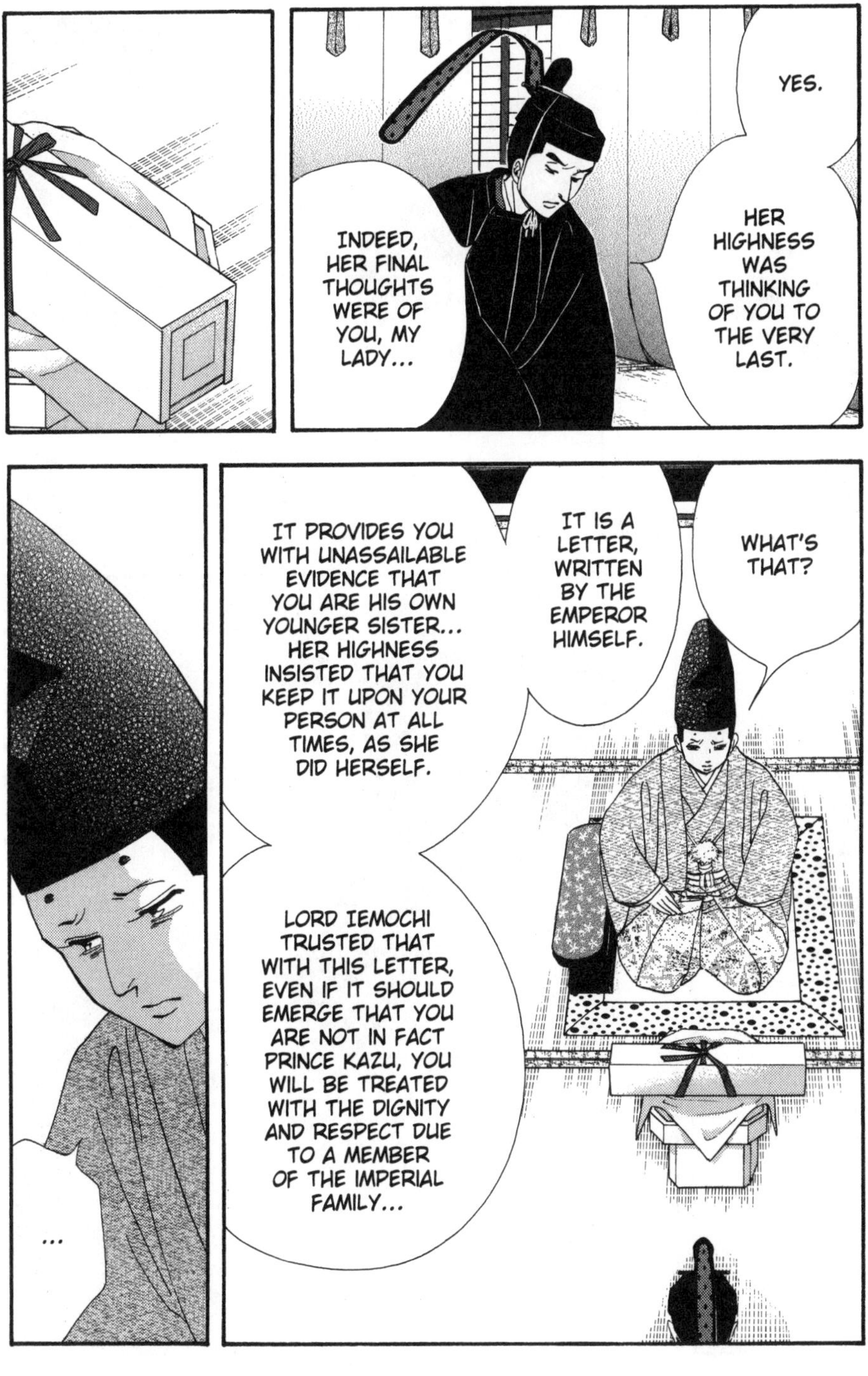
YES.
HER HIGHNESS WAS THINKING OF YOU TO THE VERY LAST.
INDEED, HER FINAL THOUGHTS WERE OF YOU, MY LADY...
WHAT'S THAT?
IT IS A LETTER, WRITTEN BY THE EMPEROR HIMSELF.
IT PROVIDES YOU WITH UNASSAILABLE EVIDENCE THAT YOU ARE HIS OWN YOUNGER SISTER... HER HIGHNESS INSISTED THAT YOU KEEP IT UPON YOUR PERSON AT ALL TIMES, AS SHE DID HERSELF.
LORD IEMOCHI TRUSTED THAT WITH THIS LETTER, EVEN IF IT SHOULD EMERGE THAT YOU ARE NOT IN FACT PRINCE KAZU, YOU WILL BE TREATED WITH THE DIGNITY AND RESPECT DUE TO A MEMBER OF THE IMPERIAL FAMILY...
...

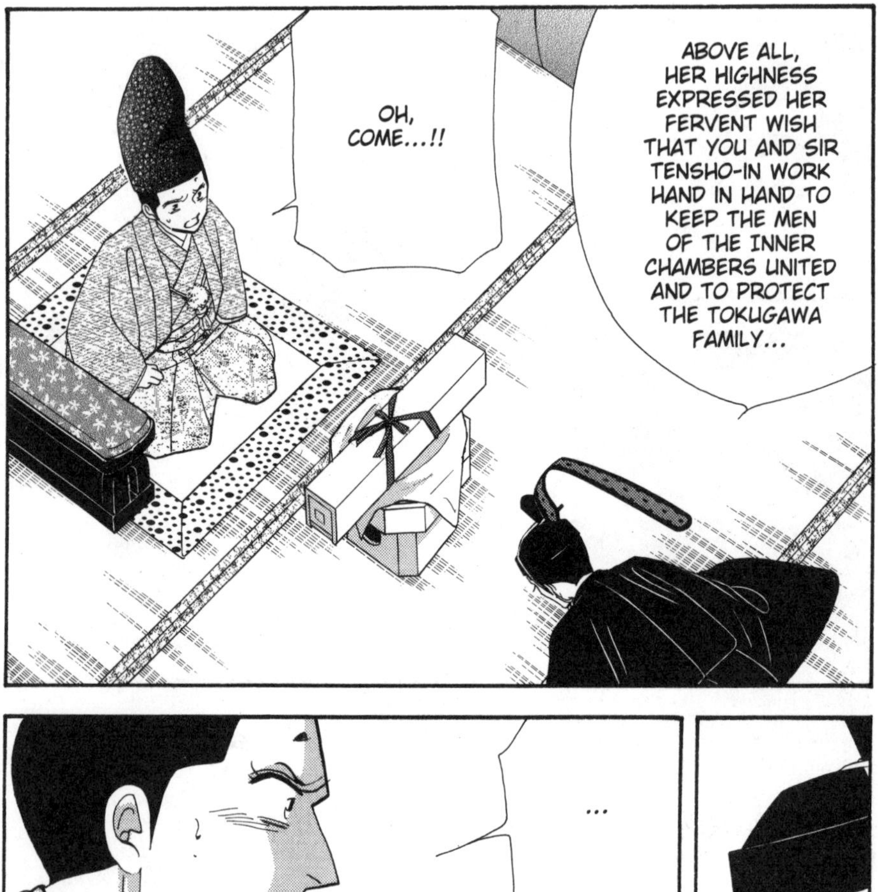
ABOVE ALL, HER HIGHNESS EXPRESSED HER FERVENT WISH THAT YOU AND SIR TENSHO-IN WORK HAND IN HAND TO KEEP THE MEN OF THE INNER CHAMBERS UNITED AND TO PROTECT THE TOKUGAWA FAMILY...
OH, COME...!!
...
I DON'T WANT TO HEAR SUCH EMPTY PLATITUDES!
HER ACTUAL WORDS!
I WANT TO HEAR THE ACTUAL WORDS SHE SPOKE ON HER DEATHBED!! DID LORD IEMOCHI SAY ANYTHING ABOUT ME?!

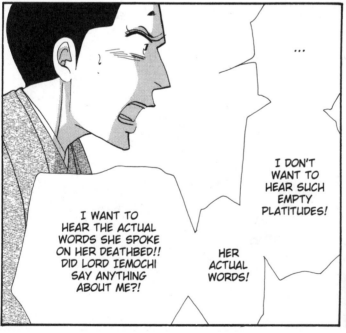

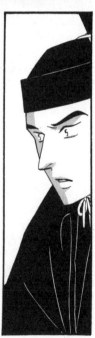

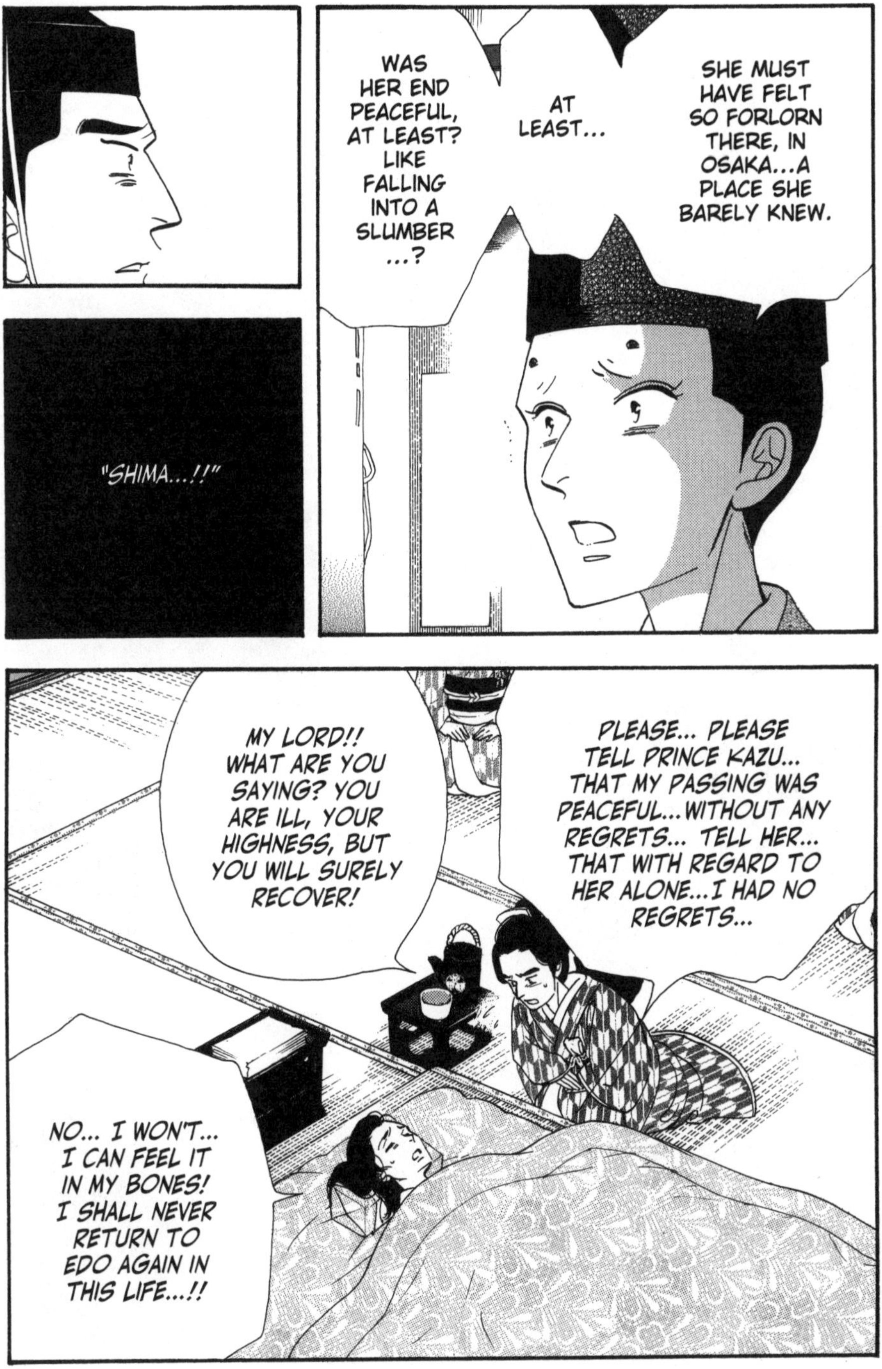
SHE MUST HAVE FELT SO FORLORN THERE, IN OSAKA...A PLACE SHE BARELY KNEW.
AT LEAST...
WAS HER END PEACEFUL, AT LEAST? LIKE FALLING INTO A SLUMBER ...?
"SHIMA...!!"
PLEASE... PLEASE TELL PRINCE KAZU... THAT MY PASSING WAS PEACEFUL...WITHOUT ANY REGRETS... TELL HER... THAT WITH REGARD TO HER ALONE...I HAD NO REGRETS...
MY LORD!! WHAT ARE YOU SAYING? YOU ARE ILL, YOUR HIGHNESS, BUT YOU WILL SURELY RECOVER!
NO... I WON'T... I CAN FEEL IT IN MY BONES! I SHALL NEVER RETURN TO EDO AGAIN IN THIS LIFE...!!

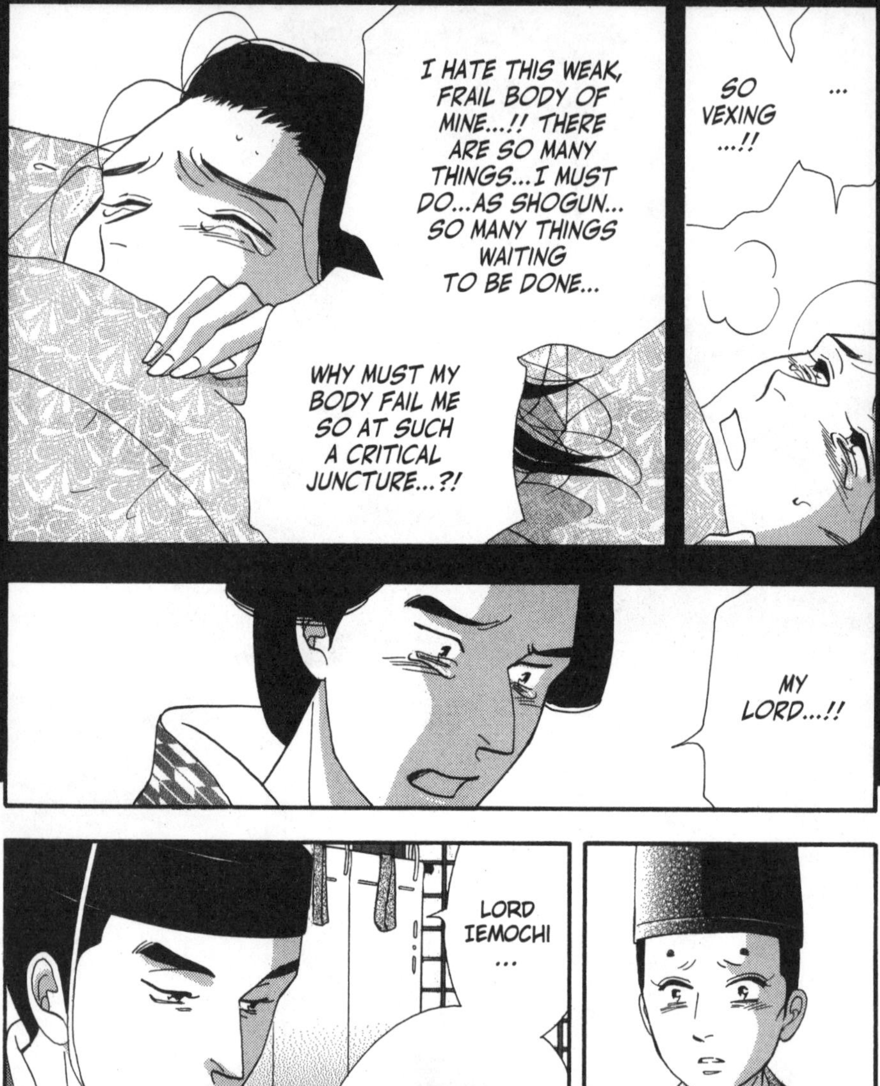
...
SO VEXING ...!!
I HATE THIS WEAK, FRAIL BODY OF MINE...!! THERE ARE SO MANY THINGS...I MUST DO...AS SHOGUN... SO MANY THINGS WAITING TO BE DONE...
WHY MUST MY BODY FAIL ME SO AT SUCH A CRITICAL JUNCTURE...?!
MY LORD...!!
LORD IEMOCHI ...
...PASSED AWAY PRAYING FOR YOUR HEALTH AND HAPPINESS, MY LADY. HER END WAS PEACEFUL, INDEED AS THOUGH SHE WERE FALLING ASLEEP.
IT WAS A QUIET END...
...

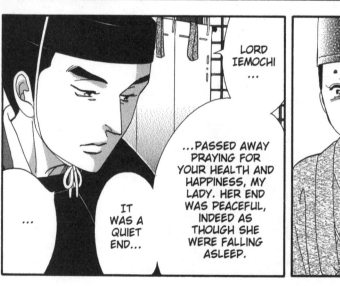

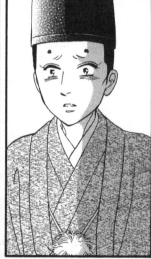

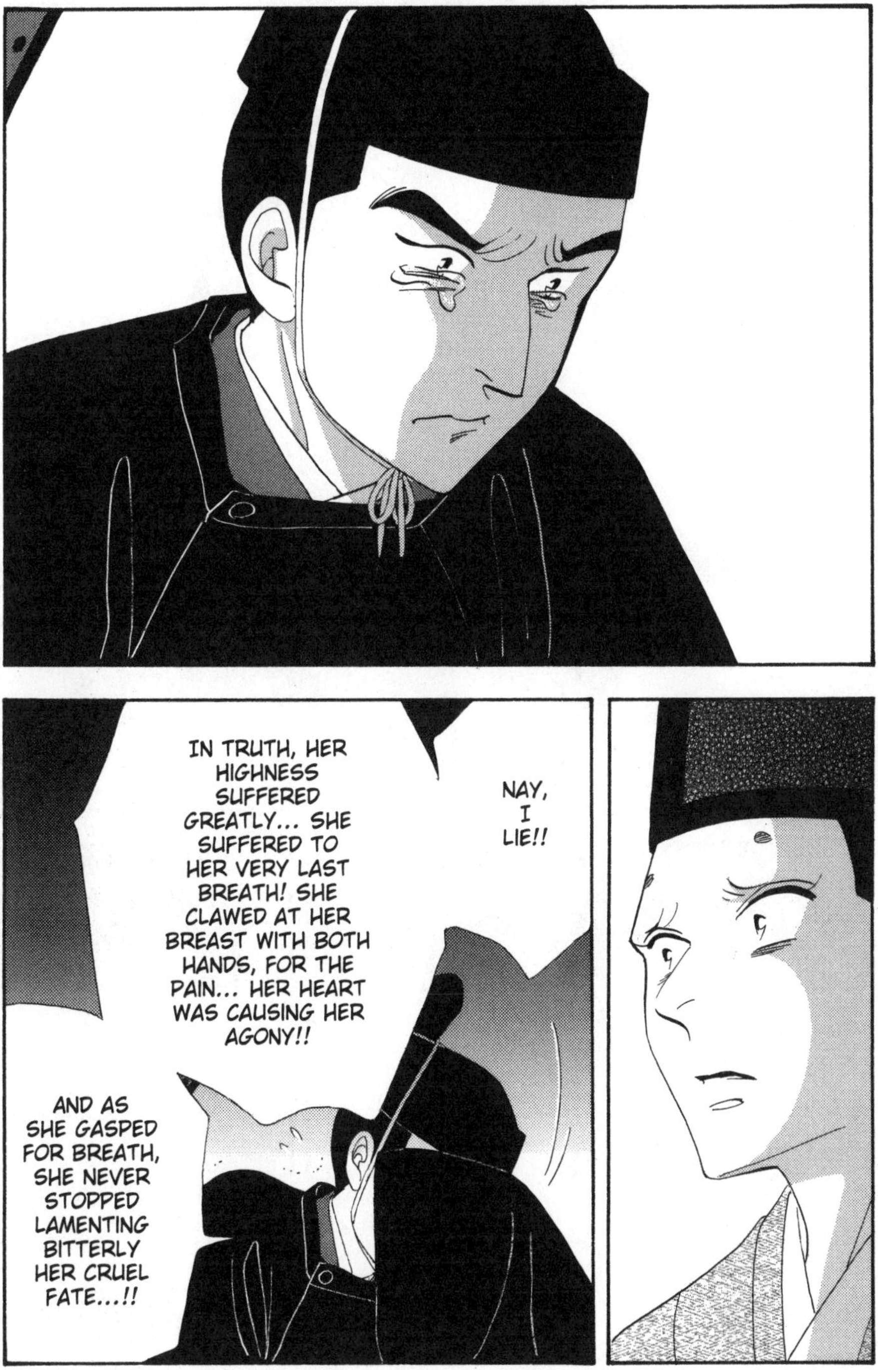
NAY, I LIE!!
IN TRUTH, HER HIGHNESS SUFFERED GREATLY... SHE SUFFERED TO HER VERY LAST BREATH! SHE CLAWED AT HER BREAST WITH BOTH HANDS, FOR THE PAIN... HER HEART WAS CAUSING HER AGONY!!
AND AS SHE GASPED FOR BREATH, SHE NEVER STOPPED LAMENTING BITTERLY HER CRUEL FATE...!!

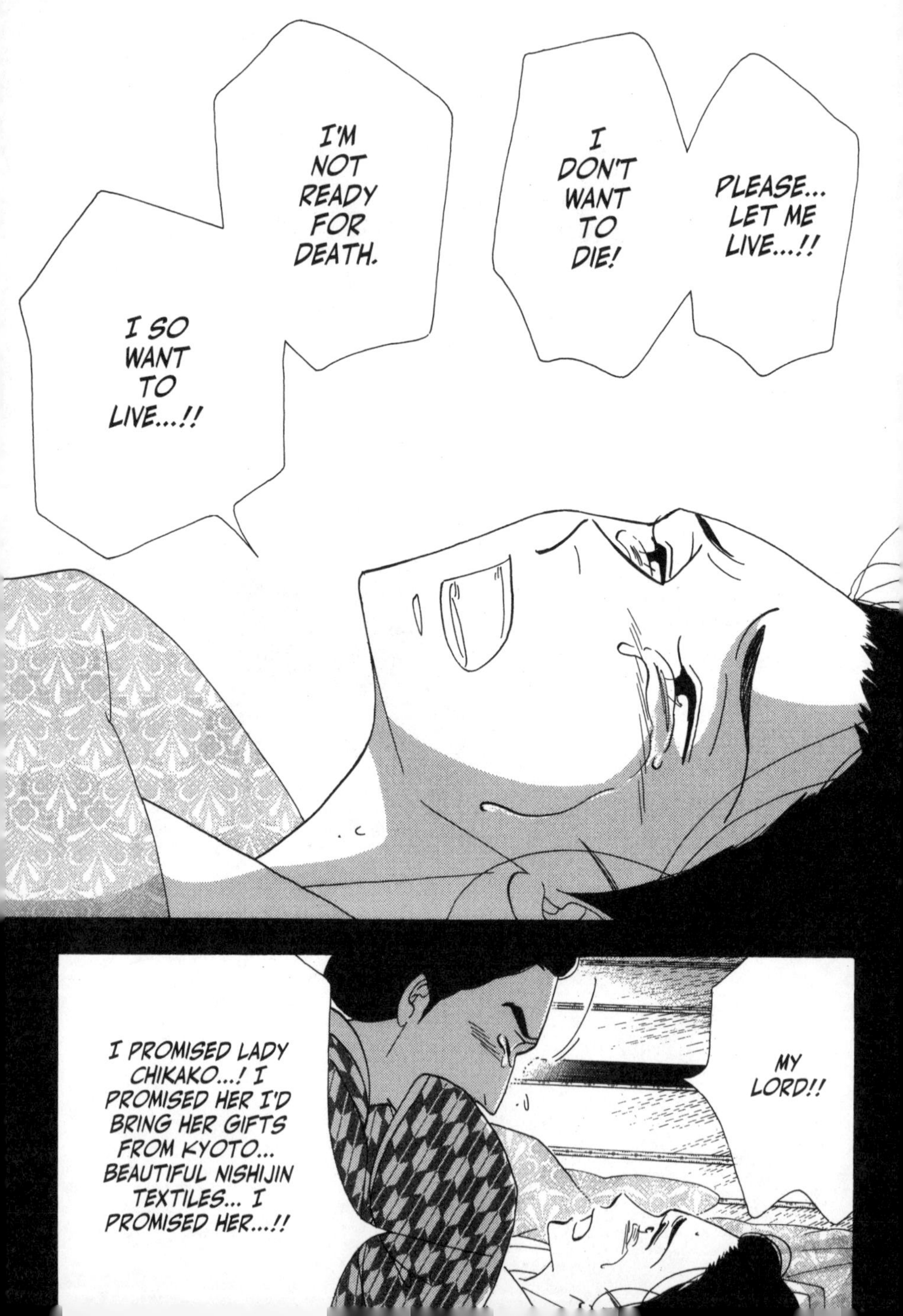
PLEASE... LET ME LIVE...!!
I DON'T WANT TO DIE!
I'M NOT READY FOR DEATH.
I SO WANT TO LIVE...!!
MY LORD!!
I PROMISED LADY CHIKAKO...! I PROMISED HER I'D BRING HER GIFTS FROM KYOTO... BEAUTIFUL NISHIJIN TEXTILES... I PROMISED HER...!!

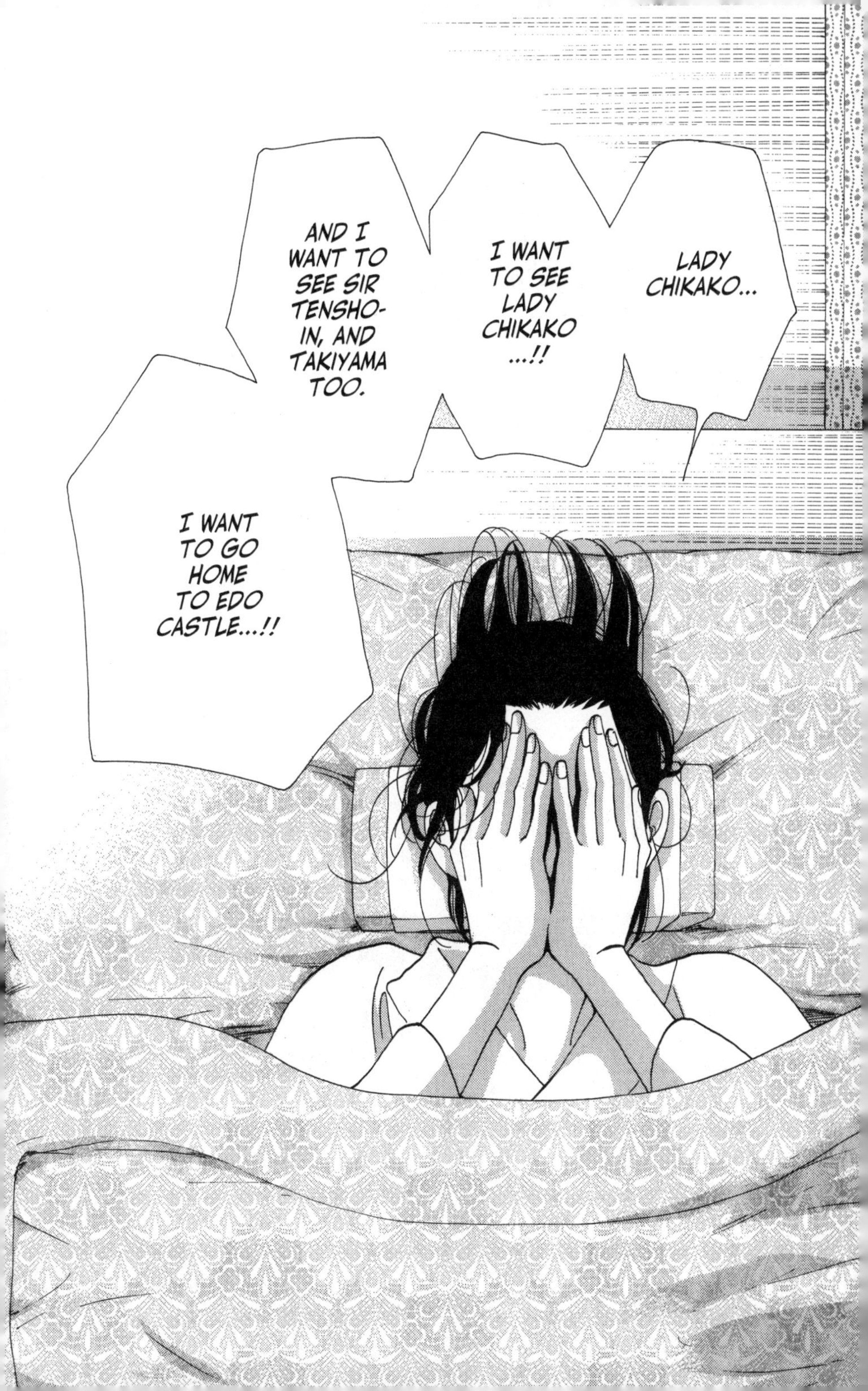
LADY CHIKAKO...
I WANT TO SEE LADY CHIKAKO ...!!
AND I WANT TO SEE SIR TENSHO-IN, AND TAKIYAMA TOO.
I WANT TO GO HOME TO EDO CASTLE...!!

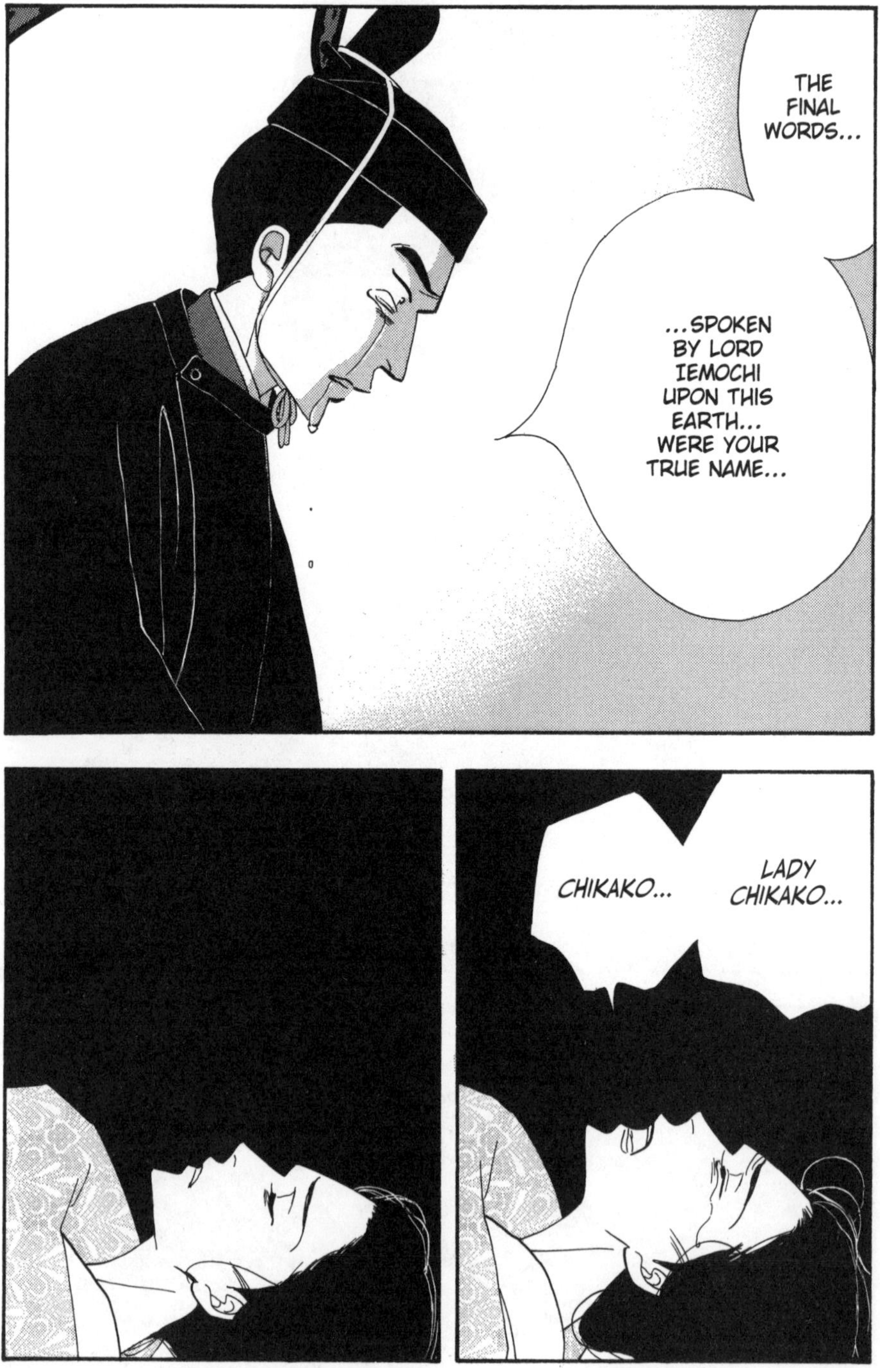
THE FINAL WORDS...
...SPOKEN BY LORD IEMOCHI UPON THIS EARTH... WERE YOUR TRUE NAME...
LADY CHIKAKO...
CHIKAKO...

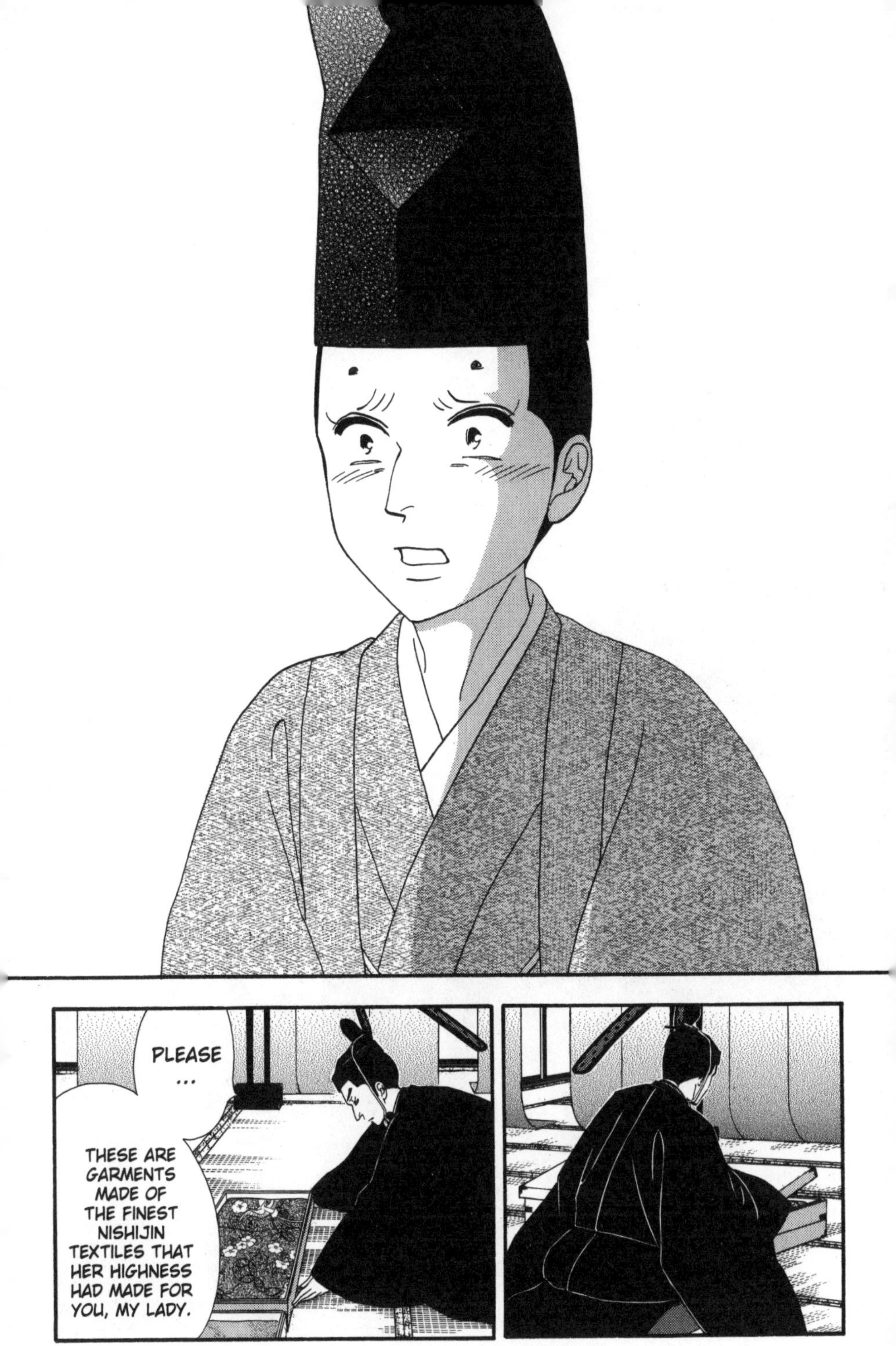
PLEASE ...
THESE ARE GARMENTS MADE OF THE FINEST NISHIJIN TEXTILES THAT HER HIGHNESS HAD MADE FOR YOU, MY LADY.

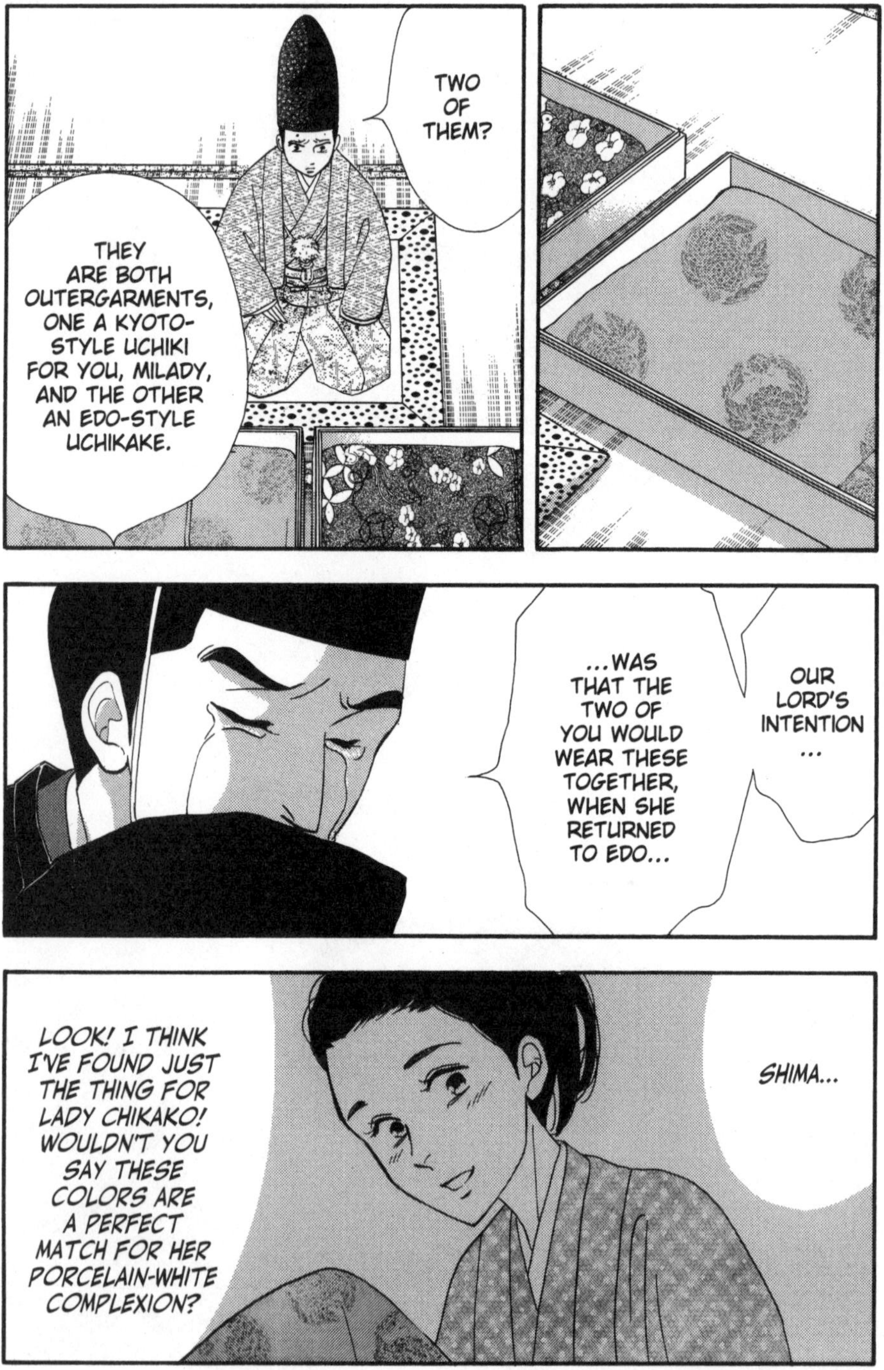
TWO OF THEM?
THEY ARE BOTH OUTERGARMENTS, ONE A KYOTO-STYLE UCHIKI FOR YOU, MILADY, AND THE OTHER AN EDO-STYLE UCHIKAKE.
OUR LORD'S INTENTION ...
...WAS THAT THE TWO OF YOU WOULD WEAR THESE TOGETHER, WHEN SHE RETURNED TO EDO...
SHIMA...
LOOK! I THINK I'VE FOUND JUST THE THING FOR LADY CHIKAKO! WOULDN'T YOU SAY THESE COLORS ARE A PERFECT MATCH FOR HER PORCELAIN-WHITE COMPLEXION?

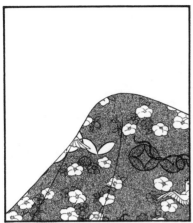
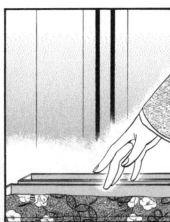
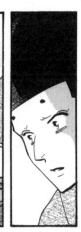
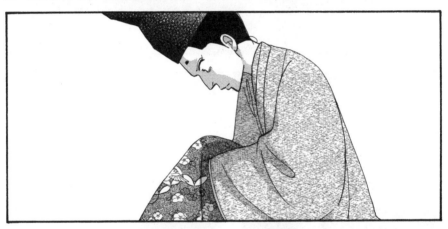
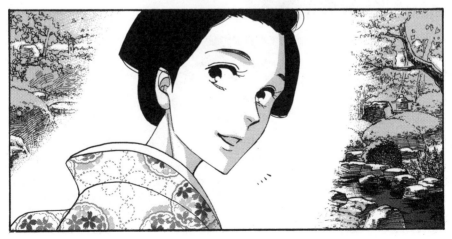

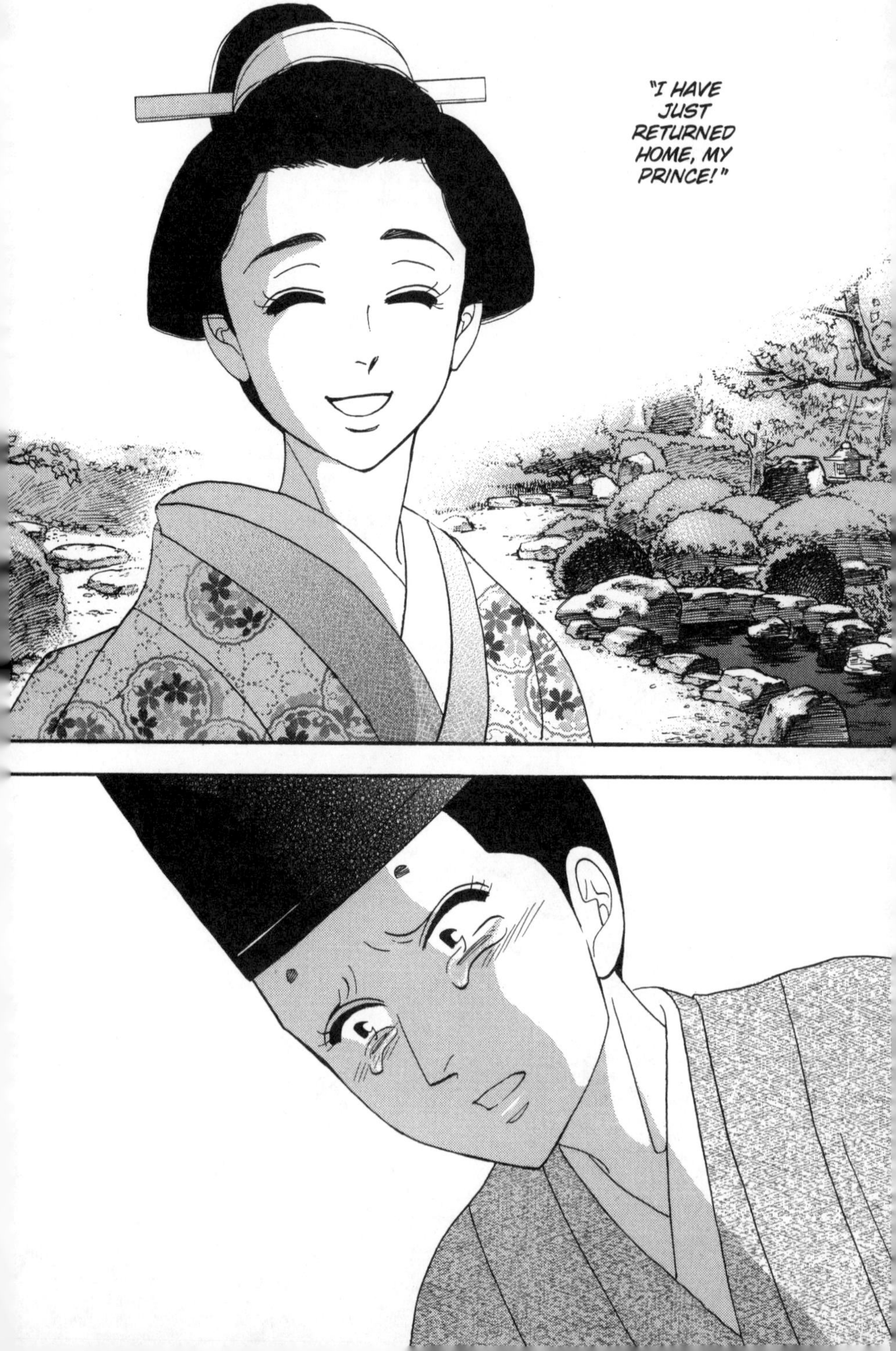
"I HAVE JUST RETURNED HOME, MY PRINCE!"

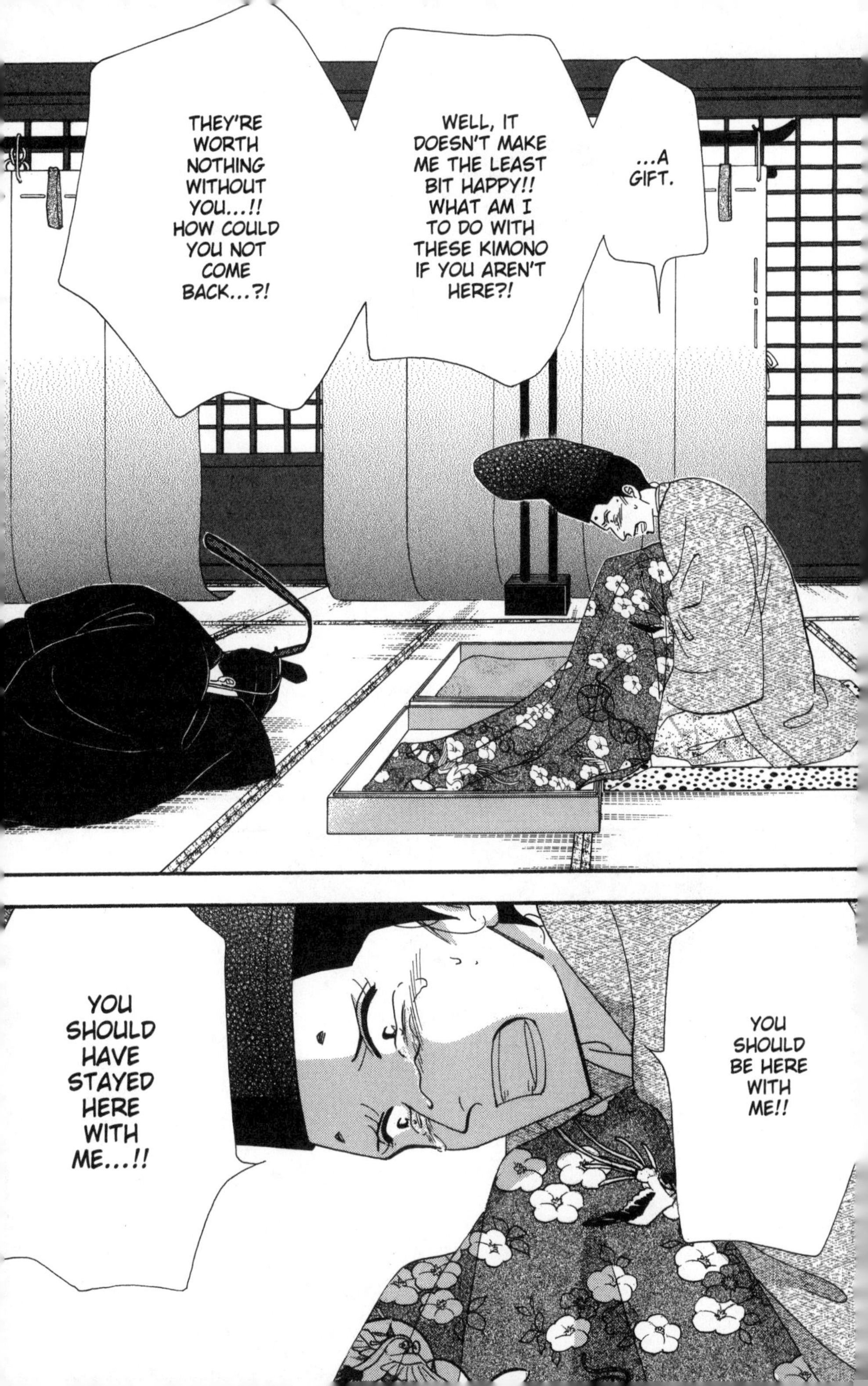
...A GIFT.
WELL, IT DOESN'T MAKE ME THE LEAST BIT HAPPY!! WHAT AM I TO DO WITH THESE KIMONO IF YOU AREN'T HERE?!
THEY'RE WORTH NOTHING WITHOUT YOU...!! HOW COULD YOU NOT COME BACK...?!
YOU SHOULD BE HERE WITH ME!!
YOU SHOULD HAVE STAYED HERE WITH ME...!!

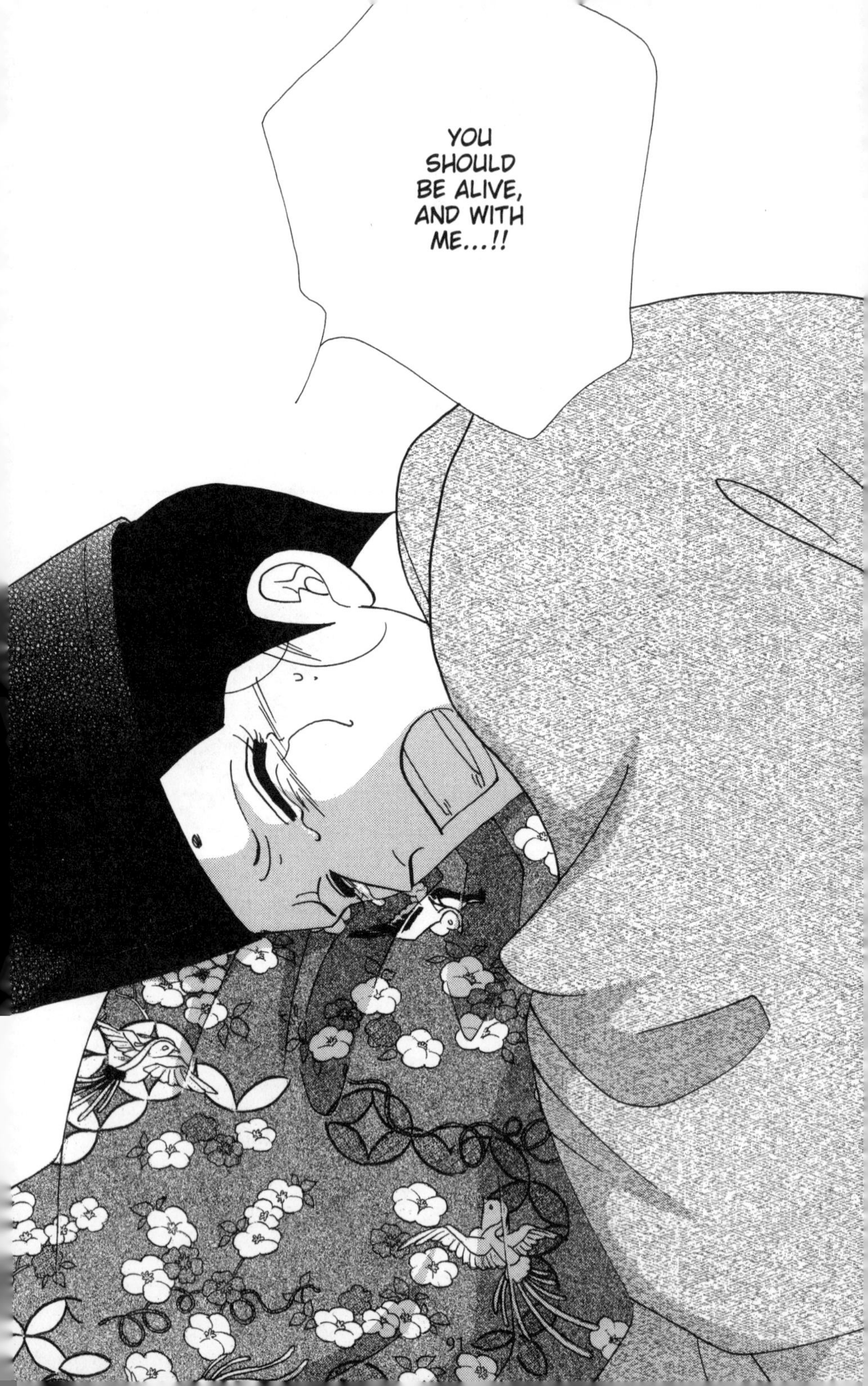
YOU SHOULD BE ALIVE, AND WITH ME...!!

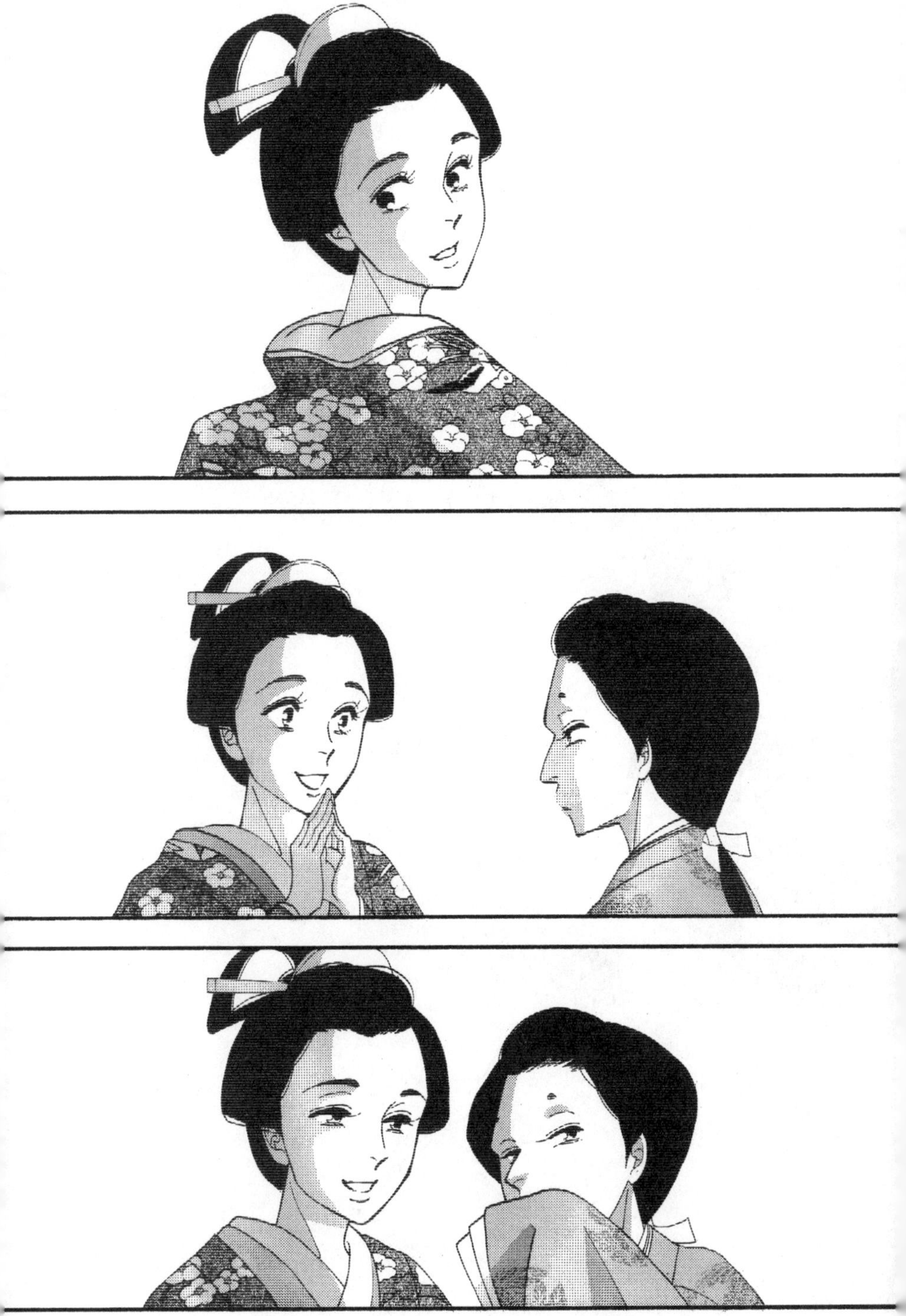

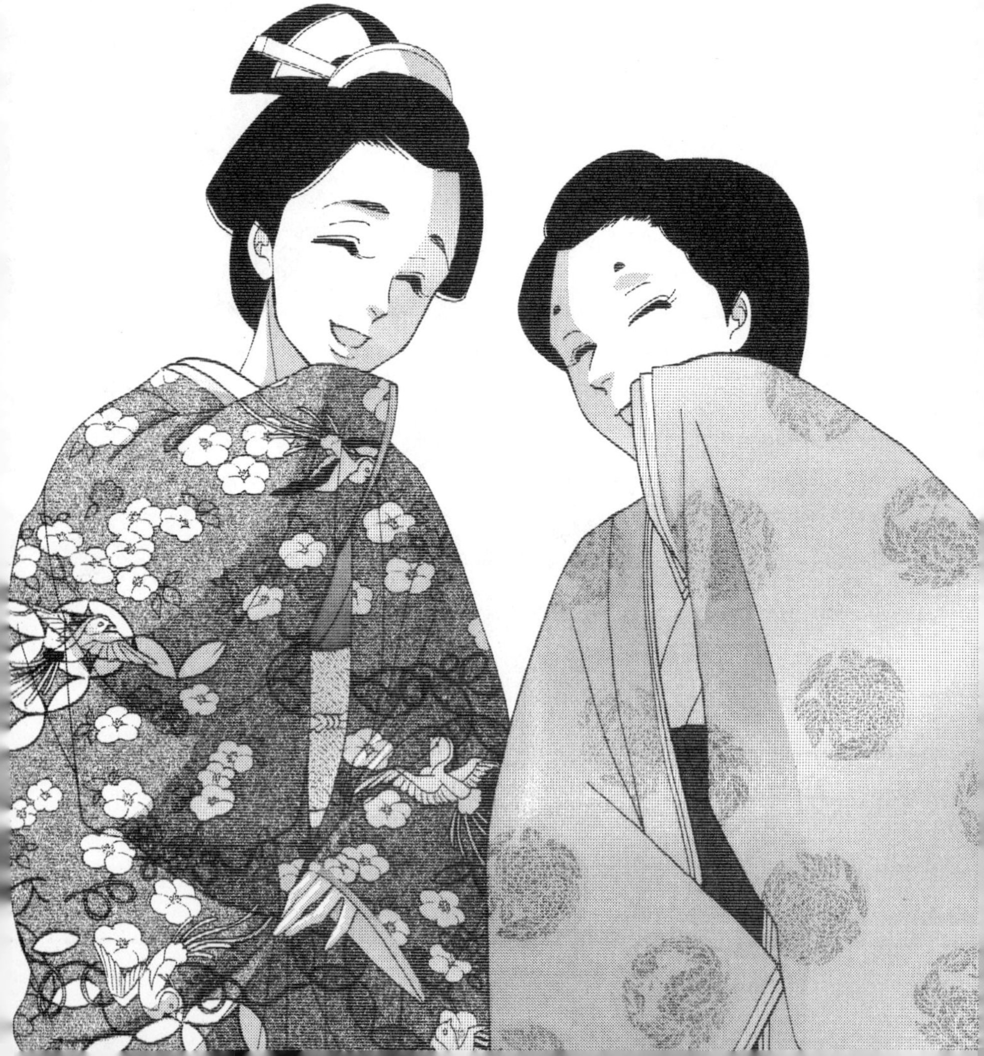

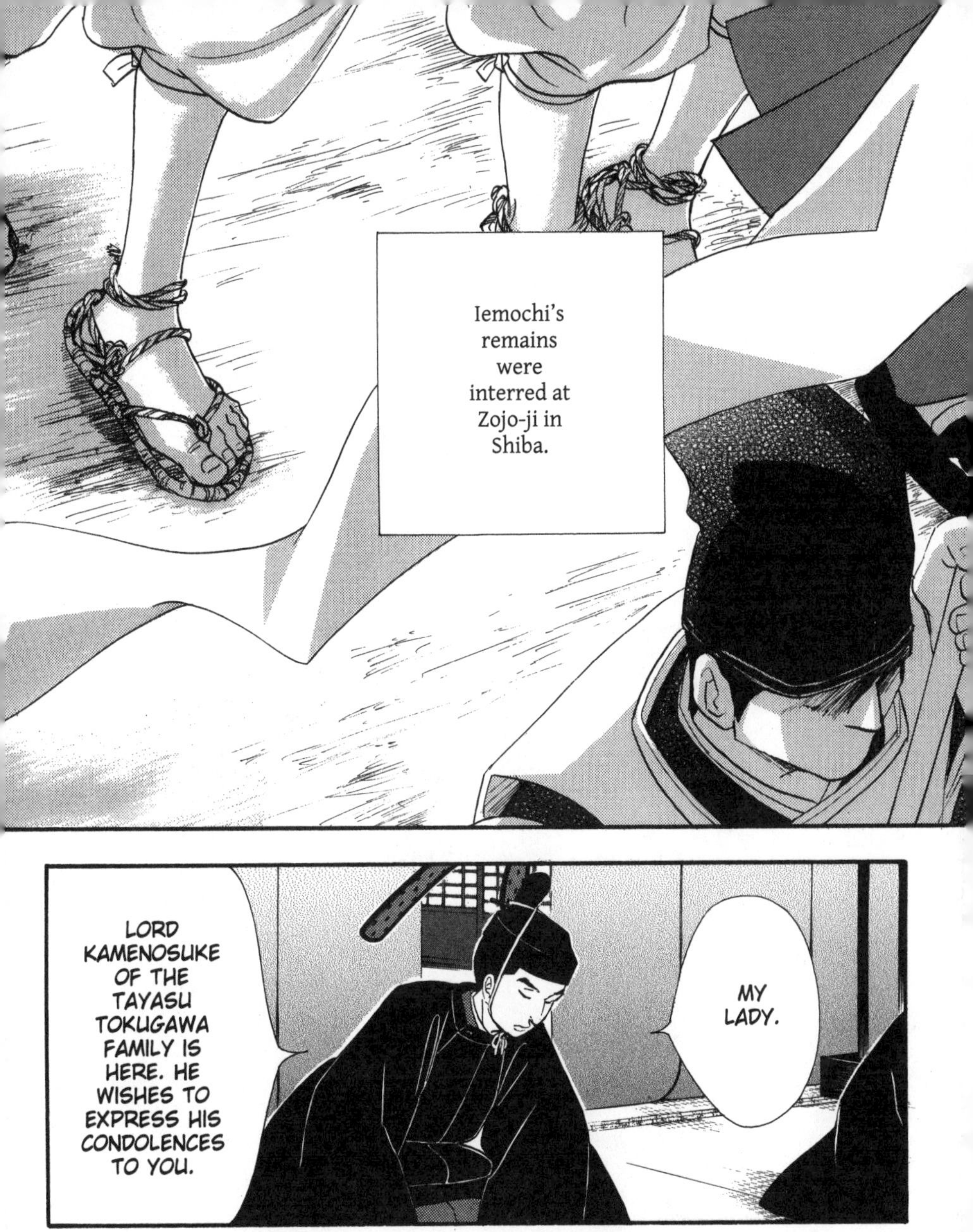
Iemochi's remains were interred at Zojo-ji in Shiba.
MY LADY.
LORD KAMENOSUKE OF THE TAYASU TOKUGAWA FAMILY IS HERE. HE WISHES TO EXPRESS HIS CONDOLENCES TO YOU.
...
I HAVE ALREADY SENT ALL THE OTHER ATTENDANTS AWAY. PLEASE MEET WITH LORD KAMENOSUKE AND SPEAK A FEW WORDS TO HIM.

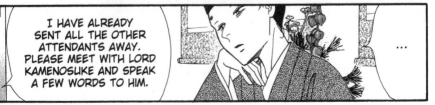

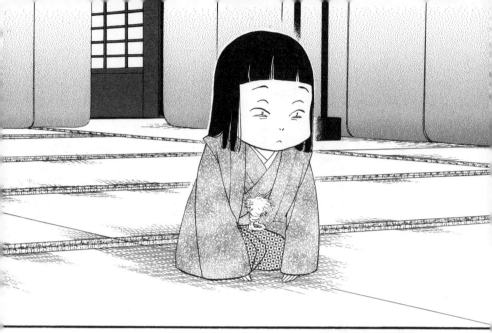

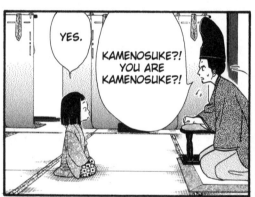

YES.

KAMENOSUKE?! YOU ARE KAMENOSUKE?!

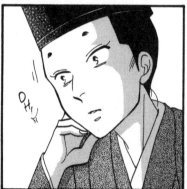

OH!

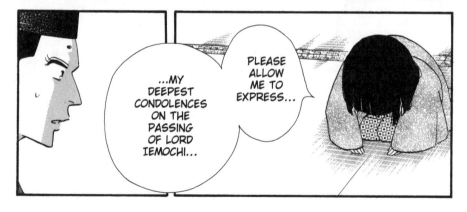

PLEASE ALLOW ME TO EXPRESS...

...MY DEEPEST CONDOLENCES ON THE PASSING OF LORD IEMOCHI...

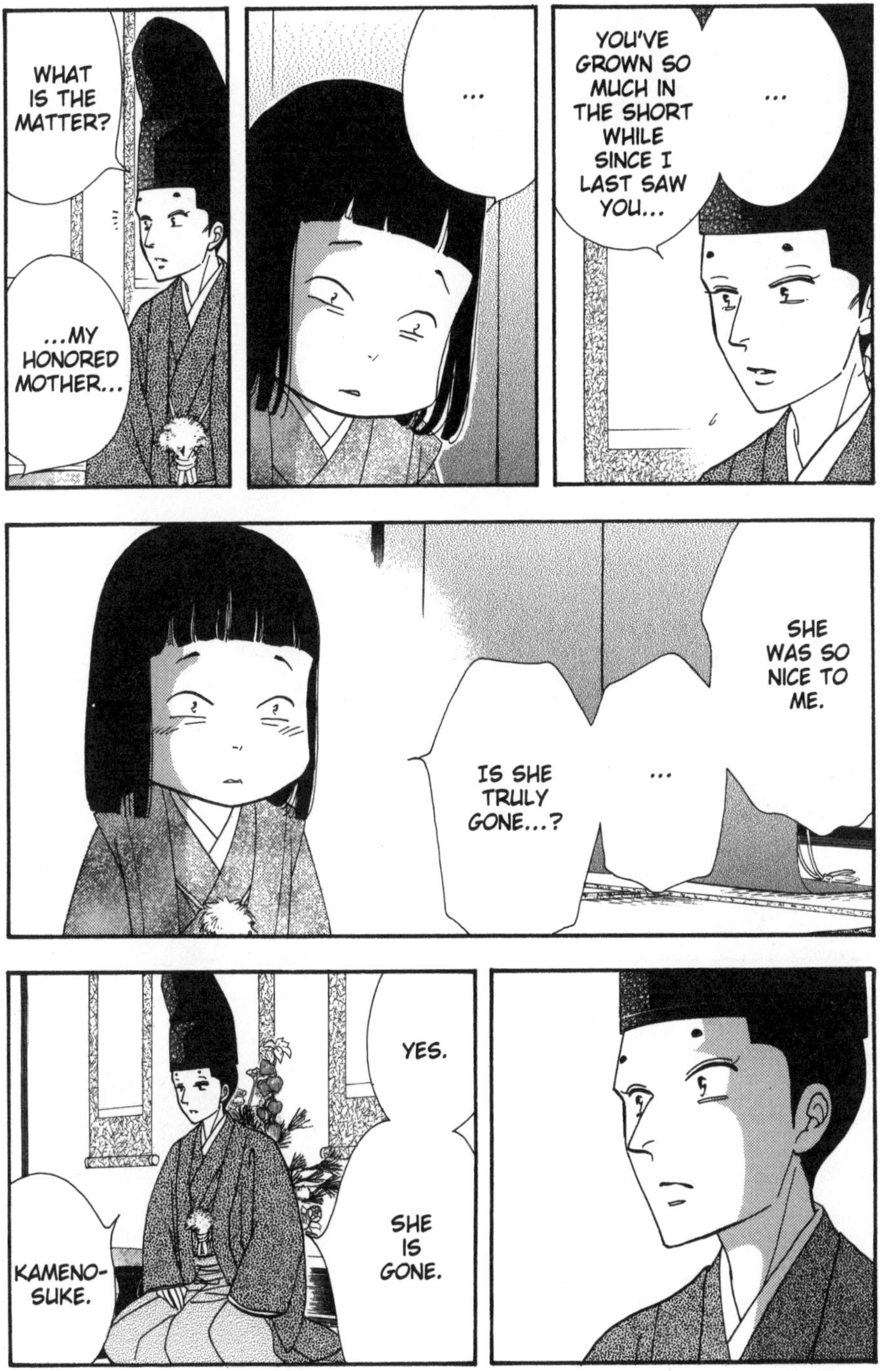
...
YOU'VE GROWN SO MUCH IN THE SHORT WHILE SINCE I LAST SAW YOU...
...
WHAT IS THE MATTER?
...MY HONORED MOTHER...
SHE WAS SO NICE TO ME.
...
IS SHE TRULY GONE...?
YES.
SHE IS GONE.
KAMENO-SUKE.

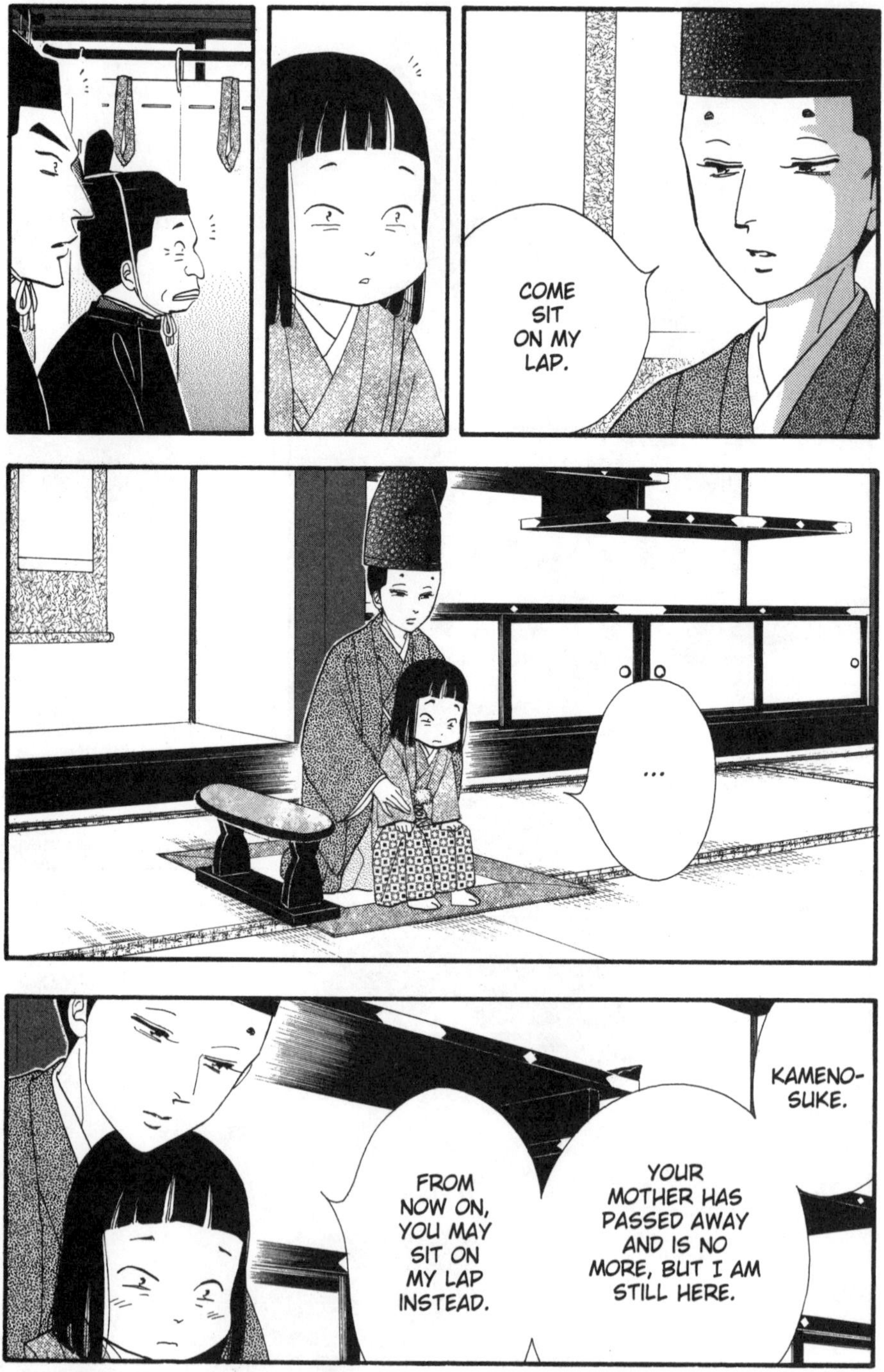
COME SIT ON MY LAP.
...
KAMENO-SUKE.
YOUR MOTHER HAS PASSED AWAY AND IS NO MORE, BUT I AM STILL HERE.
FROM NOW ON, YOU MAY SIT ON MY LAP INSTEAD.

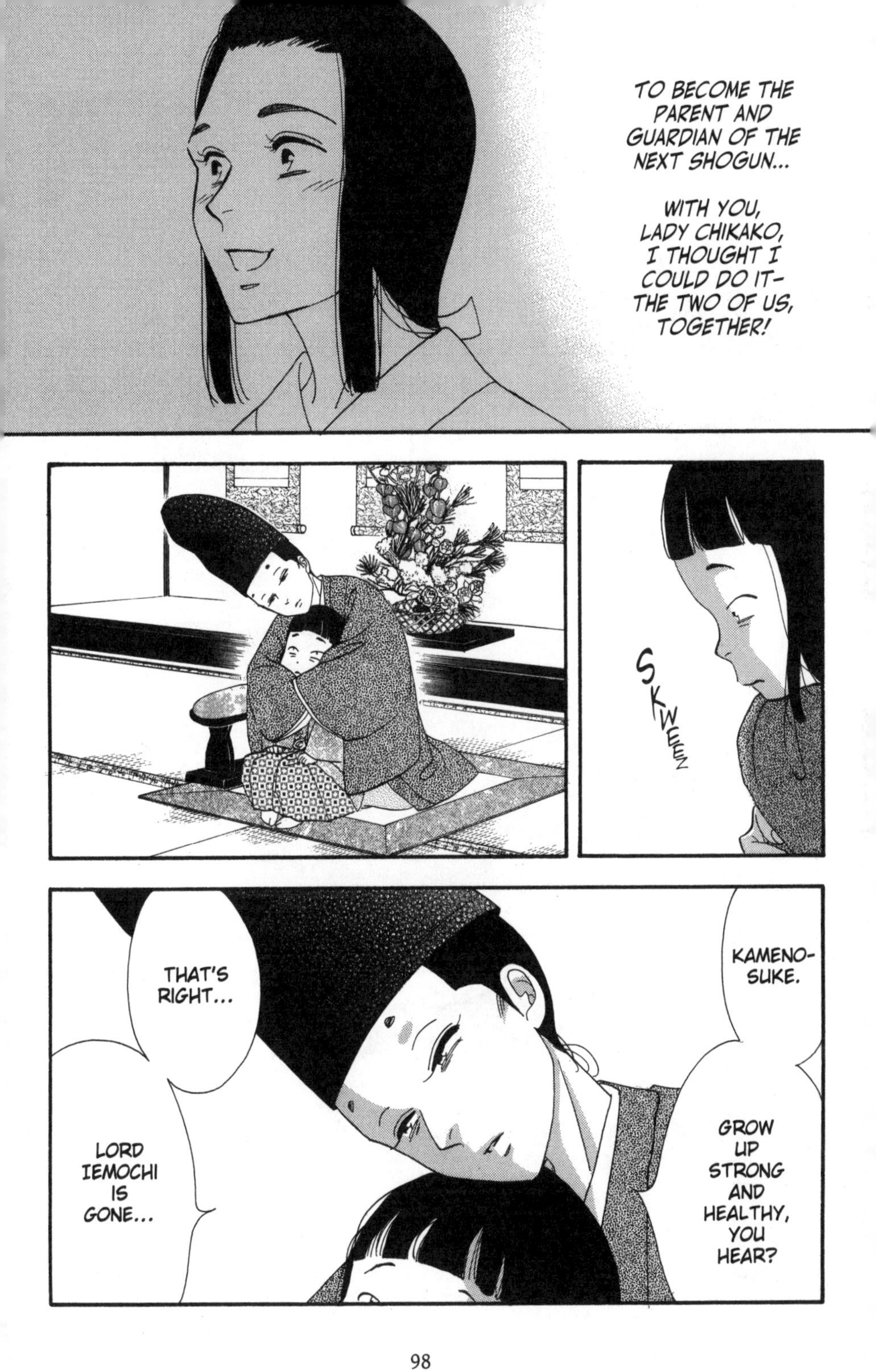
TO BECOME THE PARENT AND GUARDIAN OF THE NEXT SHOGUN...
WITH YOU, LADY CHIKAKO, I THOUGHT I COULD DO IT-THE TWO OF US, TOGETHER!
SKWEEZ
KAMENO-SUKE.
GROW UP STRONG AND HEALTHY, YOU HEAR?
THAT'S RIGHT...
LORD IEMOCHI IS GONE...

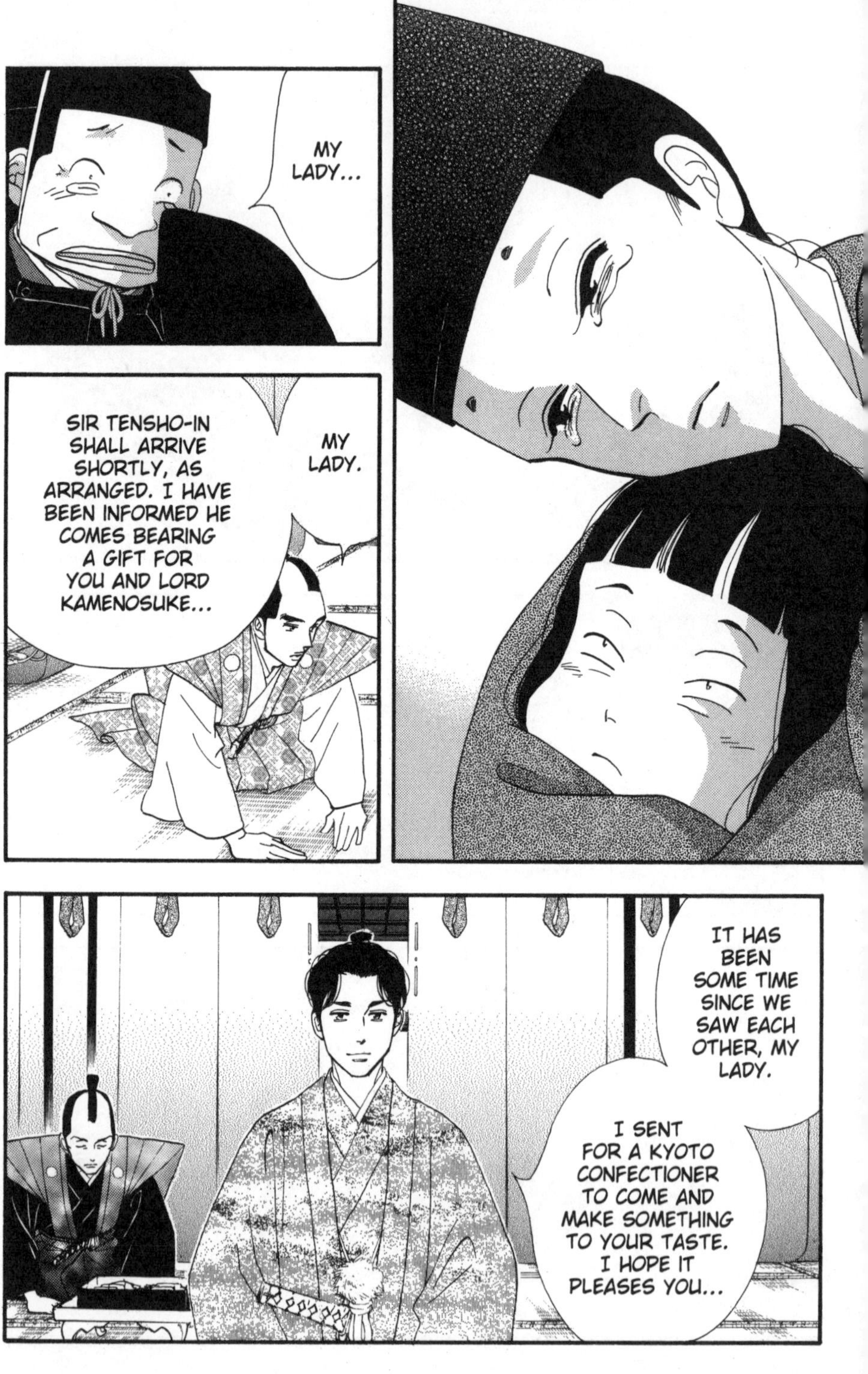
MY LADY...
MY LADY.
SIR TENSHO-IN SHALL ARRIVE SHORTLY, AS ARRANGED. I HAVE BEEN INFORMED HE COMES BEARING A GIFT FOR YOU AND LORD KAMENOSUKE...
IT HAS BEEN SOME TIME SINCE WE SAW EACH OTHER, MY LADY.
I SENT FOR A KYOTO CONFECTIONER TO COME AND MAKE SOMETHING TO YOUR TASTE. I HOPE IT PLEASES YOU...

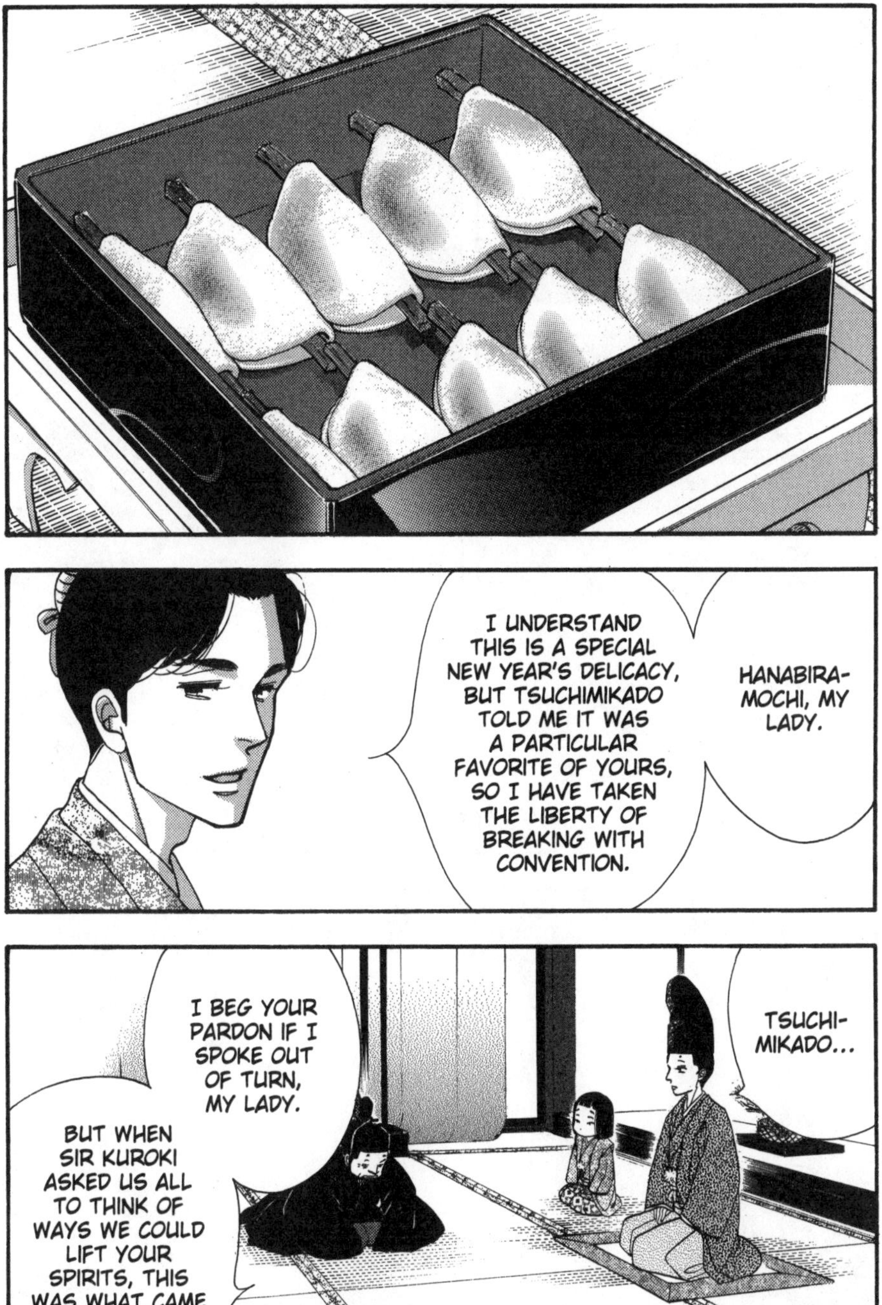
HANABIRA-MOCHI, MY LADY.
I UNDERSTAND THIS IS A SPECIAL NEW YEAR'S DELICACY, BUT TSUCHIMIKADO TOLD ME IT WAS A PARTICULAR FAVORITE OF YOURS, SO I HAVE TAKEN THE LIBERTY OF BREAKING WITH CONVENTION.
TSUCHI-MIKADO...
I BEG YOUR PARDON IF I SPOKE OUT OF TURN, MY LADY.
BUT WHEN SIR KUROKI ASKED US ALL TO THINK OF WAYS WE COULD LIFT YOUR SPIRITS, THIS WAS WHAT CAME TO MIND...

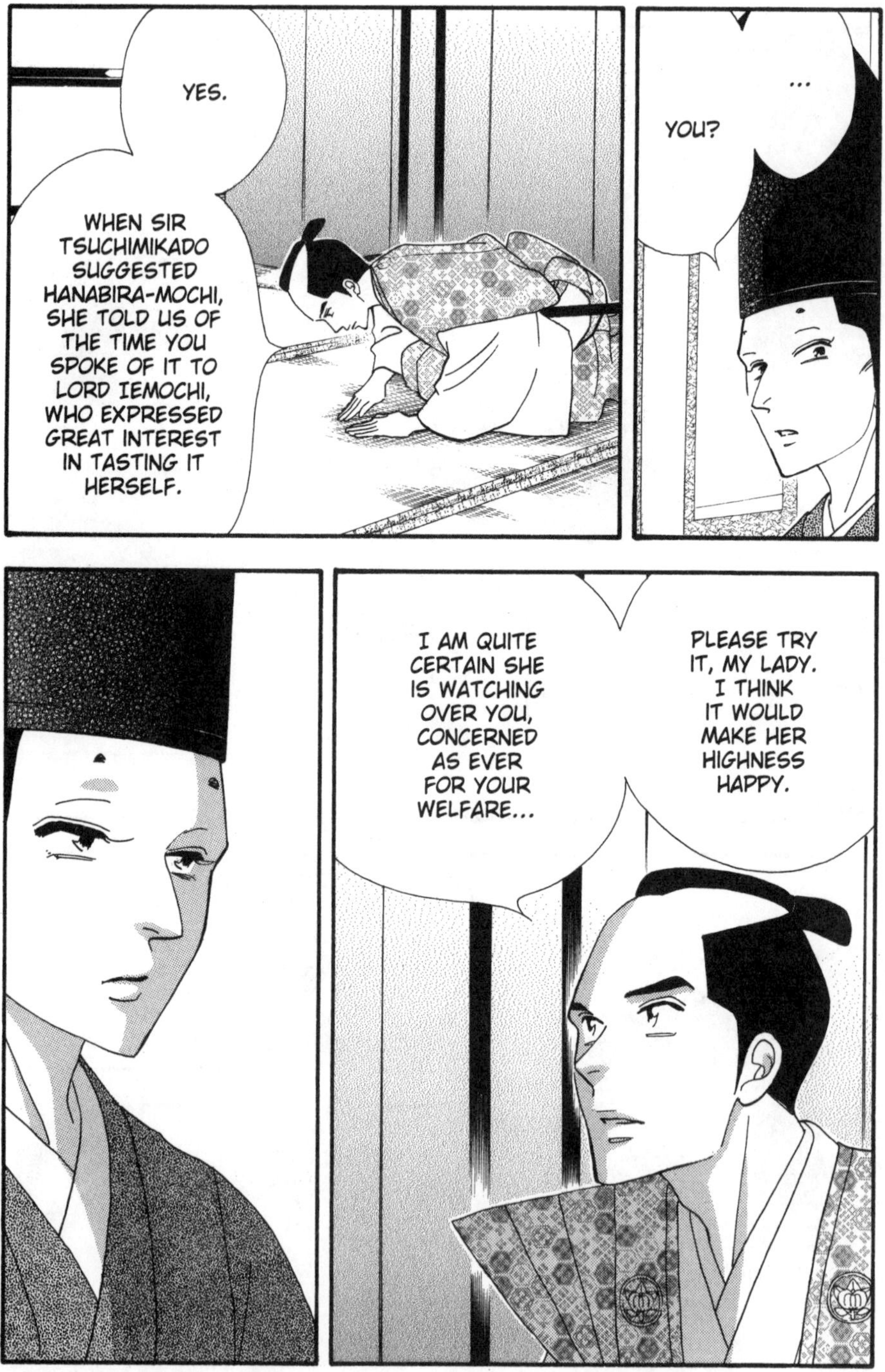
...
YOU?
YES.
WHEN SIR TSUCHIMIKADO SUGGESTED HANABIRA-MOCHI, SHE TOLD US OF THE TIME YOU SPOKE OF IT TO LORD IEMOCHI, WHO EXPRESSED GREAT INTEREST IN TASTING IT HERSELF.
PLEASE TRY IT, MY LADY. I THINK IT WOULD MAKE HER HIGHNESS HAPPY.
I AM QUITE CERTAIN SHE IS WATCHING OVER YOU, CONCERNED AS EVER FOR YOUR WELFARE...

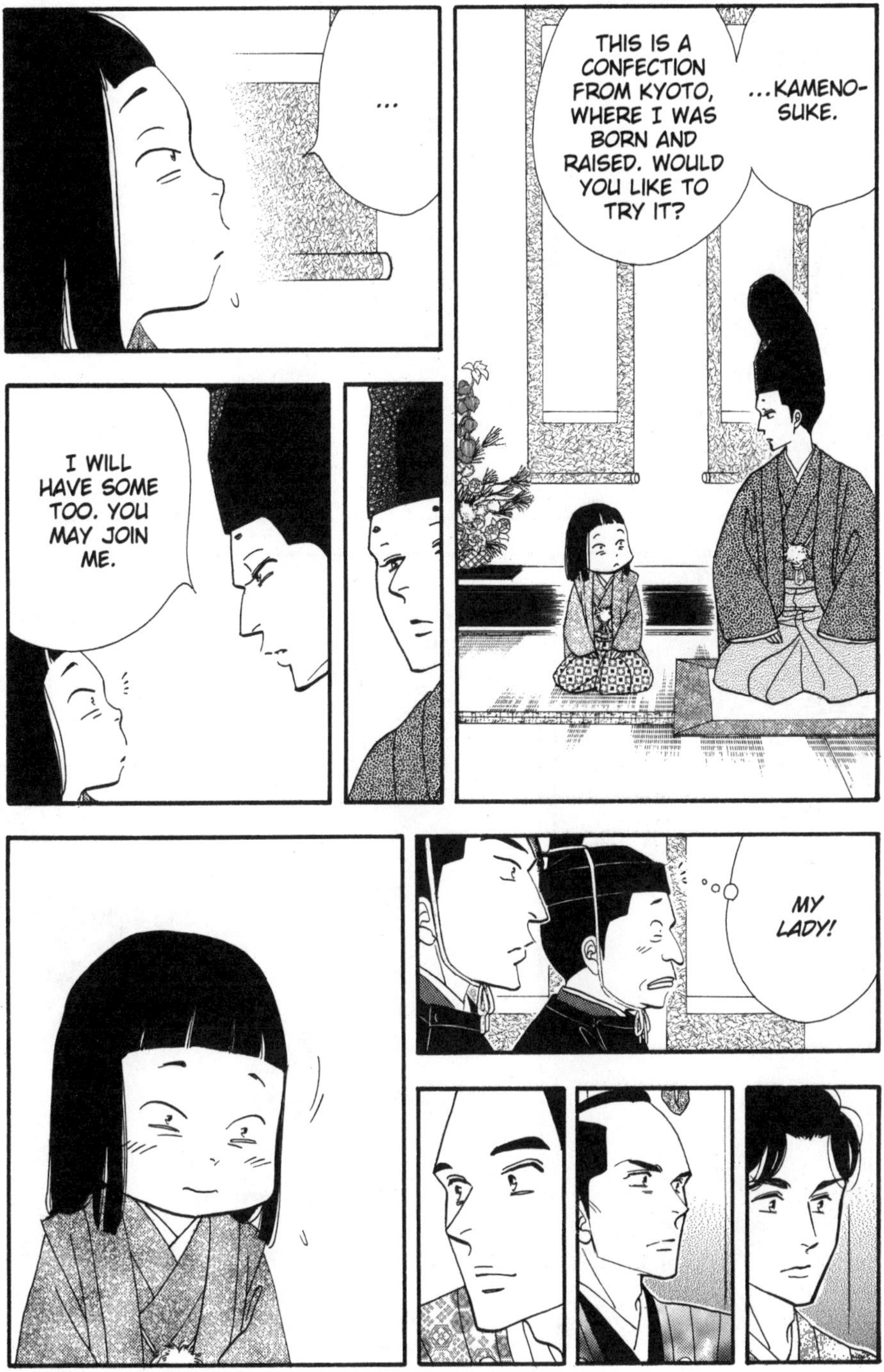
...KAMENO-SUKE.
THIS IS A CONFECTION FROM KYOTO, WHERE I WAS BORN AND RAISED. WOULD YOU LIKE TO TRY IT?
...
I WILL HAVE SOME TOO. YOU MAY JOIN ME.
MY LADY!

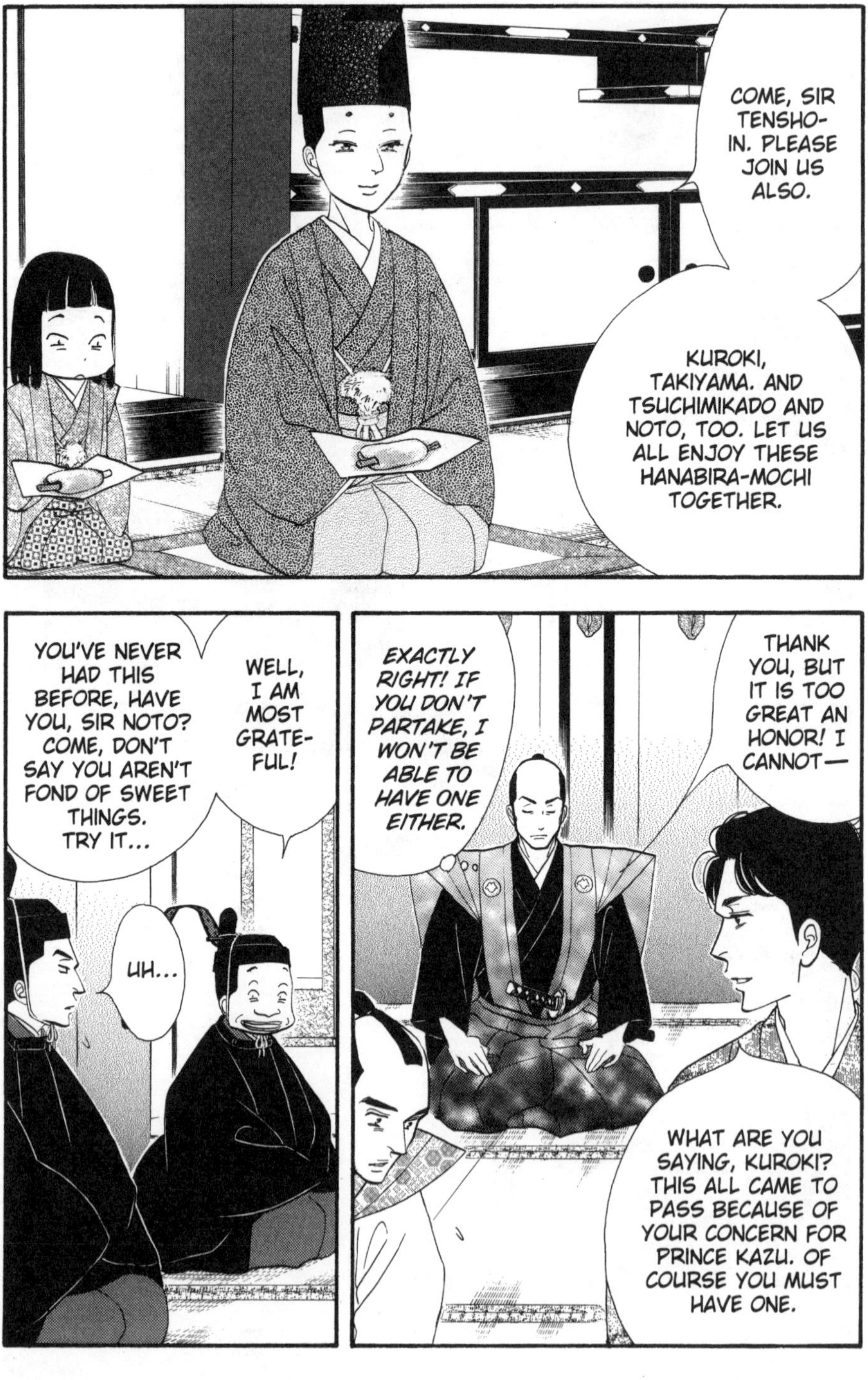
COME, SIR TENSHO-IN. PLEASE JOIN US ALSO.
KUROKI, TAKIYAMA. AND TSUCHIMIKADO AND NOTO, TOO. LET US ALL ENJOY THESE HANABIRA-MOCHI TOGETHER.
THANK YOU, BUT IT IS TOO GREAT AN HONOR! I CANNOT—
EXACTLY RIGHT! IF YOU DON'T PARTAKE, I WON'T BE ABLE TO HAVE ONE EITHER.
WHAT ARE YOU SAYING, KUROKI? THIS ALL CAME TO PASS BECAUSE OF YOUR CONCERN FOR PRINCE KAZU. OF COURSE YOU MUST HAVE ONE.
WELL, I AM MOST GRATE-FUL!
YOU'VE NEVER HAD THIS BEFORE, HAVE YOU, SIR NOTO? COME, DON'T SAY YOU AREN'T FOND OF SWEET THINGS. TRY IT...
UH...

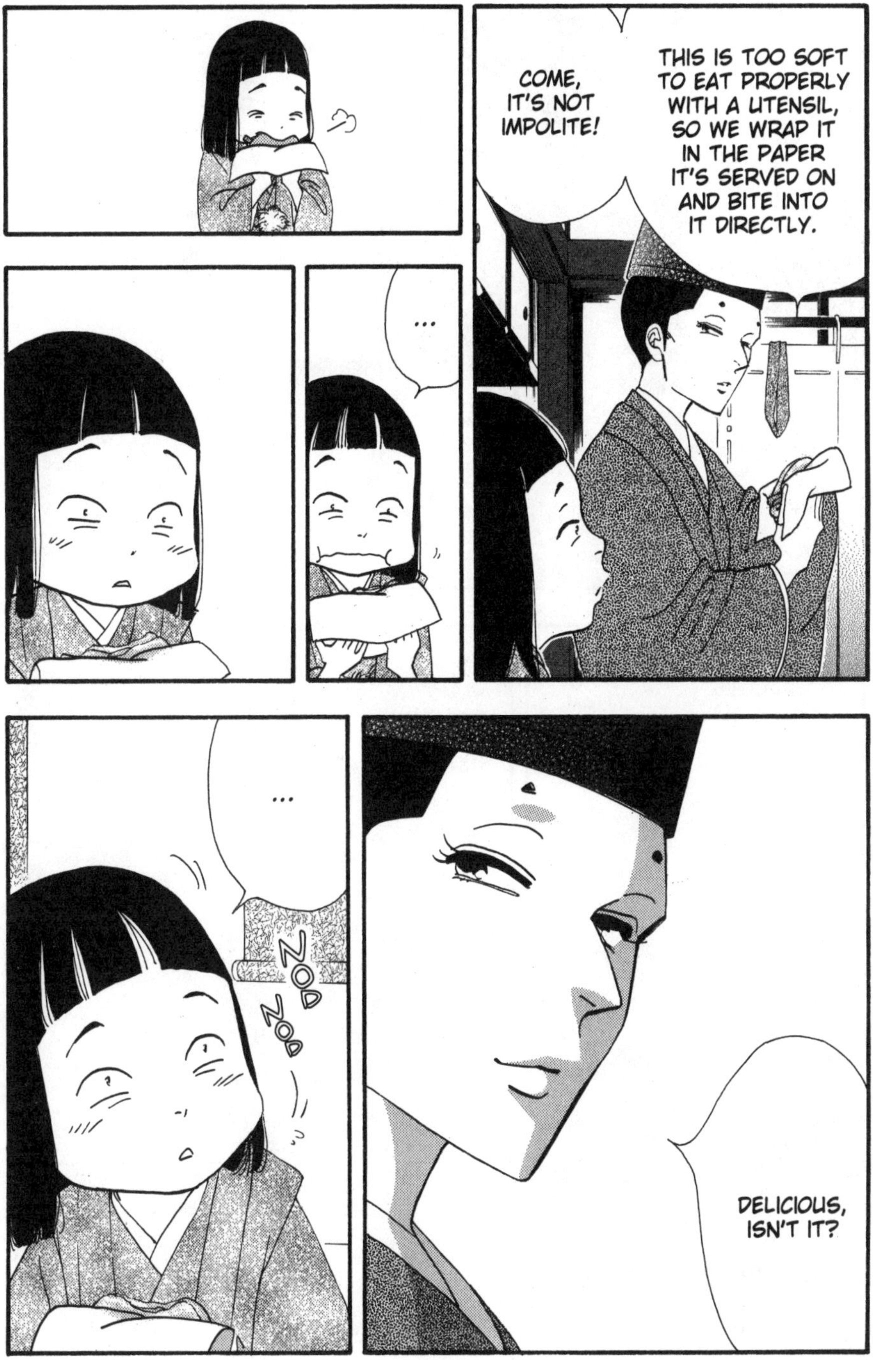

THIS IS TOO SOFT TO EAT PROPERLY WITH A UTENSIL, SO WE WRAP IT IN THE PAPER IT'S SERVED ON AND BITE INTO IT DIRECTLY.
COME, IT'S NOT IMPOLITE!
...
DELICIOUS, ISN'T IT?
...
NOD NOD

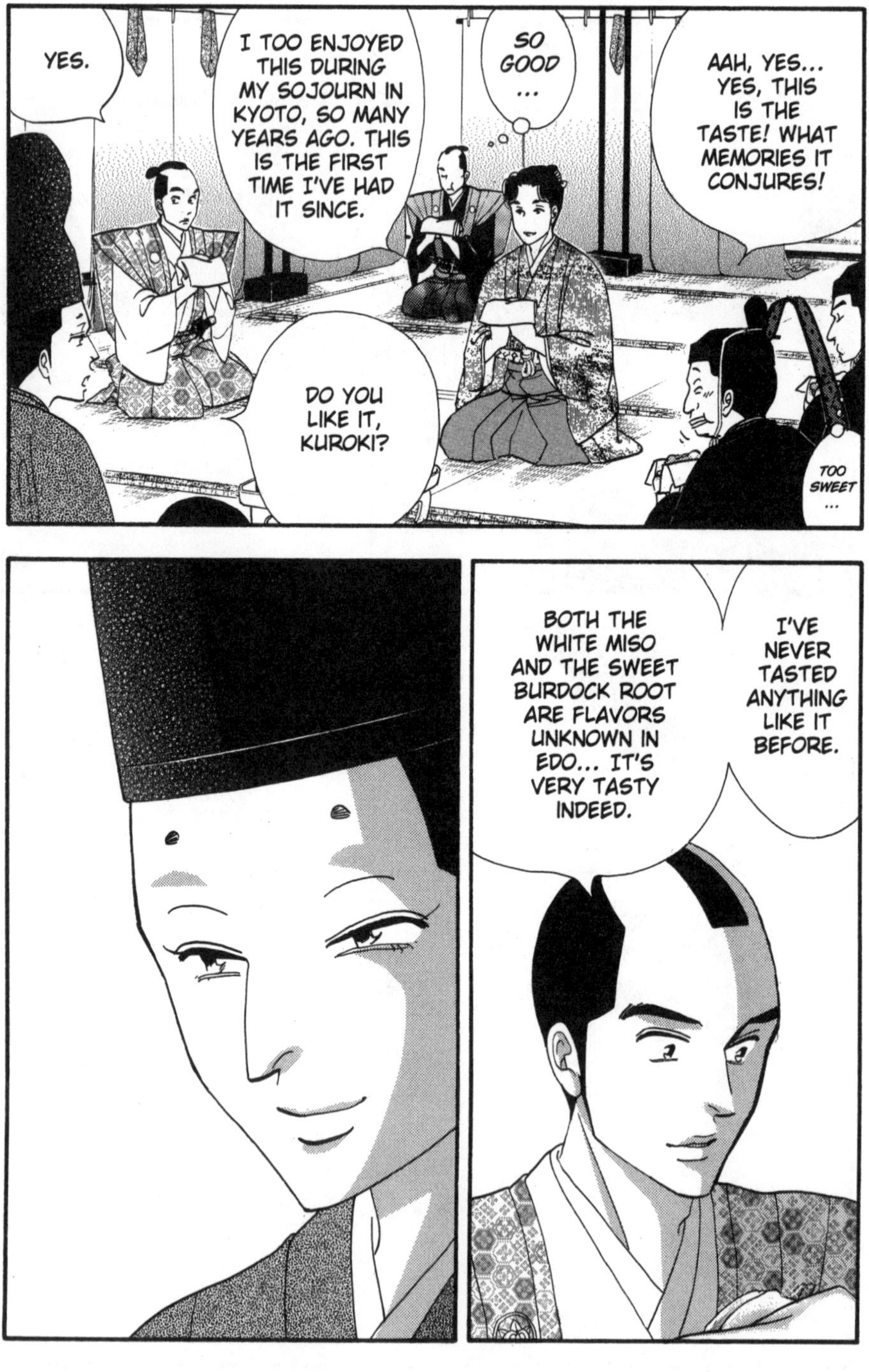
AAH, YES... YES, THIS IS THE TASTE! WHAT MEMORIES IT CONJURES!
SO GOOD ...
I TOO ENJOYED THIS DURING MY SOJOURN IN KYOTO, SO MANY YEARS AGO. THIS IS THE FIRST TIME I'VE HAD IT SINCE.
YES.
TOO SWEET ...
DO YOU LIKE IT, KUROKI?
I'VE NEVER TASTED ANYTHING LIKE IT BEFORE.
BOTH THE WHITE MISO AND THE SWEET BURDOCK ROOT ARE FLAVORS UNKNOWN IN EDO... IT'S VERY TASTY INDEED.

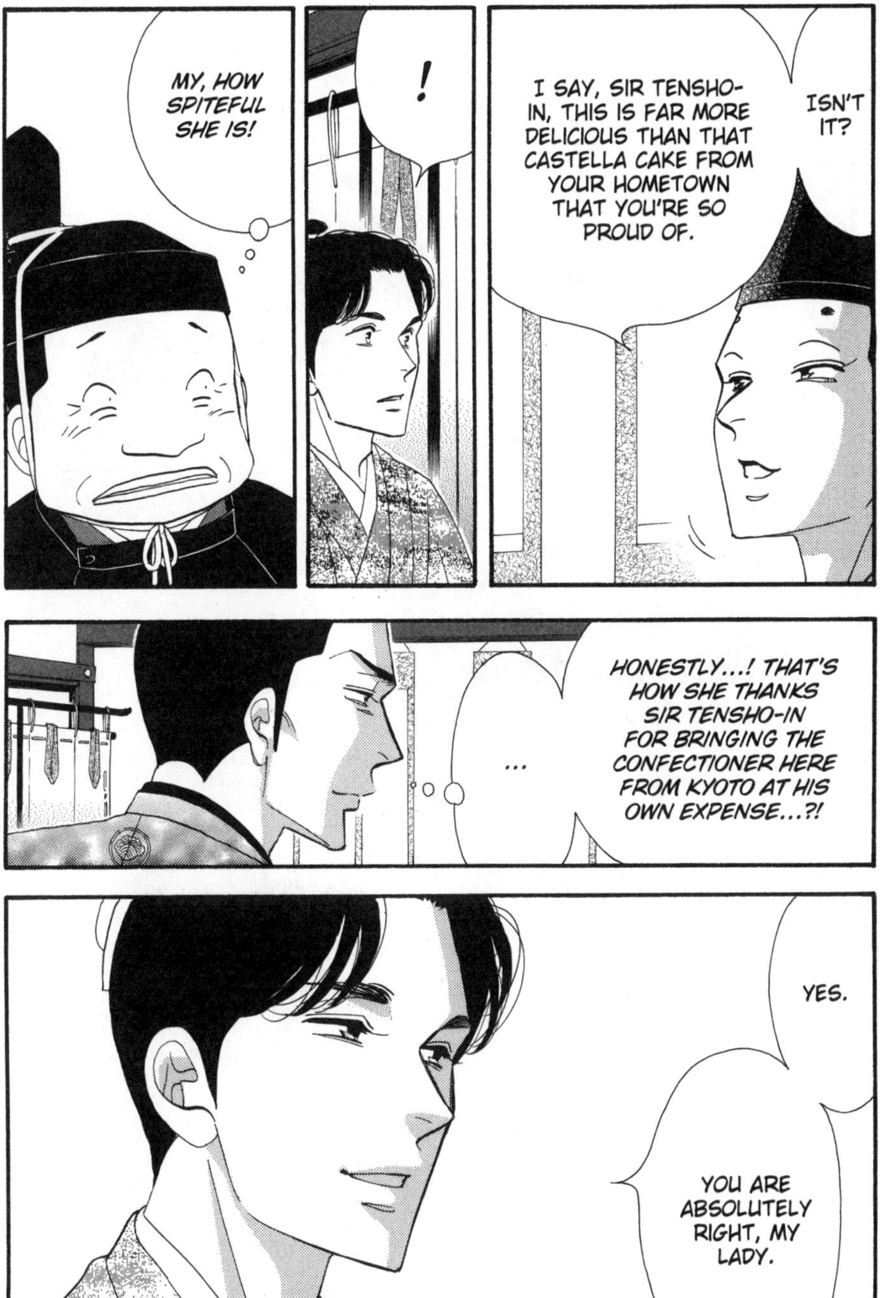
I SAY, SIR TENSHO-IN, THIS IS FAR MORE DELICIOUS THAN THAT CASTELLA CAKE FROM YOUR HOMETOWN THAT YOU'RE SO PROUD OF.
ISN'T IT?
!
MY, HOW SPITEFUL SHE IS!
HONESTLY...! THAT'S HOW SHE THANKS SIR TENSHO-IN FOR BRINGING THE CONFECTIONER HERE FROM KYOTO AT HIS OWN EXPENSE...?!
...
YES.
YOU ARE ABSOLUTELY RIGHT, MY LADY.

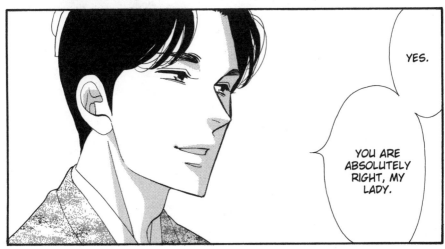

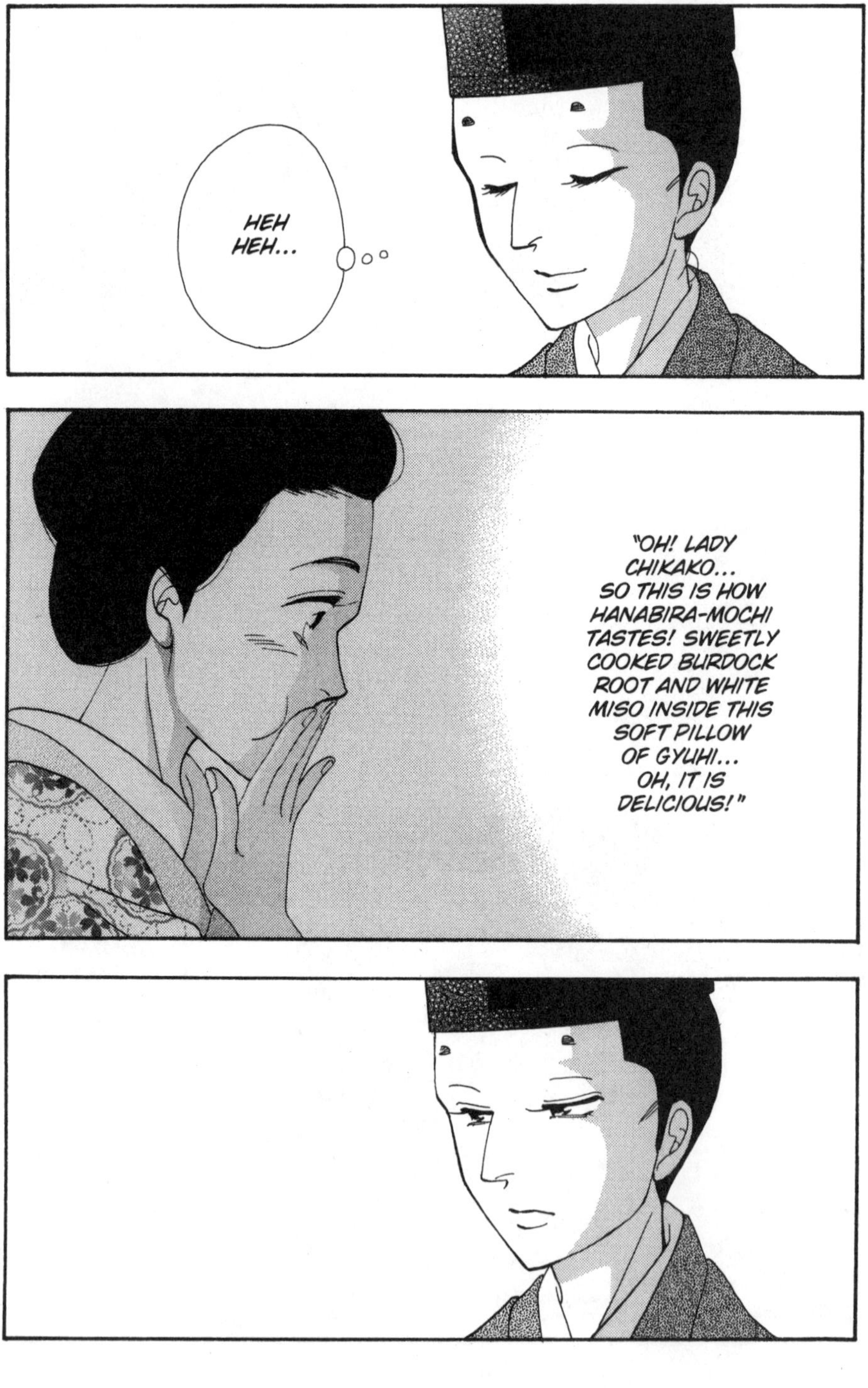
HEH HEH...
"OH! LADY CHIKAKO... SO THIS IS HOW HANABIRA-MOCHI TASTES! SWEETLY COOKED BURDOCK ROOT AND WHITE MISO INSIDE THIS SOFT PILLOW OF GYUHI... OH, IT IS DELICIOUS!"

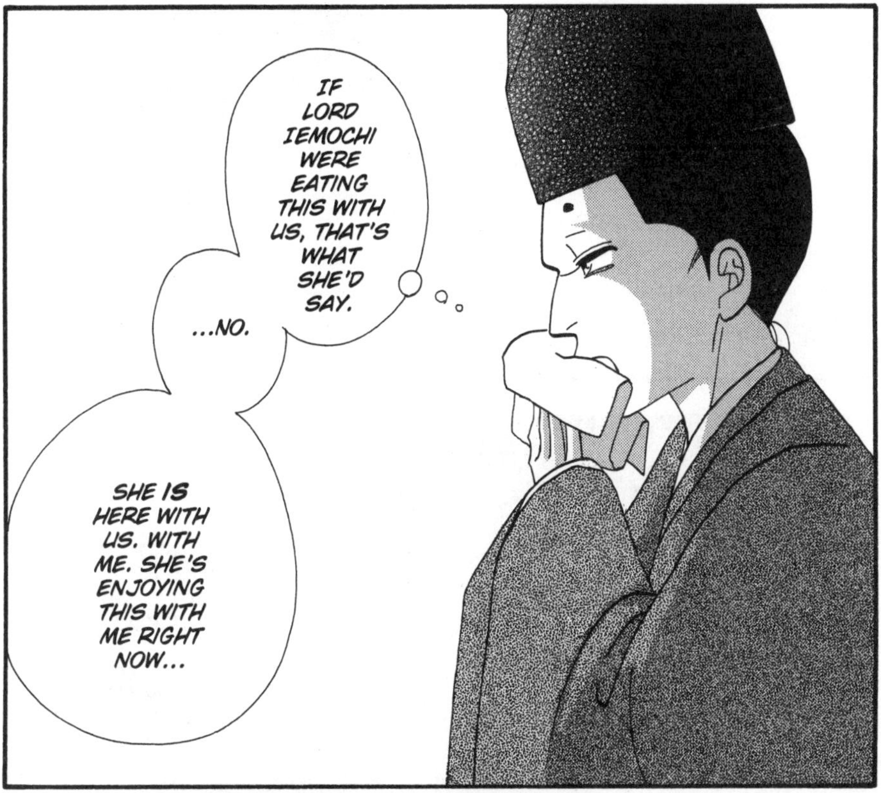
IF LORD IEMOCHI WERE EATING THIS WITH US, THAT'S WHAT SHE'D SAY.
...NO.
SHE **IS** HERE WITH US. WITH ME. SHE'S ENJOYING THIS WITH ME RIGHT NOW...

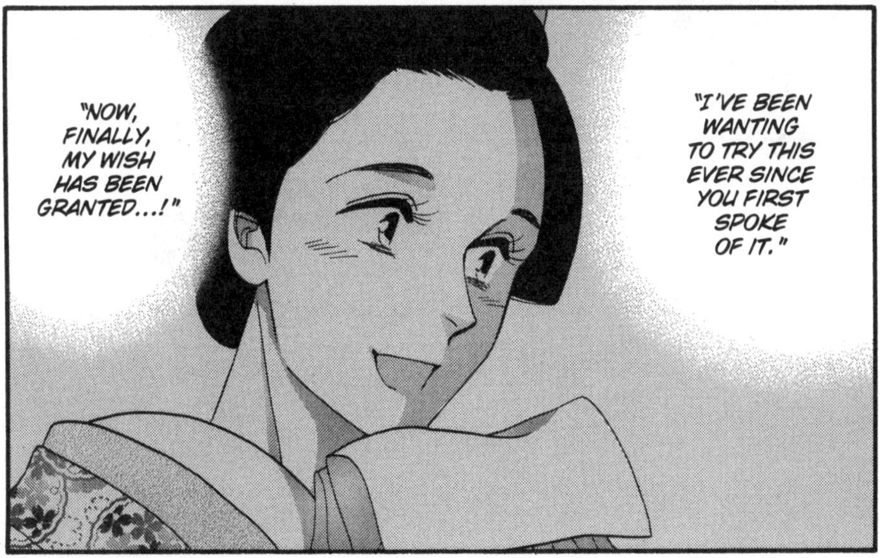
"I'VE BEEN WANTING TO TRY THIS EVER SINCE YOU FIRST SPOKE OF IT."
"NOW, FINALLY, MY WISH HAS BEEN GRANTED...!"

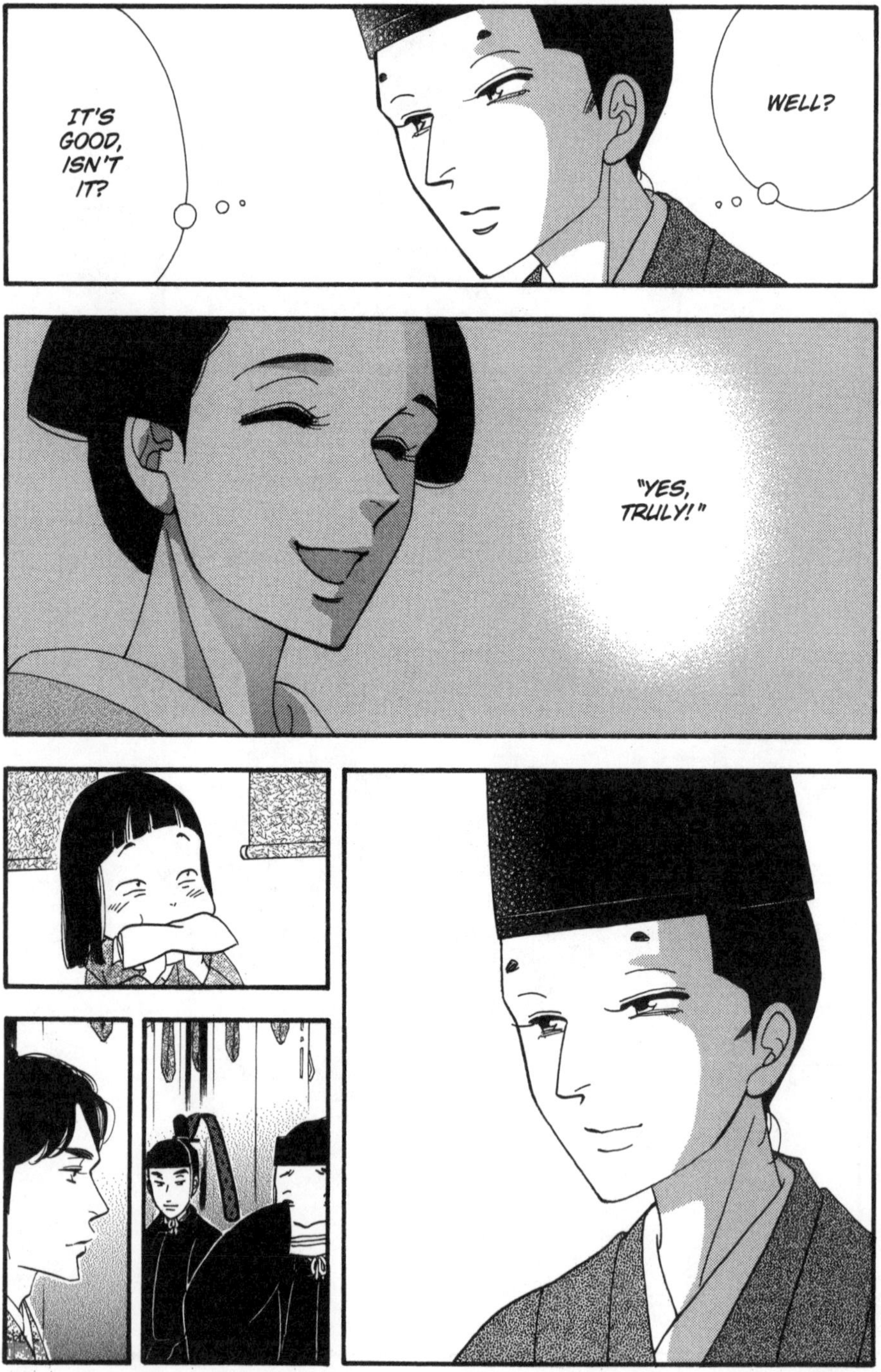
WELL?
IT'S GOOD, ISN'T IT?
"YES, TRULY!"

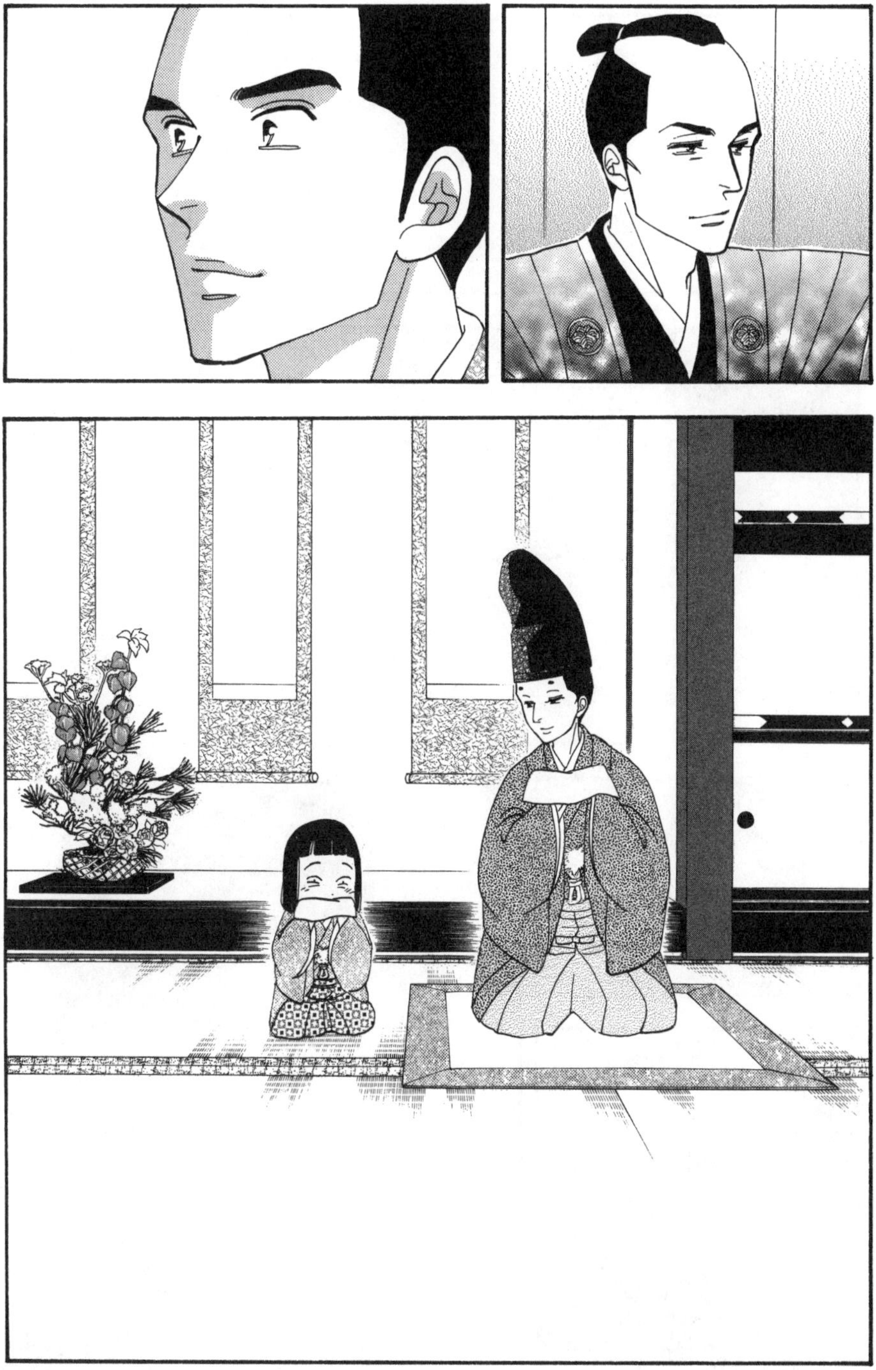

Ōoku

THE INNER CHAMBERS

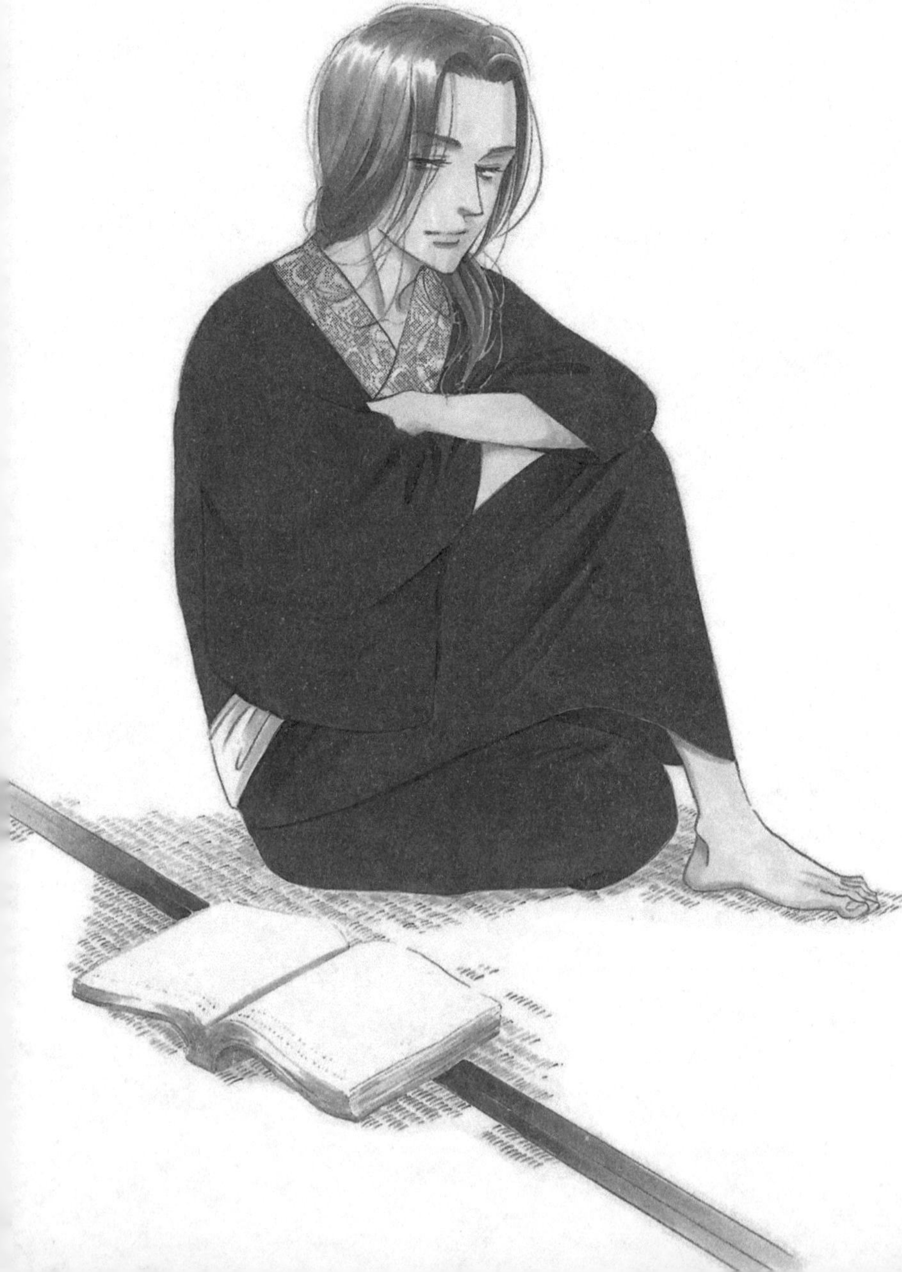

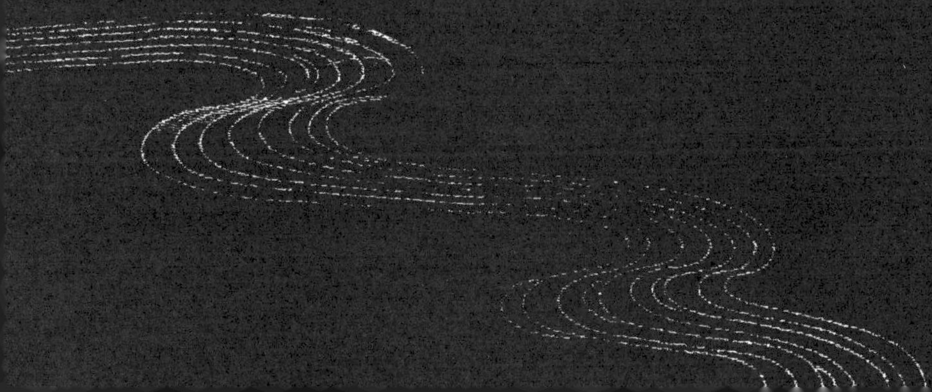

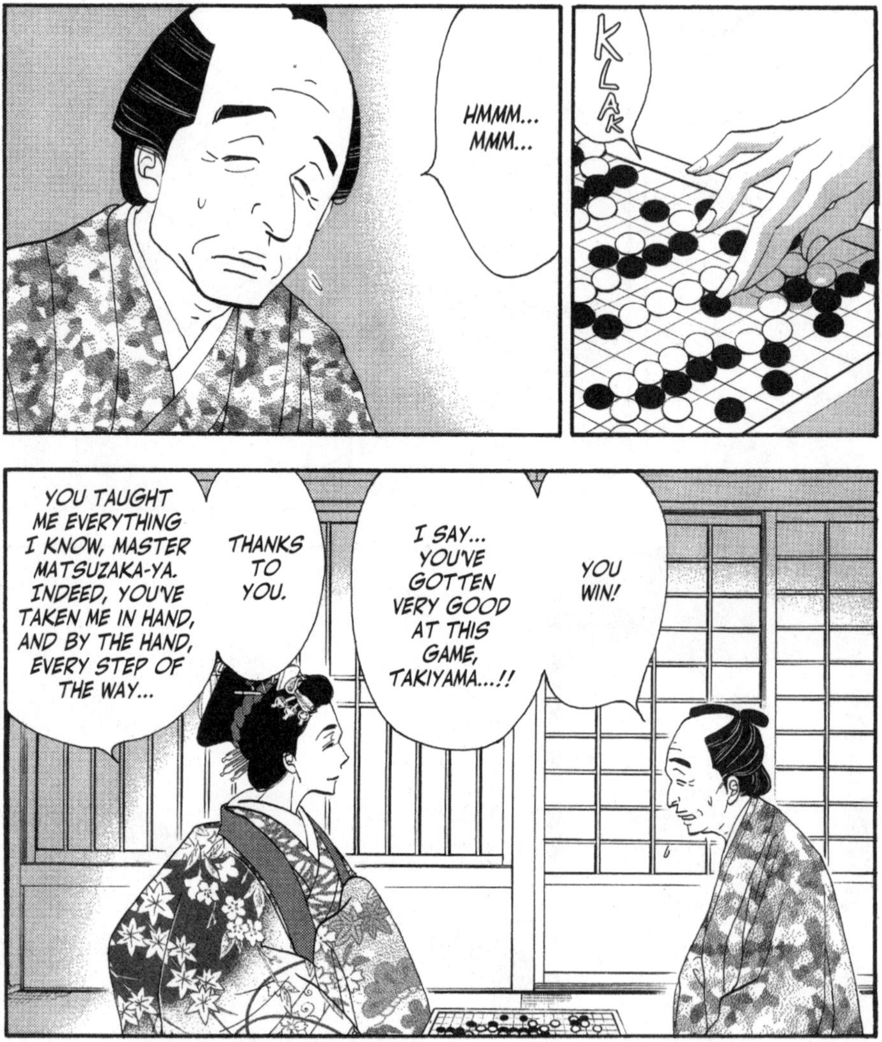
KLAK
HMMM... MMM...
YOU WIN!
I SAY... YOU'VE GOTTEN VERY GOOD AT THIS GAME, TAKIYAMA...!!
THANKS TO YOU.
YOU TAUGHT ME EVERYTHING I KNOW, MASTER MATSUZAKA-YA. INDEED, YOU'VE TAKEN ME IN HAND, AND BY THE HAND, EVERY STEP OF THE WAY...
TAKEN YOU IN HAND...
HA HA HA! I SUPPOSE I DID. I WAS STILL QUITE VIGOROUS THREE YEARS AGO!
HEE HEE HEE HEE! WELL, I WAS AT THE HEIGHT OF MY ALLURE BACK THEN AS WELL, IF I DO SAY SO MYSELF!

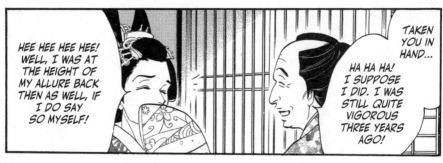

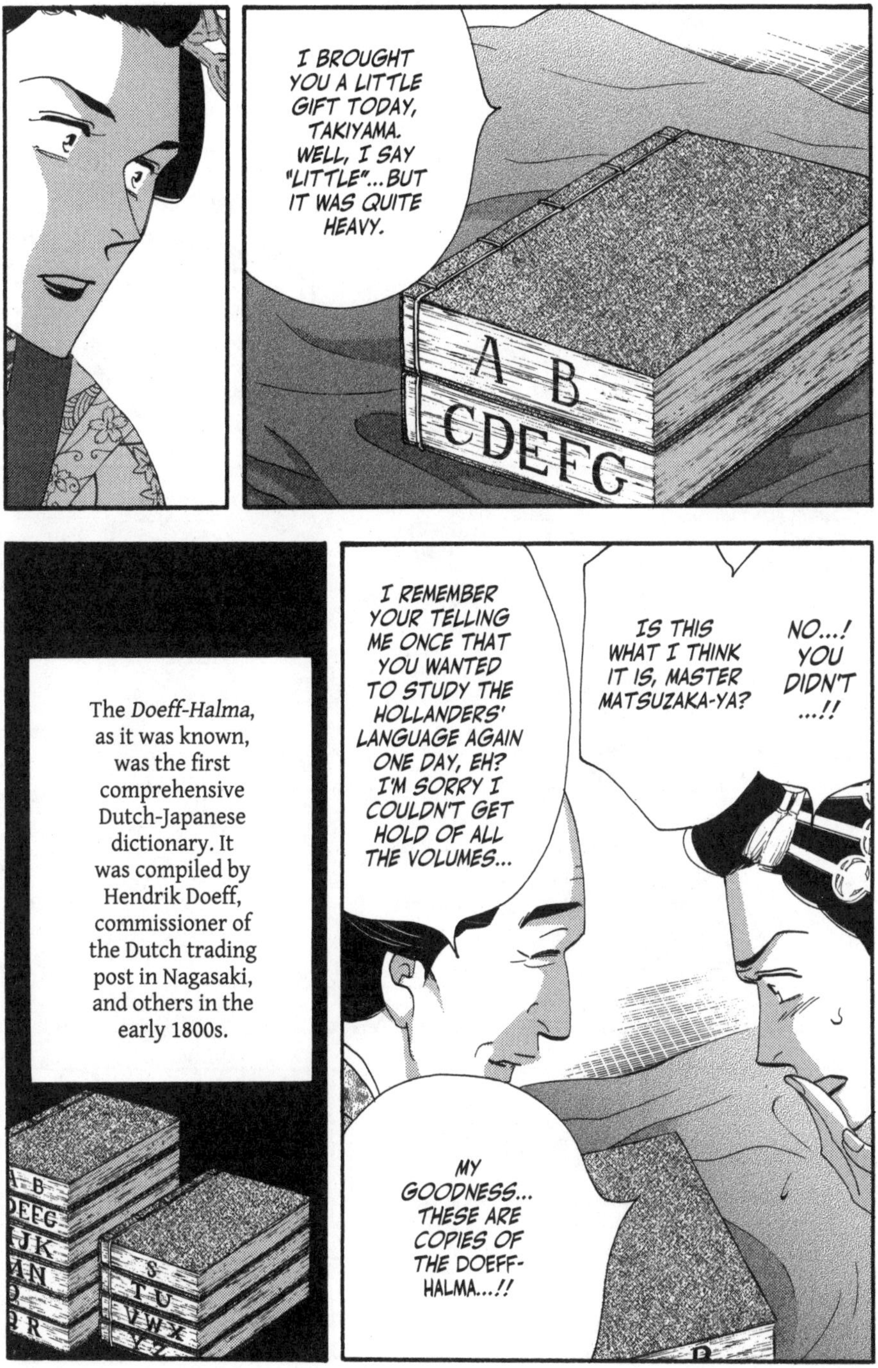
I BROUGHT YOU A LITTLE GIFT TODAY, TAKIYAMA. WELL, I SAY "LITTLE"...BUT IT WAS QUITE HEAVY.
NO...! YOU DIDN'T ...!!
IS THIS WHAT I THINK IT IS, MASTER MATSUZAKA-YA?
I REMEMBER YOUR TELLING ME ONCE THAT YOU WANTED TO STUDY THE HOLLANDERS' LANGUAGE AGAIN ONE DAY, EH? I'M SORRY I COULDN'T GET HOLD OF ALL THE VOLUMES...
MY GOODNESS... THESE ARE COPIES OF THE DOEFF-HALMA...!!
The *Doeff-Halma*, as it was known, was the first comprehensive Dutch-Japanese dictionary. It was compiled by Hendrik Doeff, commissioner of the Dutch trading post in Nagasaki, and others in the early 1800s.

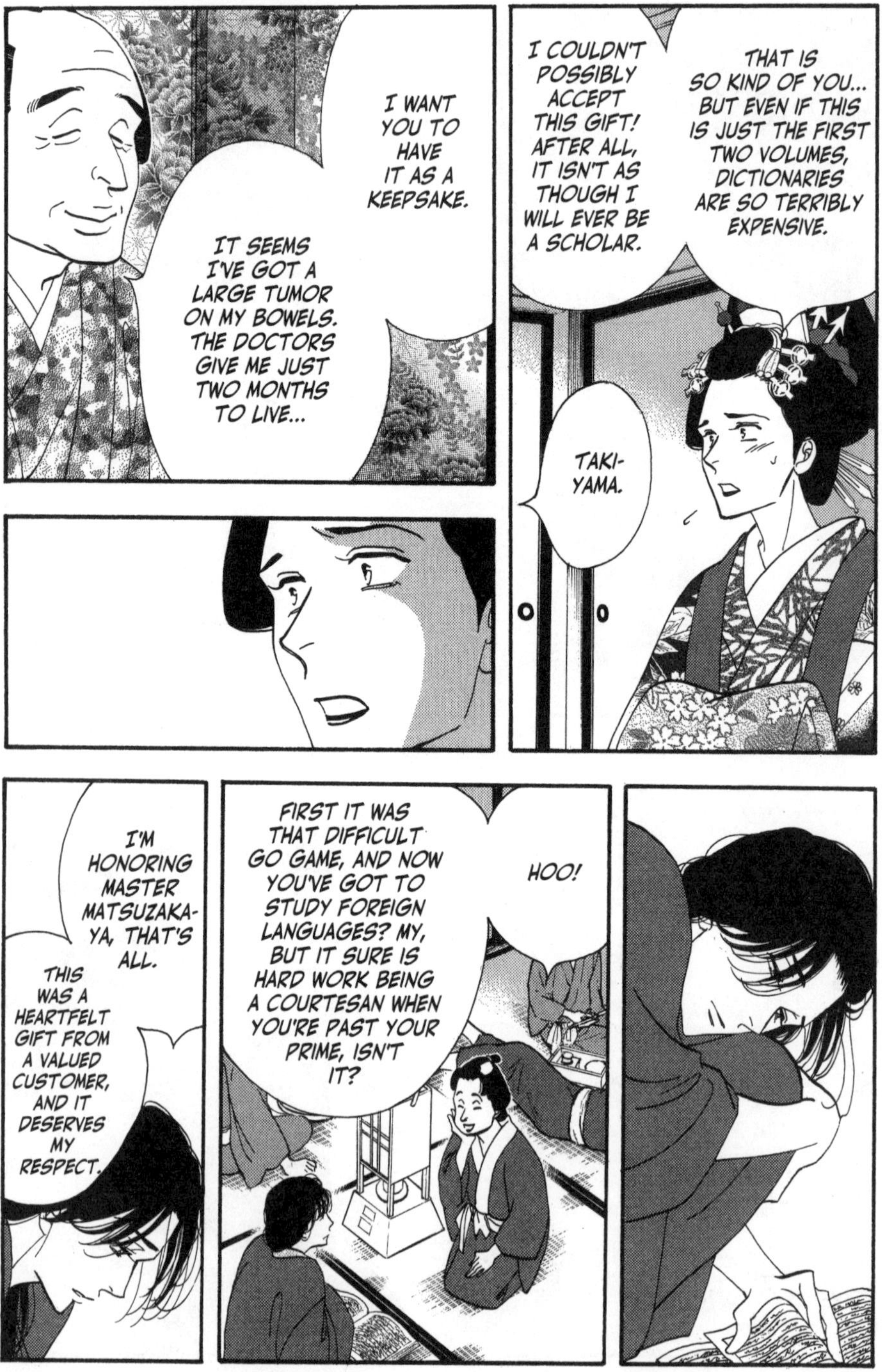
THAT IS SO KIND OF YOU... BUT EVEN IF THIS IS JUST THE FIRST TWO VOLUMES, DICTIONARIES ARE SO TERRIBLY EXPENSIVE.
I COULDN'T POSSIBLY ACCEPT THIS GIFT! AFTER ALL, IT ISN'T AS THOUGH I WILL EVER BE A SCHOLAR.
TAKI-YAMA.
I WANT YOU TO HAVE IT AS A KEEPSAKE.
IT SEEMS I'VE GOT A LARGE TUMOR ON MY BOWELS. THE DOCTORS GIVE ME JUST TWO MONTHS TO LIVE...
HOO!
FIRST IT WAS THAT DIFFICULT GO GAME, AND NOW YOU'VE GOT TO STUDY FOREIGN LANGUAGES? MY, BUT IT SURE IS HARD WORK BEING A COURTESAN WHEN YOU'RE PAST YOUR PRIME, ISN'T IT?
I'M HONORING MASTER MATSUZAKA-YA, THAT'S ALL.
THIS WAS A HEARTFELT GIFT FROM A VALUED CUSTOMER, AND IT DESERVES MY RESPECT.

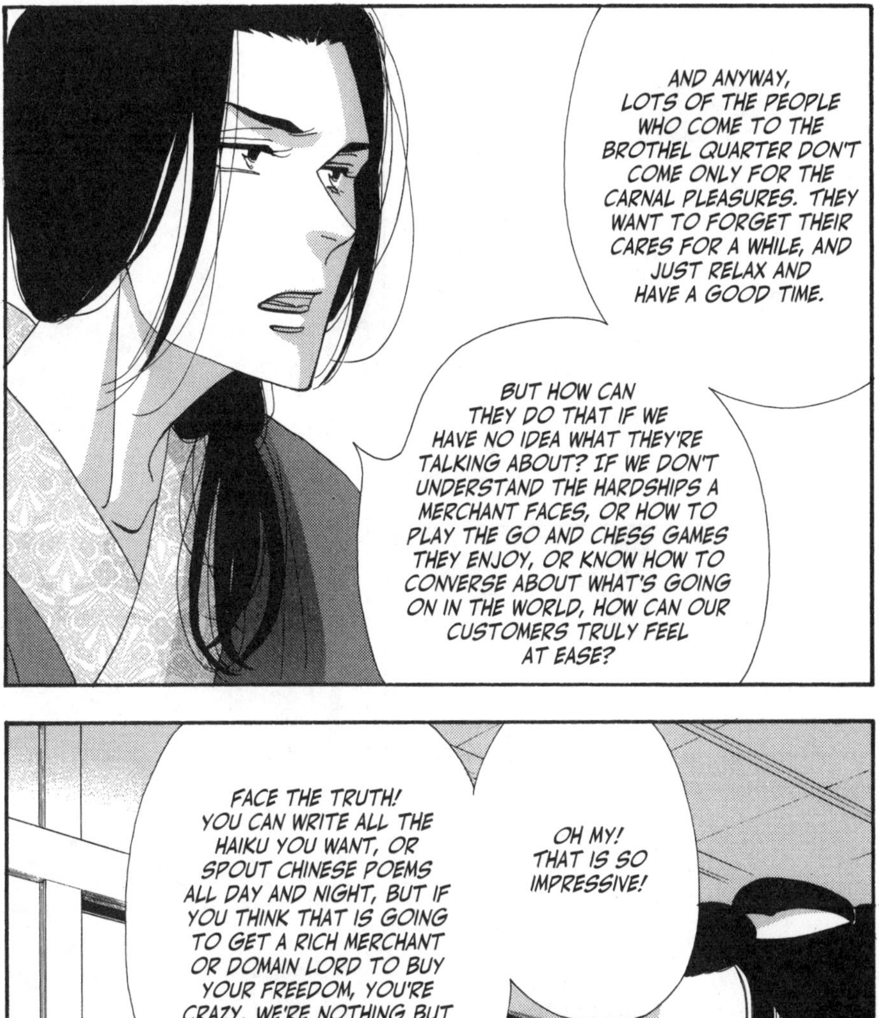
AND ANYWAY, LOTS OF THE PEOPLE WHO COME TO THE BROTHEL QUARTER DON'T COME ONLY FOR THE CARNAL PLEASURES. THEY WANT TO FORGET THEIR CARES FOR A WHILE, AND JUST RELAX AND HAVE A GOOD TIME.
BUT HOW CAN THEY DO THAT IF WE HAVE NO IDEA WHAT THEY'RE TALKING ABOUT? IF WE DON'T UNDERSTAND THE HARDSHIPS A MERCHANT FACES, OR HOW TO PLAY THE GO AND CHESS GAMES THEY ENJOY, OR KNOW HOW TO CONVERSE ABOUT WHAT'S GOING ON IN THE WORLD, HOW CAN OUR CUSTOMERS TRULY FEEL AT EASE?
OH MY! THAT IS SO IMPRESSIVE!
FACE THE TRUTH! YOU CAN WRITE ALL THE HAIKU YOU WANT, OR SPOUT CHINESE POEMS ALL DAY AND NIGHT, BUT IF YOU THINK THAT IS GOING TO GET A RICH MERCHANT OR DOMAIN LORD TO BUY YOUR FREEDOM, YOU'RE CRAZY. WE'RE NOTHING BUT KAGEMA, AND KAGEMA IS ALL WE'LL EVER BE.
WELL, MAYBE YOU SHOULD PRACTICE DANCING... FOR WHEN NOBODY WANTS TO SCREW YOU ANYMORE AND YOU HAVE TO WORK AS AN ENTERTAINER.

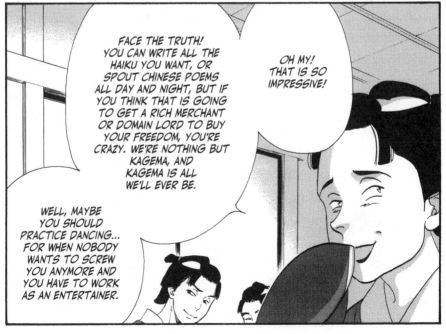

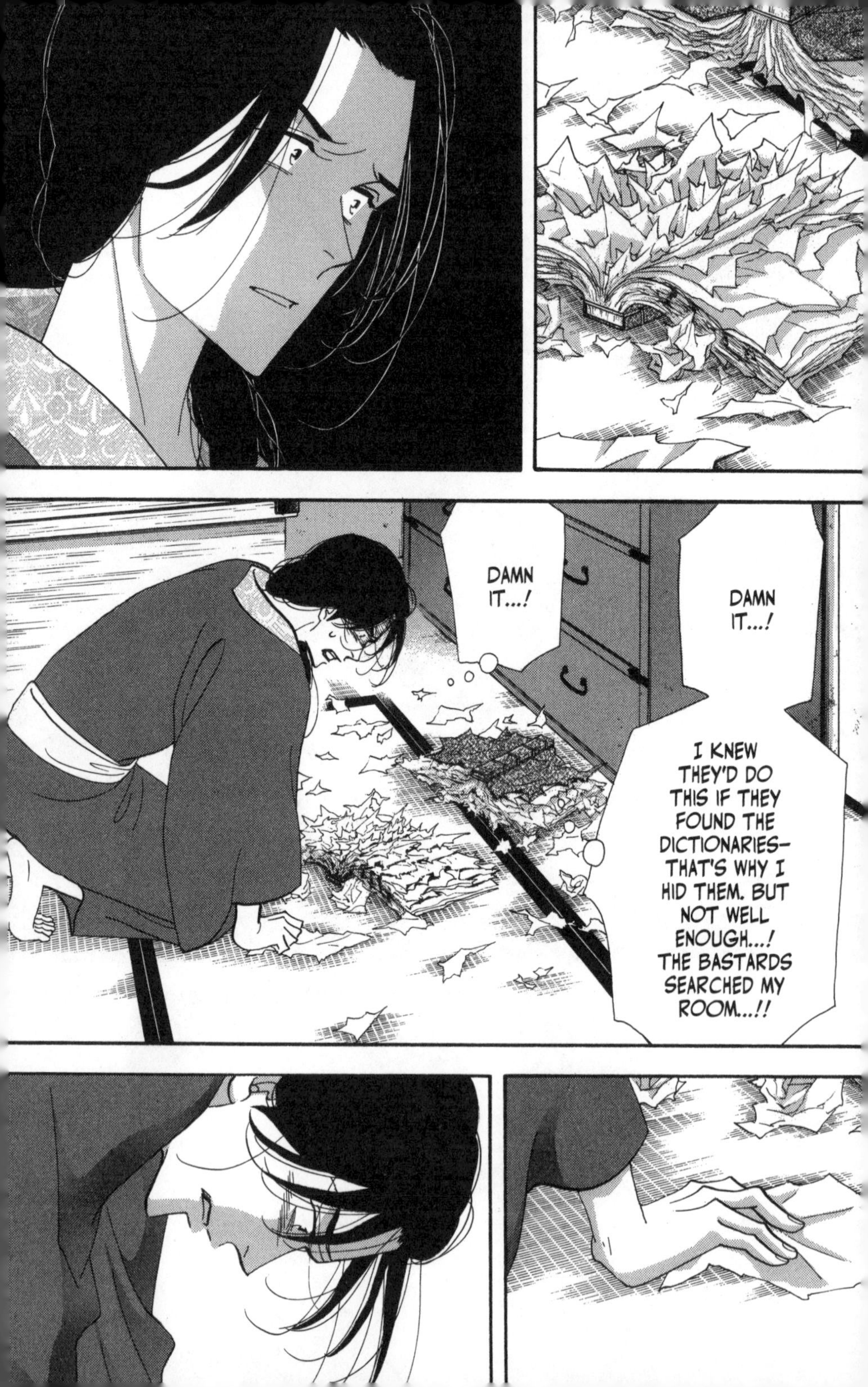
DAMN IT...!
DAMN IT...!
I KNEW THEY'D DO THIS IF THEY FOUND THE DICTIONARIES—THAT'S WHY I HID THEM. BUT NOT WELL ENOUGH...! THE BASTARDS SEARCHED MY ROOM...!!

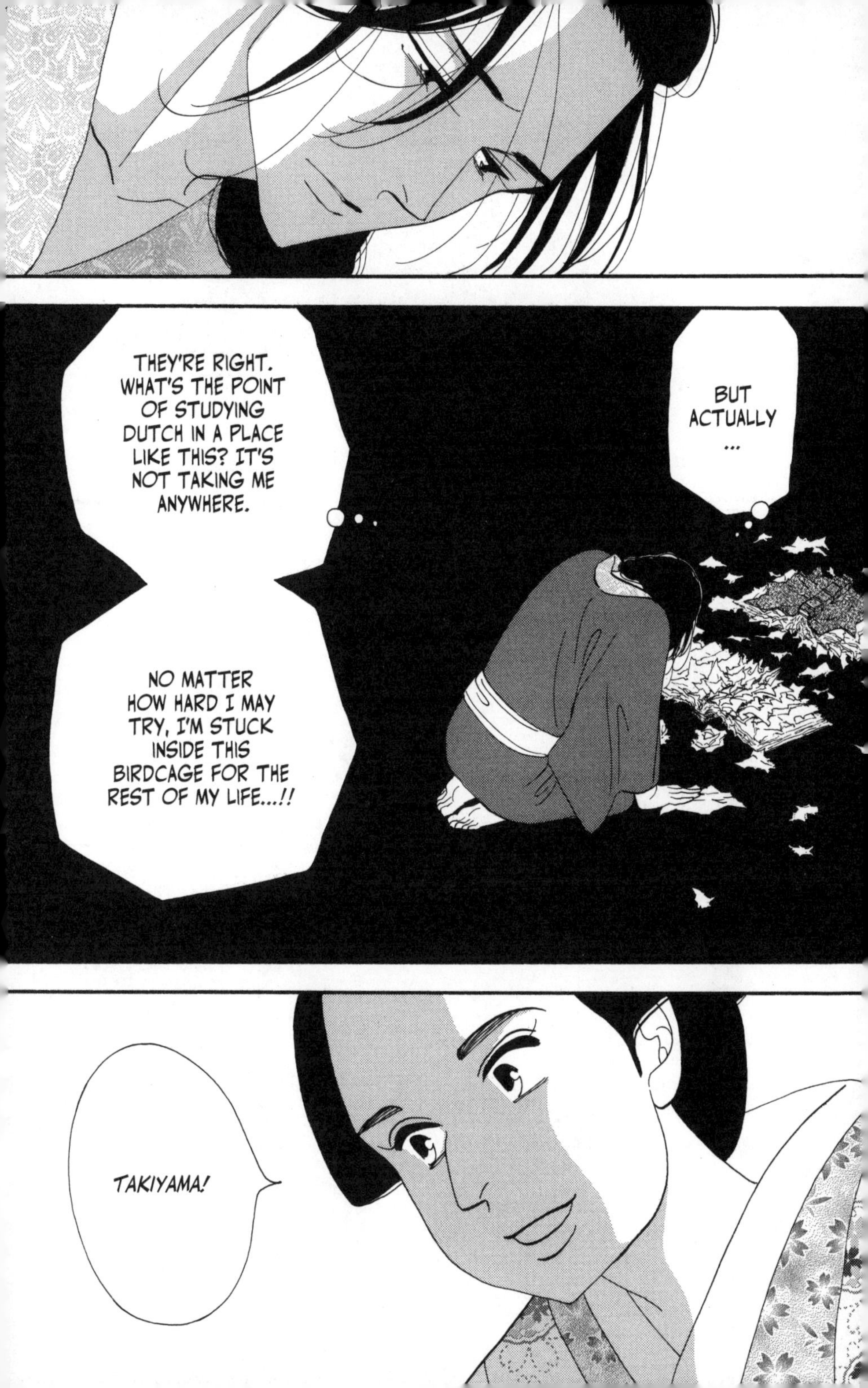
BUT ACTUALLY ...
THEY'RE RIGHT. WHAT'S THE POINT OF STUDYING DUTCH IN A PLACE LIKE THIS? IT'S NOT TAKING ME ANYWHERE.
NO MATTER HOW HARD I MAY TRY, I'M STUCK INSIDE THIS BIRDCAGE FOR THE REST OF MY LIFE...!!
TAKIYAMA!

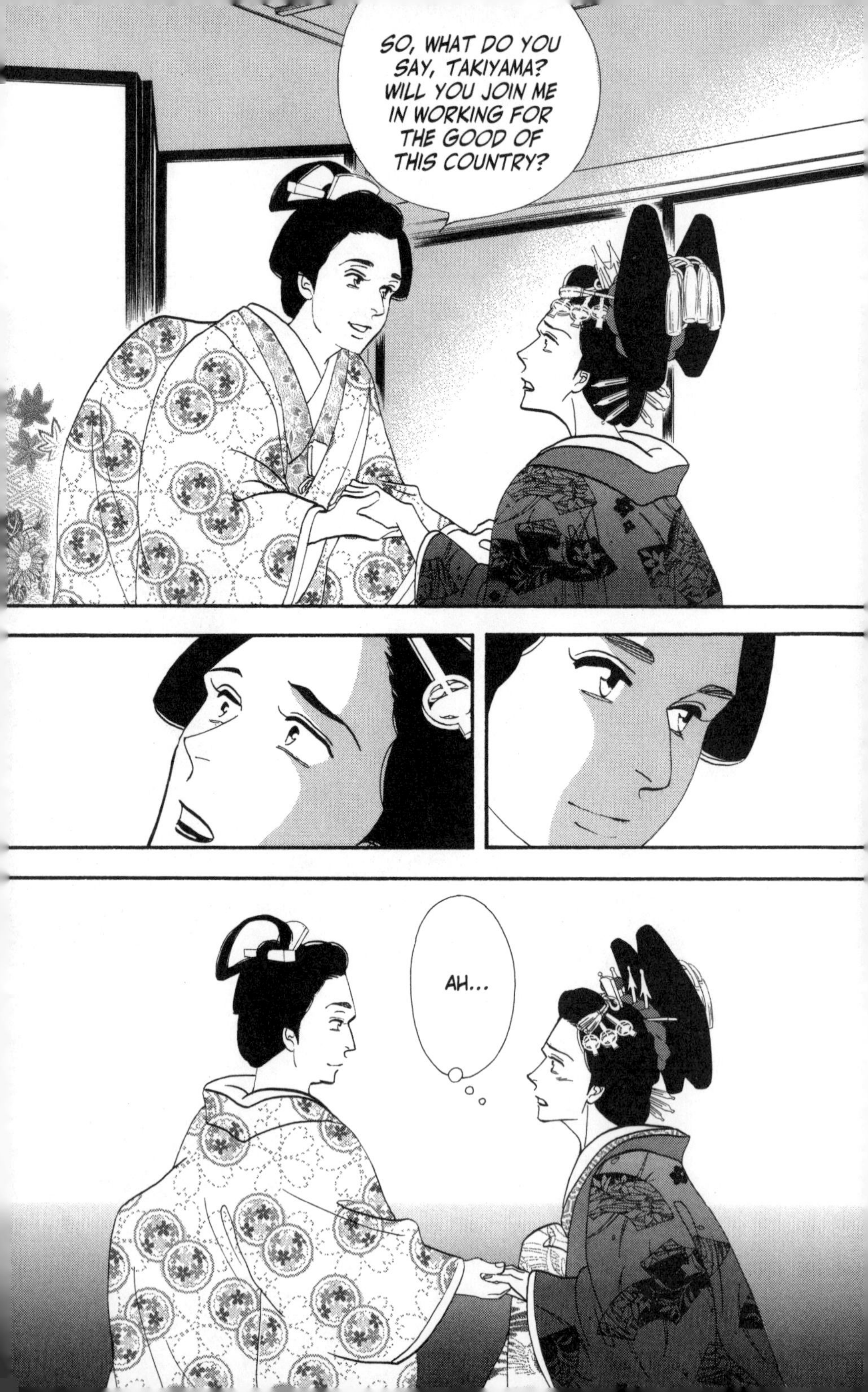
SO, WHAT DO YOU SAY, TAKIYAMA? WILL YOU JOIN ME IN WORKING FOR THE GOOD OF THIS COUNTRY?
AH...

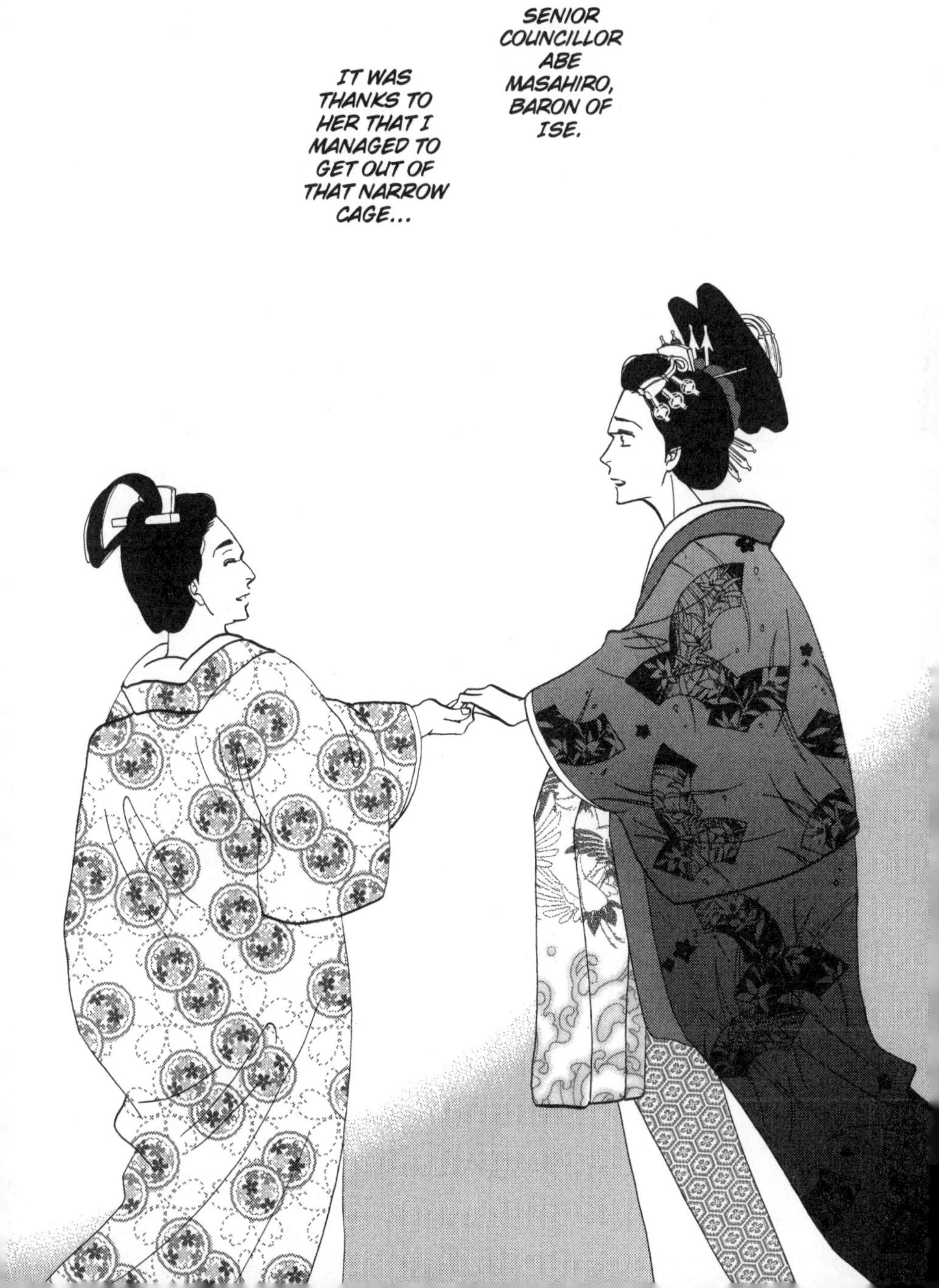
SENIOR COUNCILLOR ABE MASAHIRO, BARON OF ISE.
IT WAS THANKS TO HER THAT I MANAGED TO GET OUT OF THAT NARROW CAGE...

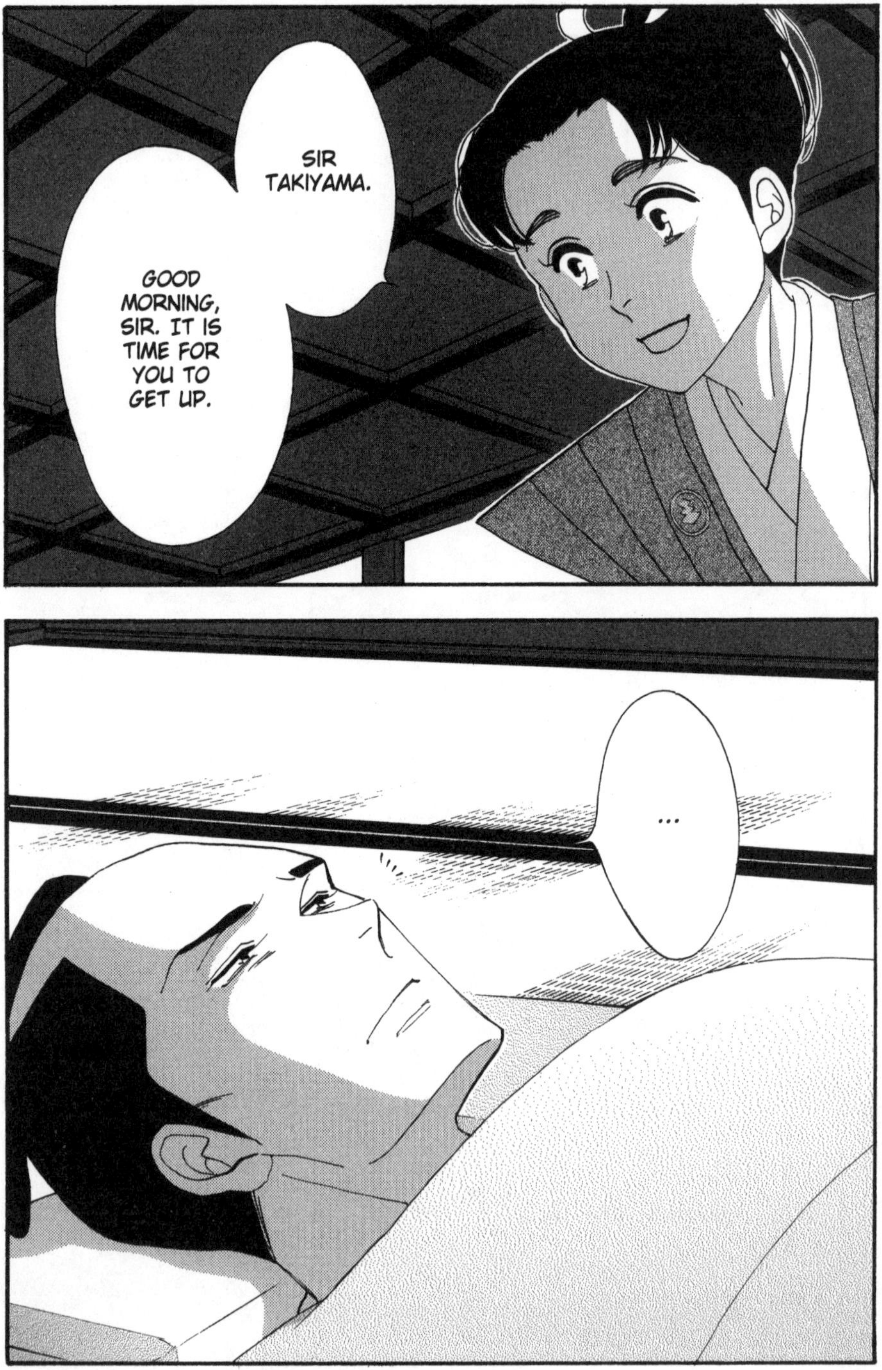
SIR TAKIYAMA.
GOOD MORNING, SIR. IT IS TIME FOR YOU TO GET UP.
...

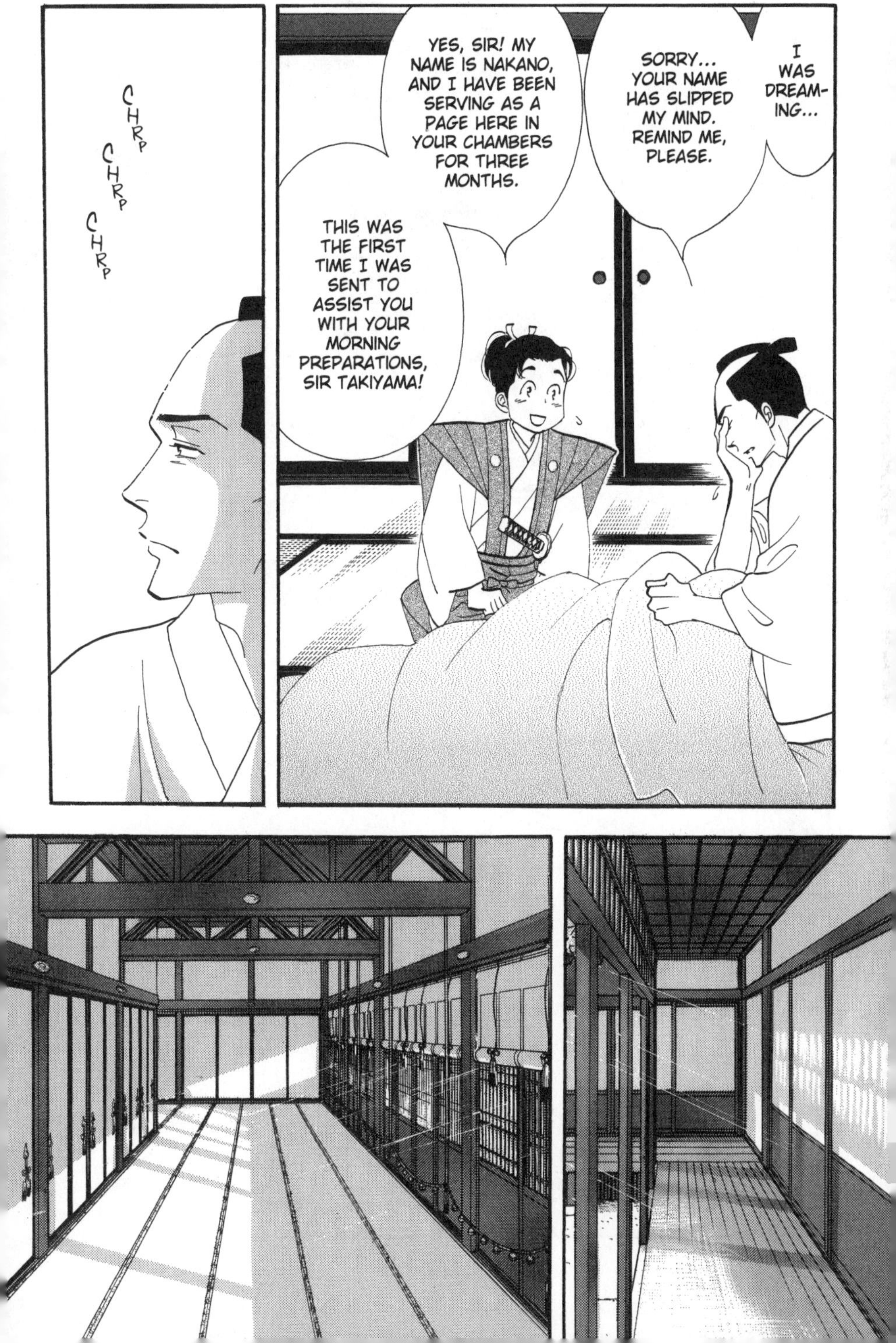
I WAS DREAMING...
SORRY... YOUR NAME HAS SLIPPED MY MIND. REMIND ME, PLEASE.
YES, SIR! MY NAME IS NAKANO, AND I HAVE BEEN SERVING AS A PAGE HERE IN YOUR CHAMBERS FOR THREE MONTHS.
THIS WAS THE FIRST TIME I WAS SENT TO ASSIST YOU WITH YOUR MORNING PREPARATIONS, SIR TAKIYAMA!
CHRP CHRP CHRP

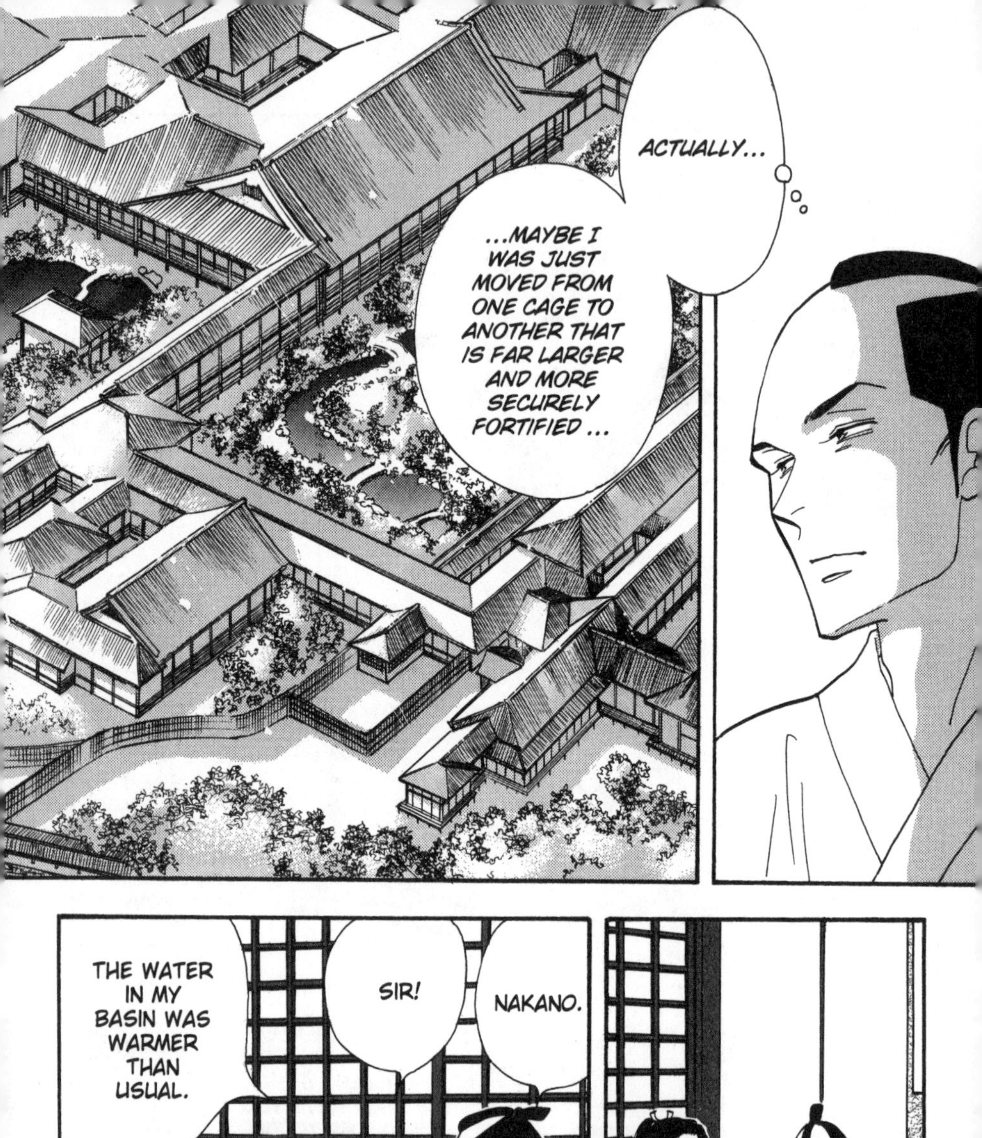
ACTUALLY...
...MAYBE I WAS JUST MOVED FROM ONE CAGE TO ANOTHER THAT IS FAR LARGER AND MORE SECURELY FORTIFIED ...
NAKANO.
SIR!
THE WATER IN MY BASIN WAS WARMER THAN USUAL.

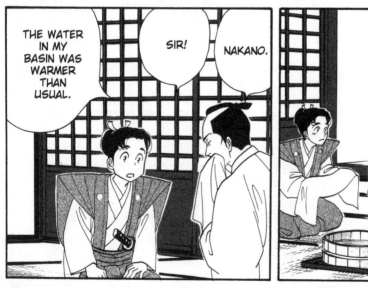

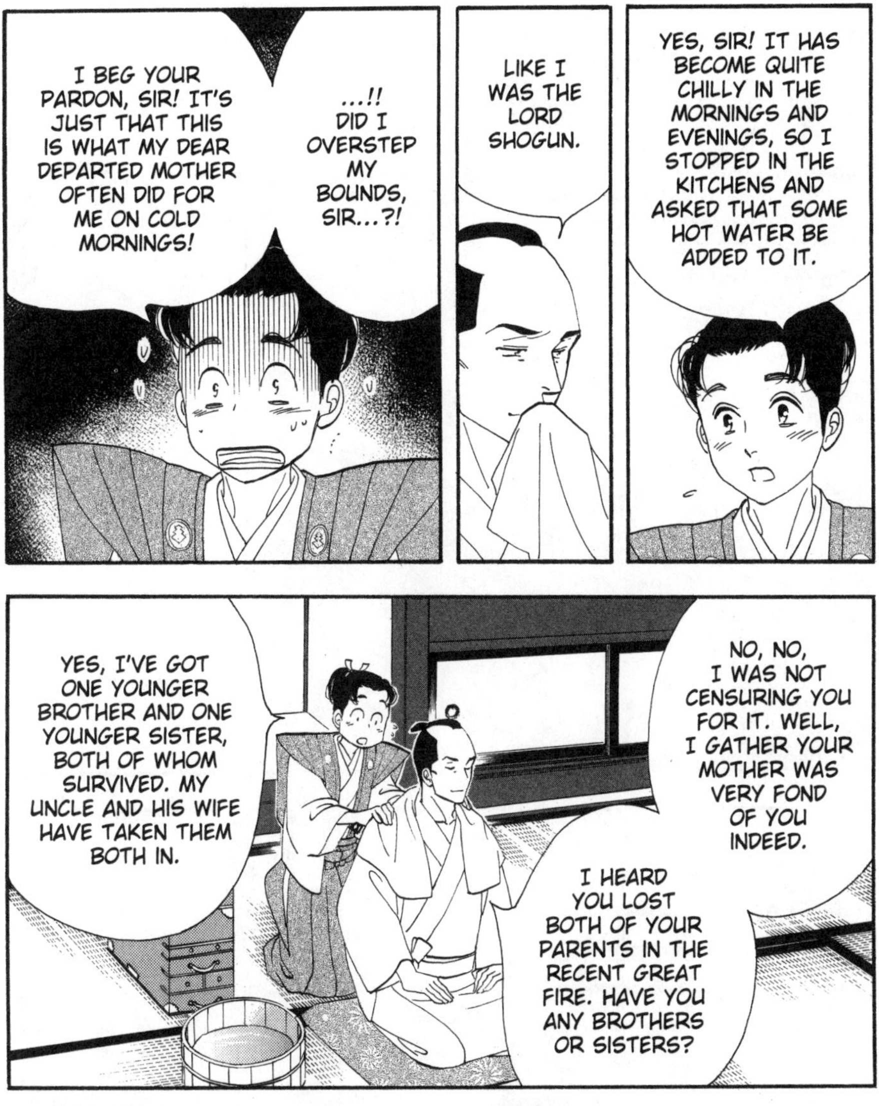
YES, SIR! IT HAS BECOME QUITE CHILLY IN THE MORNINGS AND EVENINGS, SO I STOPPED IN THE KITCHENS AND ASKED THAT SOME HOT WATER BE ADDED TO IT.
LIKE I WAS THE LORD SHOGUN.
...!! DID I OVERSTEP MY BOUNDS, SIR...?!
I BEG YOUR PARDON, SIR! IT'S JUST THAT THIS IS WHAT MY DEAR DEPARTED MOTHER OFTEN DID FOR ME ON COLD MORNINGS!
NO, NO, I WAS NOT CENSURING YOU FOR IT. WELL, I GATHER YOUR MOTHER WAS VERY FOND OF YOU INDEED.
I HEARD YOU LOST BOTH OF YOUR PARENTS IN THE RECENT GREAT FIRE. HAVE YOU ANY BROTHERS OR SISTERS?
YES, I'VE GOT ONE YOUNGER BROTHER AND ONE YOUNGER SISTER, BOTH OF WHOM SURVIVED. MY UNCLE AND HIS WIFE HAVE TAKEN THEM BOTH IN.
PLIP

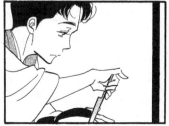

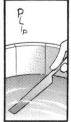

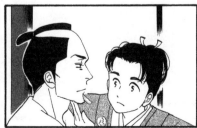

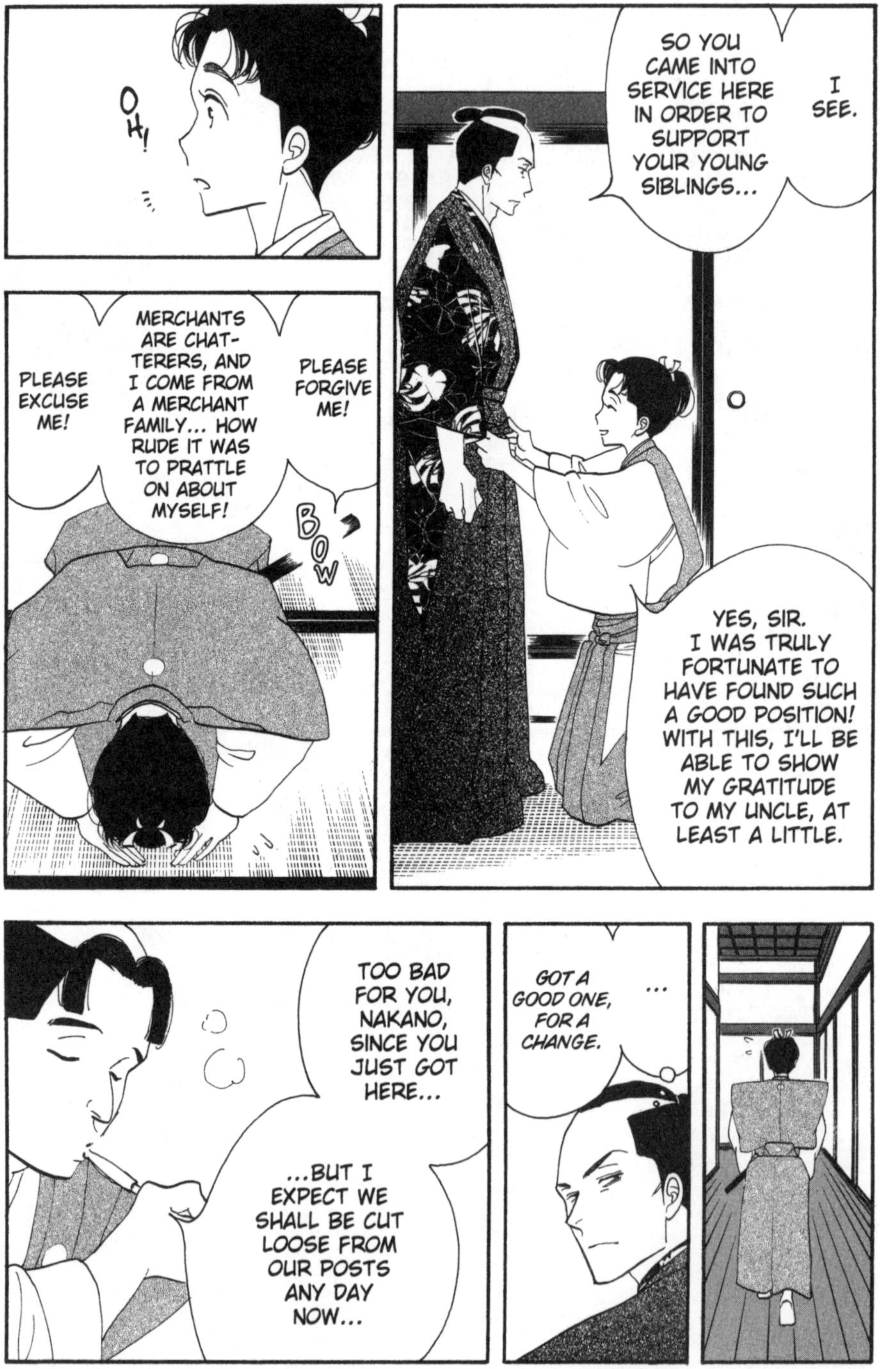
SO YOU CAME INTO SERVICE HERE IN ORDER TO SUPPORT YOUR YOUNG SIBLINGS...
I SEE.
YES, SIR. I WAS TRULY FORTUNATE TO HAVE FOUND SUCH A GOOD POSITION! WITH THIS, I'LL BE ABLE TO SHOW MY GRATITUDE TO MY UNCLE, AT LEAST A LITTLE.
OH!
PLEASE FORGIVE ME!
MERCHANTS ARE CHATTERERS, AND I COME FROM A MERCHANT FAMILY... HOW RUDE IT WAS TO PRATTLE ON ABOUT MYSELF!
PLEASE EXCUSE ME!
BOW
...
GOT A GOOD ONE, FOR A CHANGE.
TOO BAD FOR YOU, NAKANO, SINCE YOU JUST GOT HERE...
...BUT I EXPECT WE SHALL BE CUT LOOSE FROM OUR POSTS ANY DAY NOW...

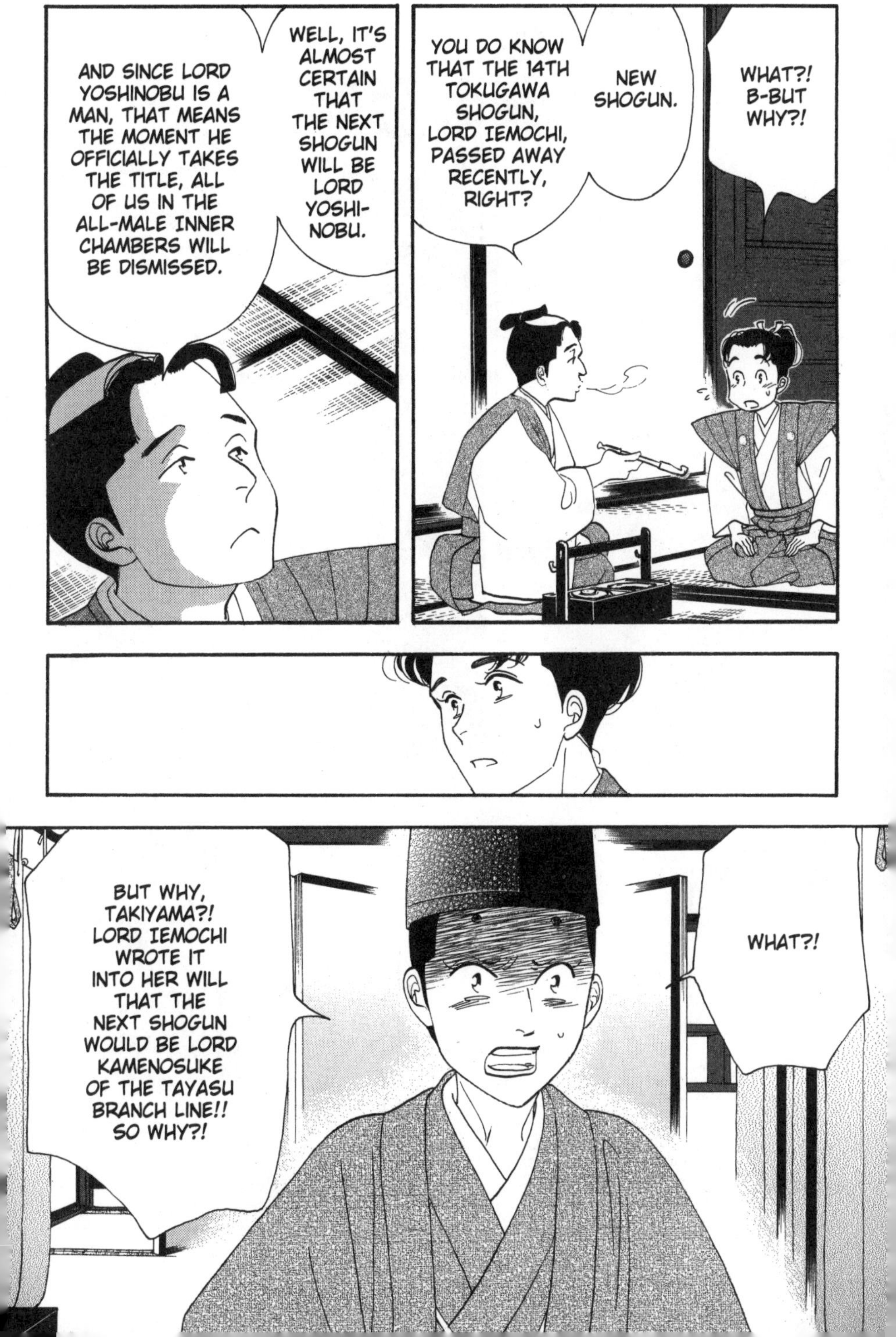
WHAT?! B-BUT WHY?!
NEW SHOGUN.
YOU DO KNOW THAT THE 14TH TOKUGAWA SHOGUN, LORD IEMOCHI, PASSED AWAY RECENTLY, RIGHT?
WELL, IT'S ALMOST CERTAIN THAT THE NEXT SHOGUN WILL BE LORD YOSHI-NOBU.
AND SINCE LORD YOSHINOBU IS A MAN, THAT MEANS THE MOMENT HE OFFICIALLY TAKES THE TITLE, ALL OF US IN THE ALL-MALE INNER CHAMBERS WILL BE DISMISSED.
WHAT?!
BUT WHY, TAKIYAMA?! LORD IEMOCHI WROTE IT INTO HER WILL THAT THE NEXT SHOGUN WOULD BE LORD KAMENOSUKE OF THE TAYASU BRANCH LINE!! SO WHY?!

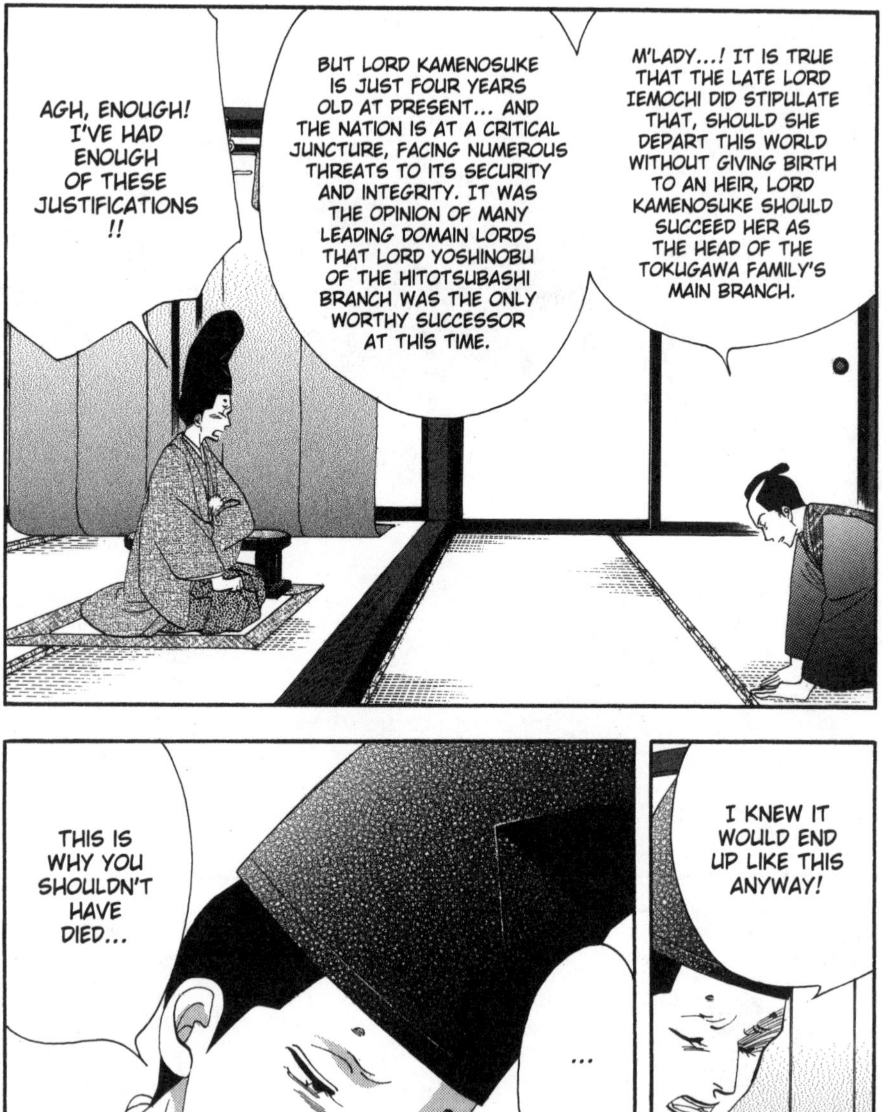
M'LADY...! IT IS TRUE THAT THE LATE LORD IEMOCHI DID STIPULATE THAT, SHOULD SHE DEPART THIS WORLD WITHOUT GIVING BIRTH TO AN HEIR, LORD KAMENOSUKE SHOULD SUCCEED HER AS THE HEAD OF THE TOKUGAWA FAMILY'S MAIN BRANCH.
BUT LORD KAMENOSUKE IS JUST FOUR YEARS OLD AT PRESENT... AND THE NATION IS AT A CRITICAL JUNCTURE, FACING NUMEROUS THREATS TO ITS SECURITY AND INTEGRITY. IT WAS THE OPINION OF MANY LEADING DOMAIN LORDS THAT LORD YOSHINOBU OF THE HITOTSUBASHI BRANCH WAS THE ONLY WORTHY SUCCESSOR AT THIS TIME.
AGH, ENOUGH! I'VE HAD ENOUGH OF THESE JUSTIFICATIONS!!
I KNEW IT WOULD END UP LIKE THIS ANYWAY!
...
THIS IS WHY YOU SHOULDN'T HAVE DIED...
SEE, MY LORD...?

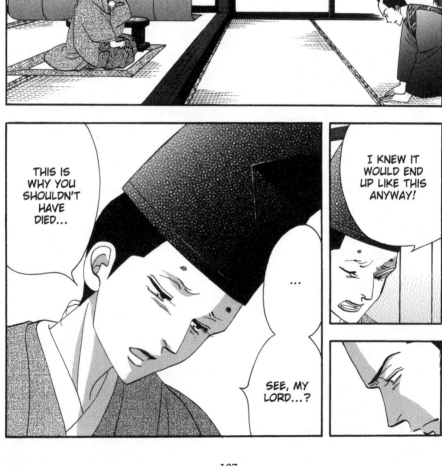

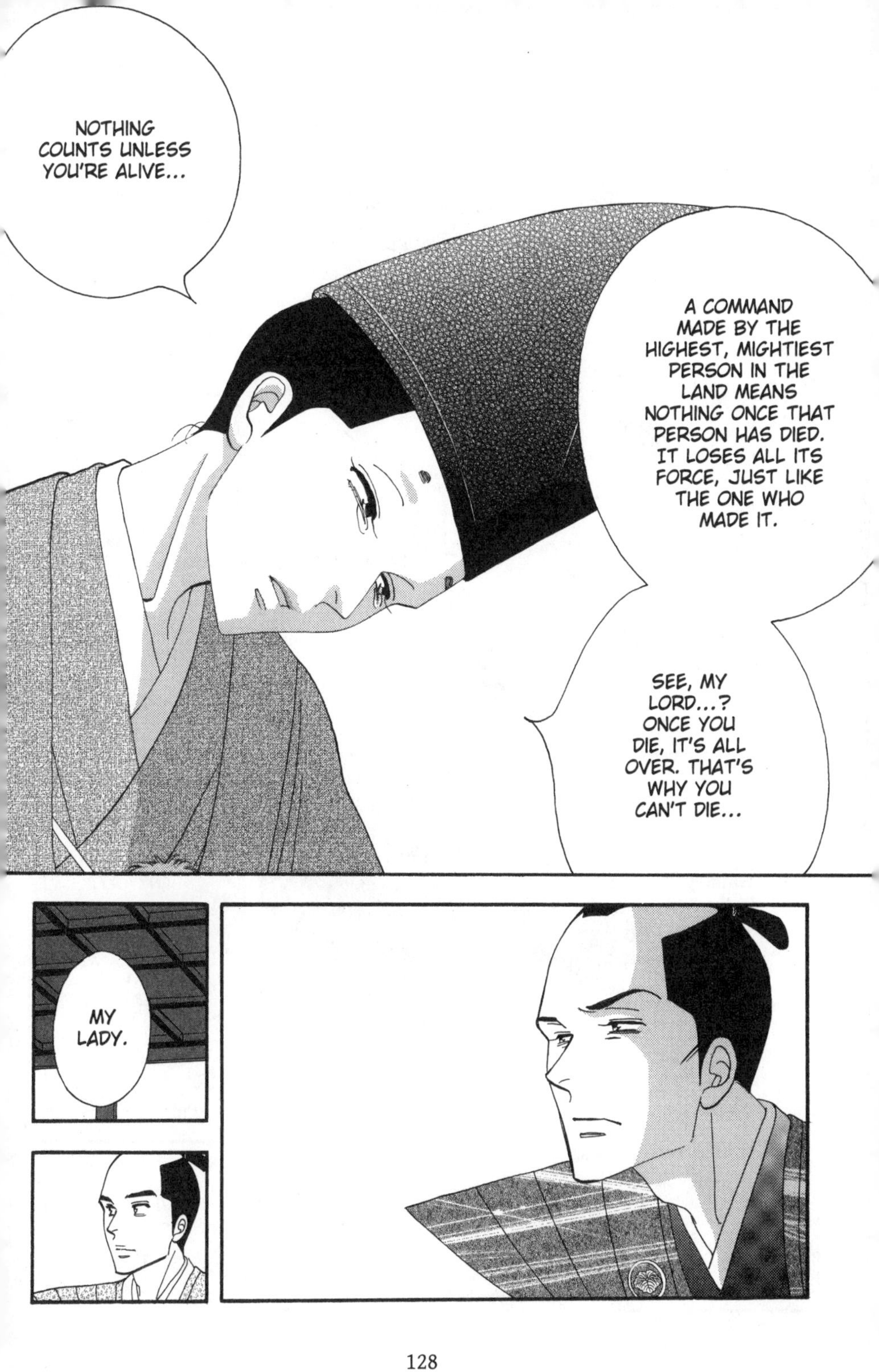
A COMMAND MADE BY THE HIGHEST, MIGHTIEST PERSON IN THE LAND MEANS NOTHING ONCE THAT PERSON HAS DIED. IT LOSES ALL ITS FORCE, JUST LIKE THE ONE WHO MADE IT.
SEE, MY LORD...? ONCE YOU DIE, IT'S ALL OVER. THAT'S WHY YOU CAN'T DIE...
NOTHING COUNTS UNLESS YOU'RE ALIVE...
MY LADY.

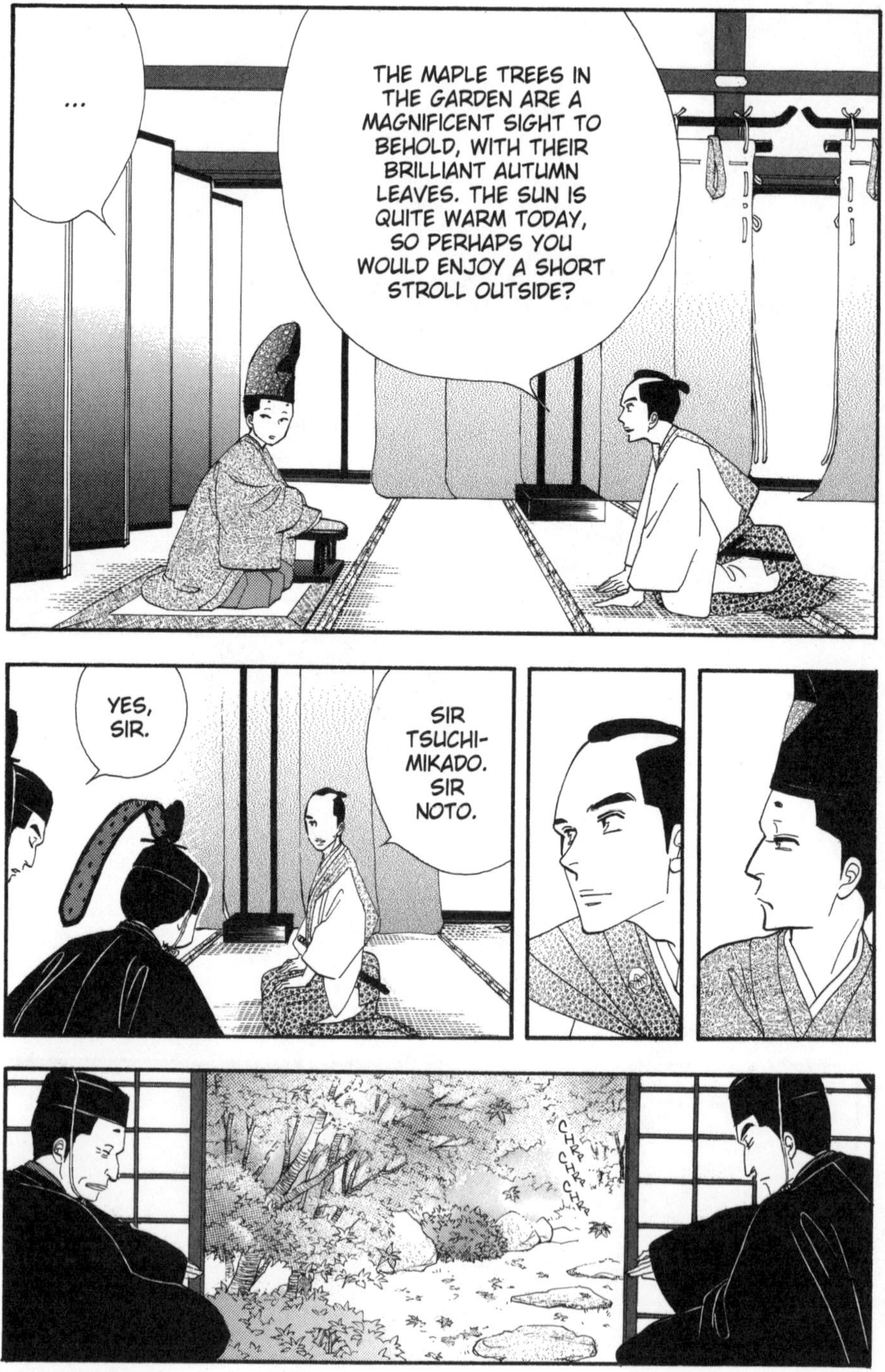
THE MAPLE TREES IN THE GARDEN ARE A MAGNIFICENT SIGHT TO BEHOLD, WITH THEIR BRILLIANT AUTUMN LEAVES. THE SUN IS QUITE WARM TODAY, SO PERHAPS YOU WOULD ENJOY A SHORT STROLL OUTSIDE?
...
SIR TSUCHI-MIKADO. SIR NOTO.
YES, SIR.
CHRP CHRP CHRP

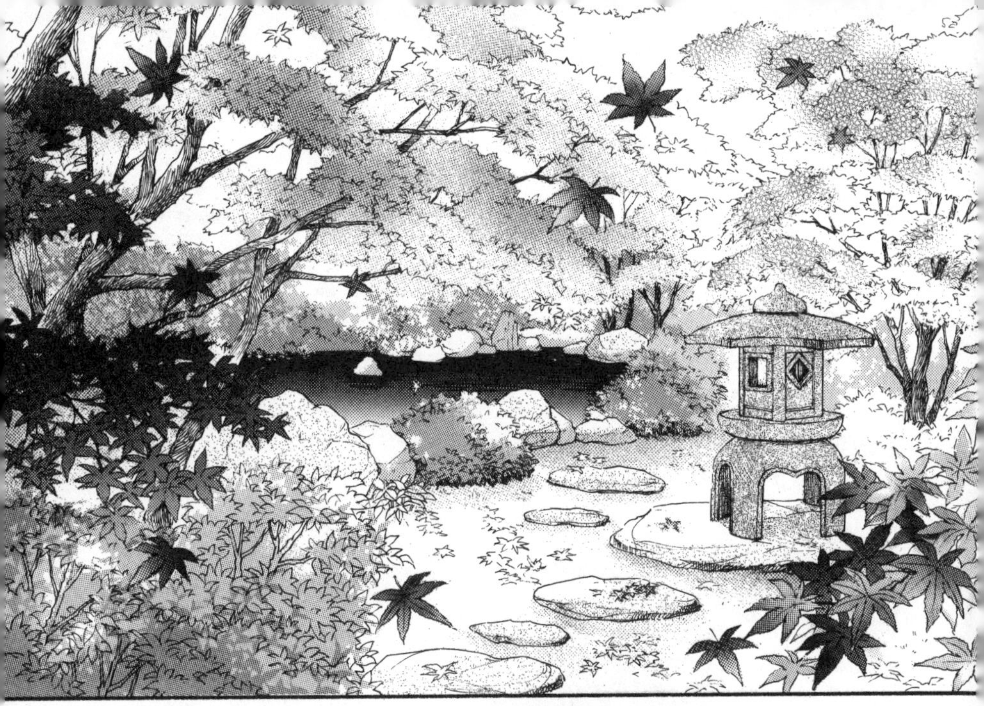
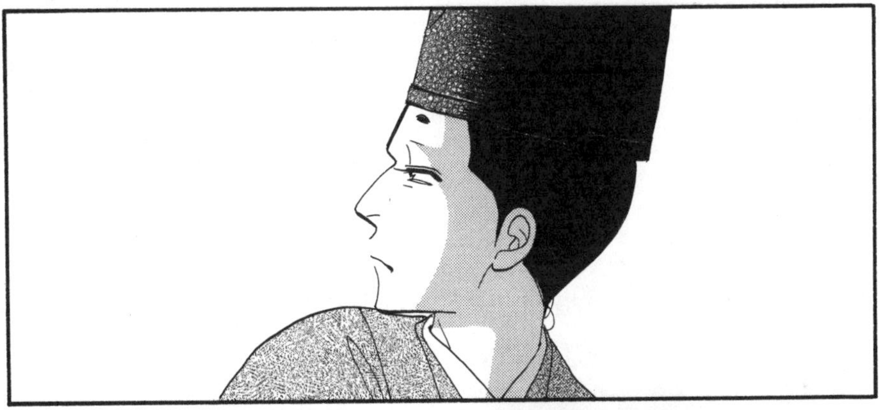
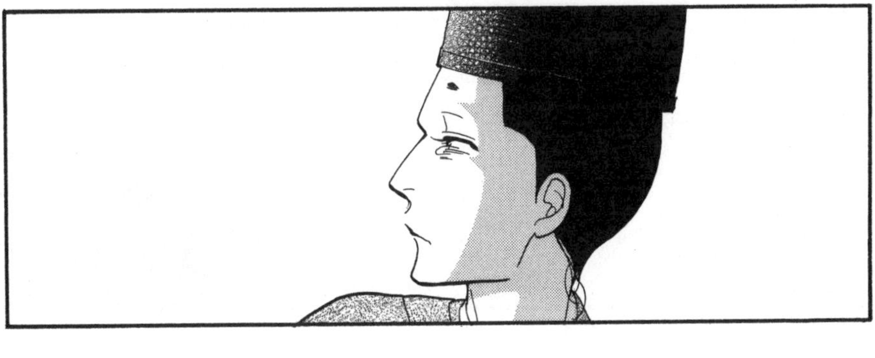

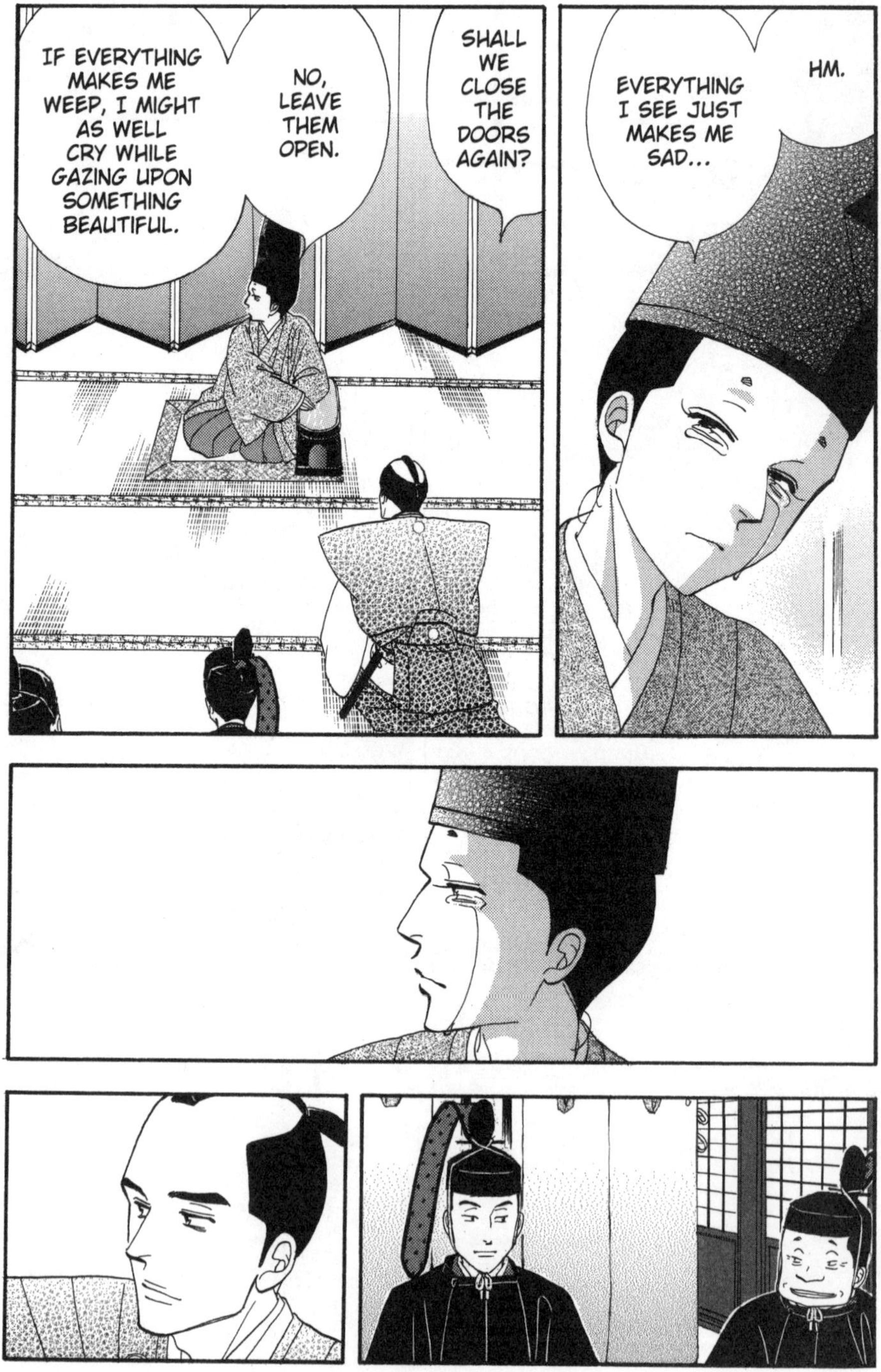
HM.
EVERYTHING I SEE JUST MAKES ME SAD...
SHALL WE CLOSE THE DOORS AGAIN?
NO, LEAVE THEM OPEN.
IF EVERYTHING MAKES ME WEEP, I MIGHT AS WELL CRY WHILE GAZING UPON SOMETHING BEAUTIFUL.

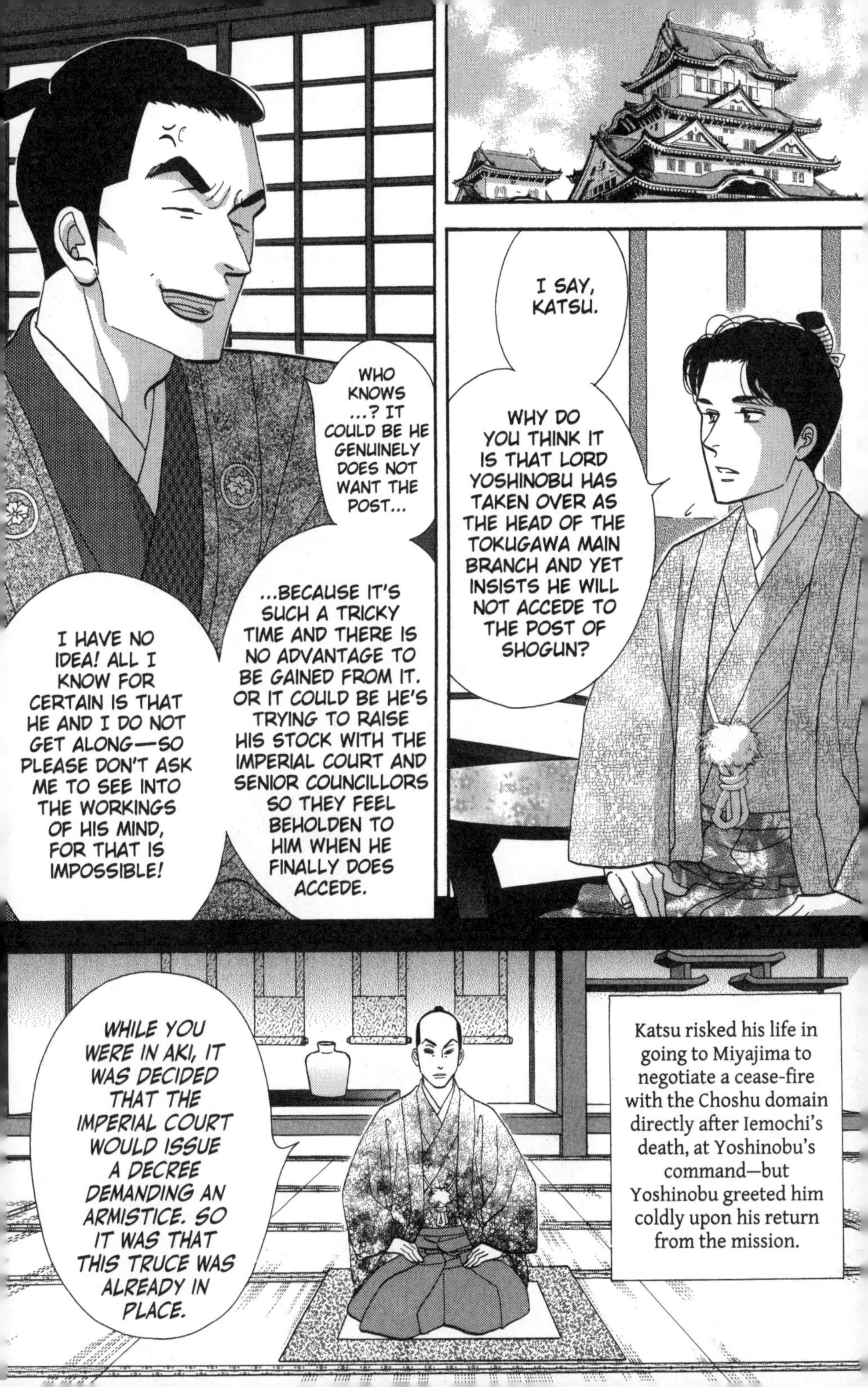
I SAY, KATSU.
WHY DO YOU THINK IT IS THAT LORD YOSHINOBU HAS TAKEN OVER AS THE HEAD OF THE TOKUGAWA MAIN BRANCH AND YET INSISTS HE WILL NOT ACCEDE TO THE POST OF SHOGUN?
WHO KNOWS ...? IT COULD BE HE GENUINELY DOES NOT WANT THE POST...
...BECAUSE IT'S SUCH A TRICKY TIME AND THERE IS NO ADVANTAGE TO BE GAINED FROM IT. OR IT COULD BE HE'S TRYING TO RAISE HIS STOCK WITH THE IMPERIAL COURT AND SENIOR COUNCILLORS SO THEY FEEL BEHOLDEN TO HIM WHEN HE FINALLY DOES ACCEDE.
I HAVE NO IDEA! ALL I KNOW FOR CERTAIN IS THAT HE AND I DO NOT GET ALONG—SO PLEASE DON'T ASK ME TO SEE INTO THE WORKINGS OF HIS MIND, FOR THAT IS IMPOSSIBLE!
Katsu risked his life in going to Miyajima to negotiate a cease-fire with the Choshu domain directly after Iemochi's death, at Yoshinobu's command—but Yoshinobu greeted him coldly upon his return from the mission.
WHILE YOU WERE IN AKI, IT WAS DECIDED THAT THE IMPERIAL COURT WOULD ISSUE A DECREE DEMANDING AN ARMISTICE. SO IT WAS THAT THIS TRUCE WAS ALREADY IN PLACE.

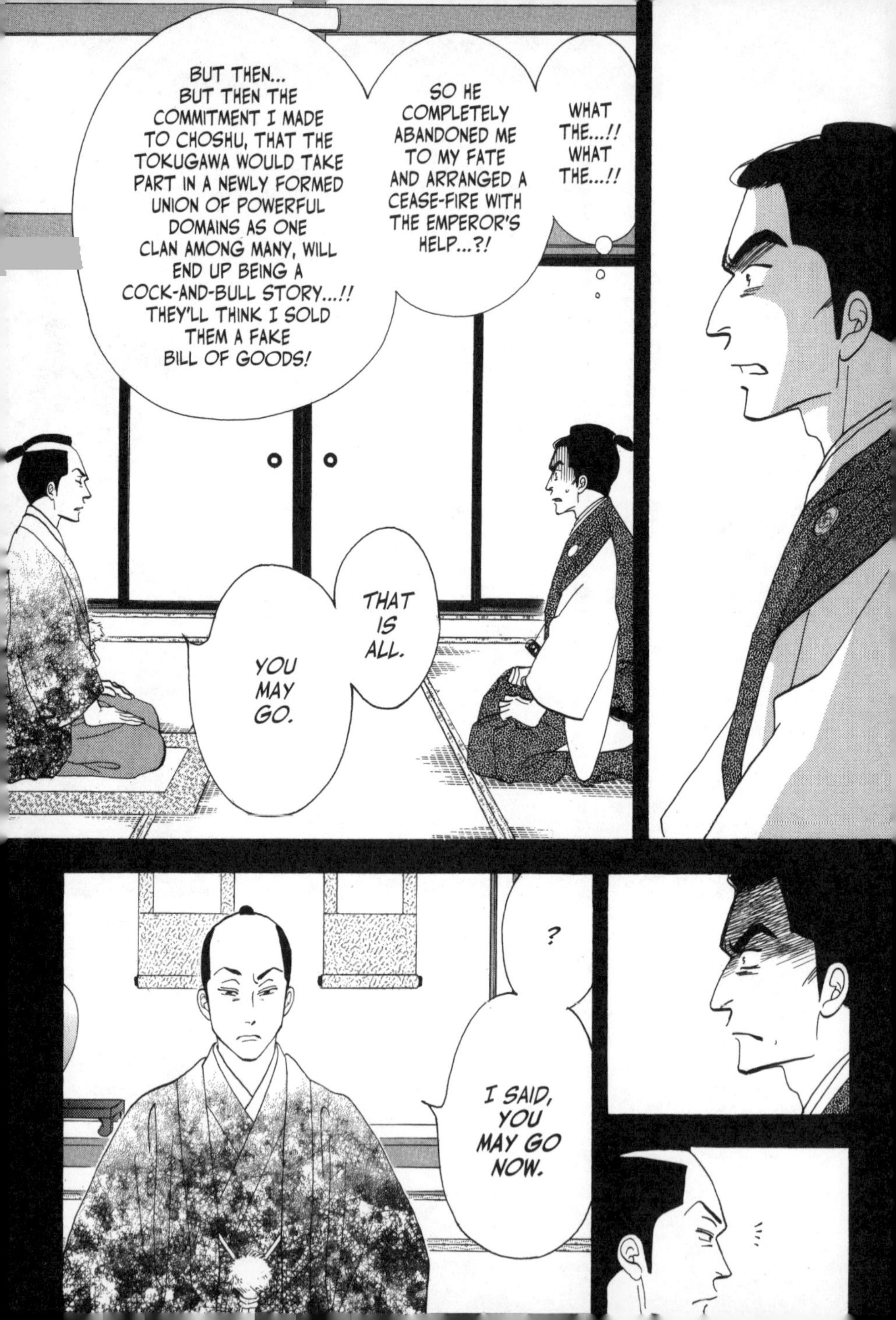
WHAT THE...!! WHAT THE...!!
SO HE COMPLETELY ABANDONED ME TO MY FATE AND ARRANGED A CEASE-FIRE WITH THE EMPEROR'S HELP...?!
BUT THEN... BUT THEN THE COMMITMENT I MADE TO CHOSHU, THAT THE TOKUGAWA WOULD TAKE PART IN A NEWLY FORMED UNION OF POWERFUL DOMAINS AS ONE CLAN AMONG MANY, WILL END UP BEING A COCK-AND-BULL STORY...!! THEY'LL THINK I SOLD THEM A FAKE BILL OF GOODS!
THAT IS ALL.
YOU MAY GO.
?
I SAID, YOU MAY GO NOW.

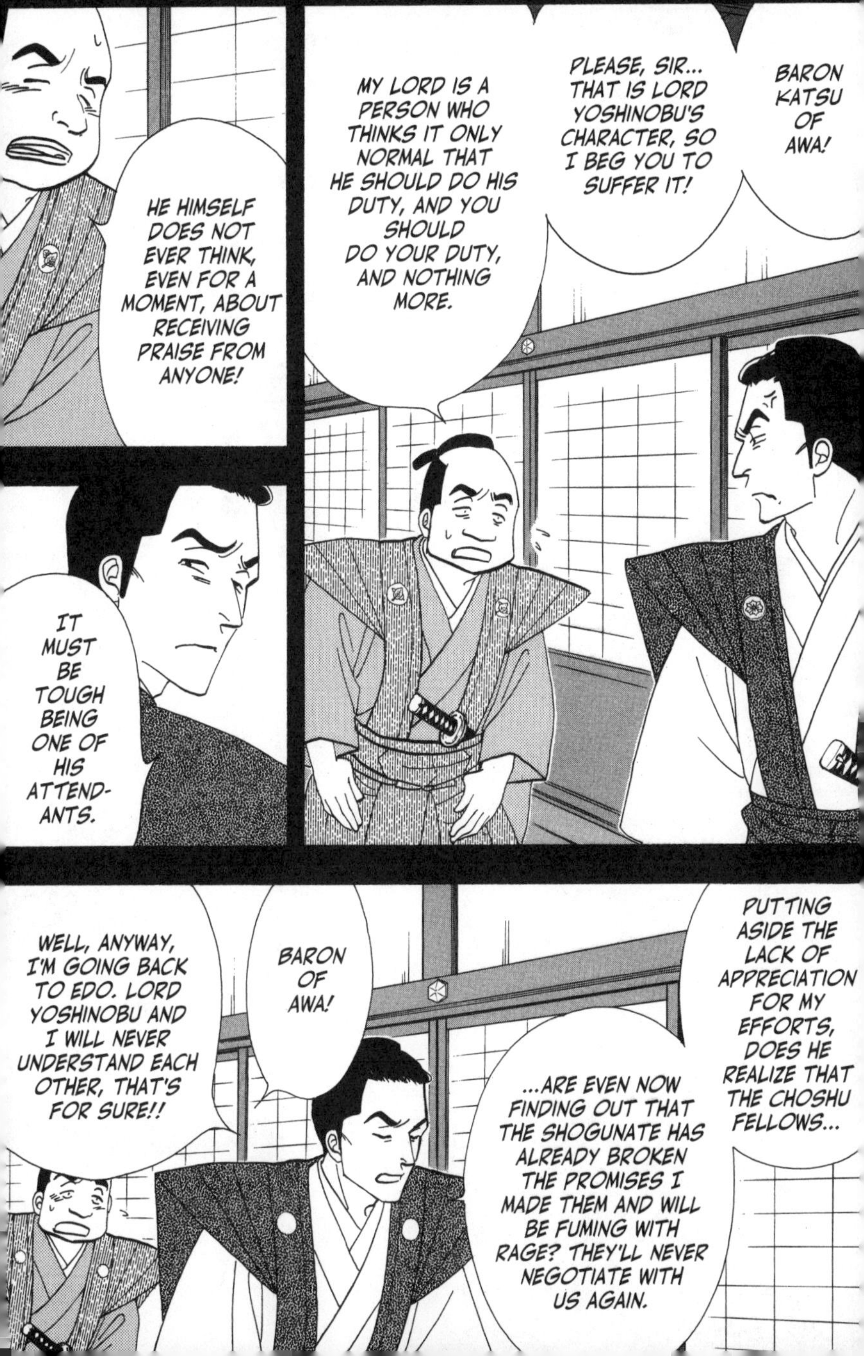
BARON KATSU OF AWA!
PLEASE, SIR... THAT IS LORD YOSHINOBU'S CHARACTER, SO I BEG YOU TO SUFFER IT!
MY LORD IS A PERSON WHO THINKS IT ONLY NORMAL THAT HE SHOULD DO HIS DUTY, AND YOU SHOULD DO YOUR DUTY, AND NOTHING MORE.
HE HIMSELF DOES NOT EVER THINK, EVEN FOR A MOMENT, ABOUT RECEIVING PRAISE FROM ANYONE!
IT MUST BE TOUGH BEING ONE OF HIS ATTEND-ANTS.
PUTTING ASIDE THE LACK OF APPRECIATION FOR MY EFFORTS, DOES HE REALIZE THAT THE CHOSHU FELLOWS...
...ARE EVEN NOW FINDING OUT THAT THE SHOGUNATE HAS ALREADY BROKEN THE PROMISES I MADE THEM AND WILL BE FUMING WITH RAGE? THEY'LL NEVER NEGOTIATE WITH US AGAIN.
BARON OF AWA!
WELL, ANYWAY, I'M GOING BACK TO EDO. LORD YOSHINOBU AND I WILL NEVER UNDERSTAND EACH OTHER, THAT'S FOR SURE!!

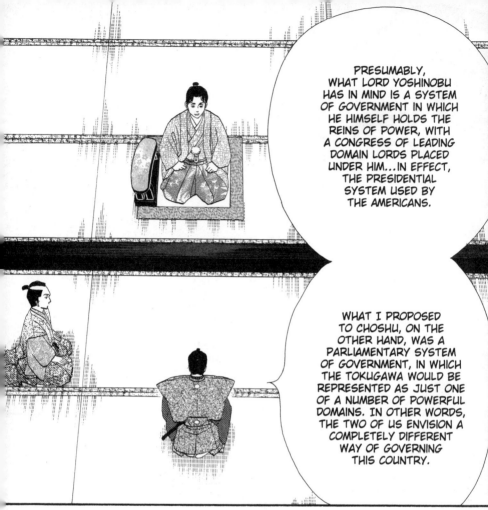

PRESUMABLY, WHAT LORD YOSHINOBU HAS IN MIND IS A SYSTEM OF GOVERNMENT IN WHICH HE HIMSELF HOLDS THE REINS OF POWER, WITH A CONGRESS OF LEADING DOMAIN LORDS PLACED UNDER HIM...IN EFFECT, THE PRESIDENTIAL SYSTEM USED BY THE AMERICANS.
WHAT I PROPOSED TO CHOSHU, ON THE OTHER HAND, WAS A PARLIAMENTARY SYSTEM OF GOVERNMENT, IN WHICH THE TOKUGAWA WOULD BE REPRESENTED AS JUST ONE OF A NUMBER OF POWERFUL DOMAINS. IN OTHER WORDS, THE TWO OF US ENVISION A COMPLETELY DIFFERENT WAY OF GOVERNING THIS COUNTRY.
IT SEEMS TO ME, HOWEVER, THAT LORD YOSHINOBU HAS FORGOTTEN ONE CRUCIAL ASPECT OF THE PRESIDENTIAL SYSTEM HE FAVORS—AND THAT IS THAT THE PRESIDENT CAN ONLY ASSUME OFFICE AFTER WINNING THE SUPPORT OF THE PEOPLE!
...
A SAMURAI OF THE LOWEST RANK DARES TO TALK ABOUT THE HEAD OF THE TOKUGAWA MAIN BRANCH IN THIS WAY... HE MAY BE THE FORMER NAVAL COMMISSIONER AND LORD YOSHINOBU IS NOT YET THE SHOGUN, BUT EVEN SO...

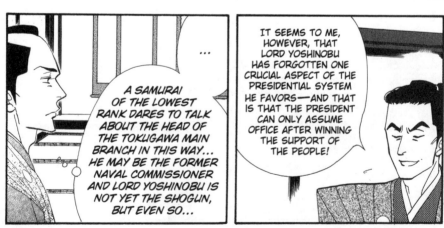

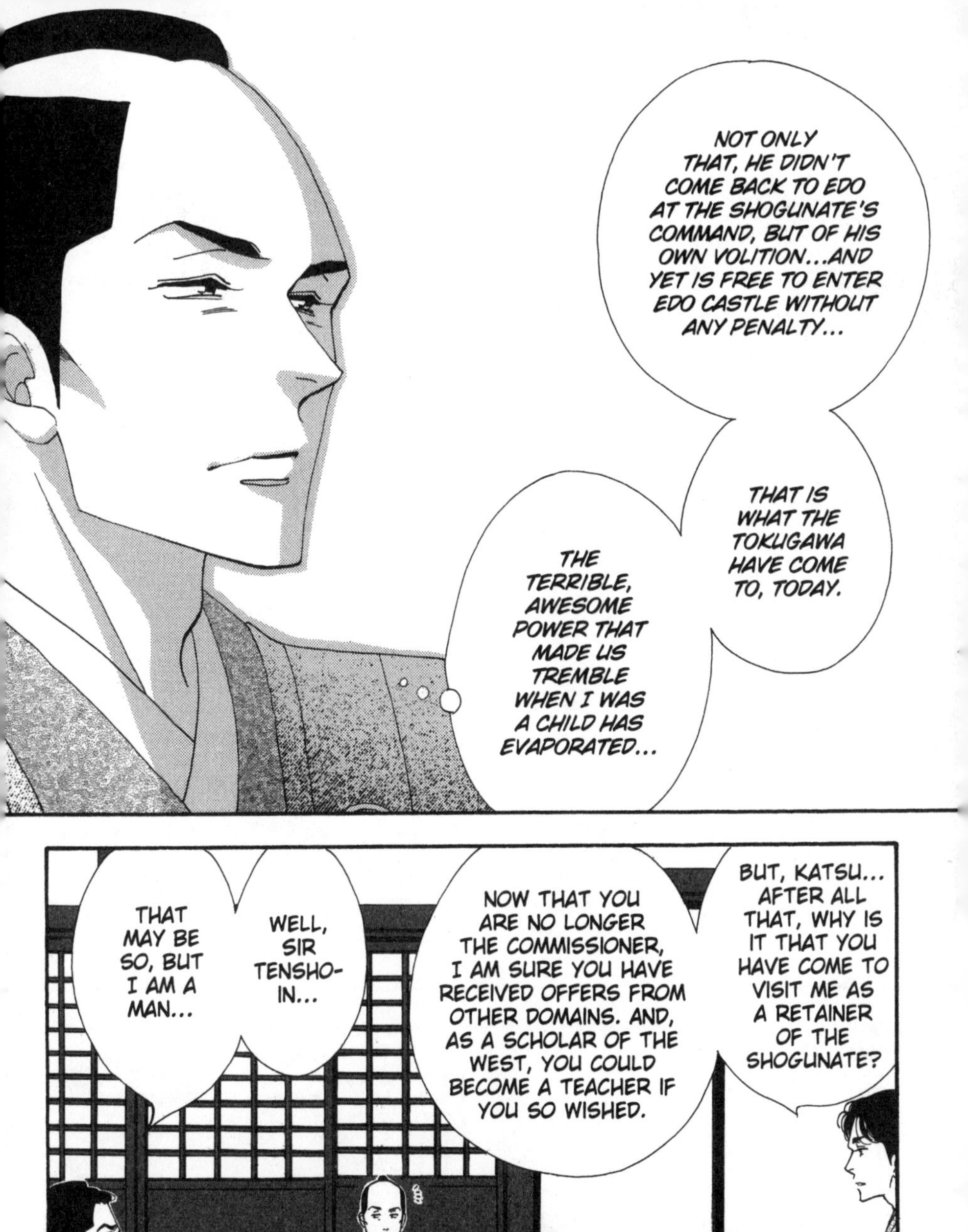
NOT ONLY THAT, HE DIDN'T COME BACK TO EDO AT THE SHOGUNATE'S COMMAND, BUT OF HIS OWN VOLITION...AND YET IS FREE TO ENTER EDO CASTLE WITHOUT ANY PENALTY...
THAT IS WHAT THE TOKUGAWA HAVE COME TO, TODAY.
THE TERRIBLE, AWESOME POWER THAT MADE US TREMBLE WHEN I WAS A CHILD HAS EVAPORATED...
BUT, KATSU... AFTER ALL THAT, WHY IS IT THAT YOU HAVE COME TO VISIT ME AS A RETAINER OF THE SHOGUNATE?
NOW THAT YOU ARE NO LONGER THE COMMISSIONER, I AM SURE YOU HAVE RECEIVED OFFERS FROM OTHER DOMAINS. AND, AS A SCHOLAR OF THE WEST, YOU COULD BECOME A TEACHER IF YOU SO WISHED.
WELL, SIR TENSHO-IN...
THAT MAY BE SO, BUT I AM A MAN...

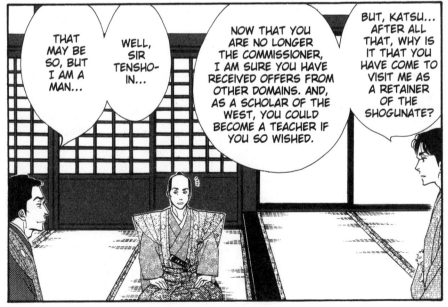

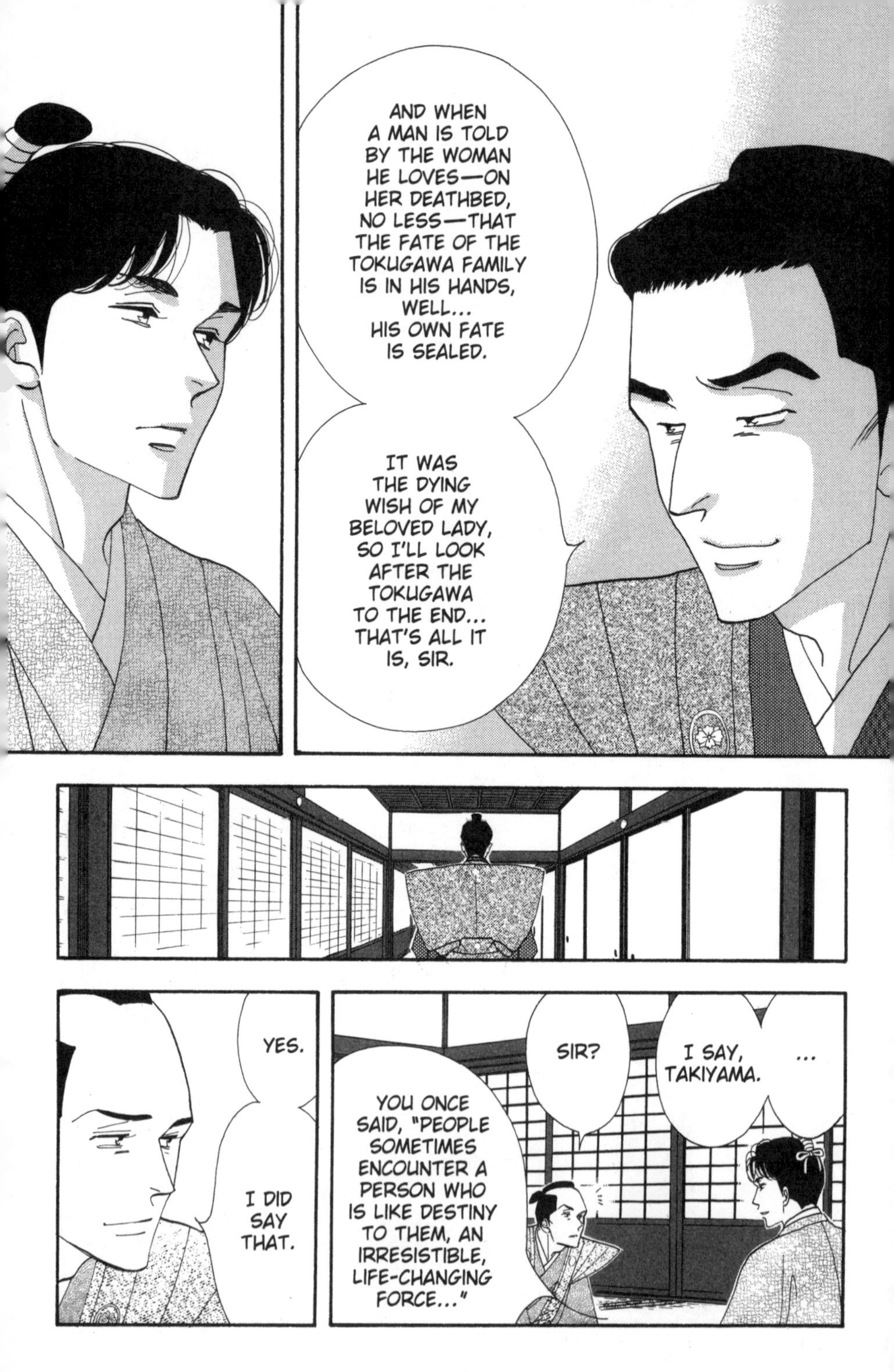
AND WHEN A MAN IS TOLD BY THE WOMAN HE LOVES—ON HER DEATHBED, NO LESS—THAT THE FATE OF THE TOKUGAWA FAMILY IS IN HIS HANDS, WELL... HIS OWN FATE IS SEALED.
IT WAS THE DYING WISH OF MY BELOVED LADY, SO I'LL LOOK AFTER THE TOKUGAWA TO THE END... THAT'S ALL IT IS, SIR.
...
I SAY, TAKIYAMA.
SIR?
YOU ONCE SAID, "PEOPLE SOMETIMES ENCOUNTER A PERSON WHO IS LIKE DESTINY TO THEM, AN IRRESISTIBLE, LIFE-CHANGING FORCE..."
YES.
I DID SAY THAT.

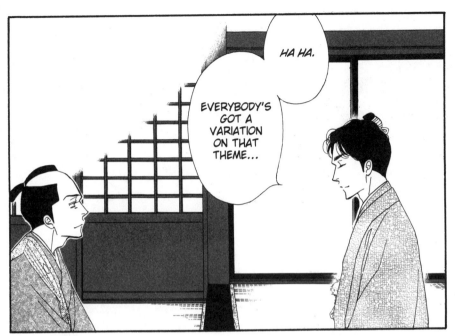

HA HA.

EVERYBODY'S GOT A VARIATION ON THAT THEME...

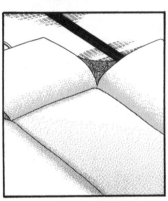

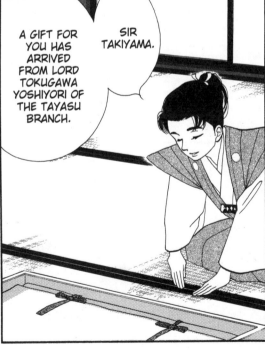

SIR TAKIYAMA.

A GIFT FOR YOU HAS ARRIVED FROM LORD TOKUGAWA YOSHIYORI OF THE TAYASU BRANCH.

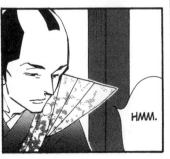

HMM.

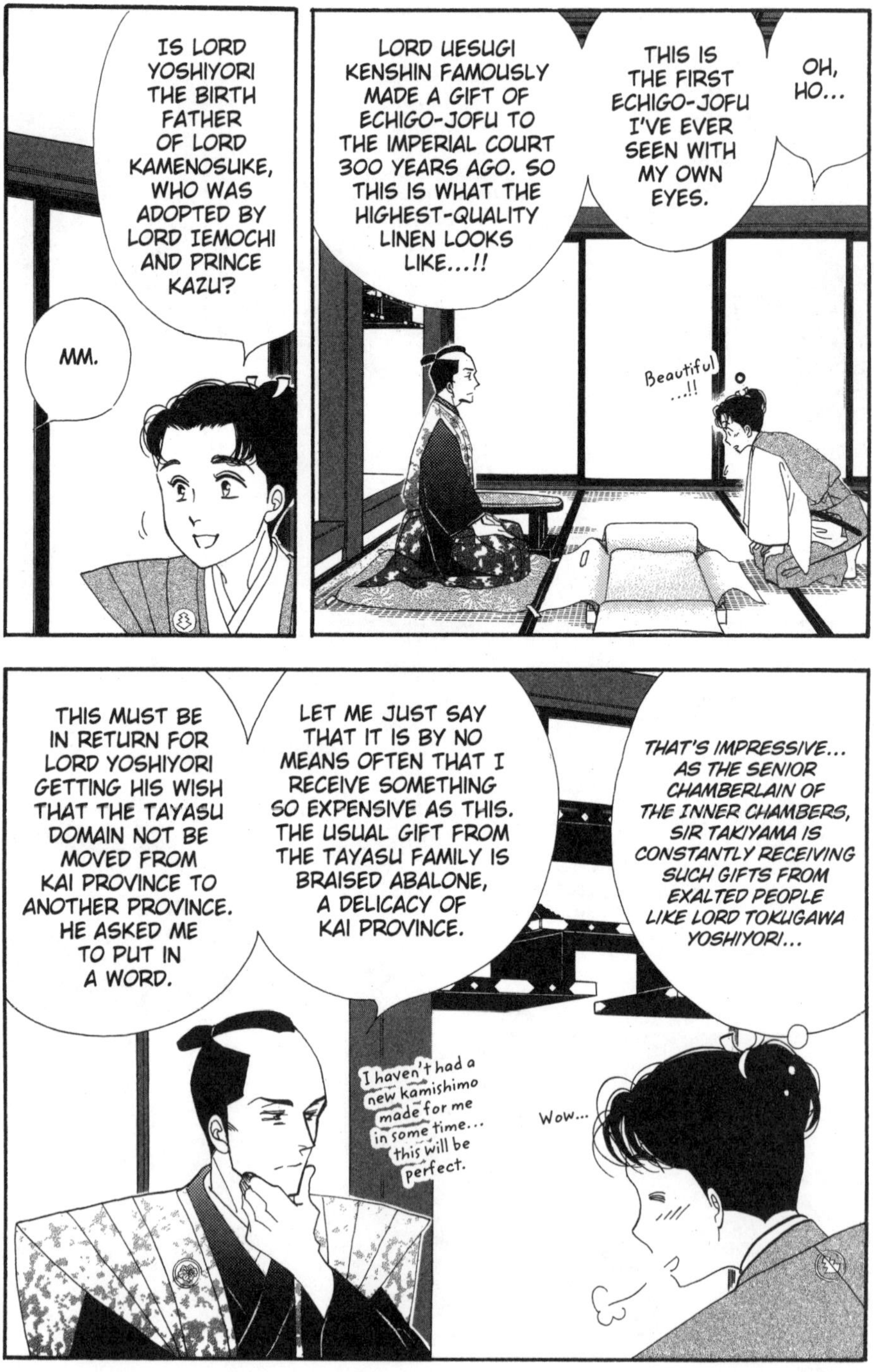
OH, HO...
THIS IS THE FIRST ECHIGO-JOFU I'VE EVER SEEN WITH MY OWN EYES.
LORD UESUGI KENSHIN FAMOUSLY MADE A GIFT OF ECHIGO-JOFU TO THE IMPERIAL COURT 300 YEARS AGO. SO THIS IS WHAT THE HIGHEST-QUALITY LINEN LOOKS LIKE...!!
Beautiful ...!!
IS LORD YOSHIYORI THE BIRTH FATHER OF LORD KAMENOSUKE, WHO WAS ADOPTED BY LORD IEMOCHI AND PRINCE KAZU?
MM.
THAT'S IMPRESSIVE... AS THE SENIOR CHAMBERLAIN OF THE INNER CHAMBERS, SIR TAKIYAMA IS CONSTANTLY RECEIVING SUCH GIFTS FROM EXALTED PEOPLE LIKE LORD TOKUGAWA YOSHIYORI...
LET ME JUST SAY THAT IT IS BY NO MEANS OFTEN THAT I RECEIVE SOMETHING SO EXPENSIVE AS THIS. THE USUAL GIFT FROM THE TAYASU FAMILY IS BRAISED ABALONE, A DELICACY OF KAI PROVINCE.
THIS MUST BE IN RETURN FOR LORD YOSHIYORI GETTING HIS WISH THAT THE TAYASU DOMAIN NOT BE MOVED FROM KAI PROVINCE TO ANOTHER PROVINCE. HE ASKED ME TO PUT IN A WORD.
Wow...
I haven't had a new kamishimo made for me in some time... this will be perfect.

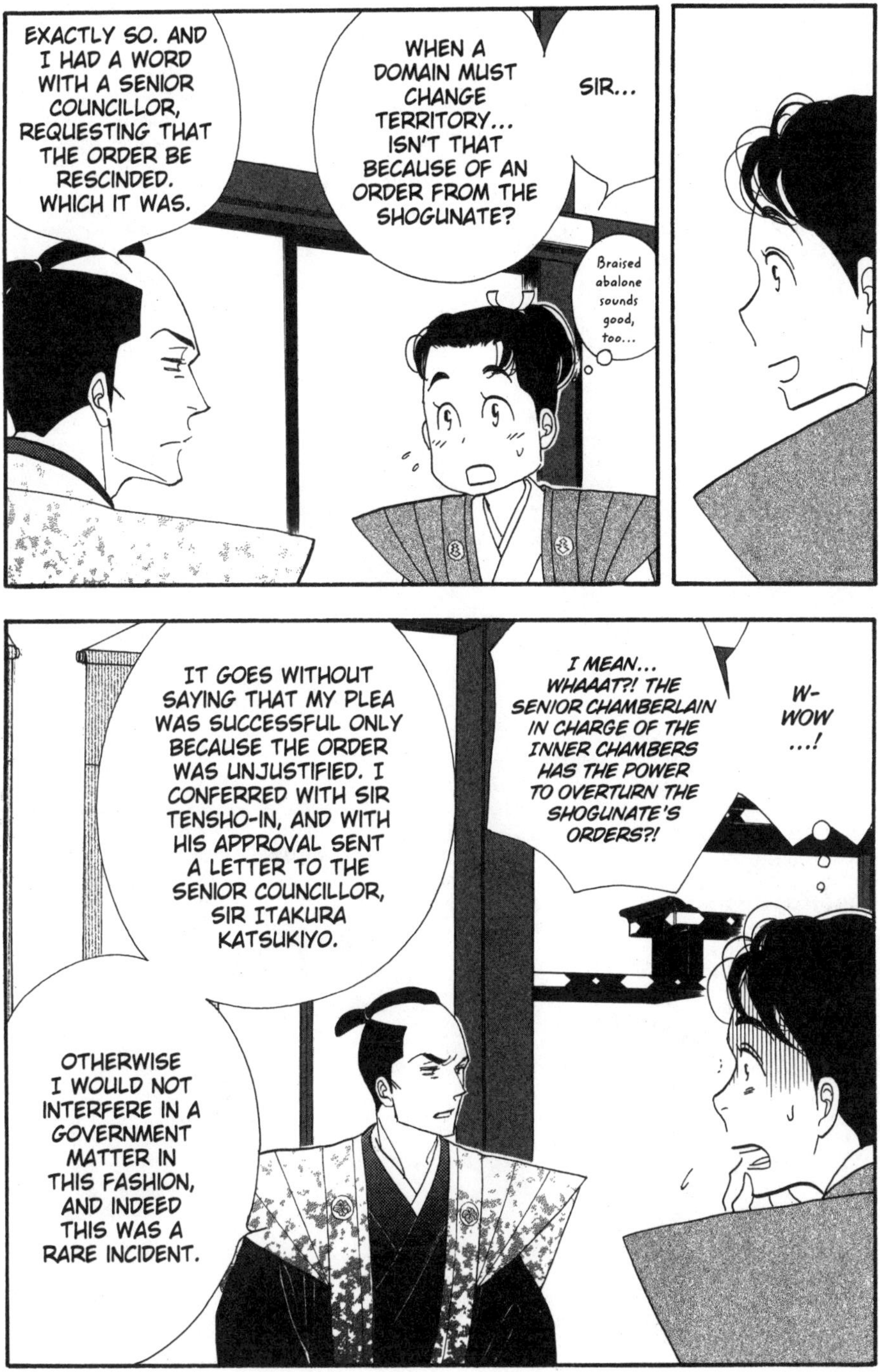
SIR...
WHEN A DOMAIN MUST CHANGE TERRITORY... ISN'T THAT BECAUSE OF AN ORDER FROM THE SHOGUNATE?
EXACTLY SO. AND I HAD A WORD WITH A SENIOR COUNCILLOR, REQUESTING THAT THE ORDER BE RESCINDED. WHICH IT WAS.
Braised abalone sounds good, too...
W-WOW...!
I MEAN... WHAAAT?! THE SENIOR CHAMBERLAIN IN CHARGE OF THE INNER CHAMBERS HAS THE POWER TO OVERTURN THE SHOGUNATE'S ORDERS?!
IT GOES WITHOUT SAYING THAT MY PLEA WAS SUCCESSFUL ONLY BECAUSE THE ORDER WAS UNJUSTIFIED. I CONFERRED WITH SIR TENSHO-IN, AND WITH HIS APPROVAL SENT A LETTER TO THE SENIOR COUNCILLOR, SIR ITAKURA KATSUKIYO.
OTHERWISE I WOULD NOT INTERFERE IN A GOVERNMENT MATTER IN THIS FASHION, AND INDEED THIS WAS A RARE INCIDENT.

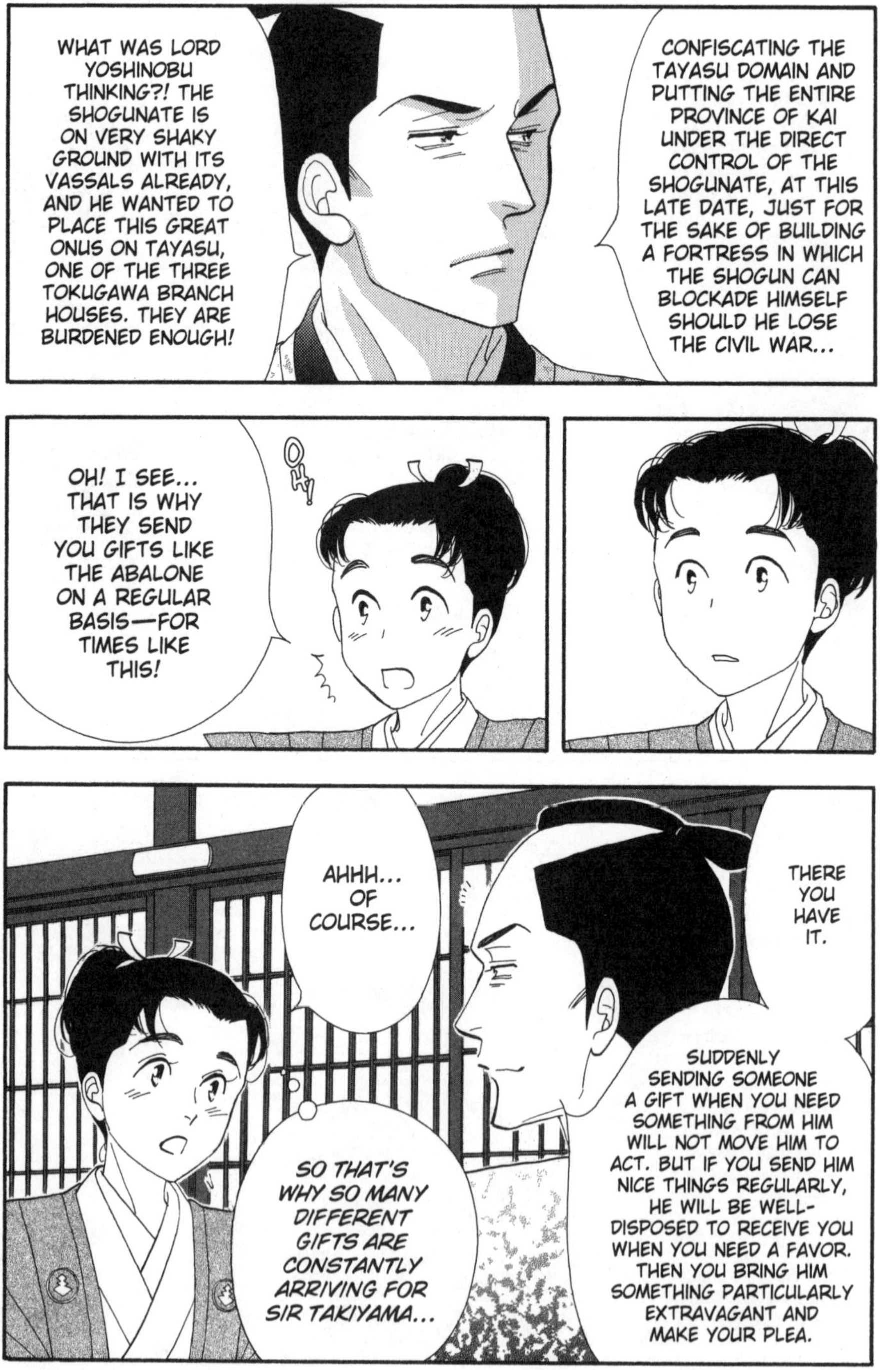
CONFISCATING THE TAYASU DOMAIN AND PUTTING THE ENTIRE PROVINCE OF KAI UNDER THE DIRECT CONTROL OF THE SHOGUNATE, AT THIS LATE DATE, JUST FOR THE SAKE OF BUILDING A FORTRESS IN WHICH THE SHOGUN CAN BLOCKADE HIMSELF SHOULD HE LOSE THE CIVIL WAR...
WHAT WAS LORD YOSHINOBU THINKING?! THE SHOGUNATE IS ON VERY SHAKY GROUND WITH ITS VASSALS ALREADY, AND HE WANTED TO PLACE THIS GREAT ONUS ON TAYASU, ONE OF THE THREE TOKUGAWA BRANCH HOUSES. THEY ARE BURDENED ENOUGH!
OH!
OH! I SEE... THAT IS WHY THEY SEND YOU GIFTS LIKE THE ABALONE ON A REGULAR BASIS—FOR TIMES LIKE THIS!
THERE YOU HAVE IT.
AHHH... OF COURSE...
SUDDENLY SENDING SOMEONE A GIFT WHEN YOU NEED SOMETHING FROM HIM WILL NOT MOVE HIM TO ACT. BUT IF YOU SEND HIM NICE THINGS REGULARLY, HE WILL BE WELL-DISPOSED TO RECEIVE YOU WHEN YOU NEED A FAVOR. THEN YOU BRING HIM SOMETHING PARTICULARLY EXTRAVAGANT AND MAKE YOUR PLEA.
SO THAT'S WHY SO MANY DIFFERENT GIFTS ARE CONSTANTLY ARRIVING FOR SIR TAKIYAMA...

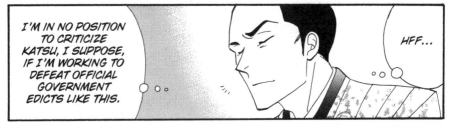

HFF...
I'M IN NO POSITION TO CRITICIZE KATSU, I SUPPOSE, IF I'M WORKING TO DEFEAT OFFICIAL GOVERNMENT EDICTS LIKE THIS.
THAT'S WHY, NAKANO...
...EVERYONE IS SAYING THAT WHEN THE NEW SHOGUN TAKES OFFICE AND SIR TAKIYAMA HAS TO RETIRE FROM THE POST OF SENIOR CHAMBERLAIN OF THE INNER CHAMBERS, HE WILL SIMPLY TAKE UP A SIMILAR POST IN THE OUTER CHAMBERS.
WHAAT?! HAS THAT EVER HAPPENED, THAT SOMEONE WHO WAS EMPLOYED IN THE INNER CHAMBERS SIMPLY MOVES INTO A NEW POST IN THE OUTER CHAMBERS??
NO, OF COURSE NOT. BUT SIR TAKIYAMA IS ON CLOSE TERMS WITH BARON ITAKURA OF SUO, THE SENIOR COUNCILLOR, FOR ONE THING.
AND THERE SEEM TO BE NEW POSTS BEING CREATED THESE DAYS—LIKE THAT NAVAL COMMISSIONER, WAS IT?—FOR DEFENDING THE COUNTRY'S SEAS AND COASTS. SO MAYBE HE COULD GET ONE OF THOSE.

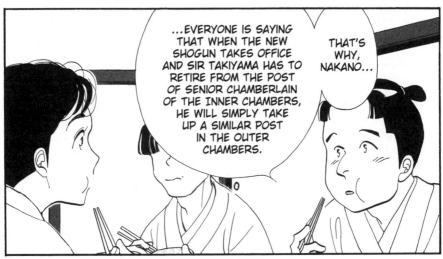

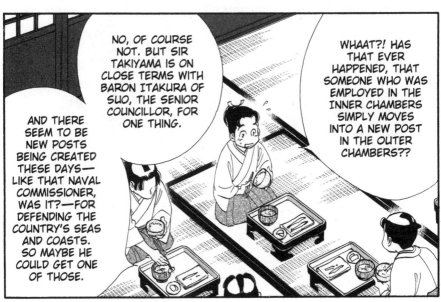

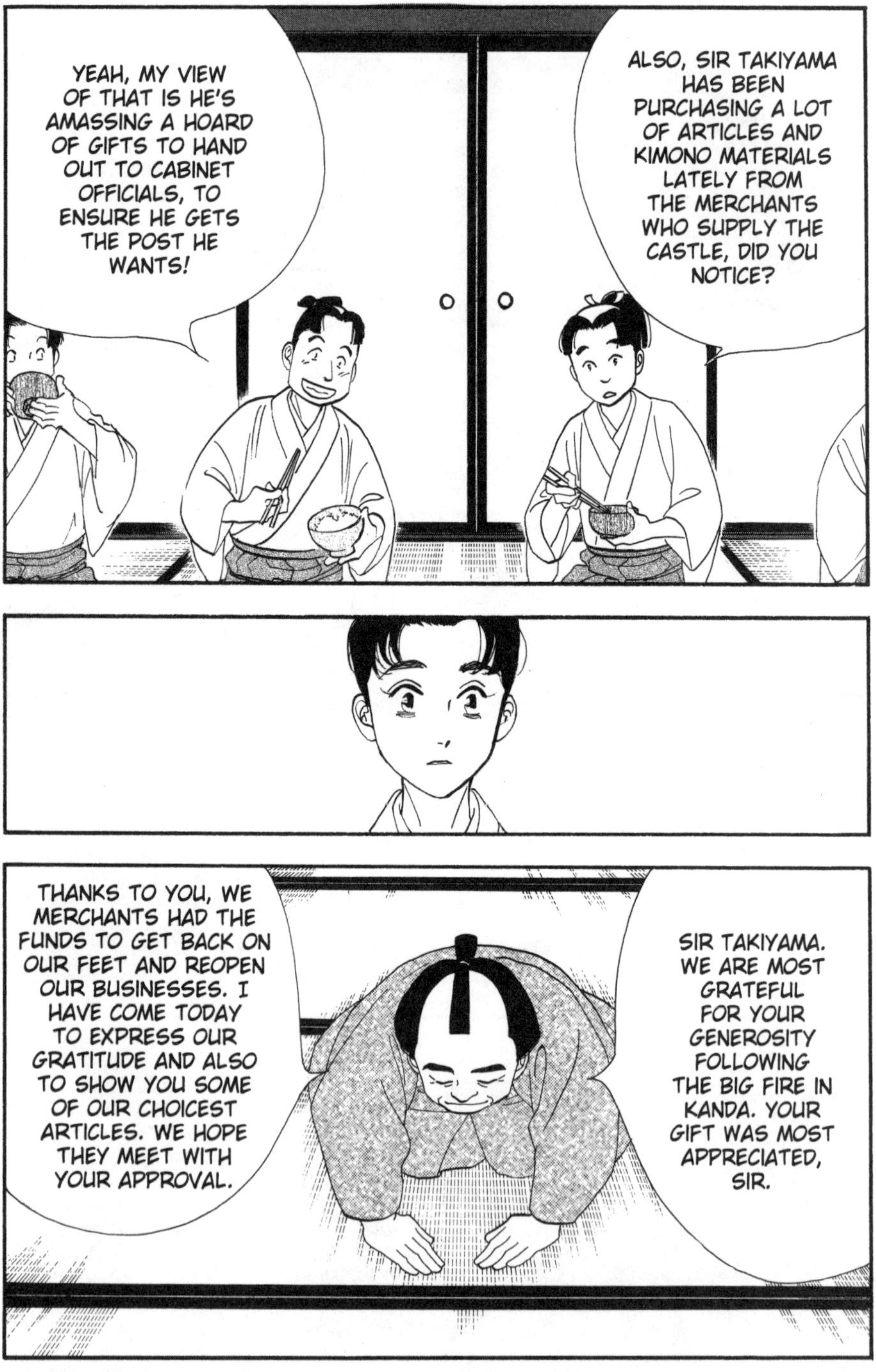
ALSO, SIR TAKIYAMA HAS BEEN PURCHASING A LOT OF ARTICLES AND KIMONO MATERIALS LATELY FROM THE MERCHANTS WHO SUPPLY THE CASTLE, DID YOU NOTICE?
YEAH, MY VIEW OF THAT IS HE'S AMASSING A HOARD OF GIFTS TO HAND OUT TO CABINET OFFICIALS, TO ENSURE HE GETS THE POST HE WANTS!
SIR TAKIYAMA. WE ARE MOST GRATEFUL FOR YOUR GENEROSITY FOLLOWING THE BIG FIRE IN KANDA. YOUR GIFT WAS MOST APPRECIATED, SIR.
THANKS TO YOU, WE MERCHANTS HAD THE FUNDS TO GET BACK ON OUR FEET AND REOPEN OUR BUSINESSES. I HAVE COME TODAY TO EXPRESS OUR GRATITUDE AND ALSO TO SHOW YOU SOME OF OUR CHOICEST ARTICLES. WE HOPE THEY MEET WITH YOUR APPROVAL.

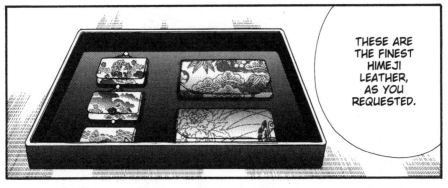

THESE ARE THE FINEST HIMEJI LEATHER, AS YOU REQUESTED.
HMM.
I'LL TAKE 50 EACH OF THAT TOBACCO POUCH AND OF THAT PAPER HOLDER.
!!
FIFTY EACH...?! A HUNDRED ARTICLES IN TOTAL, SIR?!
THAT'S RIGHT. WHAT YOU CANNOT SUPPLY NOW, YOU MAY BRING LATER WHEN YOU HAVE IT.
YES, SIR! THANK YOU, SIR...!! WE SHALL HAVE THE ARTISANS WORKING AT FULL TILT!! AND WE'LL CERTAINLY GIVE YOU A GOOD PRICE, FOR SUCH A LARGE ORDER!
WE ARE TRULY... TRULY GRATEFUL TO YOU, SIR! I BEG FOR YOUR CONTINUED GOOD FAVOR, MY LORD!

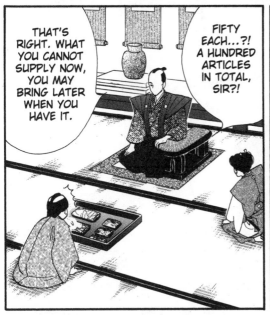

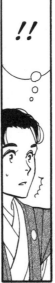

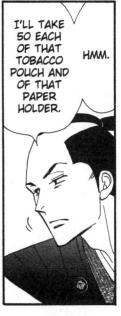

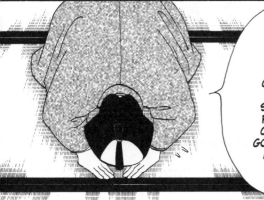

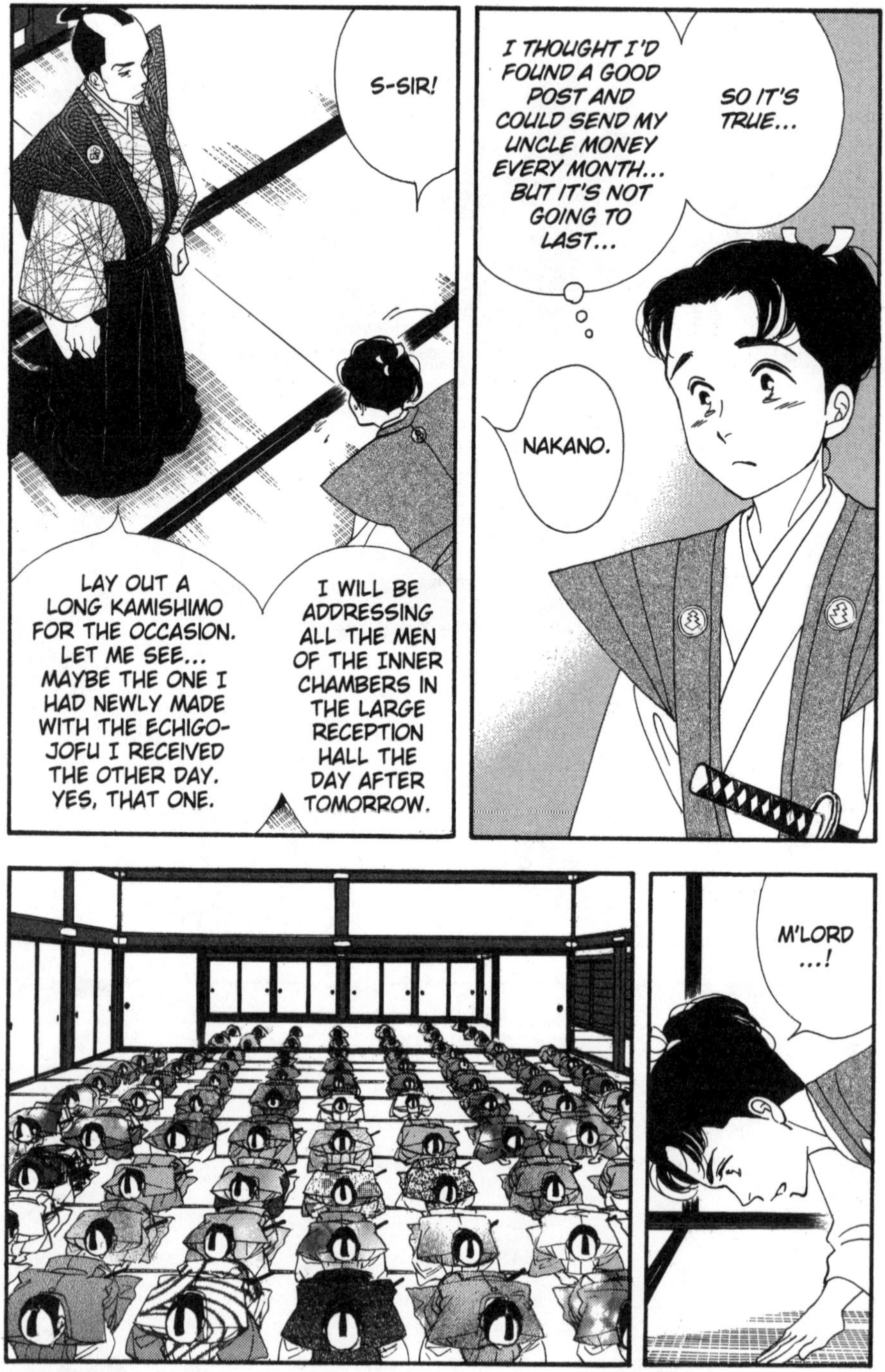
SO IT'S TRUE...
I THOUGHT I'D FOUND A GOOD POST AND COULD SEND MY UNCLE MONEY EVERY MONTH... BUT IT'S NOT GOING TO LAST...
NAKANO.
S-SIR!
I WILL BE ADDRESSING ALL THE MEN OF THE INNER CHAMBERS IN THE LARGE RECEPTION HALL THE DAY AFTER TOMORROW.
LAY OUT A LONG KAMISHIMO FOR THE OCCASION. LET ME SEE... MAYBE THE ONE I HAD NEWLY MADE WITH THE ECHIGO-JOFU I RECEIVED THE OTHER DAY. YES, THAT ONE.
M'LORD ...!

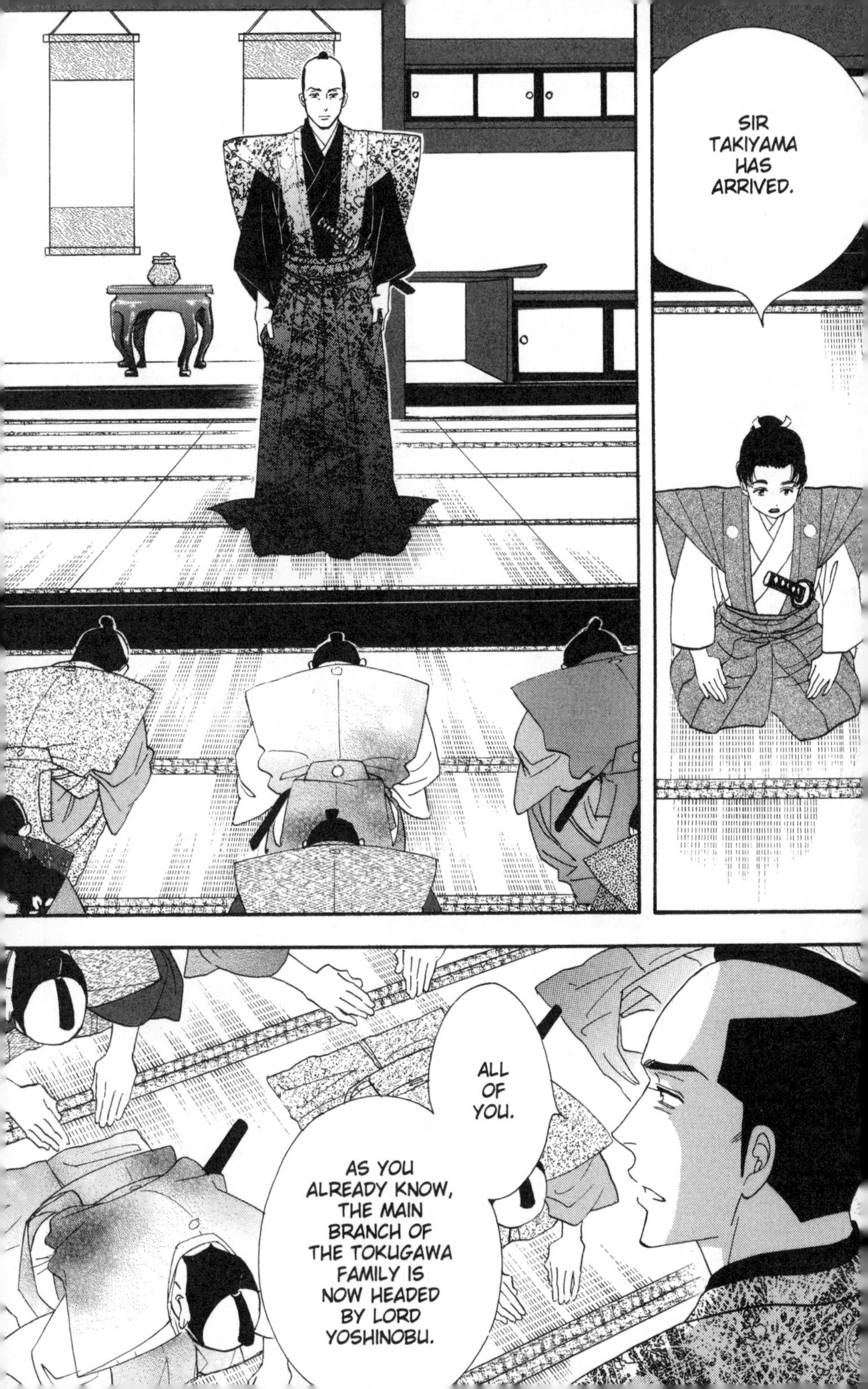
SIR TAKIYAMA HAS ARRIVED.
ALL OF YOU.
AS YOU ALREADY KNOW, THE MAIN BRANCH OF THE TOKUGAWA FAMILY IS NOW HEADED BY LORD YOSHINOBU.

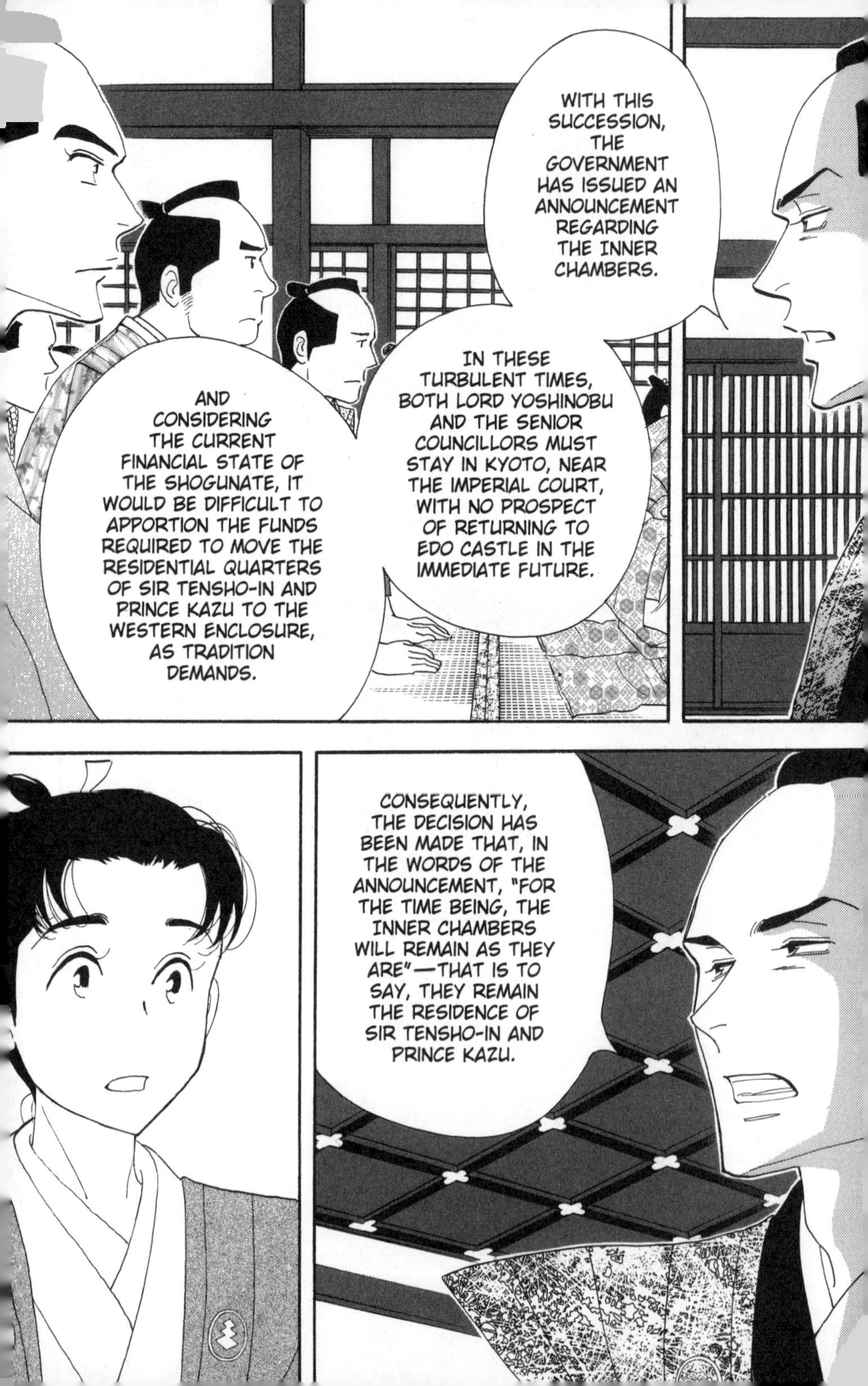
WITH THIS SUCCESSION, THE GOVERNMENT HAS ISSUED AN ANNOUNCEMENT REGARDING THE INNER CHAMBERS.
IN THESE TURBULENT TIMES, BOTH LORD YOSHINOBU AND THE SENIOR COUNCILLORS MUST STAY IN KYOTO, NEAR THE IMPERIAL COURT, WITH NO PROSPECT OF RETURNING TO EDO CASTLE IN THE IMMEDIATE FUTURE.
AND CONSIDERING THE CURRENT FINANCIAL STATE OF THE SHOGUNATE, IT WOULD BE DIFFICULT TO APPORTION THE FUNDS REQUIRED TO MOVE THE RESIDENTIAL QUARTERS OF SIR TENSHO-IN AND PRINCE KAZU TO THE WESTERN ENCLOSURE, AS TRADITION DEMANDS.
CONSEQUENTLY, THE DECISION HAS BEEN MADE THAT, IN THE WORDS OF THE ANNOUNCEMENT, "FOR THE TIME BEING, THE INNER CHAMBERS WILL REMAIN AS THEY ARE"—THAT IS TO SAY, THEY REMAIN THE RESIDENCE OF SIR TENSHO-IN AND PRINCE KAZU.

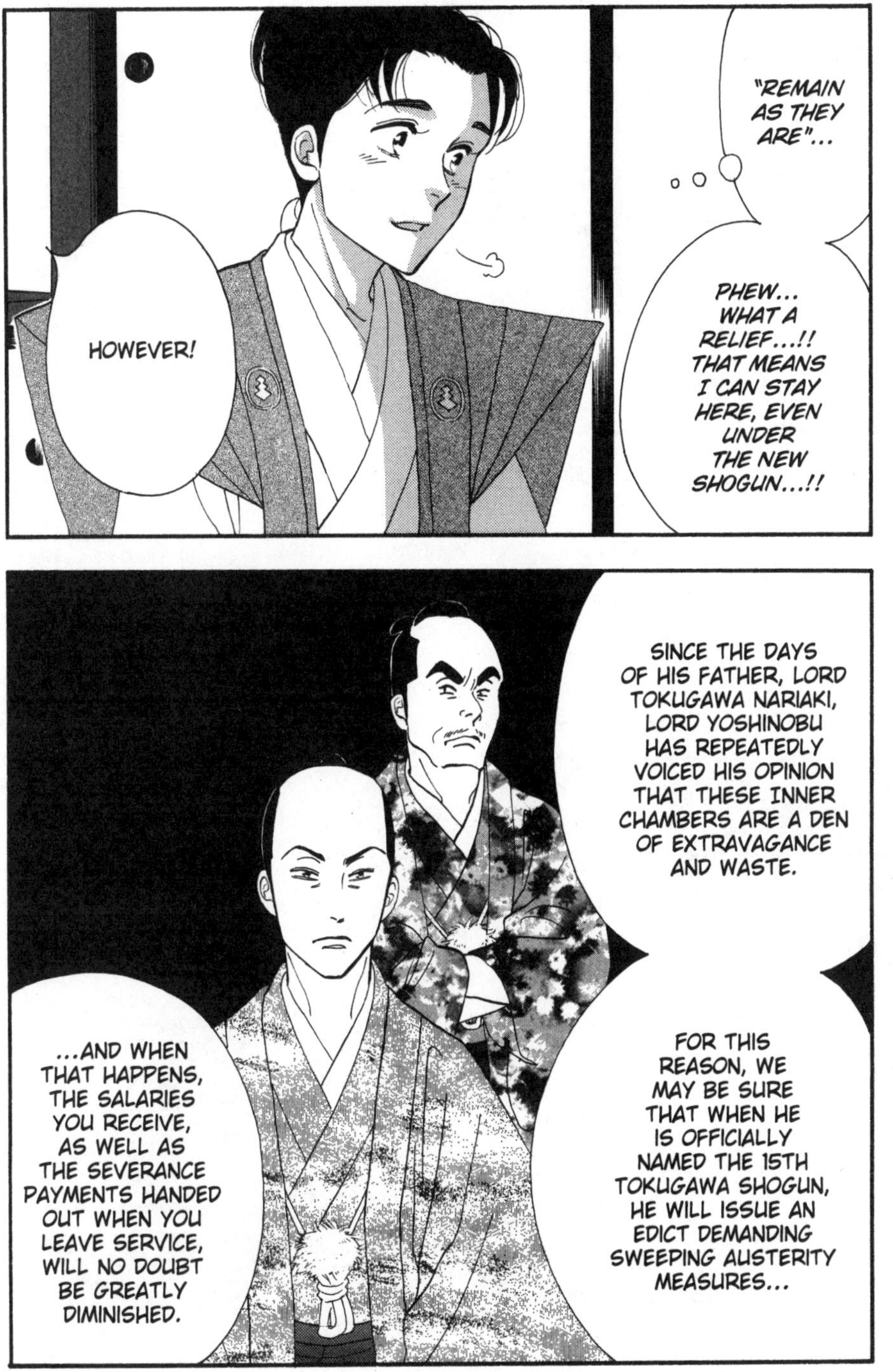
"REMAIN AS THEY ARE"...
PHEW... WHAT A RELIEF...!! THAT MEANS I CAN STAY HERE, EVEN UNDER THE NEW SHOGUN...!!
HOWEVER!
SINCE THE DAYS OF HIS FATHER, LORD TOKUGAWA NARIAKI, LORD YOSHINOBU HAS REPEATEDLY VOICED HIS OPINION THAT THESE INNER CHAMBERS ARE A DEN OF EXTRAVAGANCE AND WASTE.
FOR THIS REASON, WE MAY BE SURE THAT WHEN HE IS OFFICIALLY NAMED THE 15TH TOKUGAWA SHOGUN, HE WILL ISSUE AN EDICT DEMANDING SWEEPING AUSTERITY MEASURES...
...AND WHEN THAT HAPPENS, THE SALARIES YOU RECEIVE, AS WELL AS THE SEVERANCE PAYMENTS HANDED OUT WHEN YOU LEAVE SERVICE, WILL NO DOUBT BE GREATLY DIMINISHED.

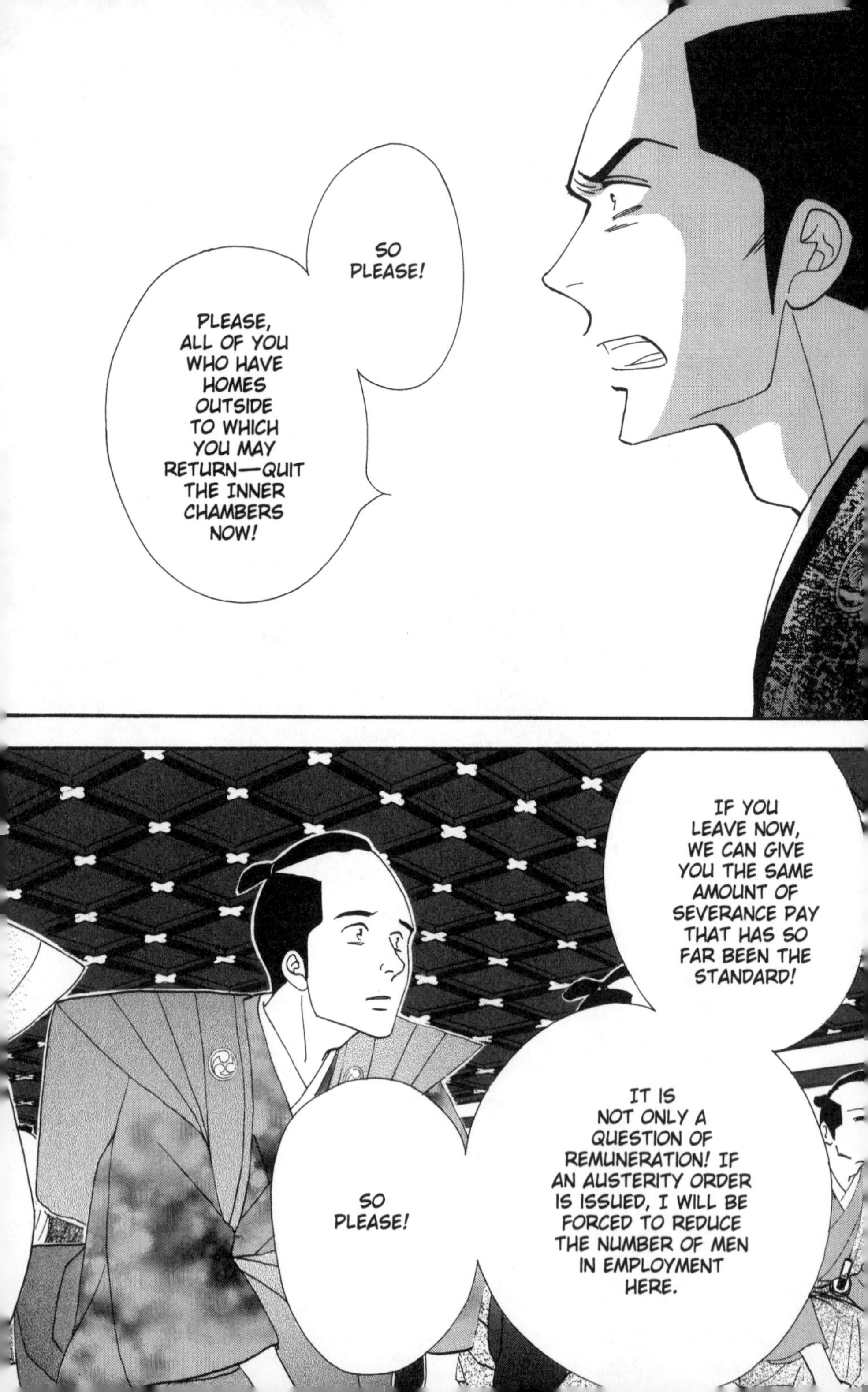
SO PLEASE!
PLEASE, ALL OF YOU WHO HAVE HOMES OUTSIDE TO WHICH YOU MAY RETURN—QUIT THE INNER CHAMBERS NOW!
IF YOU LEAVE NOW, WE CAN GIVE YOU THE SAME AMOUNT OF SEVERANCE PAY THAT HAS SO FAR BEEN THE STANDARD!
IT IS NOT ONLY A QUESTION OF REMUNERATION! IF AN AUSTERITY ORDER IS ISSUED, I WILL BE FORCED TO REDUCE THE NUMBER OF MEN IN EMPLOYMENT HERE.
SO PLEASE!

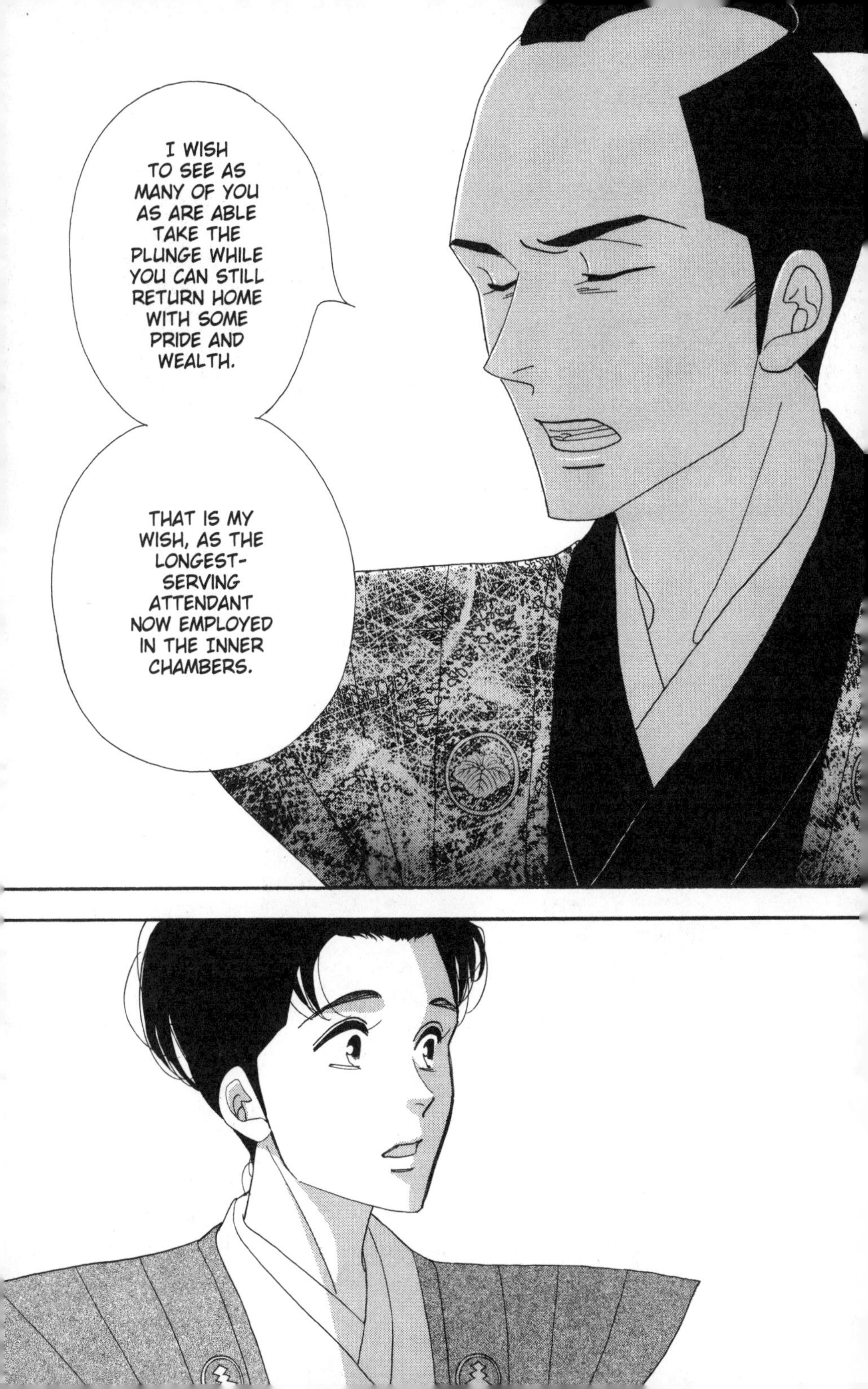
I WISH TO SEE AS MANY OF YOU AS ARE ABLE TAKE THE PLUNGE WHILE YOU CAN STILL RETURN HOME WITH SOME PRIDE AND WEALTH.
THAT IS MY WISH, AS THE LONGEST-SERVING ATTENDANT NOW EMPLOYED IN THE INNER CHAMBERS.

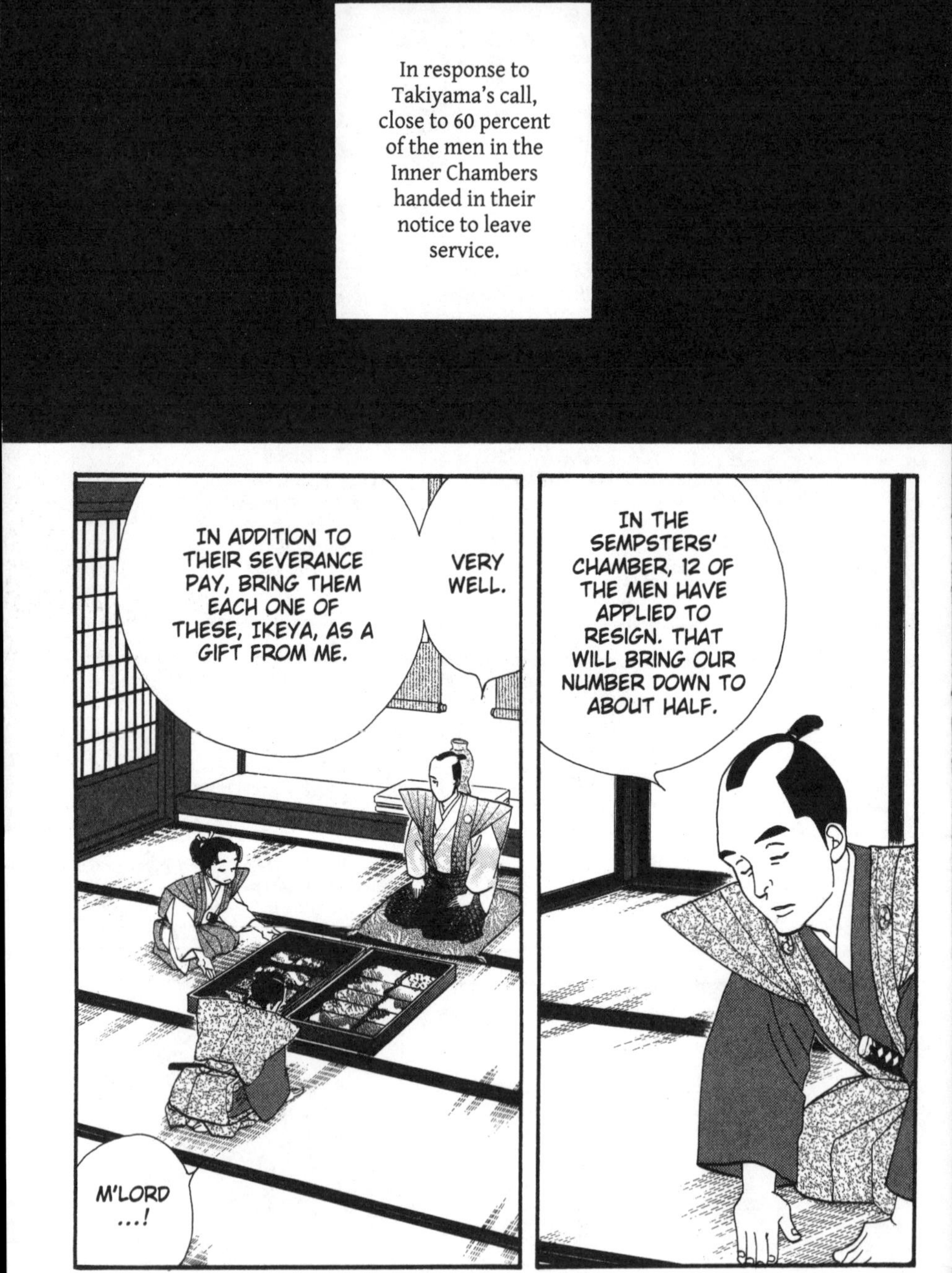
In response to Takiyama's call, close to 60 percent of the men in the Inner Chambers handed in their notice to leave service.
IN THE SEMPSTERS' CHAMBER, 12 OF THE MEN HAVE APPLIED TO RESIGN. THAT WILL BRING OUR NUMBER DOWN TO ABOUT HALF.
IN ADDITION TO THEIR SEVERANCE PAY, BRING THEM EACH ONE OF THESE, IKEYA, AS A GIFT FROM ME.
VERY WELL.
M'LORD ...!

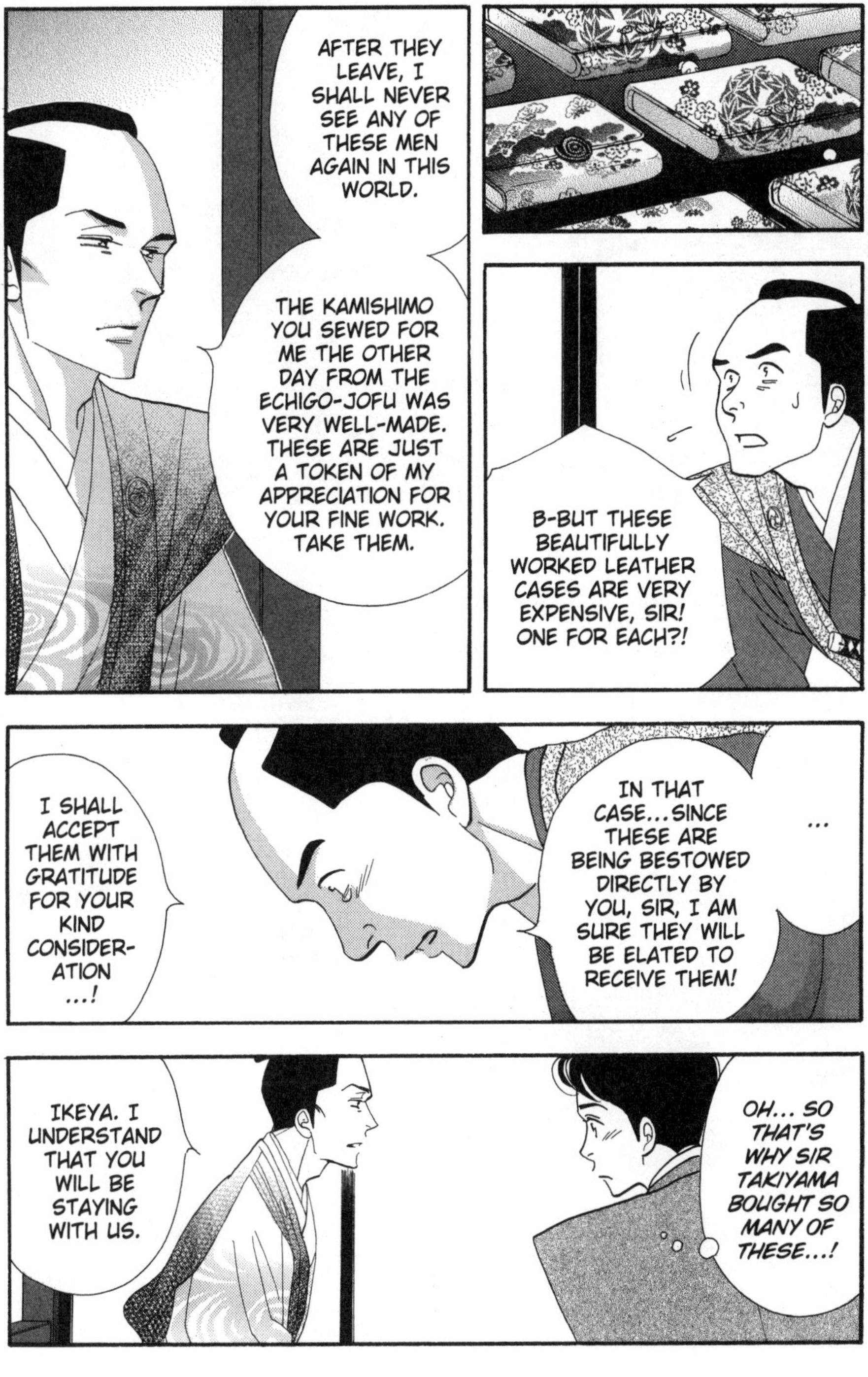
B-BUT THESE BEAUTIFULLY WORKED LEATHER CASES ARE VERY EXPENSIVE, SIR! ONE FOR EACH?!
AFTER THEY LEAVE, I SHALL NEVER SEE ANY OF THESE MEN AGAIN IN THIS WORLD.
THE KAMISHIMO YOU SEWED FOR ME THE OTHER DAY FROM THE ECHIGO-JOFU WAS VERY WELL-MADE. THESE ARE JUST A TOKEN OF MY APPRECIATION FOR YOUR FINE WORK. TAKE THEM.
...
IN THAT CASE...SINCE THESE ARE BEING BESTOWED DIRECTLY BY YOU, SIR, I AM SURE THEY WILL BE ELATED TO RECEIVE THEM!
I SHALL ACCEPT THEM WITH GRATITUDE FOR YOUR KIND CONSIDER-ATION ...!
OH... SO THAT'S WHY SIR TAKIYAMA BOUGHT SO MANY OF THESE...!
IKEYA. I UNDERSTAND THAT YOU WILL BE STAYING WITH US.

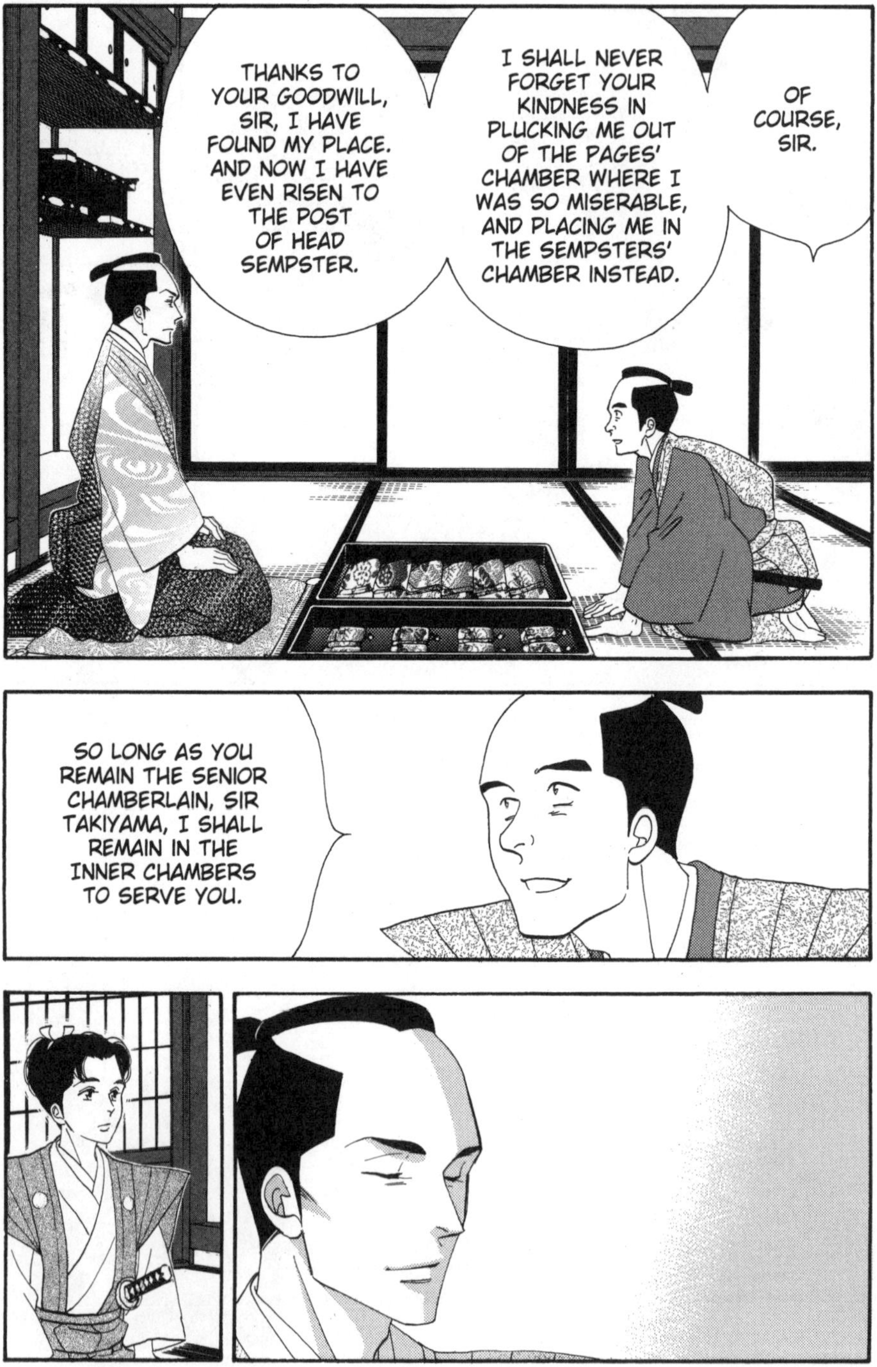
OF COURSE, SIR.
I SHALL NEVER FORGET YOUR KINDNESS IN PLUCKING ME OUT OF THE PAGES' CHAMBER WHERE I WAS SO MISERABLE, AND PLACING ME IN THE SEMPSTERS' CHAMBER INSTEAD.
THANKS TO YOUR GOODWILL, SIR, I HAVE FOUND MY PLACE. AND NOW I HAVE EVEN RISEN TO THE POST OF HEAD SEMPSTER.
SO LONG AS YOU REMAIN THE SENIOR CHAMBERLAIN, SIR TAKIYAMA, I SHALL REMAIN IN THE INNER CHAMBERS TO SERVE YOU.

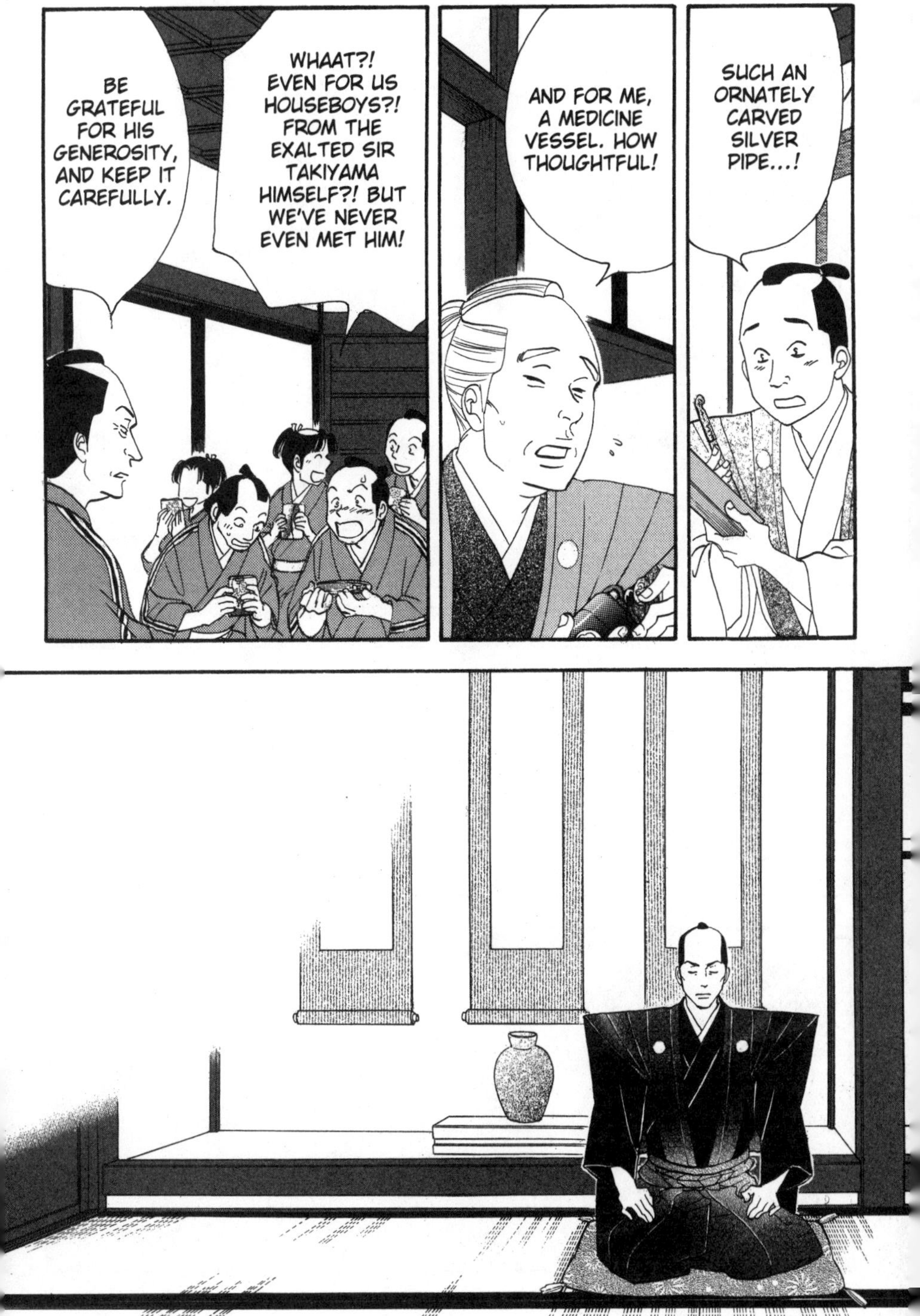
SUCH AN ORNATELY CARVED SILVER PIPE...!
AND FOR ME, A MEDICINE VESSEL. HOW THOUGHTFUL!
WHAAT?! EVEN FOR US HOUSEBOYS?! FROM THE EXALTED SIR TAKIYAMA HIMSELF?! BUT WE'VE NEVER EVEN MET HIM!
BE GRATEFUL FOR HIS GENEROSITY, AND KEEP IT CAREFULLY.

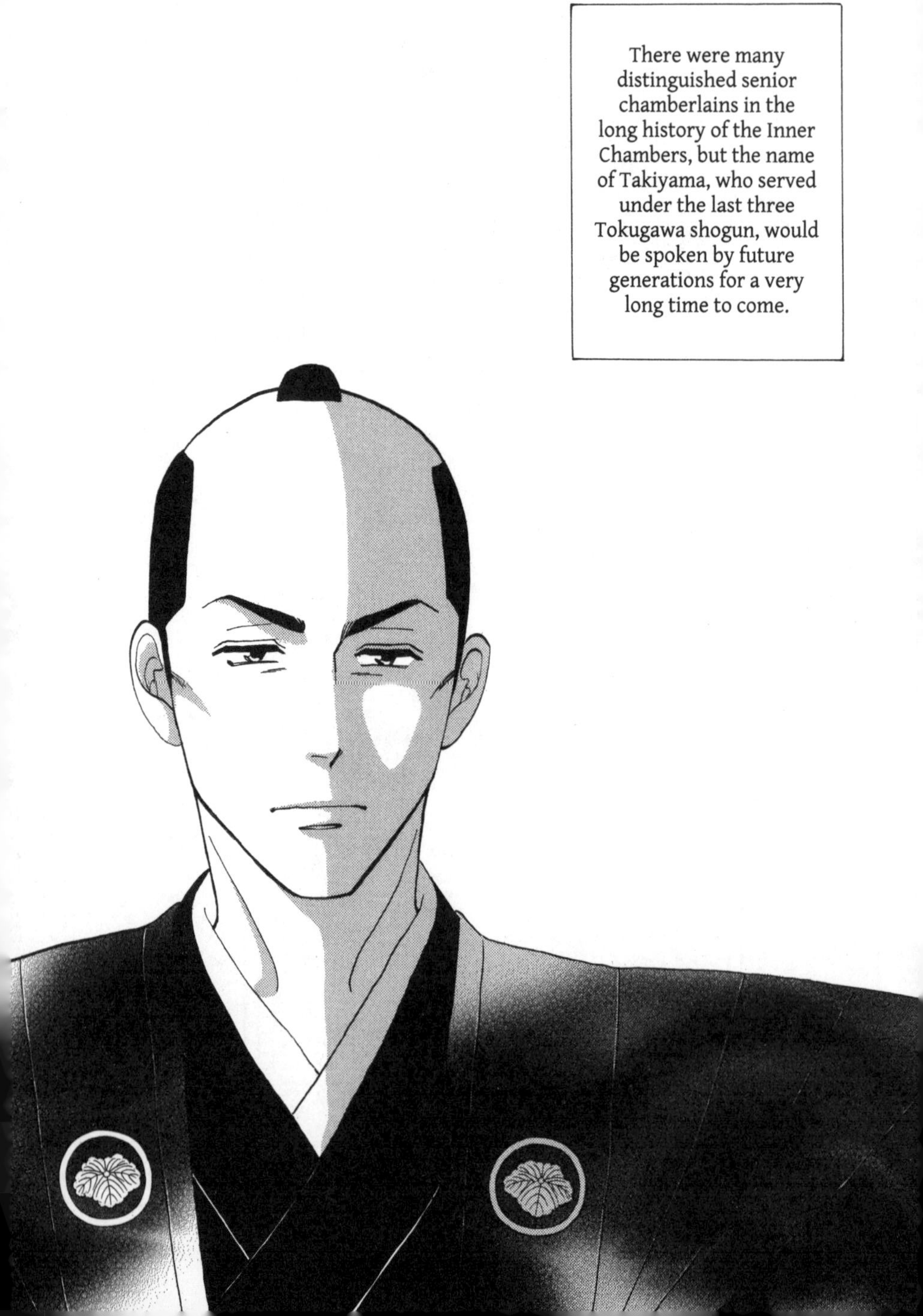
There were many distinguished senior chamberlains in the long history of the Inner Chambers, but the name of Takiyama, who served under the last three Tokugawa shogun, would be spoken by future generations for a very long time to come.

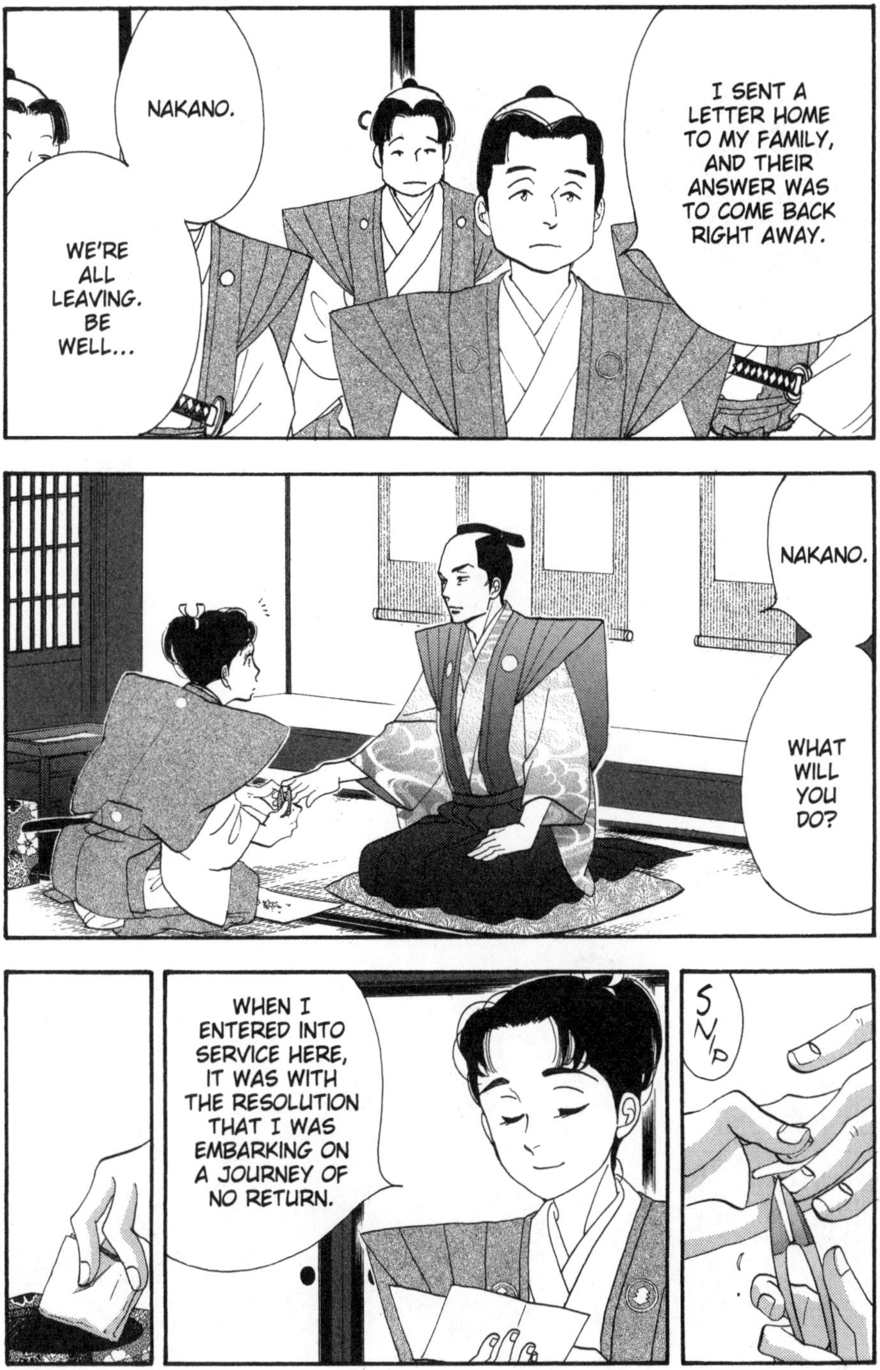

I SENT A LETTER HOME TO MY FAMILY, AND THEIR ANSWER WAS TO COME BACK RIGHT AWAY.
NAKANO.
WE'RE ALL LEAVING. BE WELL...
NAKANO.
WHAT WILL YOU DO?
SNIP
WHEN I ENTERED INTO SERVICE HERE, IT WAS WITH THE RESOLUTION THAT I WAS EMBARKING ON A JOURNEY OF NO RETURN.

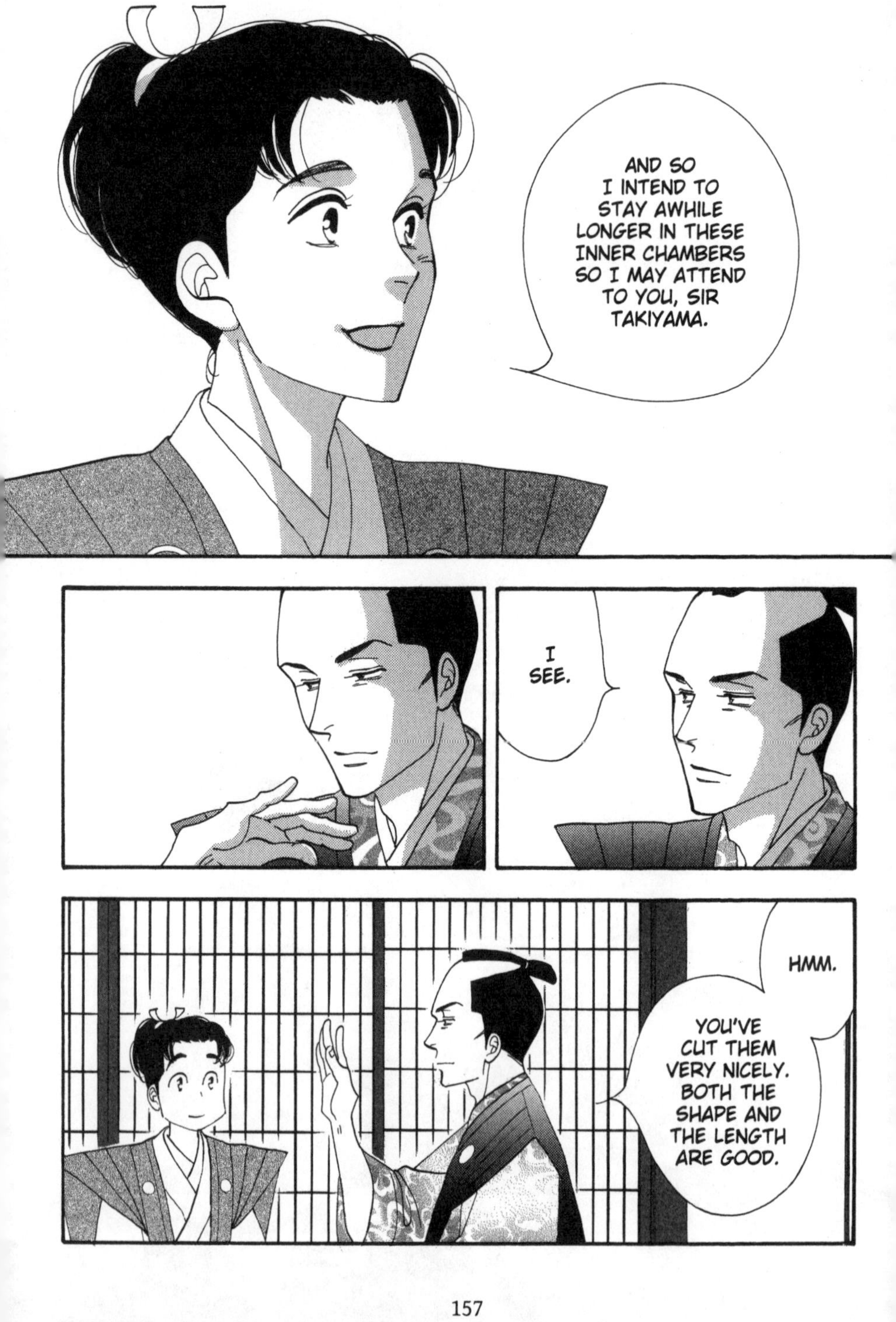
AND SO I INTEND TO STAY AWHILE LONGER IN THESE INNER CHAMBERS SO I MAY ATTEND TO YOU, SIR TAKIYAMA.
I SEE.
HMM.
YOU'VE CUT THEM VERY NICELY. BOTH THE SHAPE AND THE LENGTH ARE GOOD.

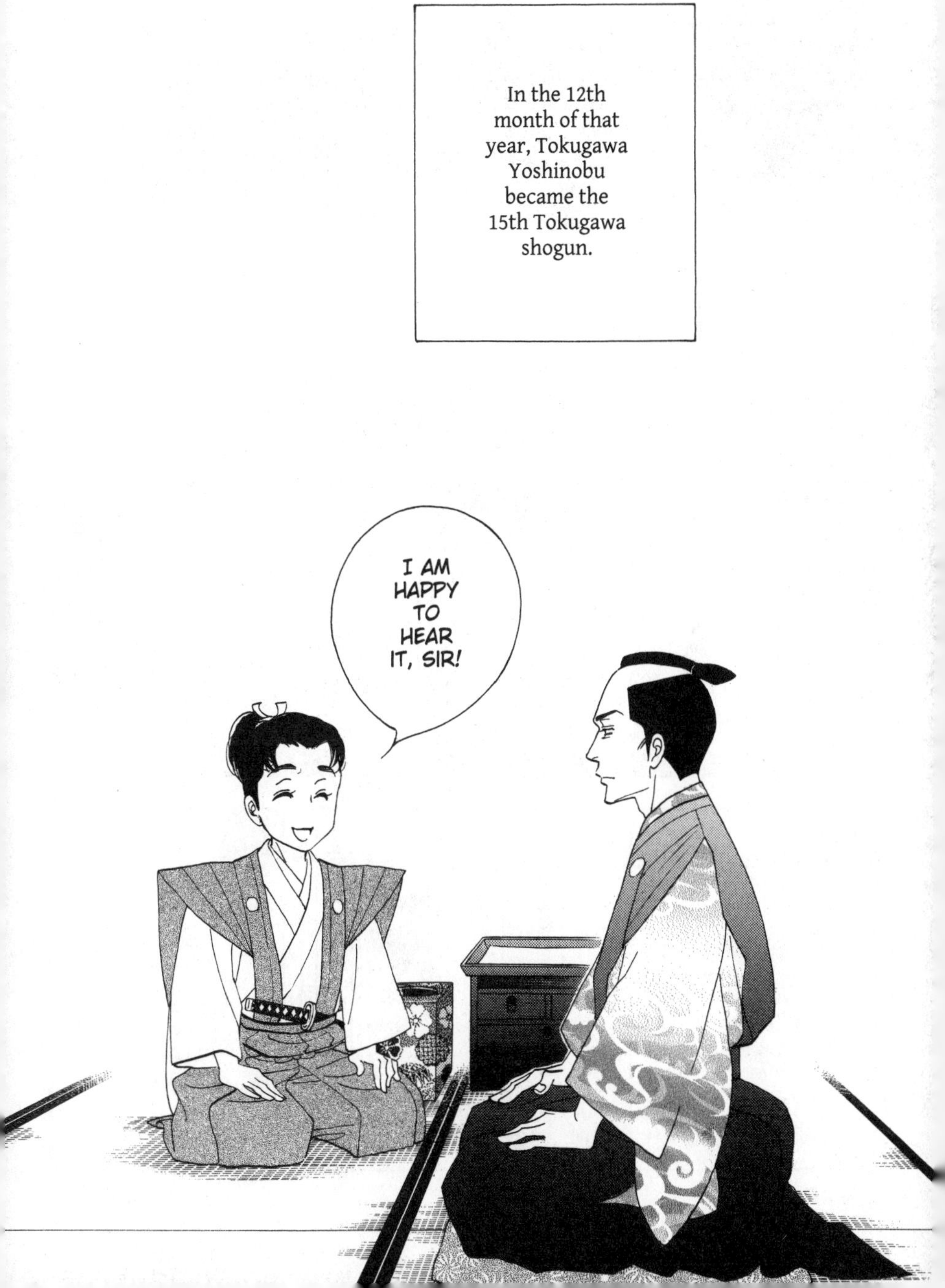
In the 12th month of that year, Tokugawa Yoshinobu became the 15th Tokugawa shogun.
I AM HAPPY TO HEAR IT, SIR!

Ōoku

🏵 THE INNER CHAMBERS

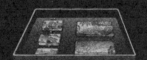

Ōoku

❀ THE INNER CHAMBERS

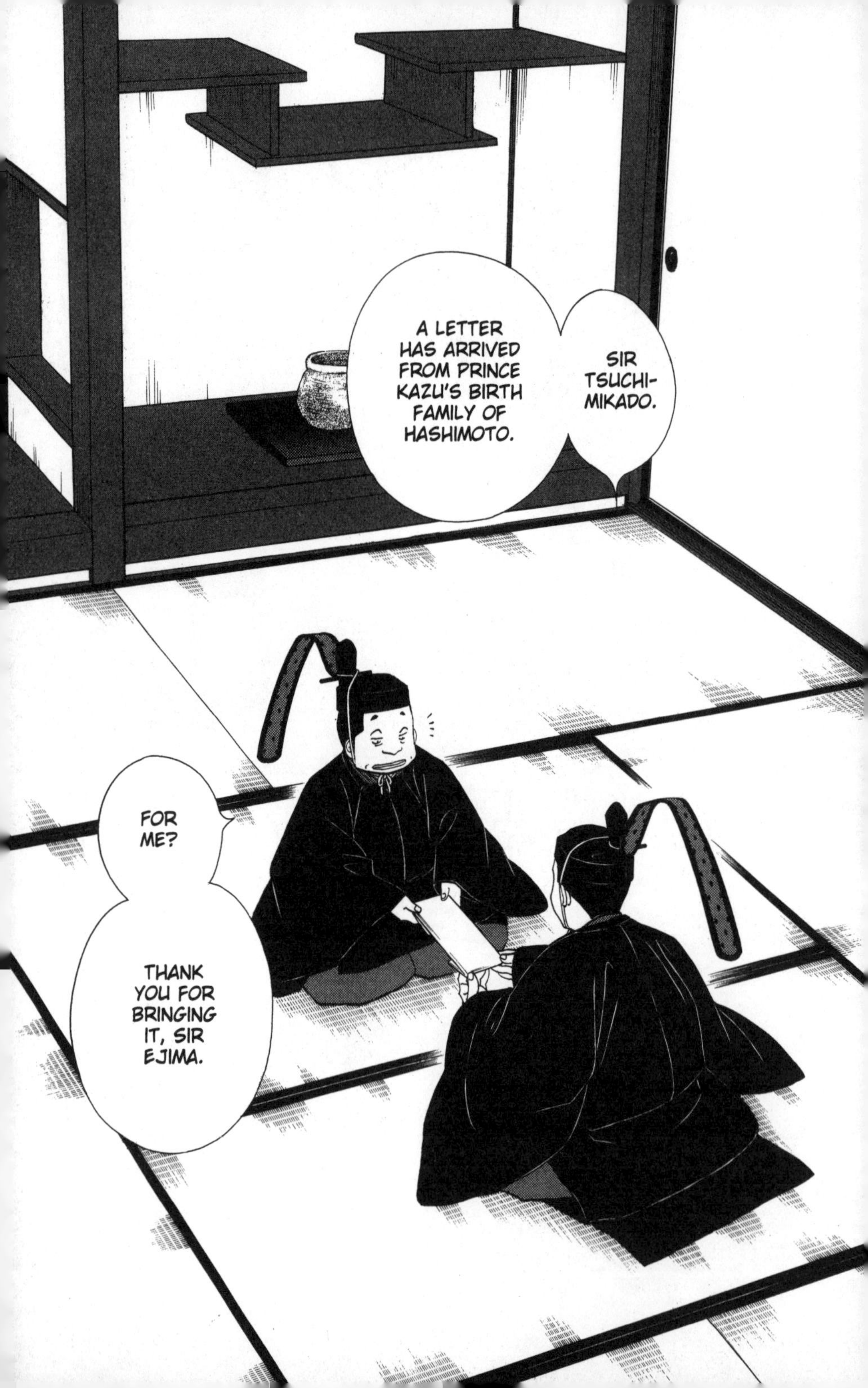
SIR TSUCHI-MIKADO.
A LETTER HAS ARRIVED FROM PRINCE KAZU'S BIRTH FAMILY OF HASHIMOTO.
FOR ME?
THANK YOU FOR BRINGING IT, SIR EJIMA.

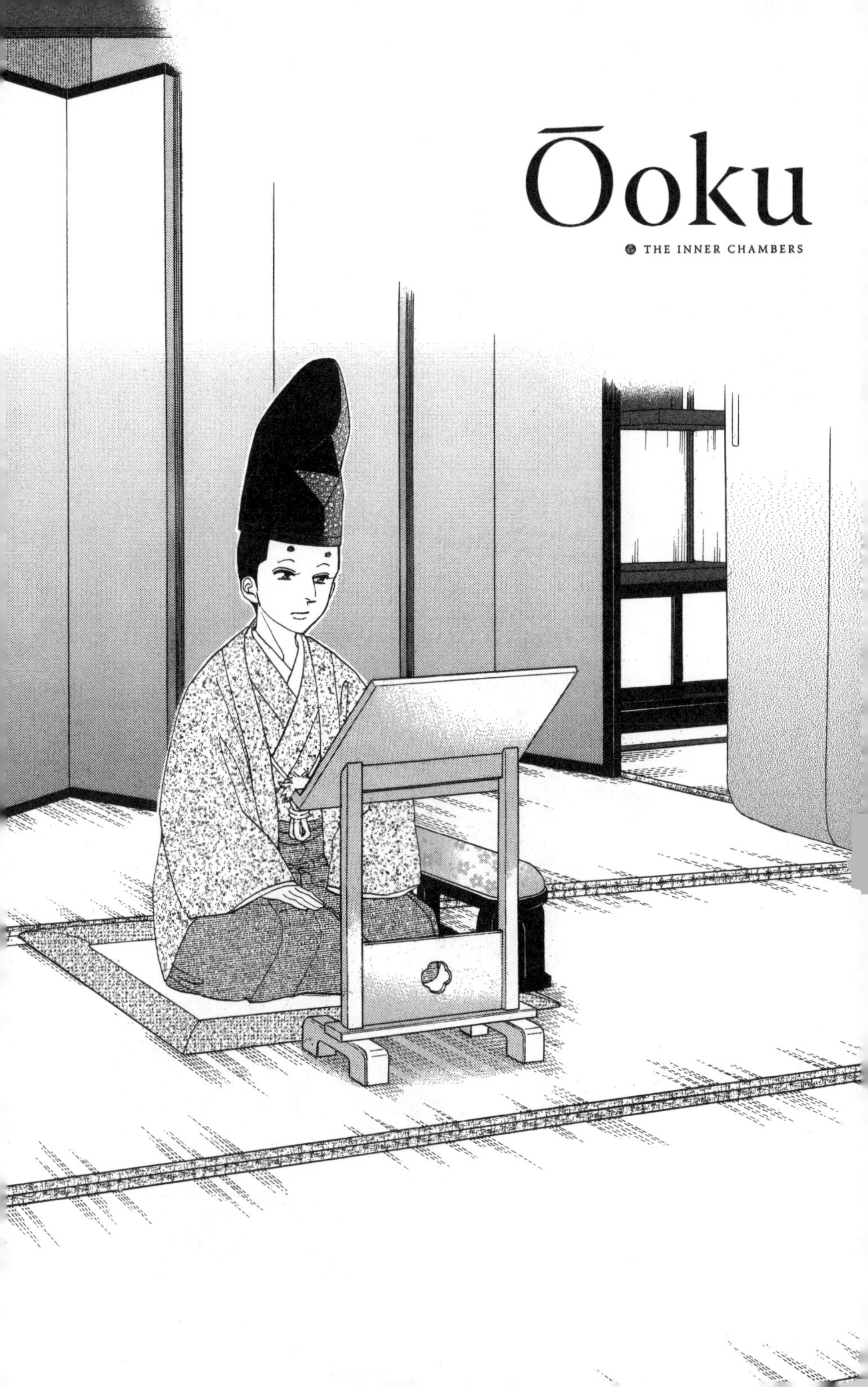
Ōoku
THE INNER CHAMBERS

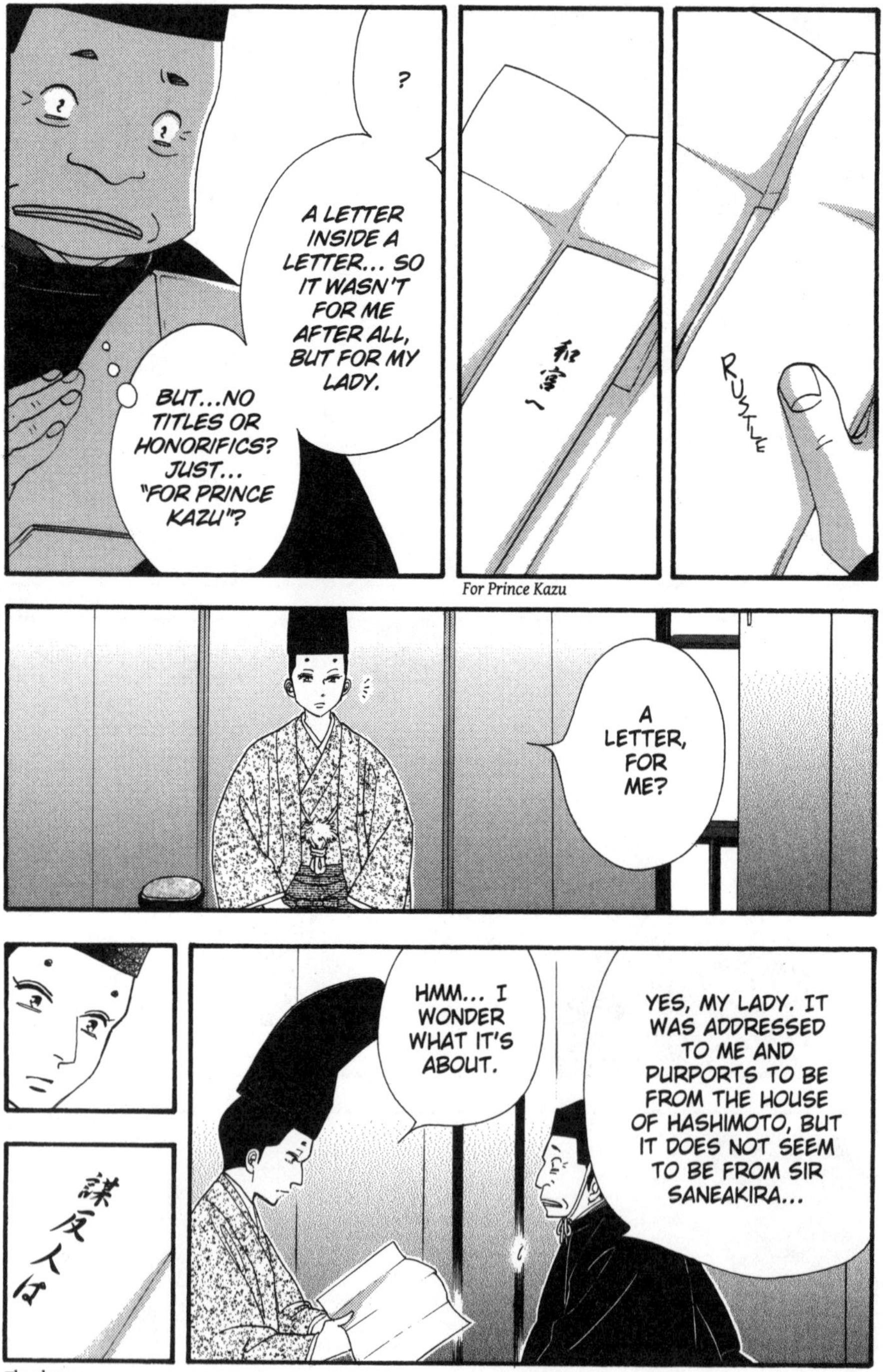
RUSTLE
和宮へ
?
A LETTER INSIDE A LETTER... SO IT WASN'T FOR ME AFTER ALL, BUT FOR MY LADY.
BUT...NO TITLES OR HONORIFICS? JUST... "FOR PRINCE KAZU"?
A LETTER, FOR ME?
YES, MY LADY. IT WAS ADDRESSED TO ME AND PURPORTS TO BE FROM THE HOUSE OF HASHIMOTO, BUT IT DOES NOT SEEM TO BE FROM SIR SANEAKIRA...
HMM... I WONDER WHAT IT'S ABOUT.
謀反人は

For Prince Kazu

The plotters

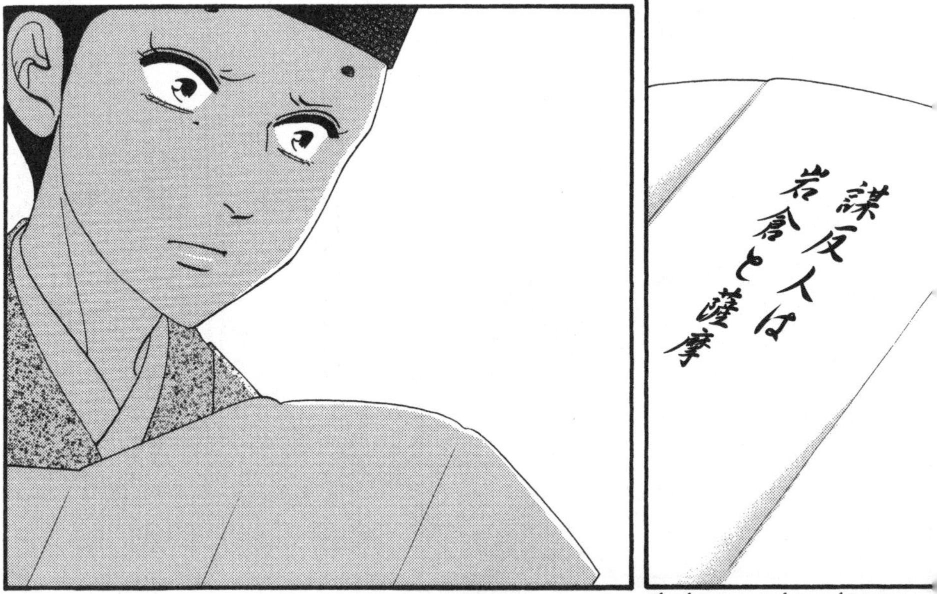
謀反人は
岩倉と薩摩

The plotters are Iwakura and Satsuma

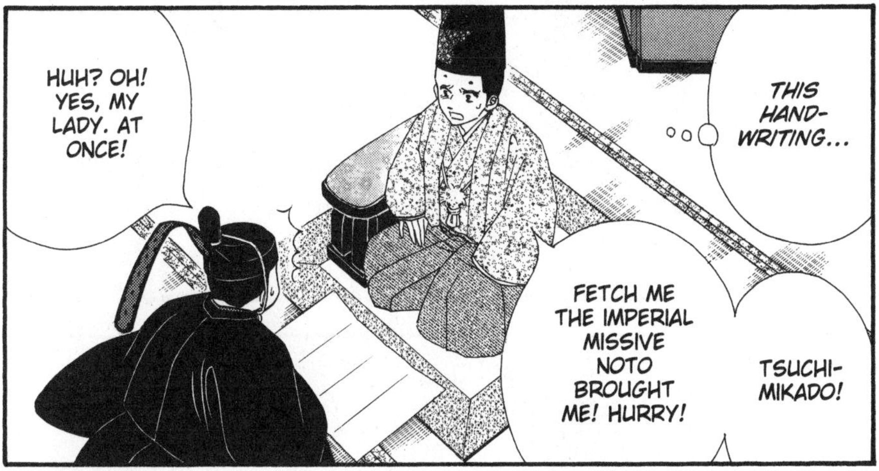
THIS HAND-WRITING...
TSUCHI-MIKADO!
FETCH ME THE IMPERIAL MISSIVE NOTO BROUGHT ME! HURRY!
HUH? OH! YES, MY LADY. AT ONCE!

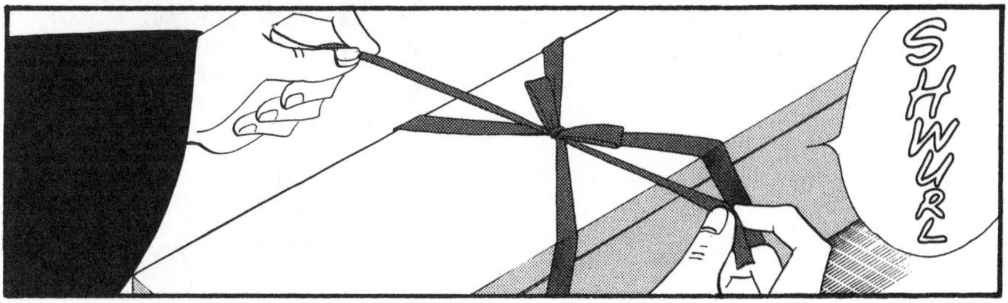
SHWURL

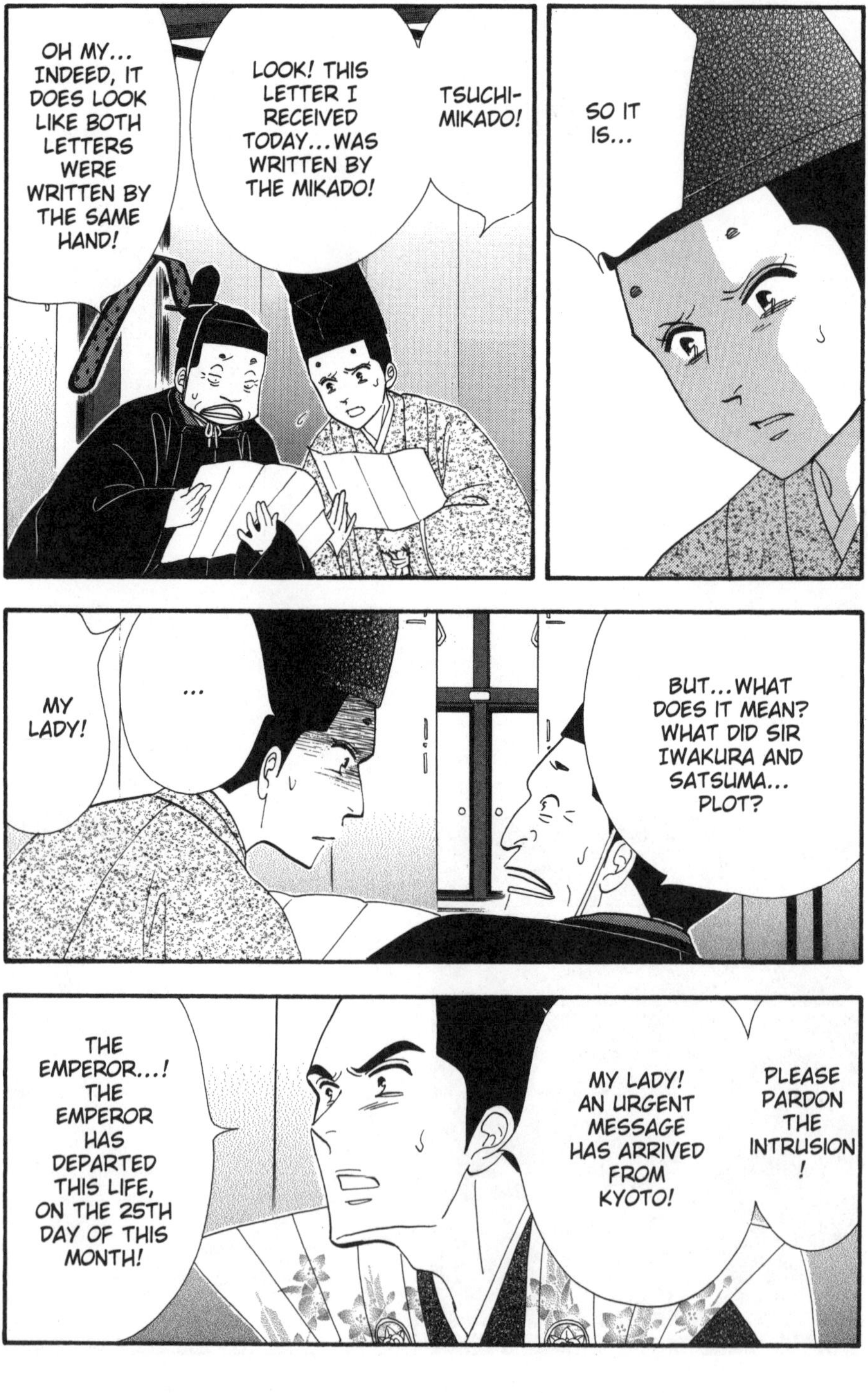
SO IT IS...
TSUCHI-MIKADO!
LOOK! THIS LETTER I RECEIVED TODAY...WAS WRITTEN BY THE MIKADO!
OH MY... INDEED, IT DOES LOOK LIKE BOTH LETTERS WERE WRITTEN BY THE SAME HAND!
BUT...WHAT DOES IT MEAN? WHAT DID SIR IWAKURA AND SATSUMA... PLOT?
...
MY LADY!
PLEASE PARDON THE INTRUSION!
MY LADY! AN URGENT MESSAGE HAS ARRIVED FROM KYOTO!
THE EMPEROR...! THE EMPEROR HAS DEPARTED THIS LIFE, ON THE 25TH DAY OF THIS MONTH!

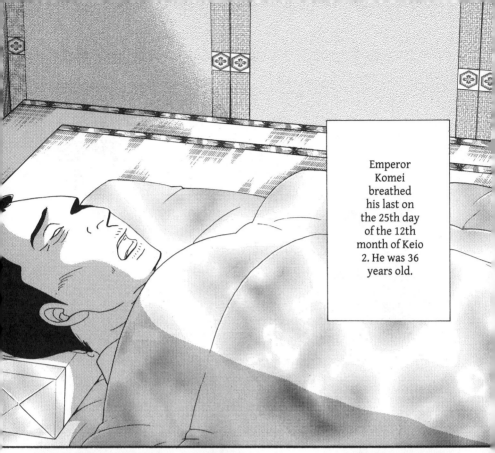

Emperor Komei breathed his last on the 25th day of the 12th month of Keio 2. He was 36 years old.

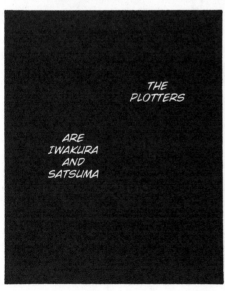

THE PLOTTERS

ARE IWAKURA AND SATSUMA

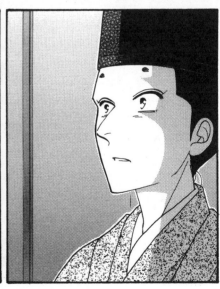

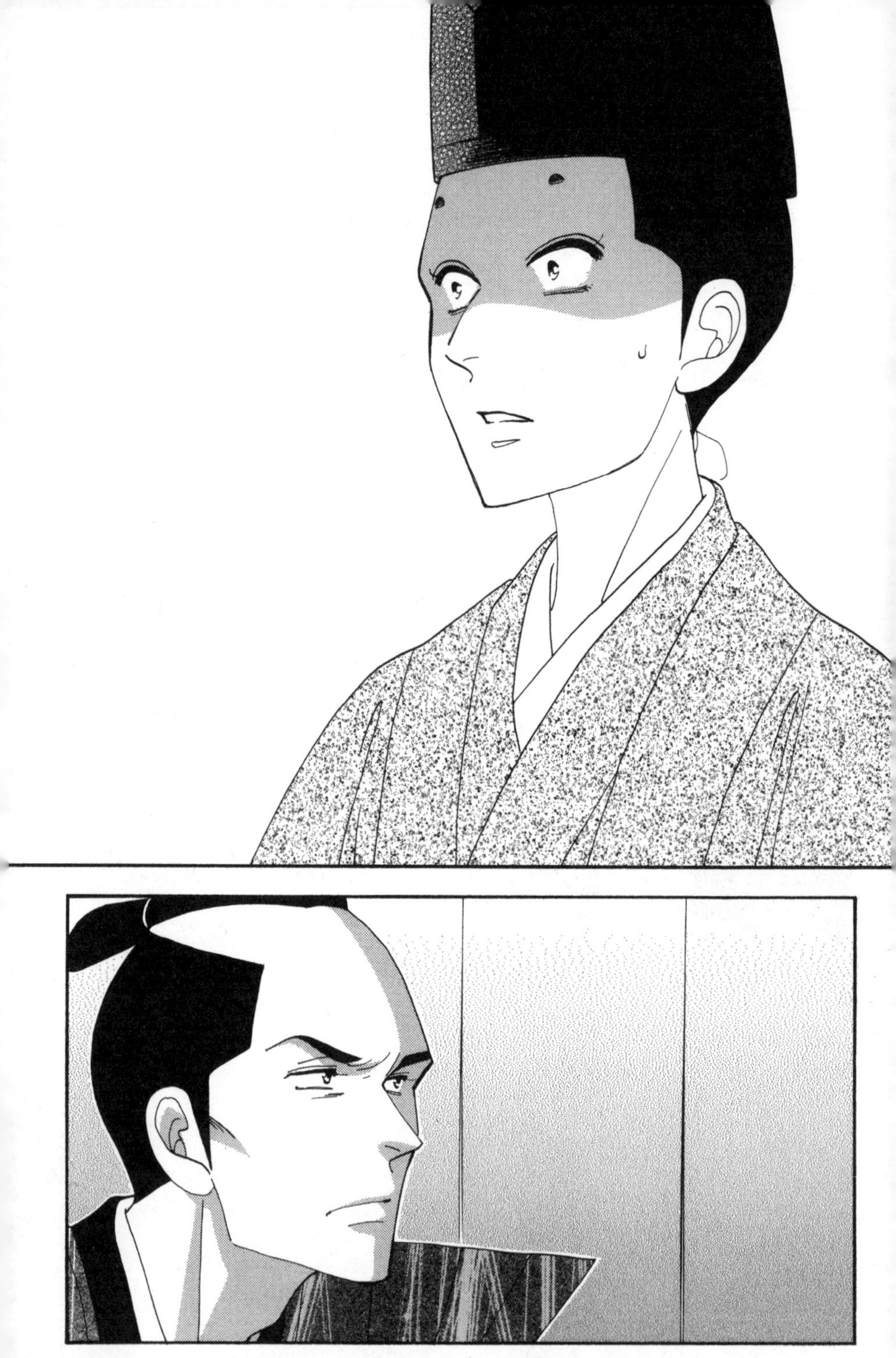

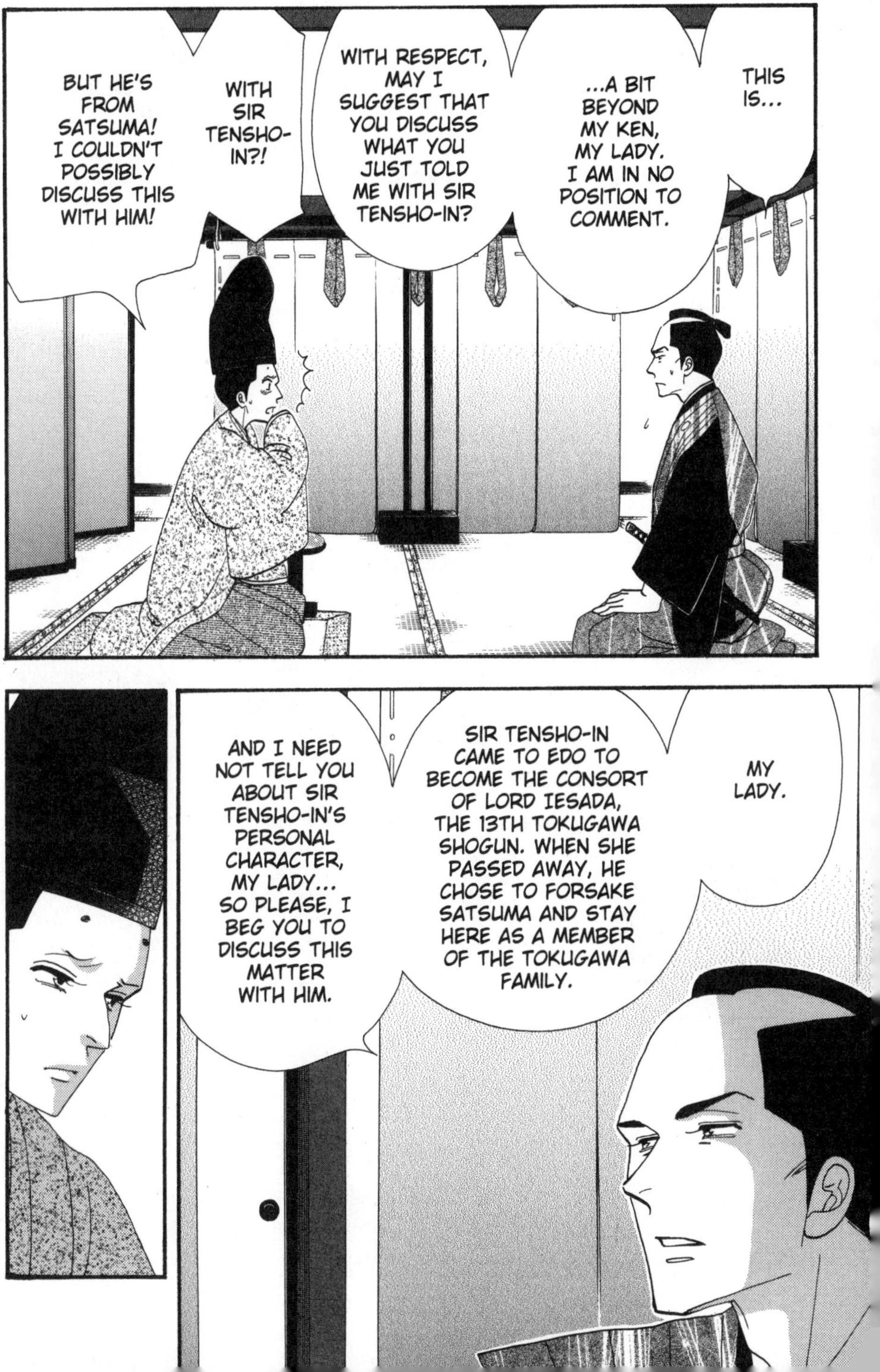
THIS IS...
...A BIT BEYOND MY KEN, MY LADY. I AM IN NO POSITION TO COMMENT.
WITH RESPECT, MAY I SUGGEST THAT YOU DISCUSS WHAT YOU JUST TOLD ME WITH SIR TENSHO-IN?
WITH SIR TENSHO-IN?!
BUT HE'S FROM SATSUMA! I COULDN'T POSSIBLY DISCUSS THIS WITH HIM!
MY LADY.
SIR TENSHO-IN CAME TO EDO TO BECOME THE CONSORT OF LORD IESADA, THE 13TH TOKUGAWA SHOGUN. WHEN SHE PASSED AWAY, HE CHOSE TO FORSAKE SATSUMA AND STAY HERE AS A MEMBER OF THE TOKUGAWA FAMILY.
AND I NEED NOT TELL YOU ABOUT SIR TENSHO-IN'S PERSONAL CHARACTER, MY LADY... SO PLEASE, I BEG YOU TO DISCUSS THIS MATTER WITH HIM.

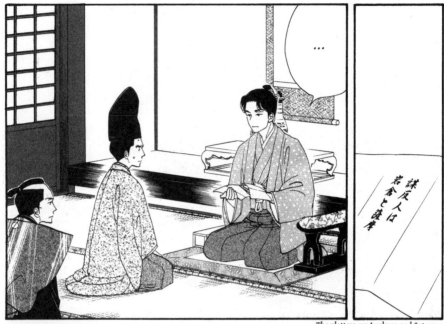

…

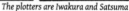

The plotters are Iwakura and Satsuma

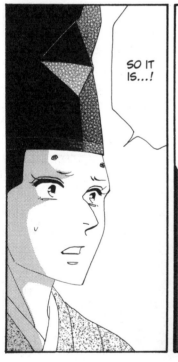

SO IT IS...!

YOUR CONJECTURE, MY PRINCE, IS BY NO MEANS EXTRAORDINARY. INDEED, RUMORS ARE ALREADY SWIRLING THROUGHOUT KYOTO THAT IWAKURA TOMOMI MURDERED THE MIKADO WITH POISON.

I SEE.

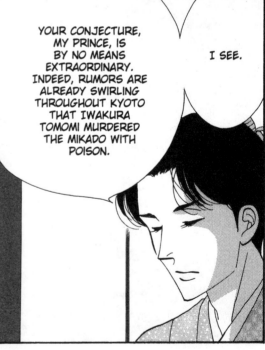

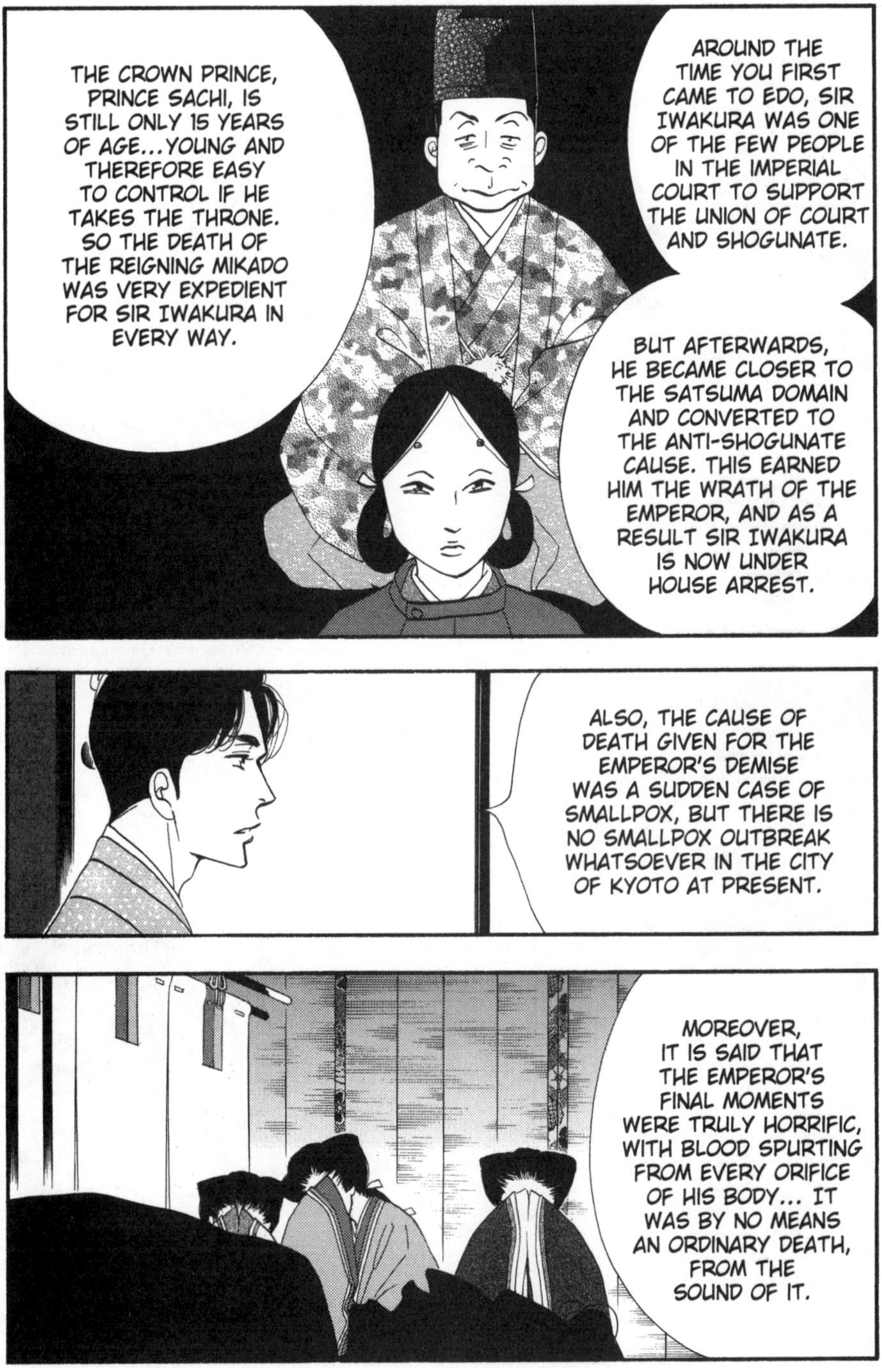
AROUND THE TIME YOU FIRST CAME TO EDO, SIR IWAKURA WAS ONE OF THE FEW PEOPLE IN THE IMPERIAL COURT TO SUPPORT THE UNION OF COURT AND SHOGUNATE.
BUT AFTERWARDS, HE BECAME CLOSER TO THE SATSUMA DOMAIN AND CONVERTED TO THE ANTI-SHOGUNATE CAUSE. THIS EARNED HIM THE WRATH OF THE EMPEROR, AND AS A RESULT SIR IWAKURA IS NOW UNDER HOUSE ARREST.
THE CROWN PRINCE, PRINCE SACHI, IS STILL ONLY 15 YEARS OF AGE...YOUNG AND THEREFORE EASY TO CONTROL IF HE TAKES THE THRONE. SO THE DEATH OF THE REIGNING MIKADO WAS VERY EXPEDIENT FOR SIR IWAKURA IN EVERY WAY.
ALSO, THE CAUSE OF DEATH GIVEN FOR THE EMPEROR'S DEMISE WAS A SUDDEN CASE OF SMALLPOX, BUT THERE IS NO SMALLPOX OUTBREAK WHATSOEVER IN THE CITY OF KYOTO AT PRESENT.
MOREOVER, IT IS SAID THAT THE EMPEROR'S FINAL MOMENTS WERE TRULY HORRIFIC, WITH BLOOD SPURTING FROM EVERY ORIFICE OF HIS BODY... IT WAS BY NO MEANS AN ORDINARY DEATH, FROM THE SOUND OF IT.

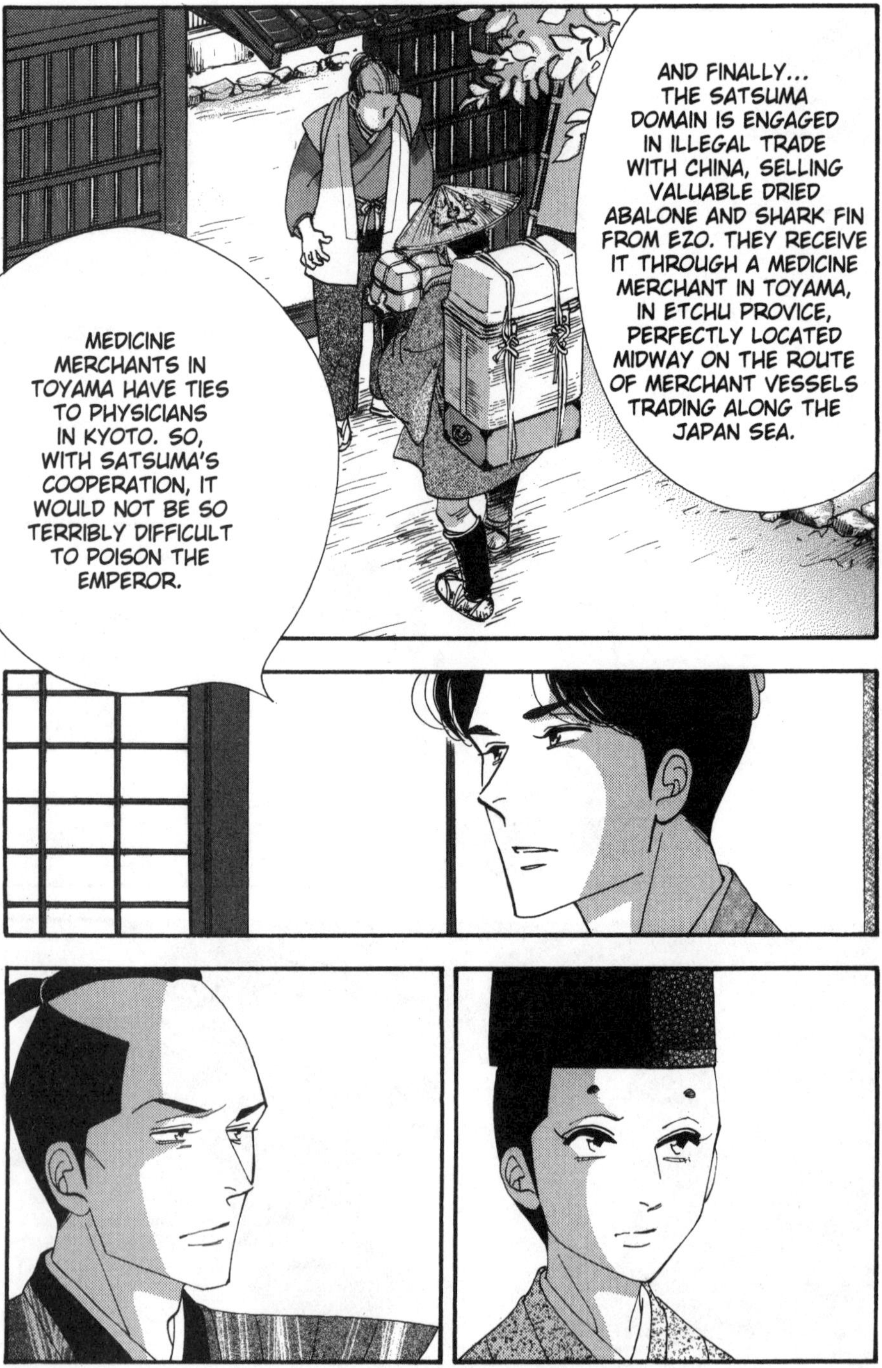
AND FINALLY... THE SATSUMA DOMAIN IS ENGAGED IN ILLEGAL TRADE WITH CHINA, SELLING VALUABLE DRIED ABALONE AND SHARK FIN FROM EZO. THEY RECEIVE IT THROUGH A MEDICINE MERCHANT IN TOYAMA, IN ETCHU PROVICE, PERFECTLY LOCATED MIDWAY ON THE ROUTE OF MERCHANT VESSELS TRADING ALONG THE JAPAN SEA.
MEDICINE MERCHANTS IN TOYAMA HAVE TIES TO PHYSICIANS IN KYOTO. SO, WITH SATSUMA'S COOPERATION, IT WOULD NOT BE SO TERRIBLY DIFFICULT TO POISON THE EMPEROR.

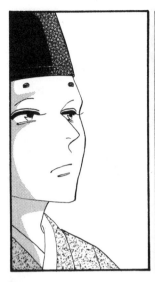

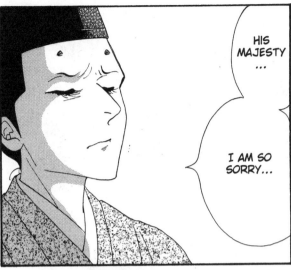

HIS MAJESTY...

I AM SO SORRY...

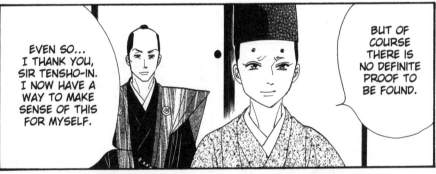

EVEN SO... I THANK YOU, SIR TENSHO-IN. I NOW HAVE A WAY TO MAKE SENSE OF THIS FOR MYSELF.

BUT OF COURSE THERE IS NO DEFINITE PROOF TO BE FOUND.

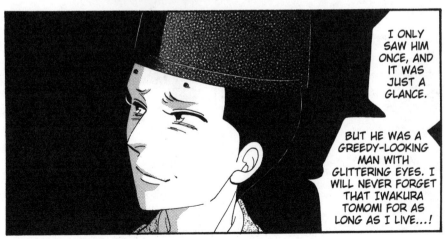

I ONLY SAW HIM ONCE, AND IT WAS JUST A GLANCE.

BUT HE WAS A GREEDY-LOOKING MAN WITH GLITTERING EYES. I WILL NEVER FORGET THAT IWAKURA TOMOMI FOR AS LONG AS I LIVE...!

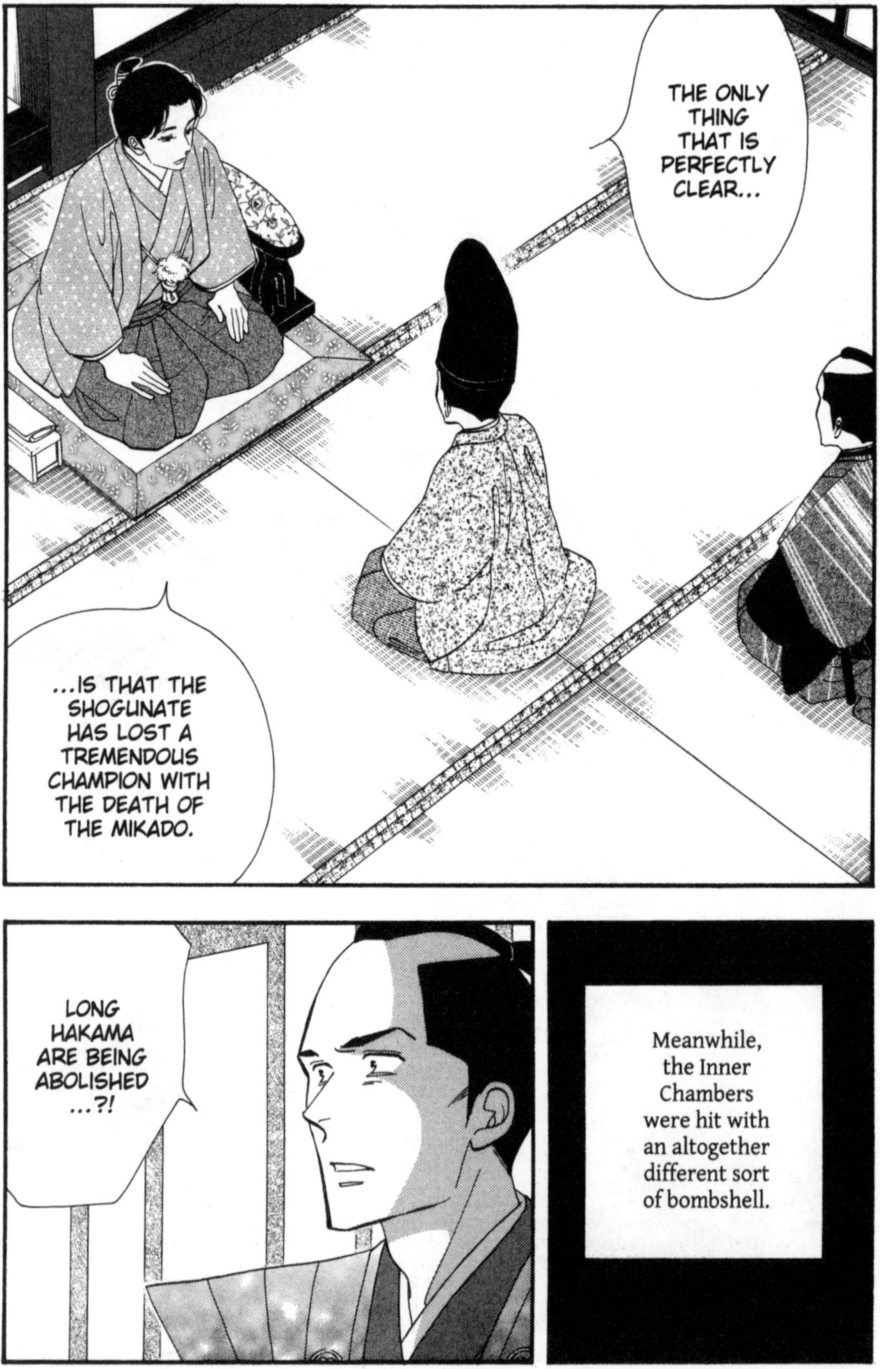
THE ONLY THING THAT IS PERFECTLY CLEAR...
...IS THAT THE SHOGUNATE HAS LOST A TREMENDOUS CHAMPION WITH THE DEATH OF THE MIKADO.
Meanwhile, the Inner Chambers were hit with an altogether different sort of bombshell.
LONG HAKAMA ARE BEING ABOLISHED ...?!

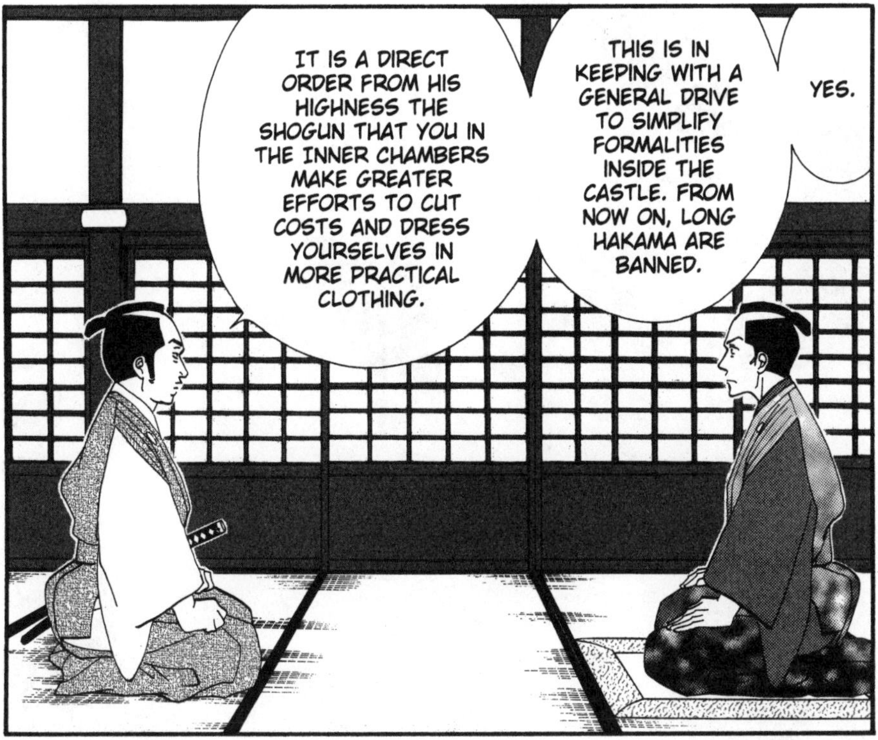
YES.
THIS IS IN KEEPING WITH A GENERAL DRIVE TO SIMPLIFY FORMALITIES INSIDE THE CASTLE. FROM NOW ON, LONG HAKAMA ARE BANNED.
IT IS A DIRECT ORDER FROM HIS HIGHNESS THE SHOGUN THAT YOU IN THE INNER CHAMBERS MAKE GREATER EFFORTS TO CUT COSTS AND DRESS YOURSELVES IN MORE PRACTICAL CLOTHING.
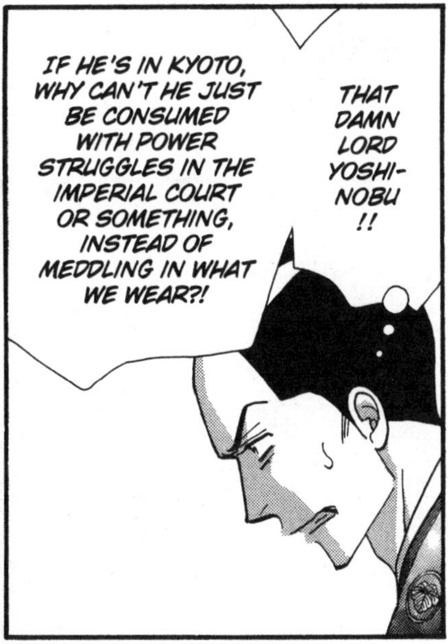
THAT DAMN LORD YOSHI-NOBU!!
IF HE'S IN KYOTO, WHY CAN'T HE JUST BE CONSUMED WITH POWER STRUGGLES IN THE IMPERIAL COURT OR SOMETHING, INSTEAD OF MEDDLING IN WHAT WE WEAR?!
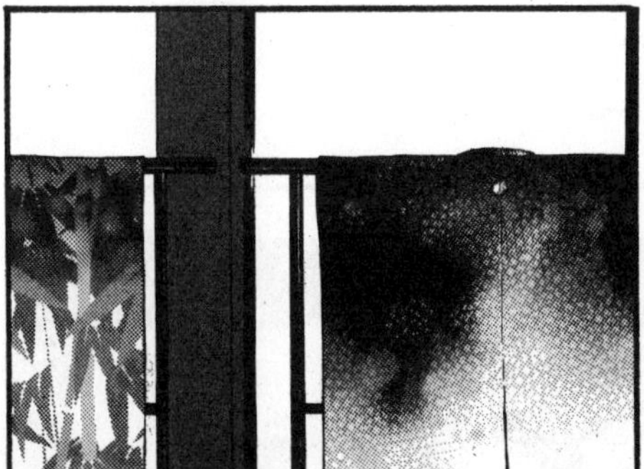

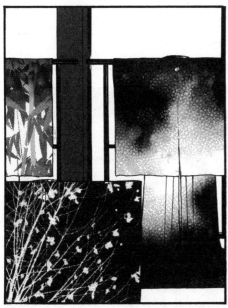

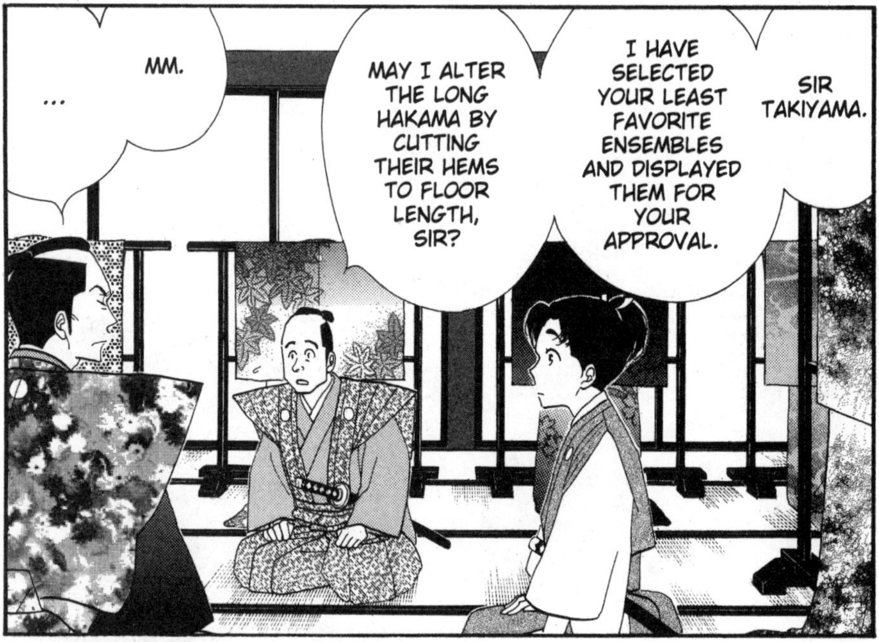
SIR TAKIYAMA.
I HAVE SELECTED YOUR LEAST FAVORITE ENSEMBLES AND DISPLAYED THEM FOR YOUR APPROVAL.
MAY I ALTER THE LONG HAKAMA BY CUTTING THEIR HEMS TO FLOOR LENGTH, SIR?
MM.
...

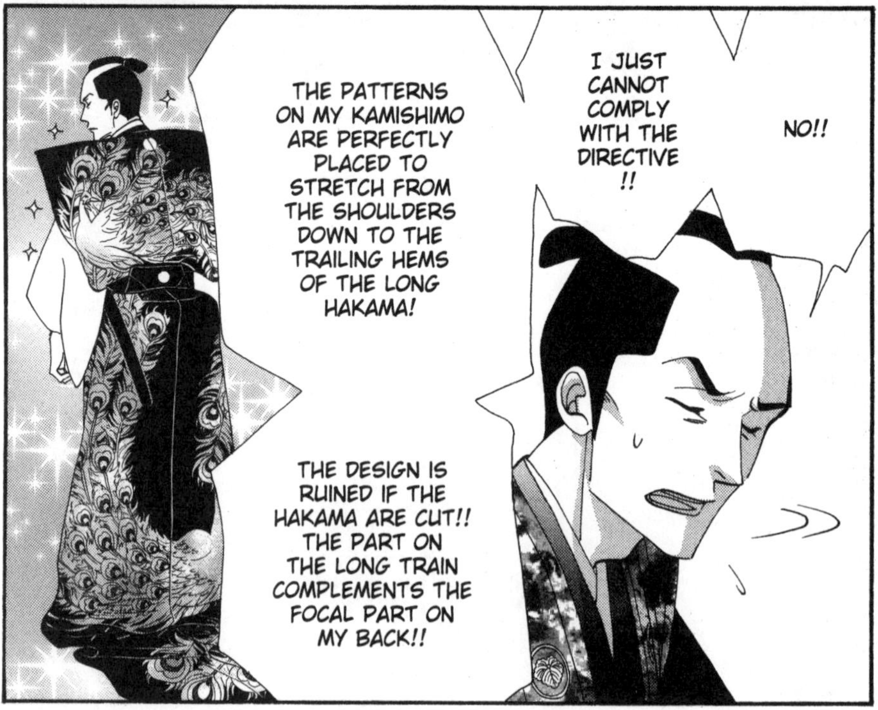
NO!!
I JUST CANNOT COMPLY WITH THE DIRECTIVE!!
THE PATTERNS ON MY KAMISHIMO ARE PERFECTLY PLACED TO STRETCH FROM THE SHOULDERS DOWN TO THE TRAILING HEMS OF THE LONG HAKAMA!
THE DESIGN IS RUINED IF THE HAKAMA ARE CUT!! THE PART ON THE LONG TRAIN COMPLEMENTS THE FOCAL PART ON MY BACK!!

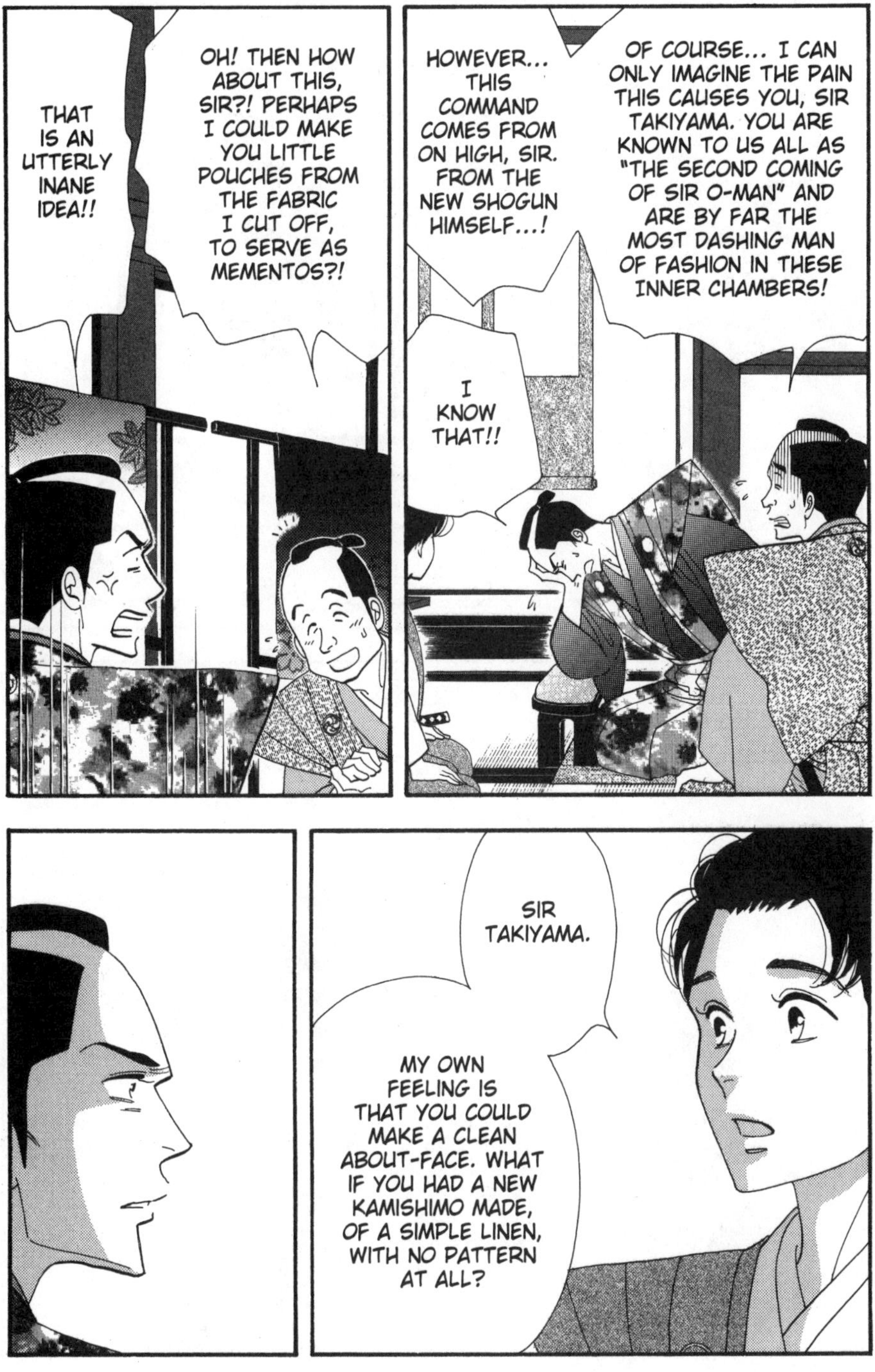
OF COURSE... I CAN ONLY IMAGINE THE PAIN THIS CAUSES YOU, SIR TAKIYAMA. YOU ARE KNOWN TO US ALL AS "THE SECOND COMING OF SIR O-MAN" AND ARE BY FAR THE MOST DASHING MAN OF FASHION IN THESE INNER CHAMBERS!
HOWEVER... THIS COMMAND COMES FROM ON HIGH, SIR. FROM THE NEW SHOGUN HIMSELF...!
I KNOW THAT!!
OH! THEN HOW ABOUT THIS, SIR?! PERHAPS I COULD MAKE YOU LITTLE POUCHES FROM THE FABRIC I CUT OFF, TO SERVE AS MEMENTOS?!
THAT IS AN UTTERLY INANE IDEA!!
SIR TAKIYAMA.
MY OWN FEELING IS THAT YOU COULD MAKE A CLEAN ABOUT-FACE. WHAT IF YOU HAD A NEW KAMISHIMO MADE, OF A SIMPLE LINEN, WITH NO PATTERN AT ALL?

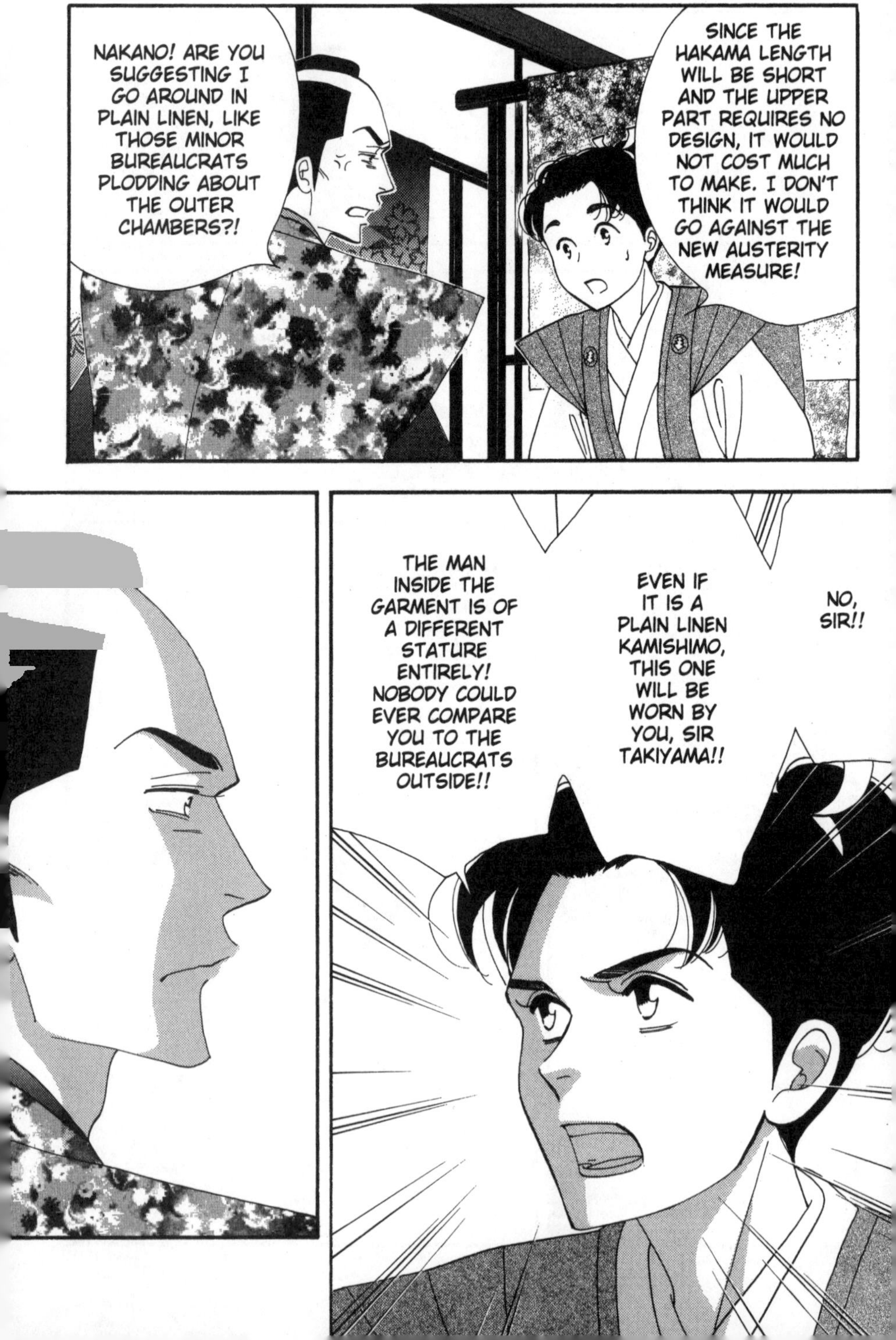
SINCE THE HAKAMA LENGTH WILL BE SHORT AND THE UPPER PART REQUIRES NO DESIGN, IT WOULD NOT COST MUCH TO MAKE. I DON'T THINK IT WOULD GO AGAINST THE NEW AUSTERITY MEASURE!
NAKANO! ARE YOU SUGGESTING I GO AROUND IN PLAIN LINEN, LIKE THOSE MINOR BUREAUCRATS PLODDING ABOUT THE OUTER CHAMBERS?!
NO, SIR!!
EVEN IF IT IS A PLAIN LINEN KAMISHIMO, THIS ONE WILL BE WORN BY YOU, SIR TAKIYAMA!!
THE MAN INSIDE THE GARMENT IS OF A DIFFERENT STATURE ENTIRELY! NOBODY COULD EVER COMPARE YOU TO THE BUREAUCRATS OUTSIDE!!

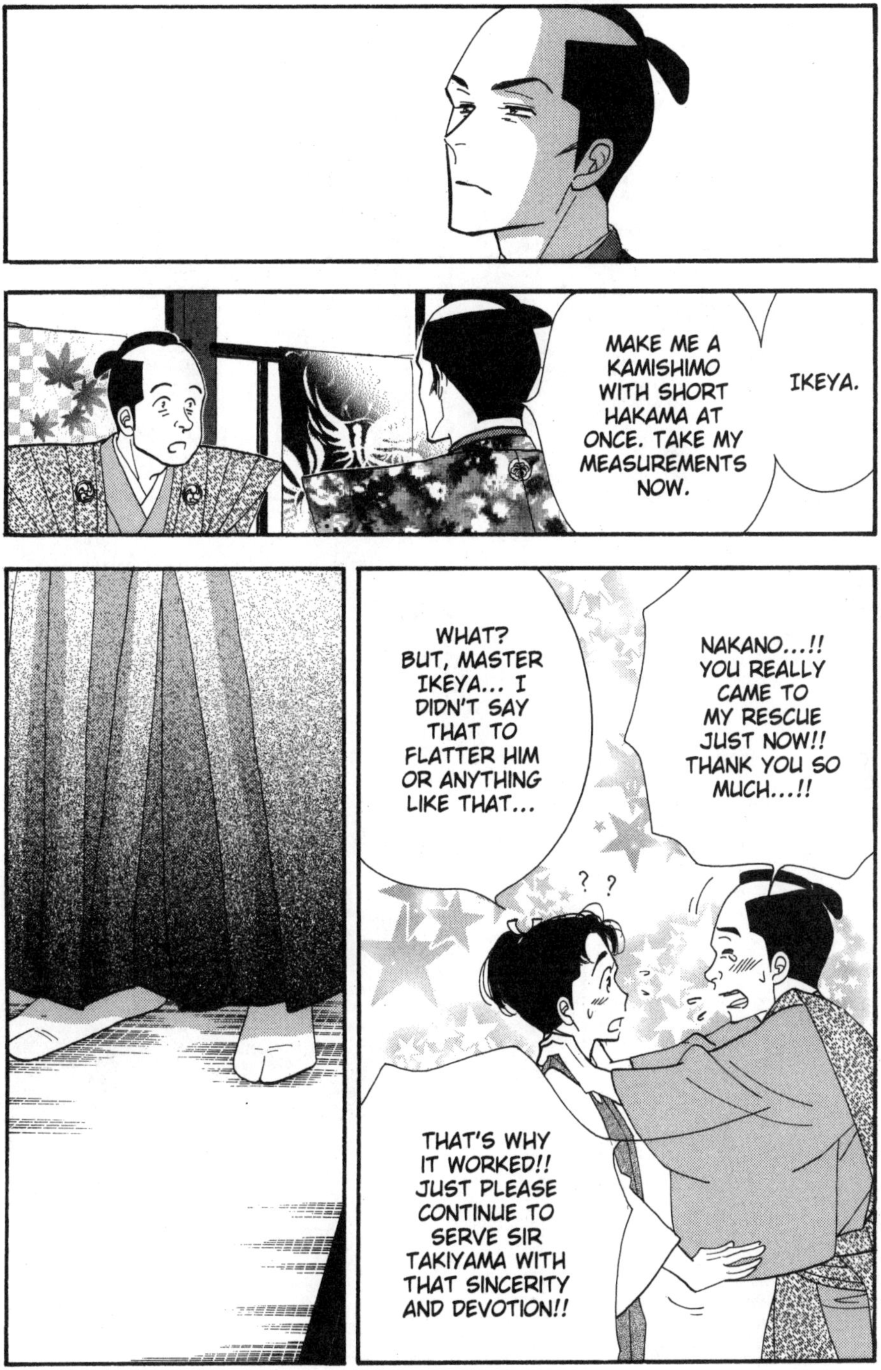
IKEYA.
MAKE ME A KAMISHIMO WITH SHORT HAKAMA AT ONCE. TAKE MY MEASUREMENTS NOW.
NAKANO...!! YOU REALLY CAME TO MY RESCUE JUST NOW!! THANK YOU SO MUCH...!!
WHAT? BUT, MASTER IKEYA... I DIDN'T SAY THAT TO FLATTER HIM OR ANYTHING LIKE THAT...
? ?
THAT'S WHY IT WORKED!! JUST PLEASE CONTINUE TO SERVE SIR TAKIYAMA WITH THAT SINCERITY AND DEVOTION!!

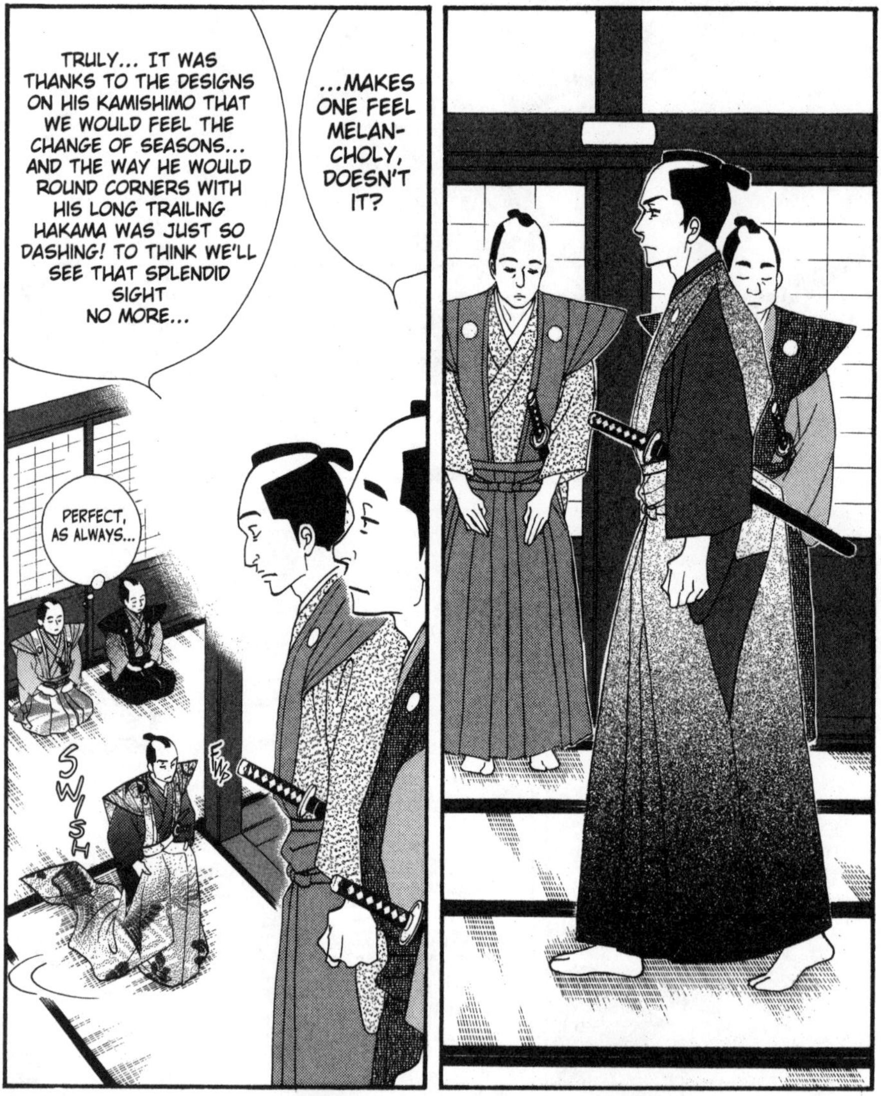
...MAKES ONE FEEL MELANCHOLY, DOESN'T IT?
TRULY... IT WAS THANKS TO THE DESIGNS ON HIS KAMISHIMO THAT WE WOULD FEEL THE CHANGE OF SEASONS... AND THE WAY HE WOULD ROUND CORNERS WITH HIS LONG TRAILING HAKAMA WAS JUST SO DASHING! TO THINK WE'LL SEE THAT SPLENDID SIGHT NO MORE...
FWP
PERFECT, AS ALWAYS...
SWISH
I HAPPENED TO HEAR THAT THE NEW PAGE YOU HAVE SERVING YOU MEETS WITH YOUR FAVOR, SIR. THAT'S QUITE UNUSUAL!

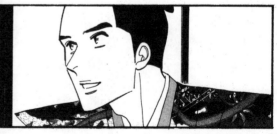

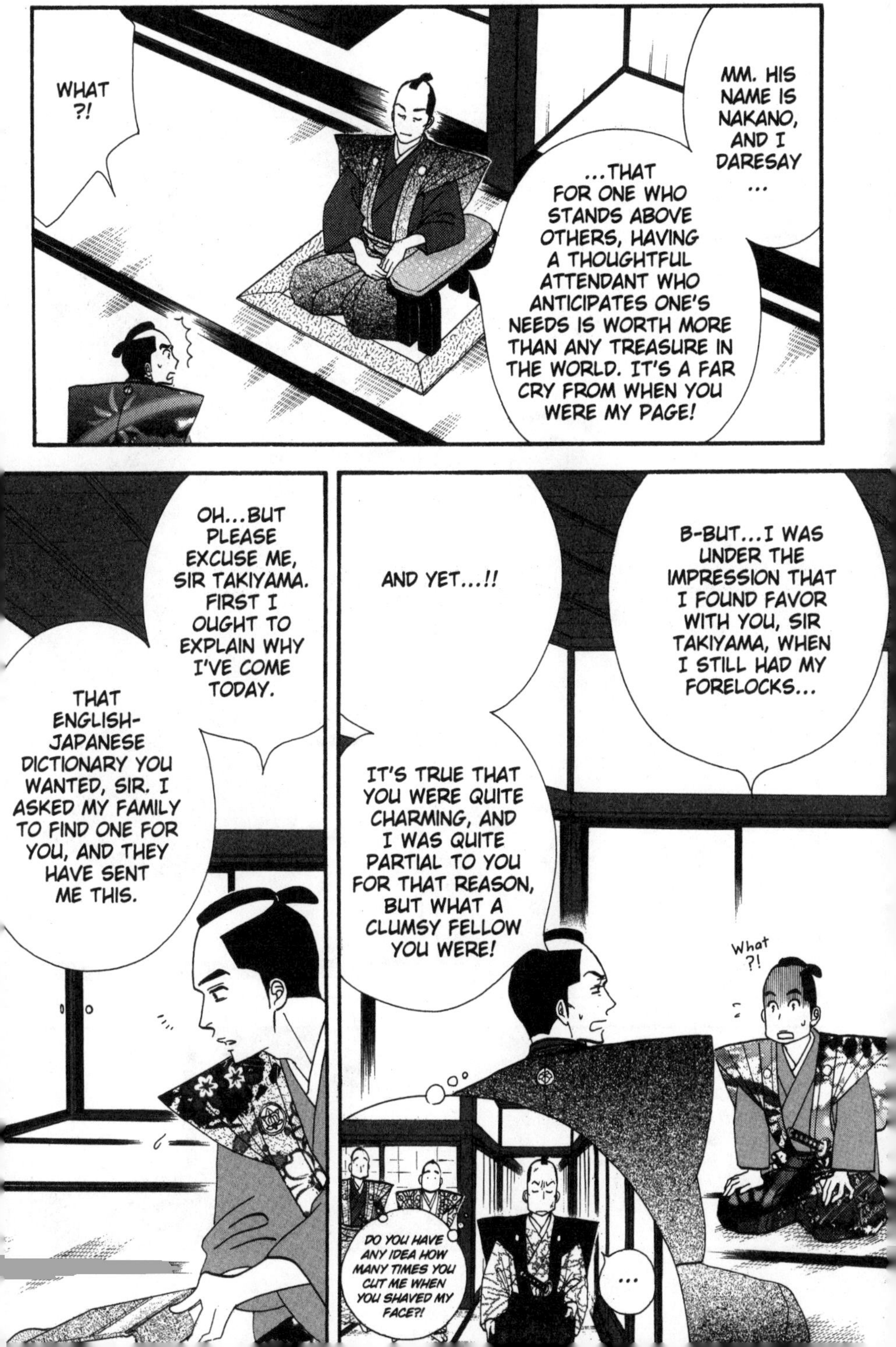
MM. HIS NAME IS NAKANO, AND I DARESAY ...
...THAT FOR ONE WHO STANDS ABOVE OTHERS, HAVING A THOUGHTFUL ATTENDANT WHO ANTICIPATES ONE'S NEEDS IS WORTH MORE THAN ANY TREASURE IN THE WORLD. IT'S A FAR CRY FROM WHEN YOU WERE MY PAGE!
WHAT ?!
B-BUT...I WAS UNDER THE IMPRESSION THAT I FOUND FAVOR WITH YOU, SIR TAKIYAMA, WHEN I STILL HAD MY FORELOCKS...
AND YET...!!
IT'S TRUE THAT YOU WERE QUITE CHARMING, AND I WAS QUITE PARTIAL TO YOU FOR THAT REASON, BUT WHAT A CLUMSY FELLOW YOU WERE!
What ?!
DO YOU HAVE ANY IDEA HOW MANY TIMES YOU CUT ME WHEN YOU SHAVED MY FACE?!
...
OH...BUT PLEASE EXCUSE ME, SIR TAKIYAMA. FIRST I OUGHT TO EXPLAIN WHY I'VE COME TODAY.
THAT ENGLISH-JAPANESE DICTIONARY YOU WANTED, SIR. I ASKED MY FAMILY TO FIND ONE FOR YOU, AND THEY HAVE SENT ME THIS.

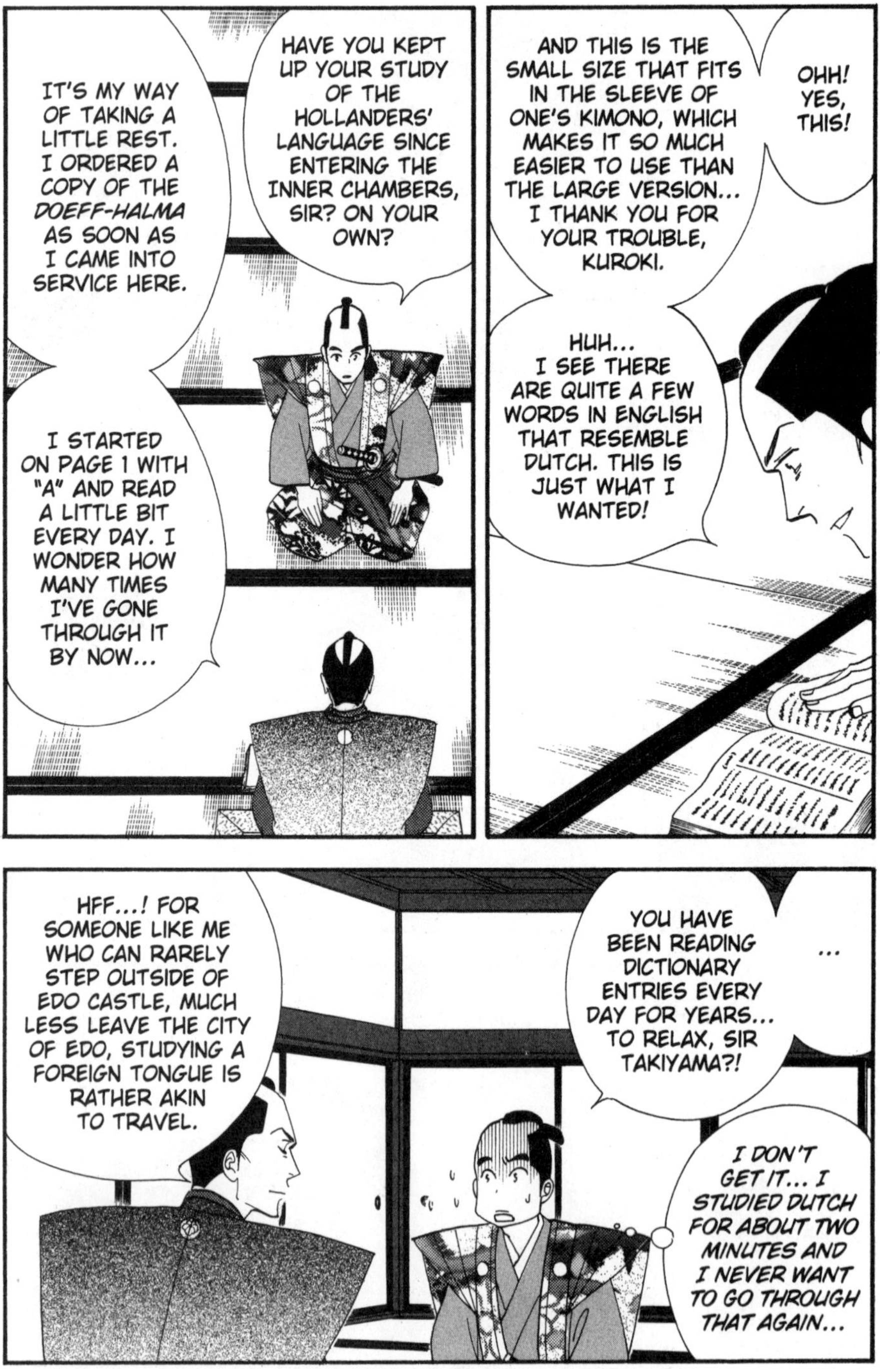
OHH! YES, THIS!
AND THIS IS THE SMALL SIZE THAT FITS IN THE SLEEVE OF ONE'S KIMONO, WHICH MAKES IT SO MUCH EASIER TO USE THAN THE LARGE VERSION... I THANK YOU FOR YOUR TROUBLE, KUROKI.
HUH... I SEE THERE ARE QUITE A FEW WORDS IN ENGLISH THAT RESEMBLE DUTCH. THIS IS JUST WHAT I WANTED!
HAVE YOU KEPT UP YOUR STUDY OF THE HOLLANDERS' LANGUAGE SINCE ENTERING THE INNER CHAMBERS, SIR? ON YOUR OWN?
IT'S MY WAY OF TAKING A LITTLE REST. I ORDERED A COPY OF THE *DOEFF-HALMA* AS SOON AS I CAME INTO SERVICE HERE.
I STARTED ON PAGE 1 WITH "A" AND READ A LITTLE BIT EVERY DAY. I WONDER HOW MANY TIMES I'VE GONE THROUGH IT BY NOW...
...
YOU HAVE BEEN READING DICTIONARY ENTRIES EVERY DAY FOR YEARS... TO RELAX, SIR TAKIYAMA?!
HFF...! FOR SOMEONE LIKE ME WHO CAN RARELY STEP OUTSIDE OF EDO CASTLE, MUCH LESS LEAVE THE CITY OF EDO, STUDYING A FOREIGN TONGUE IS RATHER AKIN TO TRAVEL.
I DON'T GET IT... I STUDIED DUTCH FOR ABOUT TWO MINUTES AND I NEVER WANT TO GO THROUGH THAT AGAIN...

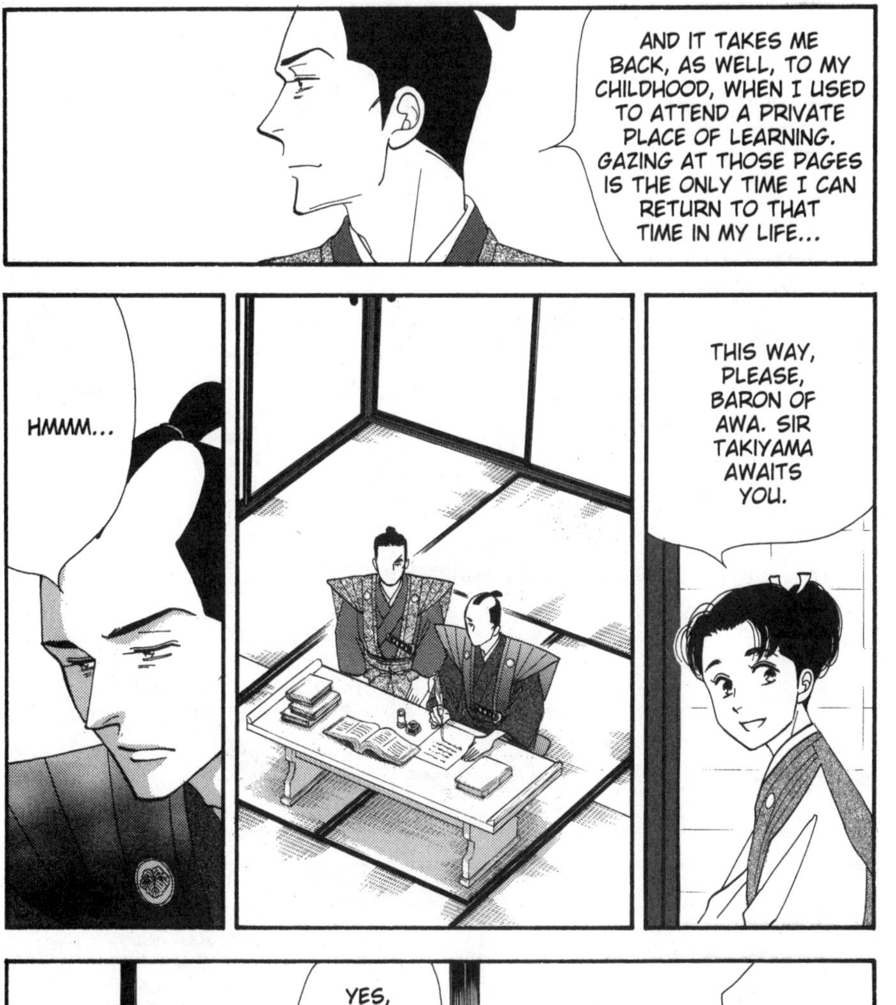
AND IT TAKES ME BACK, AS WELL, TO MY CHILDHOOD, WHEN I USED TO ATTEND A PRIVATE PLACE OF LEARNING. GAZING AT THOSE PAGES IS THE ONLY TIME I CAN RETURN TO THAT TIME IN MY LIFE...
THIS WAY, PLEASE, BARON OF AWA. SIR TAKIYAMA AWAITS YOU.
HMMM...
KATSU!!
HOW IS IT THAT THIS LANGUAGE CALLED ENGLISH IS SO CLEAR AND EASY TO UNDERSTAND?! THERE ARE NO SPLIT VERBS LIKE IN DUTCH, IS THAT CORRECT?!
YES, SIR. THAT'S RIGHT.
AND THE NOUNS ARE NEITHER MALE NOR FEMALE, SO THE DEFINITE ARTICLE IS ALWAYS "THE," FOR EVERYTHING!

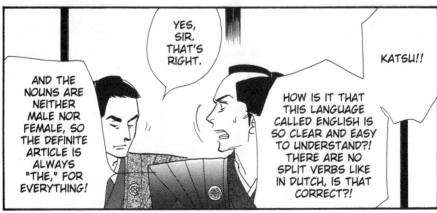

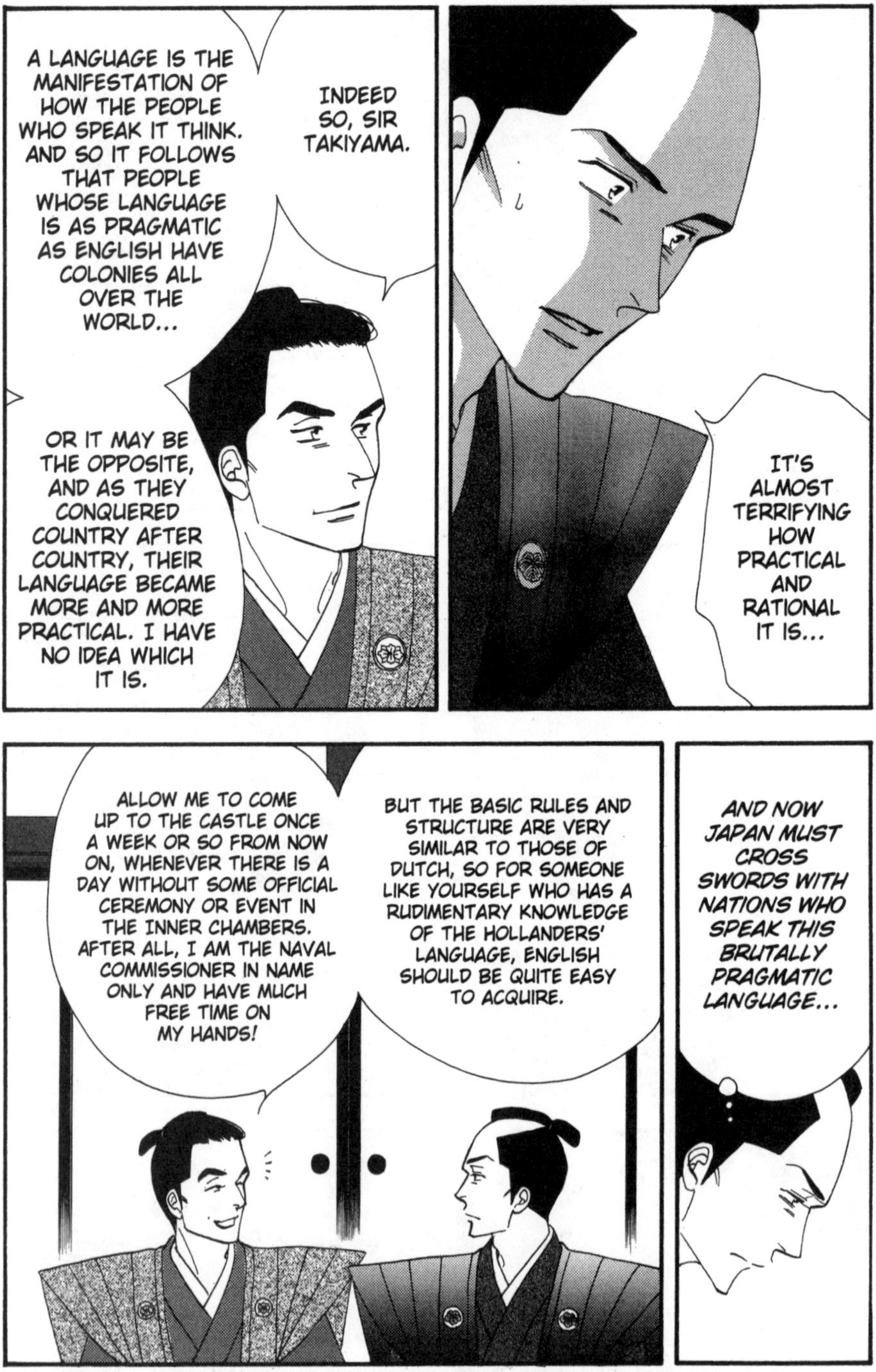
IT'S ALMOST TERRIFYING HOW PRACTICAL AND RATIONAL IT IS...
INDEED SO, SIR TAKIYAMA.
A LANGUAGE IS THE MANIFESTATION OF HOW THE PEOPLE WHO SPEAK IT THINK. AND SO IT FOLLOWS THAT PEOPLE WHOSE LANGUAGE IS AS PRAGMATIC AS ENGLISH HAVE COLONIES ALL OVER THE WORLD...
OR IT MAY BE THE OPPOSITE, AND AS THEY CONQUERED COUNTRY AFTER COUNTRY, THEIR LANGUAGE BECAME MORE AND MORE PRACTICAL. I HAVE NO IDEA WHICH IT IS.
AND NOW JAPAN MUST CROSS SWORDS WITH NATIONS WHO SPEAK THIS BRUTALLY PRAGMATIC LANGUAGE...
BUT THE BASIC RULES AND STRUCTURE ARE VERY SIMILAR TO THOSE OF DUTCH, SO FOR SOMEONE LIKE YOURSELF WHO HAS A RUDIMENTARY KNOWLEDGE OF THE HOLLANDERS' LANGUAGE, ENGLISH SHOULD BE QUITE EASY TO ACQUIRE.
ALLOW ME TO COME UP TO THE CASTLE ONCE A WEEK OR SO FROM NOW ON, WHENEVER THERE IS A DAY WITHOUT SOME OFFICIAL CEREMONY OR EVENT IN THE INNER CHAMBERS. AFTER ALL, I AM THE NAVAL COMMISSIONER IN NAME ONLY AND HAVE MUCH FREE TIME ON MY HANDS!

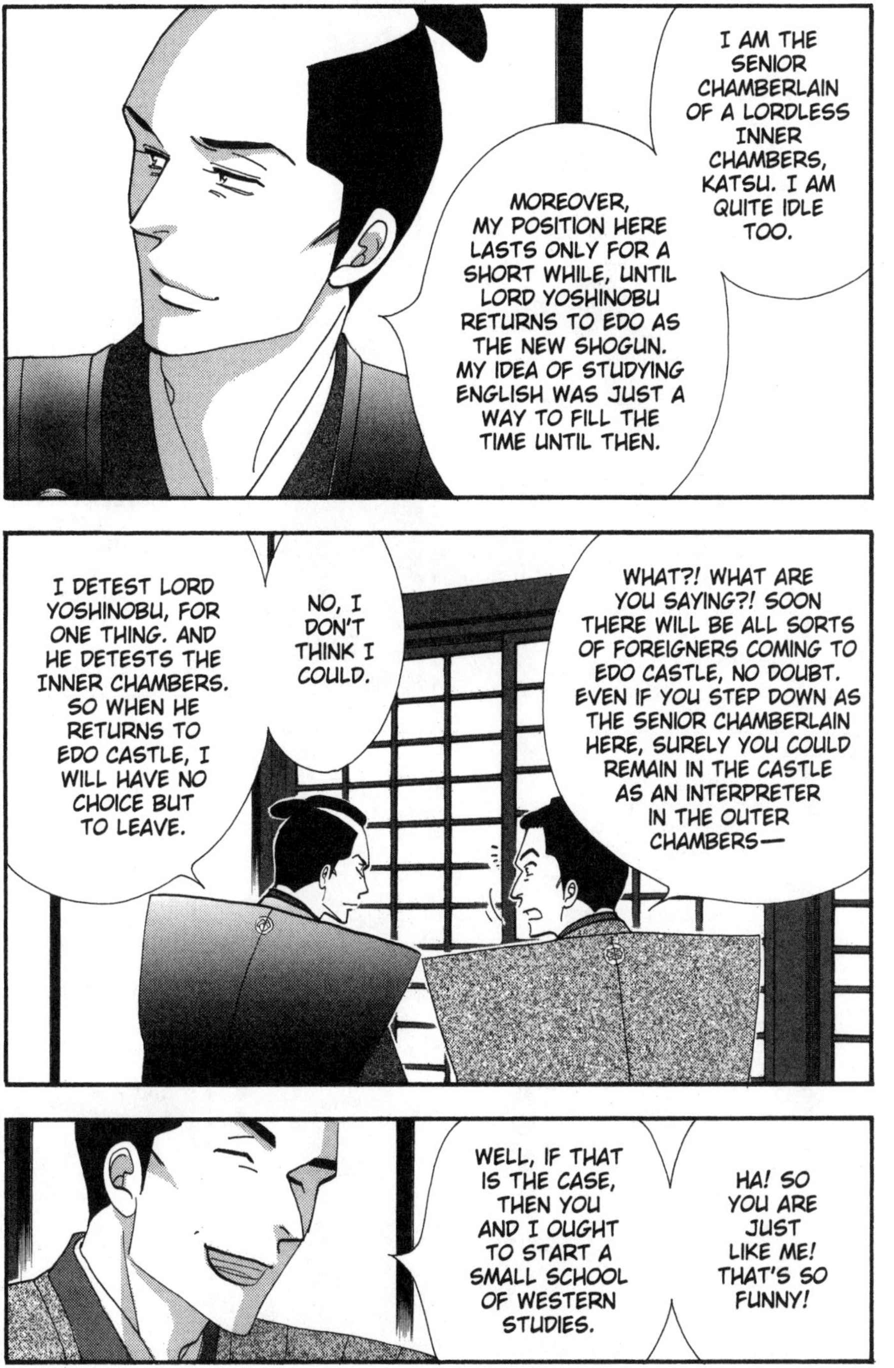
I AM THE SENIOR CHAMBERLAIN OF A LORDLESS INNER CHAMBERS, KATSU. I AM QUITE IDLE TOO.
MOREOVER, MY POSITION HERE LASTS ONLY FOR A SHORT WHILE, UNTIL LORD YOSHINOBU RETURNS TO EDO AS THE NEW SHOGUN. MY IDEA OF STUDYING ENGLISH WAS JUST A WAY TO FILL THE TIME UNTIL THEN.
WHAT?! WHAT ARE YOU SAYING?! SOON THERE WILL BE ALL SORTS OF FOREIGNERS COMING TO EDO CASTLE, NO DOUBT. EVEN IF YOU STEP DOWN AS THE SENIOR CHAMBERLAIN HERE, SURELY YOU COULD REMAIN IN THE CASTLE AS AN INTERPRETER IN THE OUTER CHAMBERS—
NO, I DON'T THINK I COULD.
I DETEST LORD YOSHINOBU, FOR ONE THING. AND HE DETESTS THE INNER CHAMBERS. SO WHEN HE RETURNS TO EDO CASTLE, I WILL HAVE NO CHOICE BUT TO LEAVE.
HA! SO YOU ARE JUST LIKE ME! THAT'S SO FUNNY!
WELL, IF THAT IS THE CASE, THEN YOU AND I OUGHT TO START A SMALL SCHOOL OF WESTERN STUDIES.

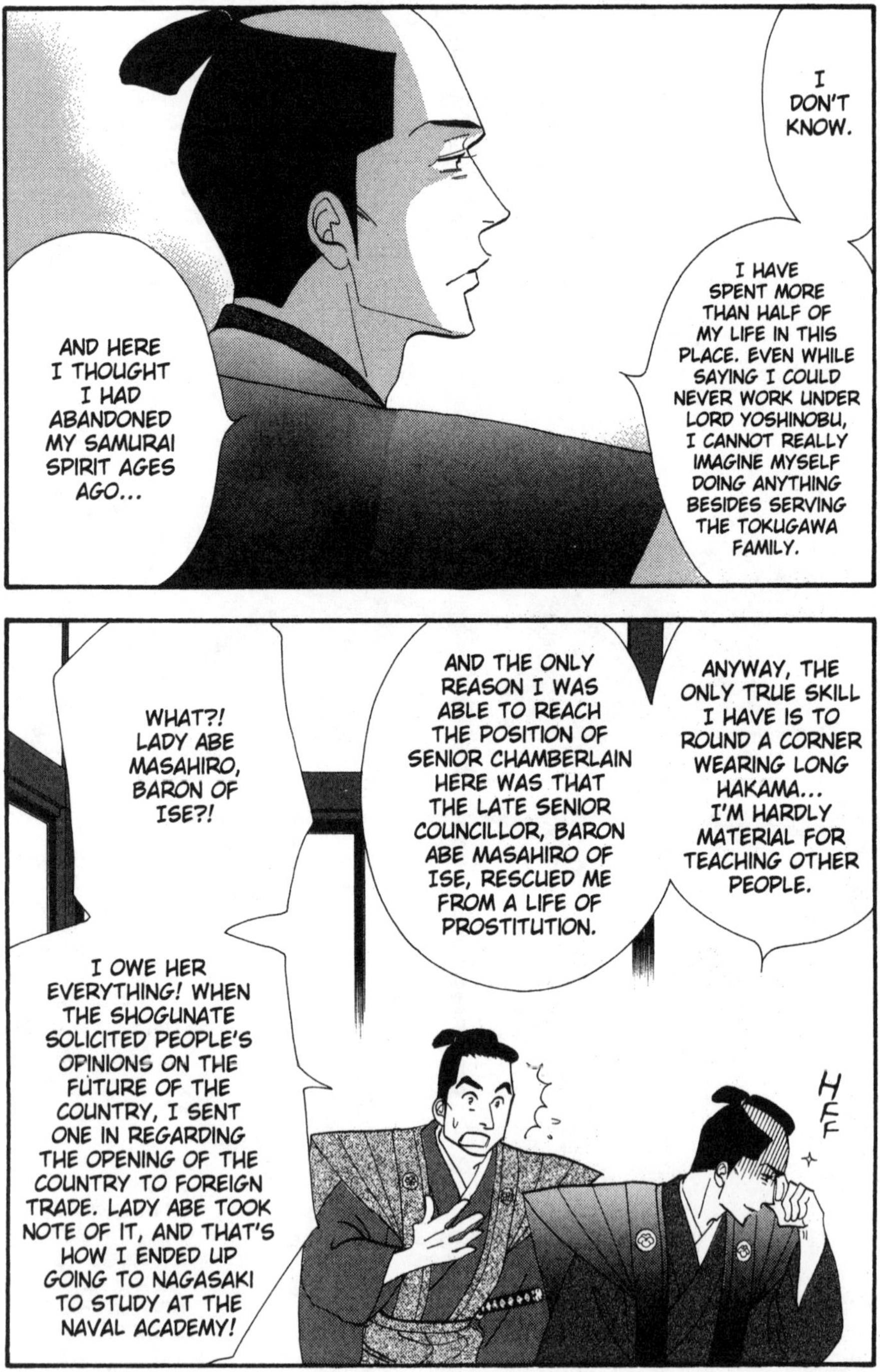
I DON'T KNOW.
I HAVE SPENT MORE THAN HALF OF MY LIFE IN THIS PLACE. EVEN WHILE SAYING I COULD NEVER WORK UNDER LORD YOSHINOBU, I CANNOT REALLY IMAGINE MYSELF DOING ANYTHING BESIDES SERVING THE TOKUGAWA FAMILY.
AND HERE I THOUGHT I HAD ABANDONED MY SAMURAI SPIRIT AGES AGO...
ANYWAY, THE ONLY TRUE SKILL I HAVE IS TO ROUND A CORNER WEARING LONG HAKAMA... I'M HARDLY MATERIAL FOR TEACHING OTHER PEOPLE.
AND THE ONLY REASON I WAS ABLE TO REACH THE POSITION OF SENIOR CHAMBERLAIN HERE WAS THAT THE LATE SENIOR COUNCILLOR, BARON ABE MASAHIRO OF ISE, RESCUED ME FROM A LIFE OF PROSTITUTION.
WHAT?! LADY ABE MASAHIRO, BARON OF ISE?!
I OWE HER EVERYTHING! WHEN THE SHOGUNATE SOLICITED PEOPLE'S OPINIONS ON THE FUTURE OF THE COUNTRY, I SENT ONE IN REGARDING THE OPENING OF THE COUNTRY TO FOREIGN TRADE. LADY ABE TOOK NOTE OF IT, AND THAT'S HOW I ENDED UP GOING TO NAGASAKI TO STUDY AT THE NAVAL ACADEMY!
HFF

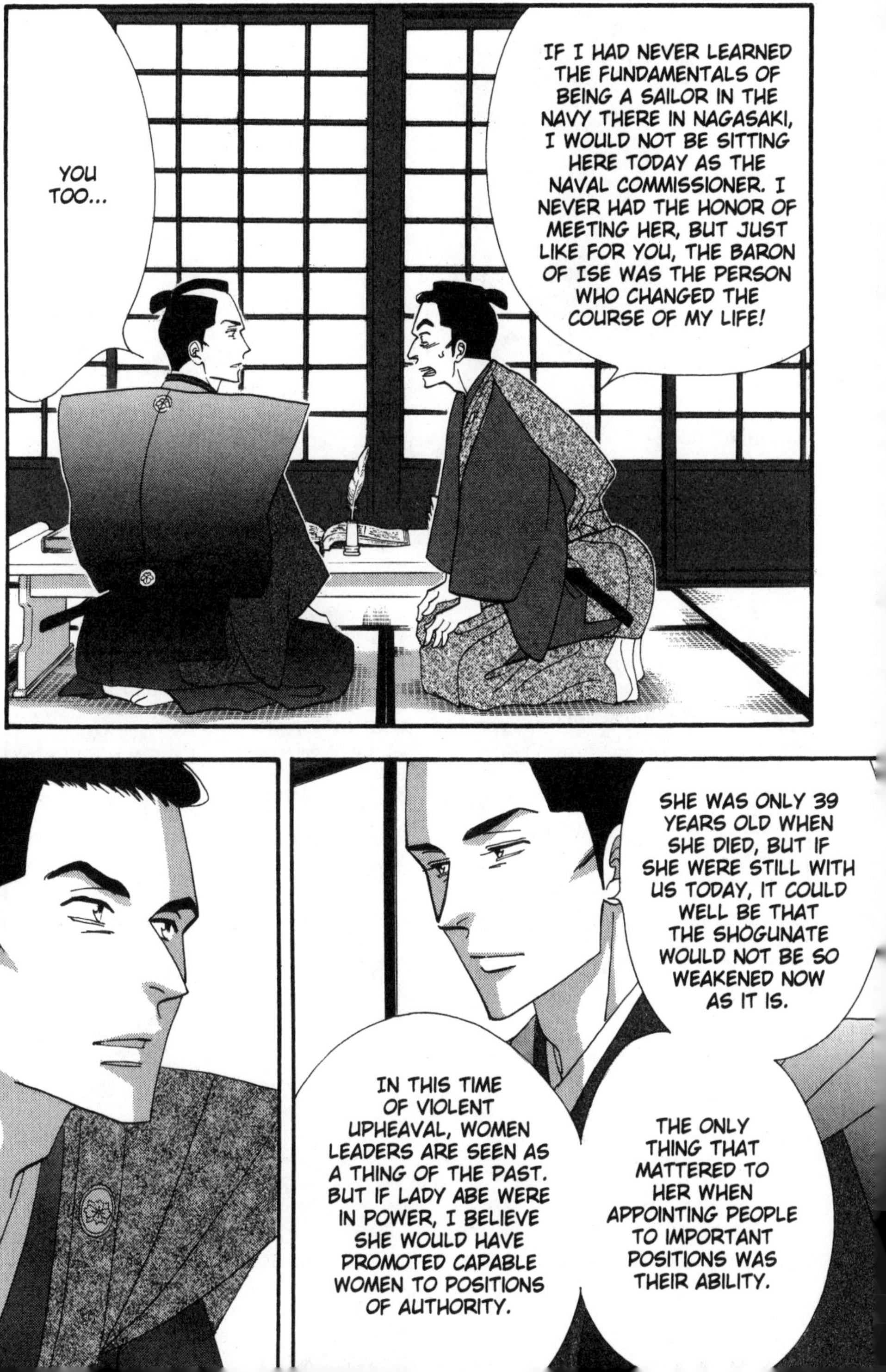
IF I HAD NEVER LEARNED THE FUNDAMENTALS OF BEING A SAILOR IN THE NAVY THERE IN NAGASAKI, I WOULD NOT BE SITTING HERE TODAY AS THE NAVAL COMMISSIONER. I NEVER HAD THE HONOR OF MEETING HER, BUT JUST LIKE FOR YOU, THE BARON OF ISE WAS THE PERSON WHO CHANGED THE COURSE OF MY LIFE!
YOU TOO...
SHE WAS ONLY 39 YEARS OLD WHEN SHE DIED, BUT IF SHE WERE STILL WITH US TODAY, IT COULD WELL BE THAT THE SHOGUNATE WOULD NOT BE SO WEAKENED NOW AS IT IS.
THE ONLY THING THAT MATTERED TO HER WHEN APPOINTING PEOPLE TO IMPORTANT POSITIONS WAS THEIR ABILITY.
IN THIS TIME OF VIOLENT UPHEAVAL, WOMEN LEADERS ARE SEEN AS A THING OF THE PAST. BUT IF LADY ABE WERE IN POWER, I BELIEVE SHE WOULD HAVE PROMOTED CAPABLE WOMEN TO POSITIONS OF AUTHORITY.

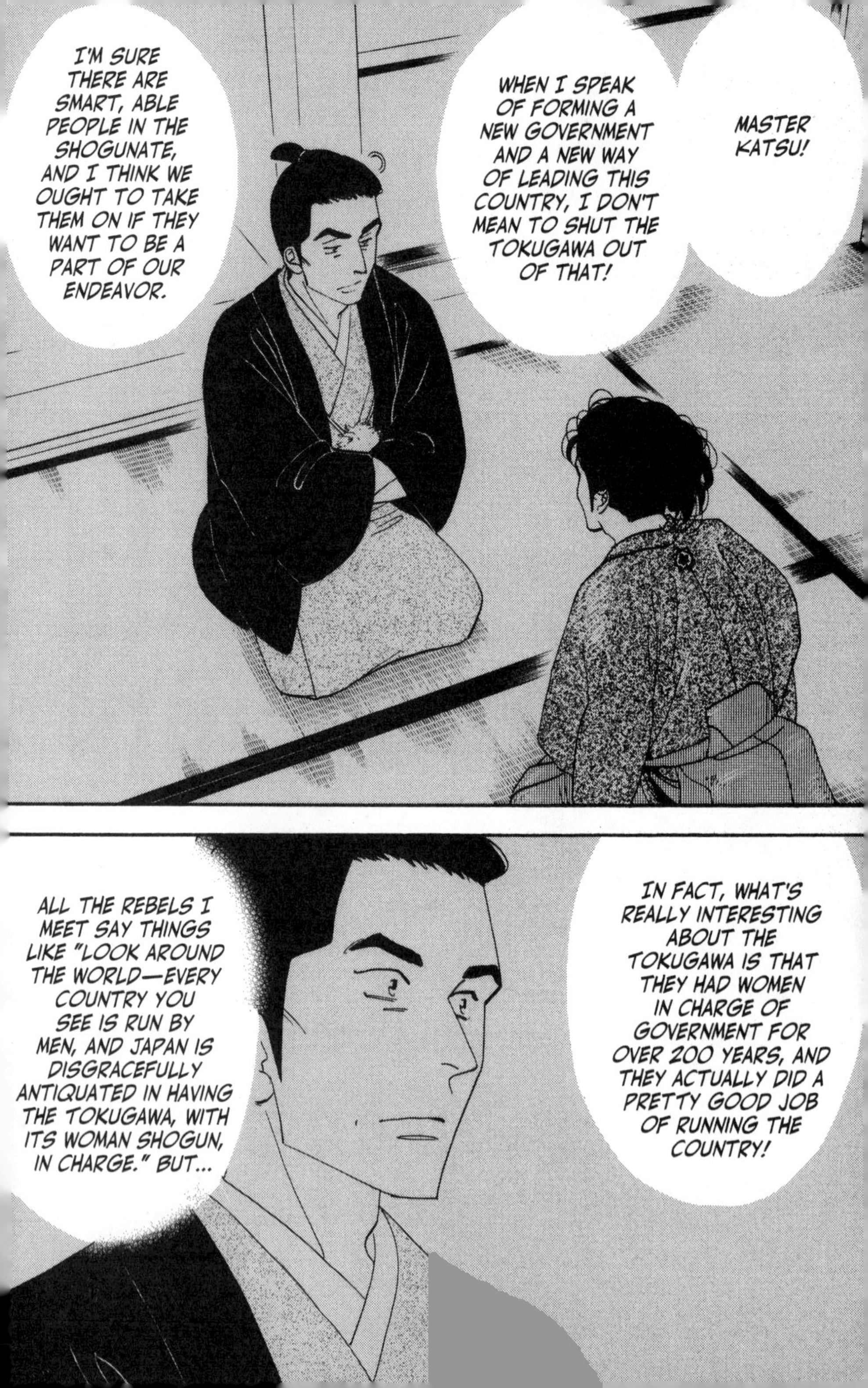
MASTER KATSU!
WHEN I SPEAK OF FORMING A NEW GOVERNMENT AND A NEW WAY OF LEADING THIS COUNTRY, I DON'T MEAN TO SHUT THE TOKUGAWA OUT OF THAT!
I'M SURE THERE ARE SMART, ABLE PEOPLE IN THE SHOGUNATE, AND I THINK WE OUGHT TO TAKE THEM ON IF THEY WANT TO BE A PART OF OUR ENDEAVOR.
IN FACT, WHAT'S REALLY INTERESTING ABOUT THE TOKUGAWA IS THAT THEY HAD WOMEN IN CHARGE OF GOVERNMENT FOR OVER 200 YEARS, AND THEY ACTUALLY DID A PRETTY GOOD JOB OF RUNNING THE COUNTRY!
ALL THE REBELS I MEET SAY THINGS LIKE "LOOK AROUND THE WORLD—EVERY COUNTRY YOU SEE IS RUN BY MEN, AND JAPAN IS DISGRACEFULLY ANTIQUATED IN HAVING THE TOKUGAWA, WITH ITS WOMAN SHOGUN, IN CHARGE." BUT...

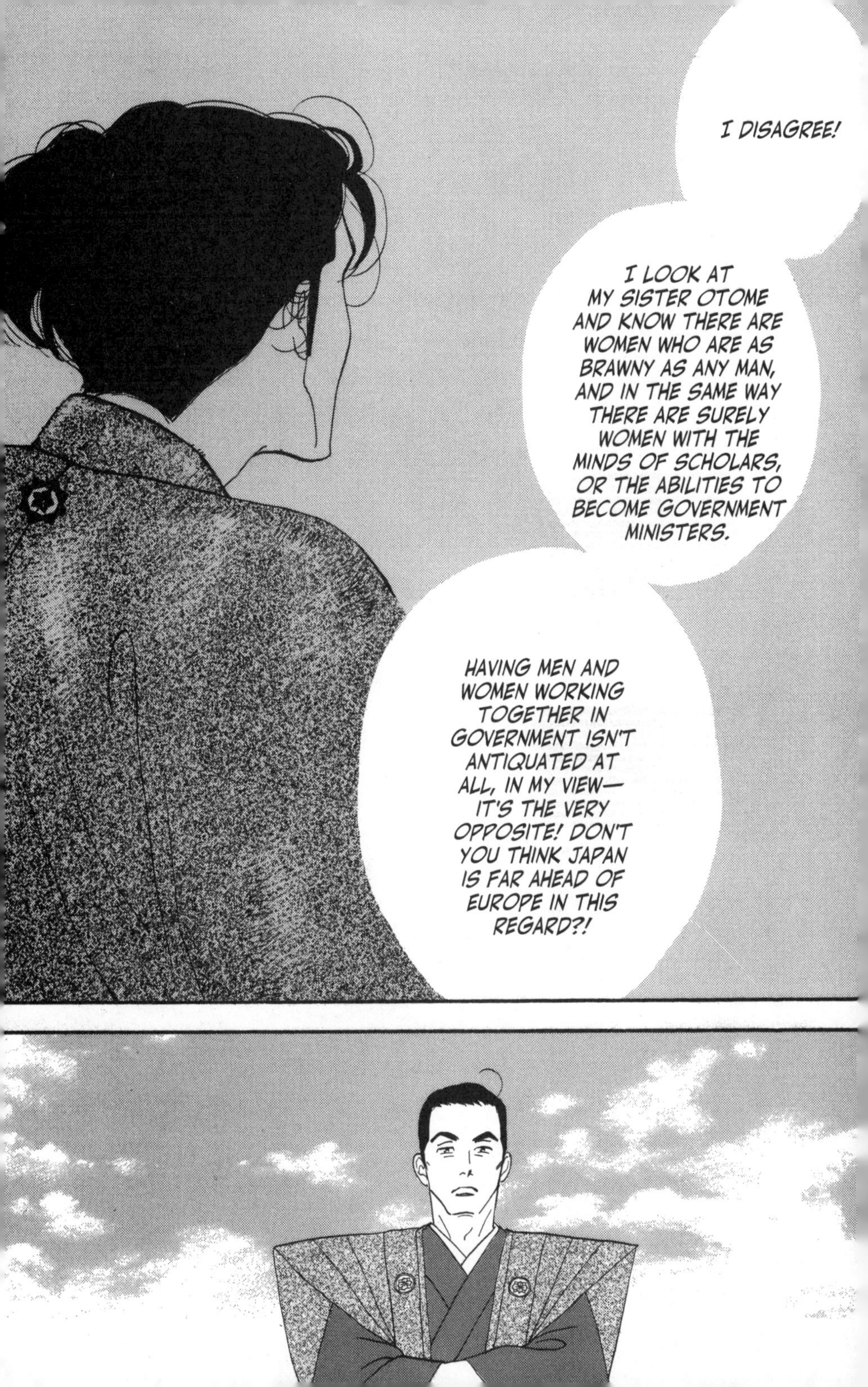
I DISAGREE!
I LOOK AT MY SISTER OTOME AND KNOW THERE ARE WOMEN WHO ARE AS BRAWNY AS ANY MAN, AND IN THE SAME WAY THERE ARE SURELY WOMEN WITH THE MINDS OF SCHOLARS, OR THE ABILITIES TO BECOME GOVERNMENT MINISTERS.
HAVING MEN AND WOMEN WORKING TOGETHER IN GOVERNMENT ISN'T ANTIQUATED AT ALL, IN MY VIEW— IT'S THE VERY OPPOSITE! DON'T YOU THINK JAPAN IS FAR AHEAD OF EUROPE IN THIS REGARD?!

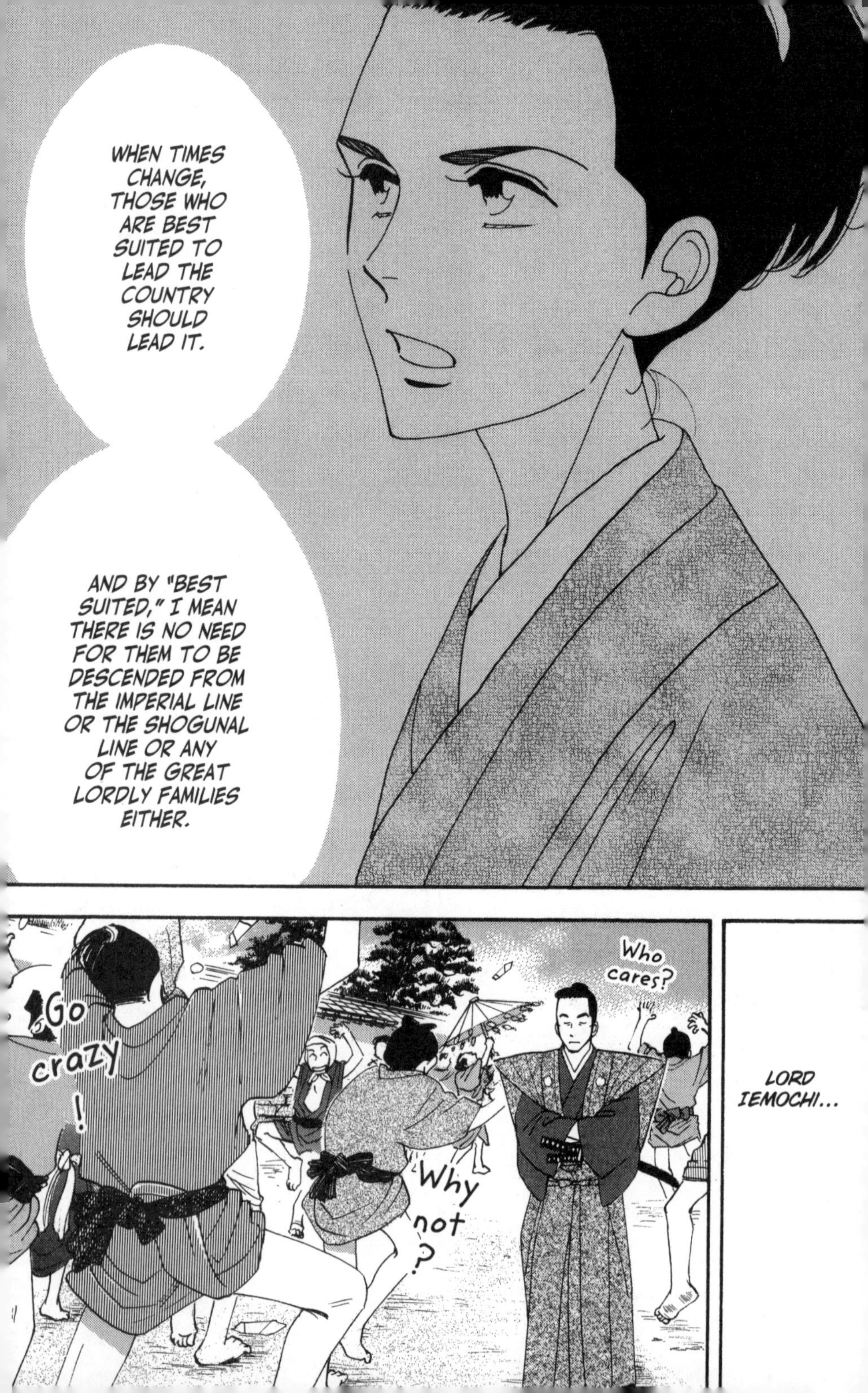
WHEN TIMES CHANGE, THOSE WHO ARE BEST SUITED TO LEAD THE COUNTRY SHOULD LEAD IT.
AND BY "BEST SUITED," I MEAN THERE IS NO NEED FOR THEM TO BE DESCENDED FROM THE IMPERIAL LINE OR THE SHOGUNAL LINE OR ANY OF THE GREAT LORDLY FAMILIES EITHER.
LORD IEMOCHI...
Who cares?
Go crazy!
Why not?

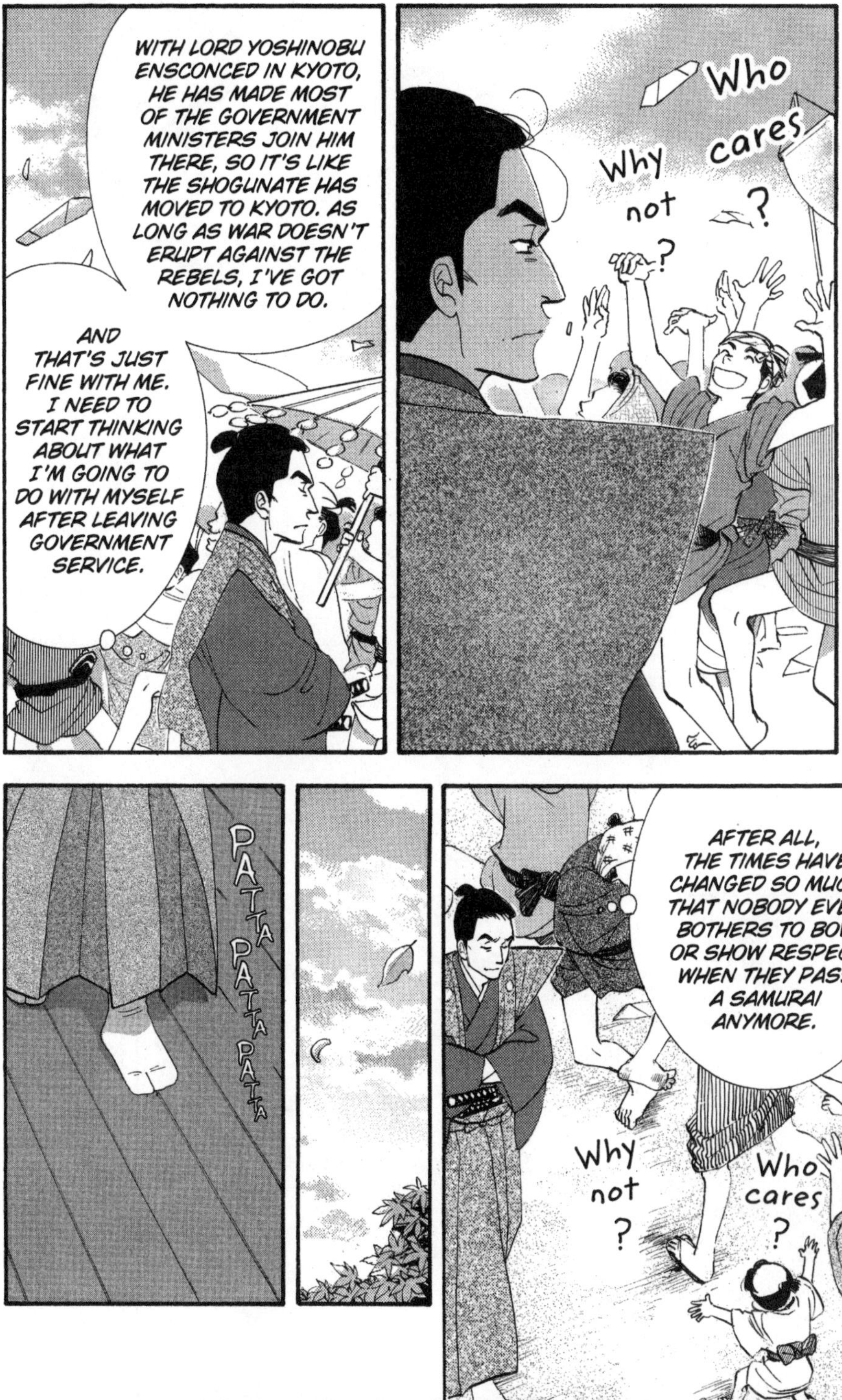
Who cares?
Why not?
WITH LORD YOSHINOBU ENSCONCED IN KYOTO, HE HAS MADE MOST OF THE GOVERNMENT MINISTERS JOIN HIM THERE, SO IT'S LIKE THE SHOGUNATE HAS MOVED TO KYOTO. AS LONG AS WAR DOESN'T ERUPT AGAINST THE REBELS, I'VE GOT NOTHING TO DO.
AND THAT'S JUST FINE WITH ME. I NEED TO START THINKING ABOUT WHAT I'M GOING TO DO WITH MYSELF AFTER LEAVING GOVERNMENT SERVICE.
AFTER ALL, THE TIMES HAVE CHANGED SO MUCH THAT NOBODY EVEN BOTHERS TO BOW OR SHOW RESPECT WHEN THEY PASS A SAMURAI ANYMORE.
Who cares?
Why not?
PATTA PATTA PATTA PATTA

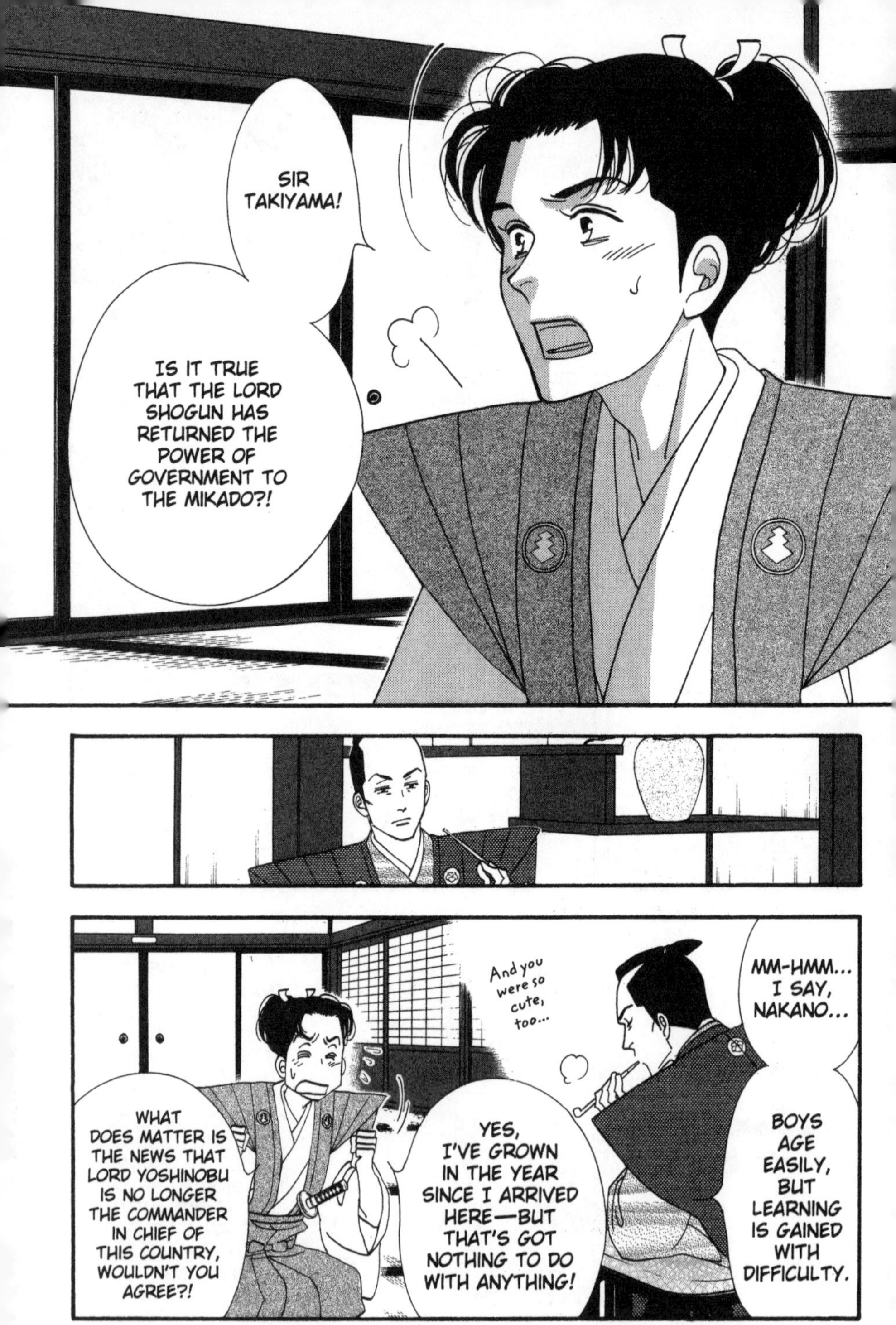
SIR TAKIYAMA!
IS IT TRUE THAT THE LORD SHOGUN HAS RETURNED THE POWER OF GOVERNMENT TO THE MIKADO?!
MM-HMM... I SAY, NAKANO...
BOYS AGE EASILY, BUT LEARNING IS GAINED WITH DIFFICULTY.
And you were so cute, too...
YES, I'VE GROWN IN THE YEAR SINCE I ARRIVED HERE—BUT THAT'S GOT NOTHING TO DO WITH ANYTHING!
WHAT DOES MATTER IS THE NEWS THAT LORD YOSHINOBU IS NO LONGER THE COMMANDER IN CHIEF OF THIS COUNTRY, WOULDN'T YOU AGREE?!

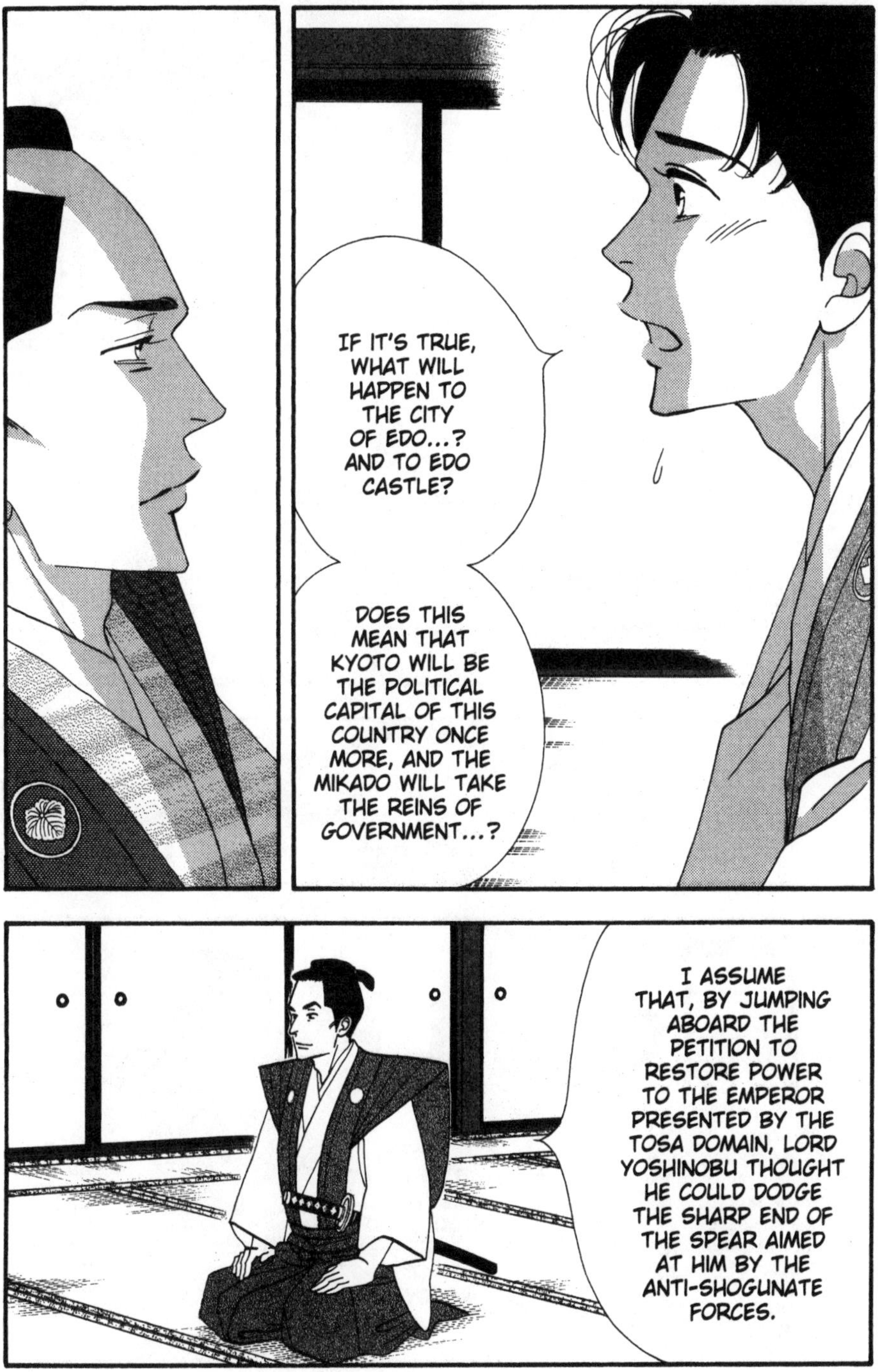
IF IT'S TRUE, WHAT WILL HAPPEN TO THE CITY OF EDO...? AND TO EDO CASTLE?
DOES THIS MEAN THAT KYOTO WILL BE THE POLITICAL CAPITAL OF THIS COUNTRY ONCE MORE, AND THE MIKADO WILL TAKE THE REINS OF GOVERNMENT...?
I ASSUME THAT, BY JUMPING ABOARD THE PETITION TO RESTORE POWER TO THE EMPEROR PRESENTED BY THE TOSA DOMAIN, LORD YOSHINOBU THOUGHT HE COULD DODGE THE SHARP END OF THE SPEAR AIMED AT HIM BY THE ANTI-SHOGUNATE FORCES.

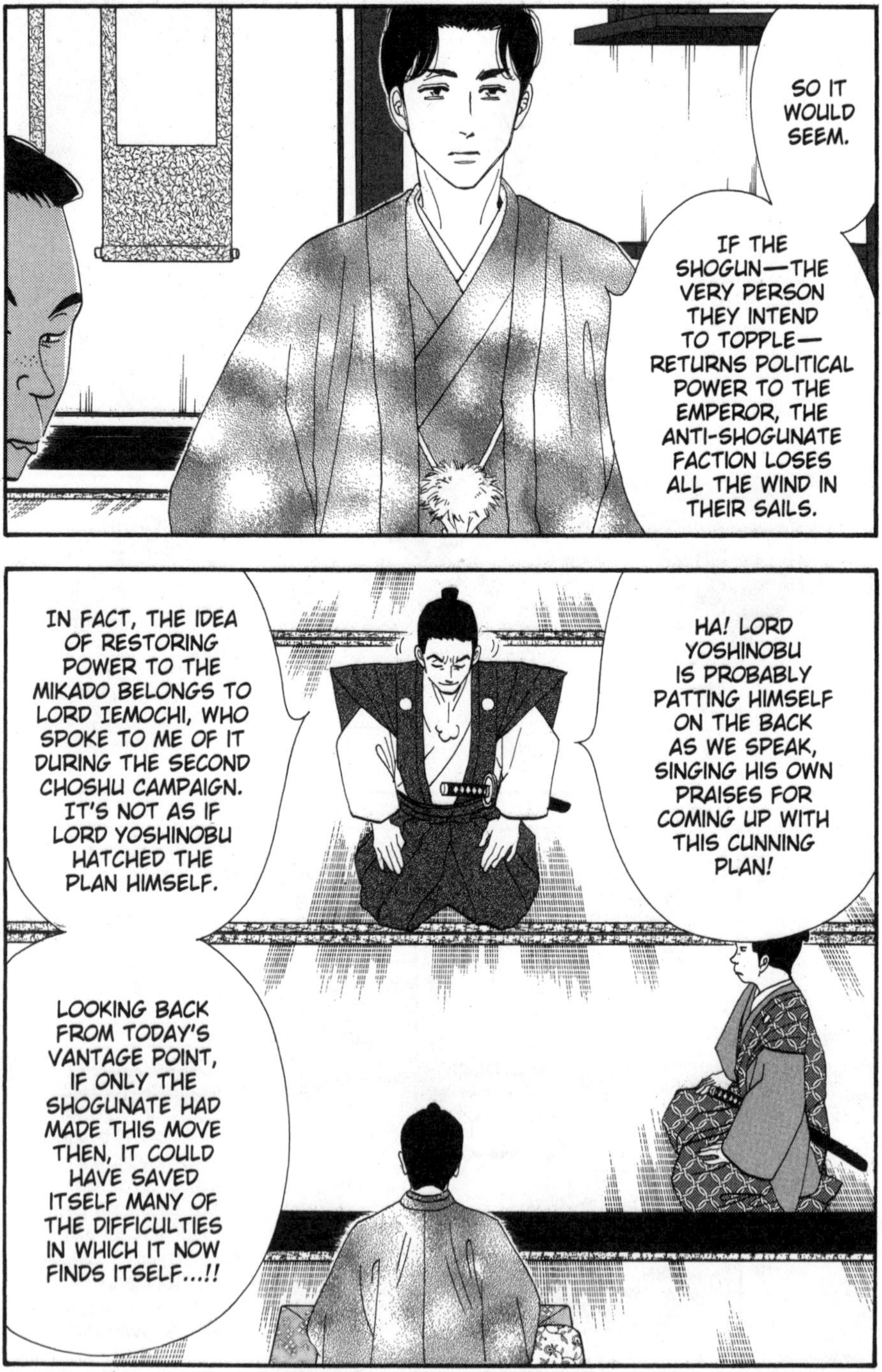
SO IT WOULD SEEM.
IF THE SHOGUN—THE VERY PERSON THEY INTEND TO TOPPLE—RETURNS POLITICAL POWER TO THE EMPEROR, THE ANTI-SHOGUNATE FACTION LOSES ALL THE WIND IN THEIR SAILS.
HA! LORD YOSHINOBU IS PROBABLY PATTING HIMSELF ON THE BACK AS WE SPEAK, SINGING HIS OWN PRAISES FOR COMING UP WITH THIS CUNNING PLAN!
IN FACT, THE IDEA OF RESTORING POWER TO THE MIKADO BELONGS TO LORD IEMOCHI, WHO SPOKE TO ME OF IT DURING THE SECOND CHOSHU CAMPAIGN. IT'S NOT AS IF LORD YOSHINOBU HATCHED THE PLAN HIMSELF.
LOOKING BACK FROM TODAY'S VANTAGE POINT, IF ONLY THE SHOGUNATE HAD MADE THIS MOVE THEN, IT COULD HAVE SAVED ITSELF MANY OF THE DIFFICULTIES IN WHICH IT NOW FINDS ITSELF...!!

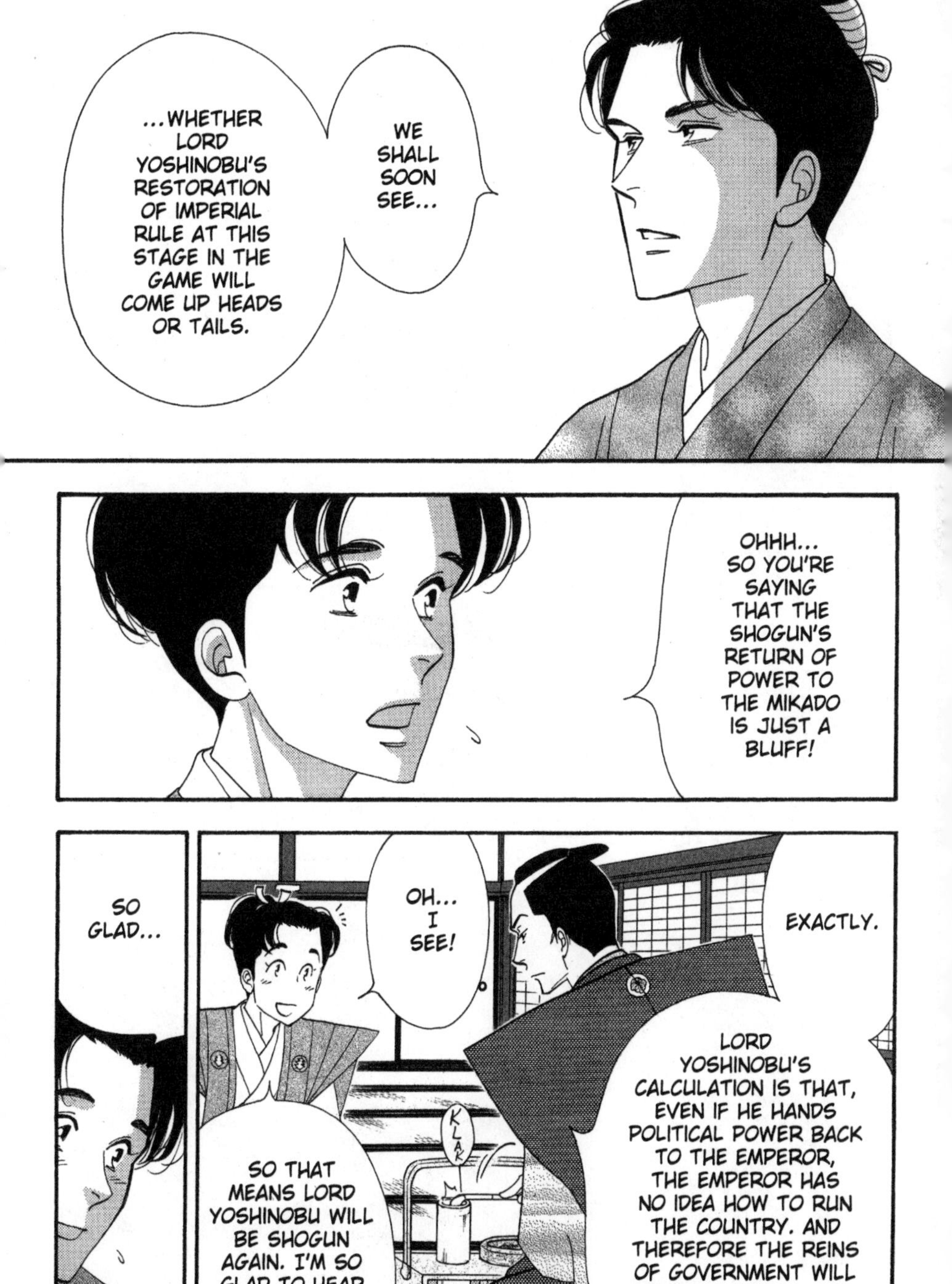
WE SHALL SOON SEE...
...WHETHER LORD YOSHINOBU'S RESTORATION OF IMPERIAL RULE AT THIS STAGE IN THE GAME WILL COME UP HEADS OR TAILS.
OHHH... SO YOU'RE SAYING THAT THE SHOGUN'S RETURN OF POWER TO THE MIKADO IS JUST A BLUFF!
EXACTLY.
OH... I SEE!
LORD YOSHINOBU'S CALCULATION IS THAT, EVEN IF HE HANDS POLITICAL POWER BACK TO THE EMPEROR, THE EMPEROR HAS NO IDEA HOW TO RUN THE COUNTRY. AND THEREFORE THE REINS OF GOVERNMENT WILL EVENTUALLY BE PLACED BACK IN HIS OWN HANDS.
KLAK
SO THAT MEANS LORD YOSHINOBU WILL BE SHOGUN AGAIN. I'M SO GLAD TO HEAR THAT...!
SO GLAD...

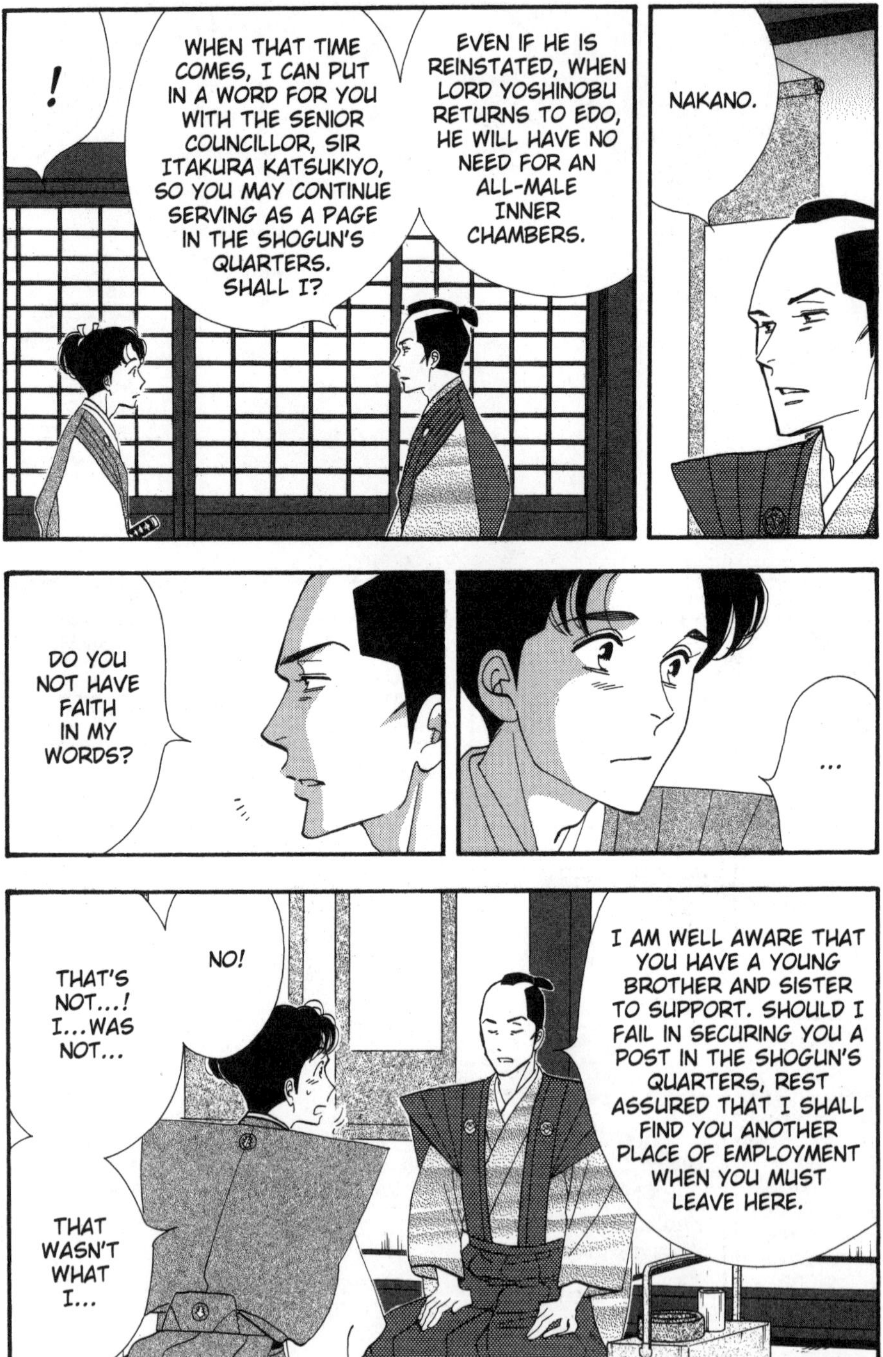
NAKANO.
EVEN IF HE IS REINSTATED, WHEN LORD YOSHINOBU RETURNS TO EDO, HE WILL HAVE NO NEED FOR AN ALL-MALE INNER CHAMBERS.
WHEN THAT TIME COMES, I CAN PUT IN A WORD FOR YOU WITH THE SENIOR COUNCILLOR, SIR ITAKURA KATSUKIYO, SO YOU MAY CONTINUE SERVING AS A PAGE IN THE SHOGUN'S QUARTERS. SHALL I?
!
...
DO YOU NOT HAVE FAITH IN MY WORDS?
I AM WELL AWARE THAT YOU HAVE A YOUNG BROTHER AND SISTER TO SUPPORT. SHOULD I FAIL IN SECURING YOU A POST IN THE SHOGUN'S QUARTERS, REST ASSURED THAT I SHALL FIND YOU ANOTHER PLACE OF EMPLOYMENT WHEN YOU MUST LEAVE HERE.
NO!
THAT'S NOT...! I...WAS NOT...
THAT WASN'T WHAT I...

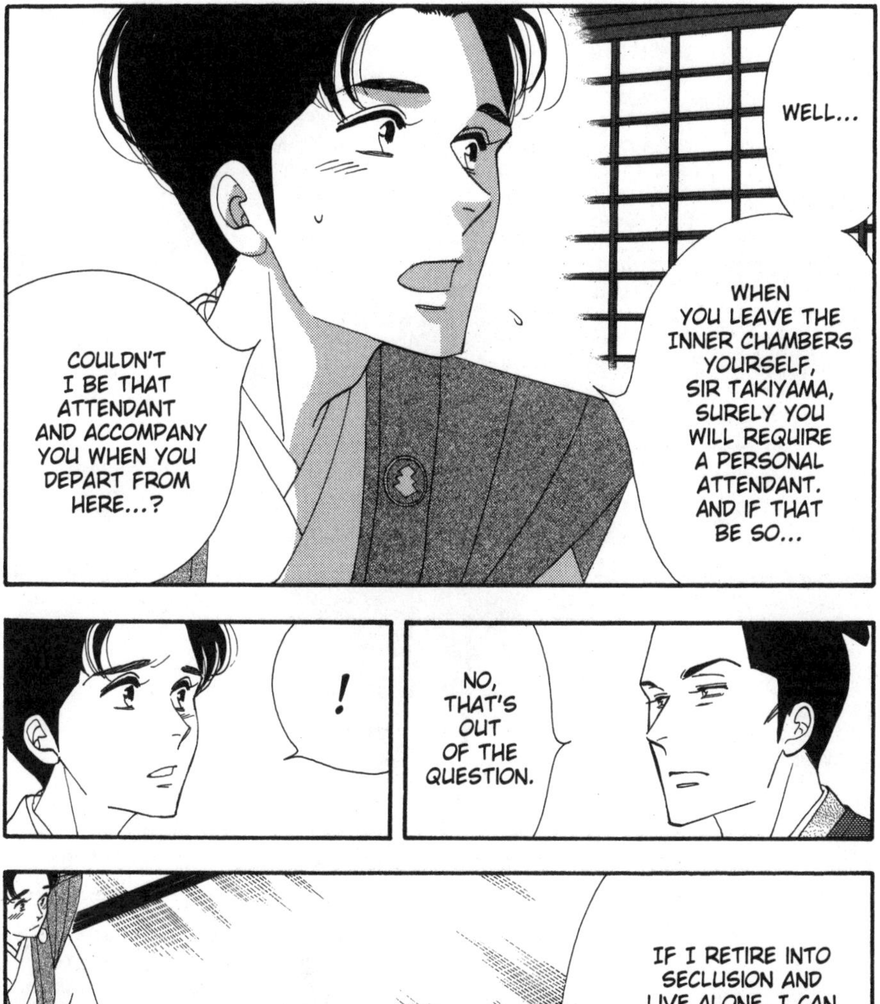
WELL...
WHEN YOU LEAVE THE INNER CHAMBERS YOURSELF, SIR TAKIYAMA, SURELY YOU WILL REQUIRE A PERSONAL ATTENDANT. AND IF THAT BE SO...
COULDN'T I BE THAT ATTENDANT AND ACCOMPANY YOU WHEN YOU DEPART FROM HERE...?
NO, THAT'S OUT OF THE QUESTION.
!
IF I RETIRE INTO SECLUSION AND LIVE ALONE, I CAN CUT MY OWN NAILS AND GET DRESSED BY MYSELF AS WELL. THE ONLY HELP I WILL NEED IS ONE SERVANT TO DO THE COOKING AND CLEANING.
TAKE MY ADVICE. IF YOU SERVE THE SHOGUN AS HIS VALET, YOU COULD QUITE POSSIBLY RISE VERY HIGH IN THE WORLD, TO PRIVY COUNCILLOR, EVEN.
IT WOULD BE BETTER FOR YOU TO STAY HERE IN EDO CASTLE.

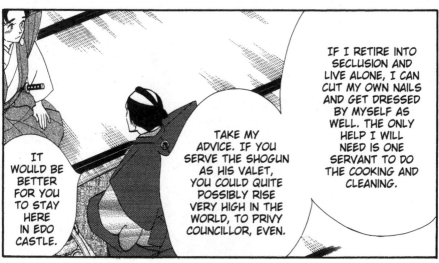

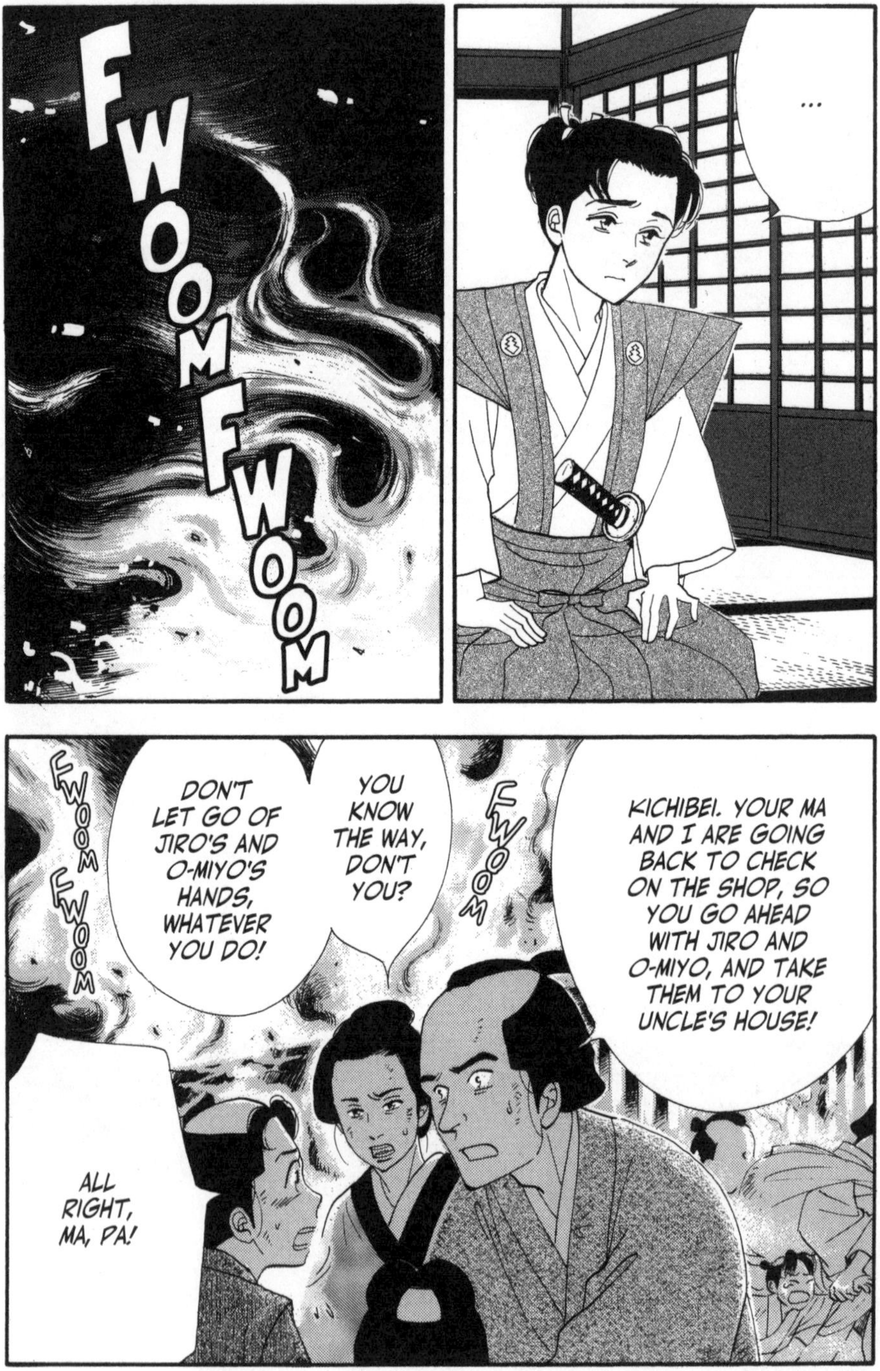
...
FWOOM FWOOM FWOOM FWOOM
KICHIBEI. YOUR MA AND I ARE GOING BACK TO CHECK ON THE SHOP, SO YOU GO AHEAD WITH JIRO AND O-MIYO, AND TAKE THEM TO YOUR UNCLE'S HOUSE!
FWOOM
YOU KNOW THE WAY, DON'T YOU?
DON'T LET GO OF JIRO'S AND O-MIYO'S HANDS, WHATEVER YOU DO!
FWOOM FWOOM
ALL RIGHT, MA, PA!

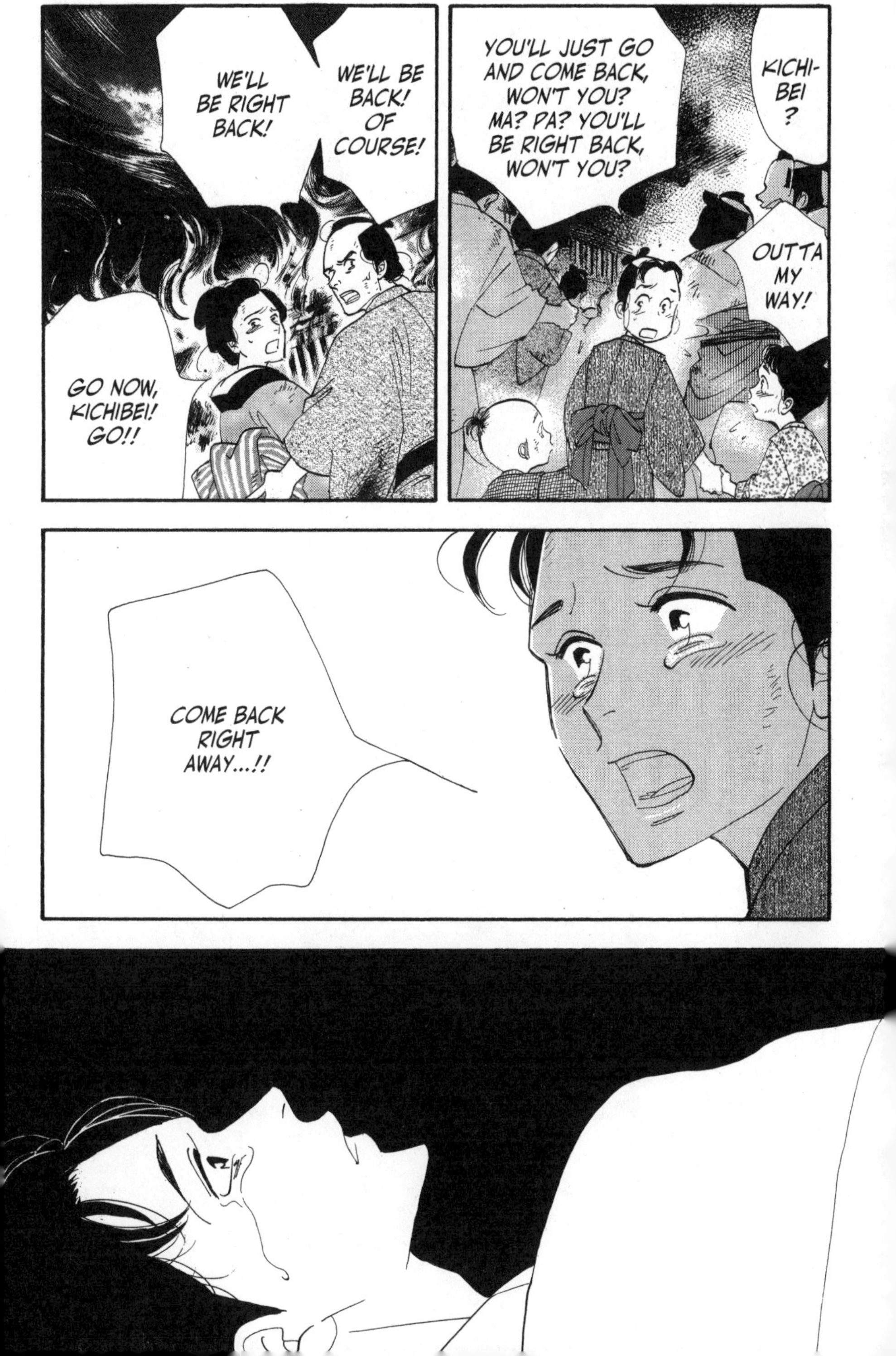
KICHI-BEI?
YOU'LL JUST GO AND COME BACK, WON'T YOU? MA? PA? YOU'LL BE RIGHT BACK, WON'T YOU?
OUTTA MY WAY!
WE'LL BE BACK! OF COURSE!
WE'LL BE RIGHT BACK!
GO NOW, KICHIBEI! GO!!
COME BACK RIGHT AWAY...!!

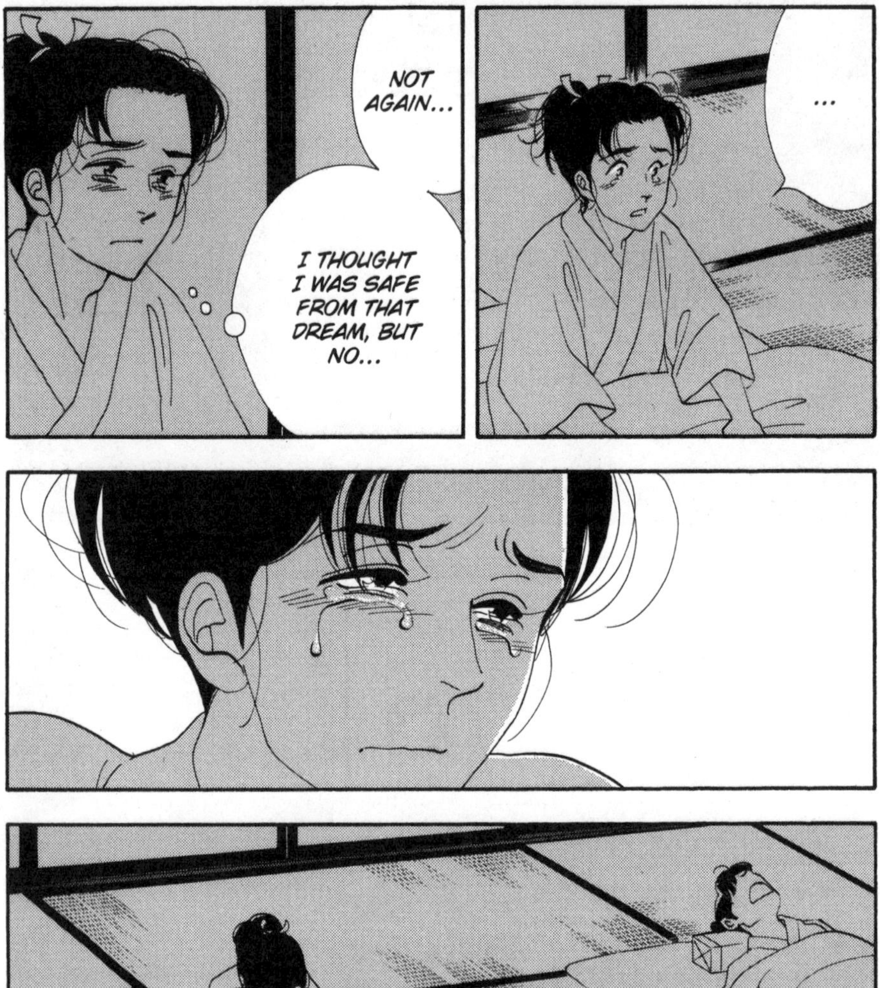
...
NOT AGAIN...
I THOUGHT I WAS SAFE FROM THAT DREAM, BUT NO...

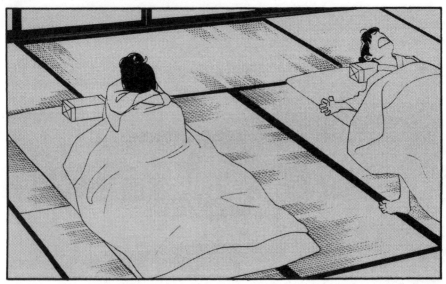

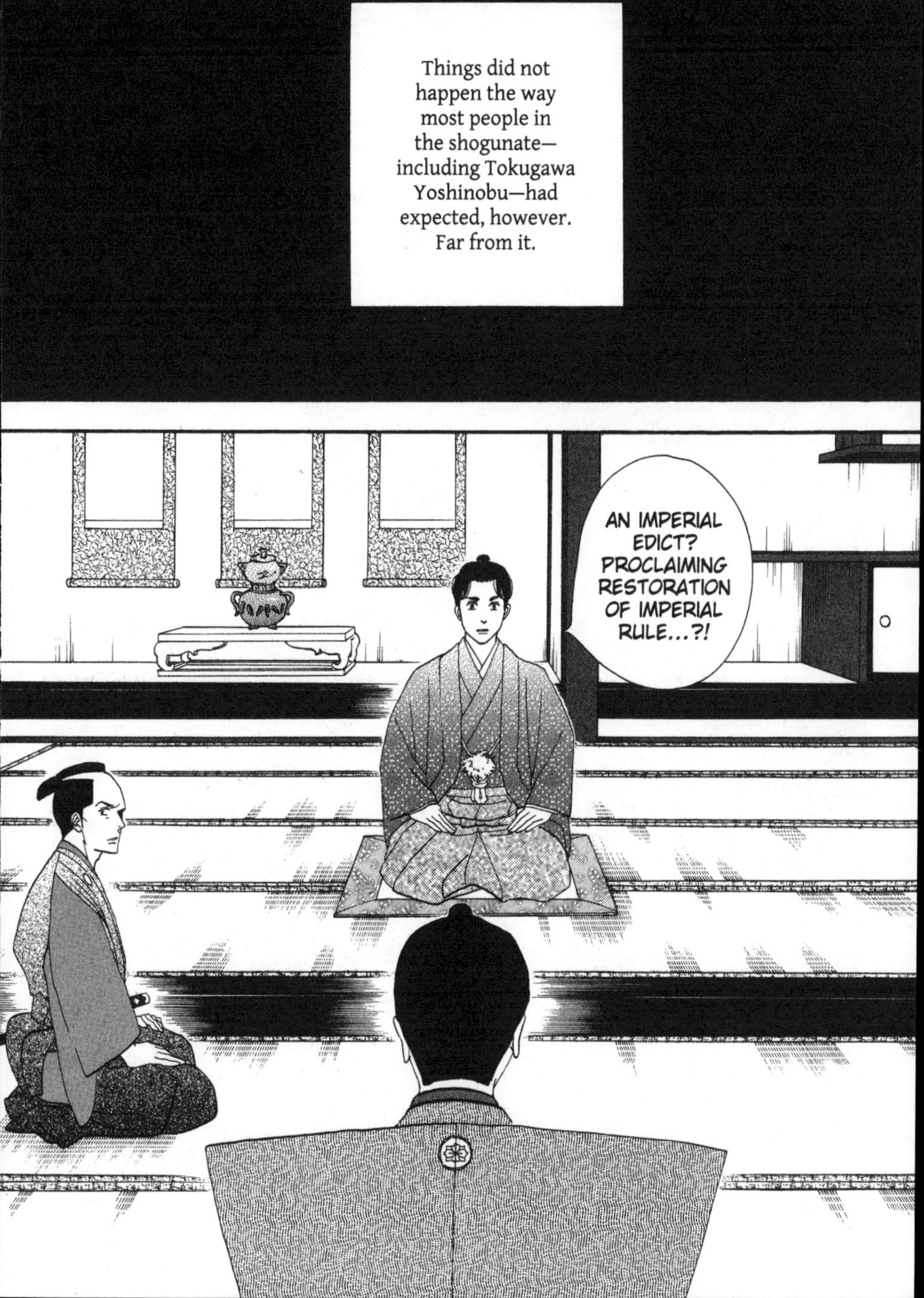
Things did not happen the way most people in the shogunate—including Tokugawa Yoshinobu—had expected, however. Far from it.
AN IMPERIAL EDICT? PROCLAIMING RESTORATION OF IMPERIAL RULE...?!

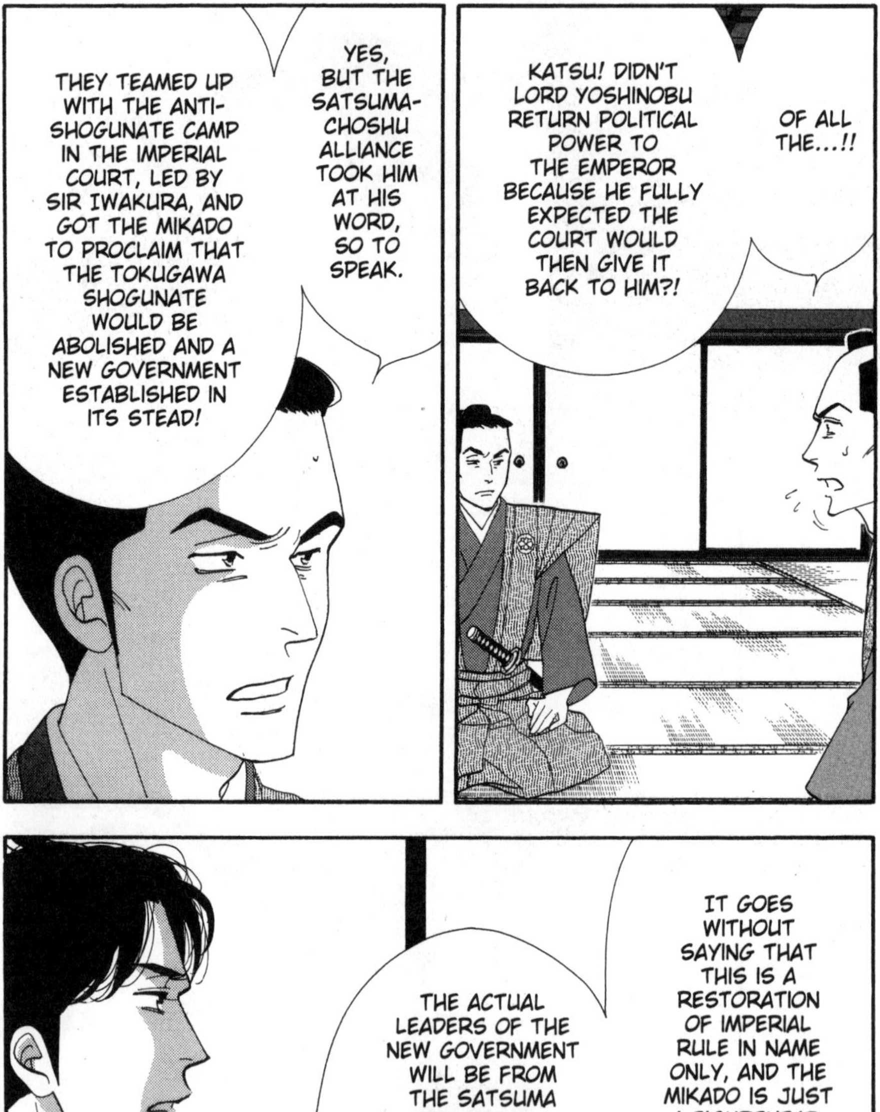
OF ALL THE...!!
KATSU! DIDN'T LORD YOSHINOBU RETURN POLITICAL POWER TO THE EMPEROR BECAUSE HE FULLY EXPECTED THE COURT WOULD THEN GIVE IT BACK TO HIM?!
YES, BUT THE SATSUMA-CHOSHU ALLIANCE TOOK HIM AT HIS WORD, SO TO SPEAK.
THEY TEAMED UP WITH THE ANTI-SHOGUNATE CAMP IN THE IMPERIAL COURT, LED BY SIR IWAKURA, AND GOT THE MIKADO TO PROCLAIM THAT THE TOKUGAWA SHOGUNATE WOULD BE ABOLISHED AND A NEW GOVERNMENT ESTABLISHED IN ITS STEAD!
IT GOES WITHOUT SAYING THAT THIS IS A RESTORATION OF IMPERIAL RULE IN NAME ONLY, AND THE MIKADO IS JUST A FIGUREHEAD.
THE ACTUAL LEADERS OF THE NEW GOVERNMENT WILL BE FROM THE SATSUMA AND CHOSHU DOMAINS. BUT THE PLAN ITSELF WAS DRAWN UP BY TWO SAMURAI OF THE SATSUMA DOMAIN—SAIGO TAKAMORI AND OKUBO TOSHIMICHI.

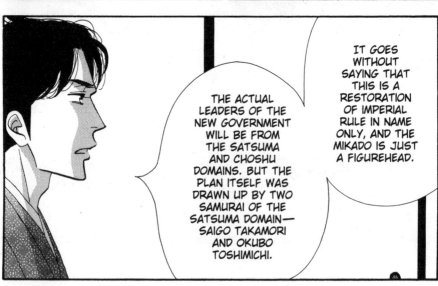

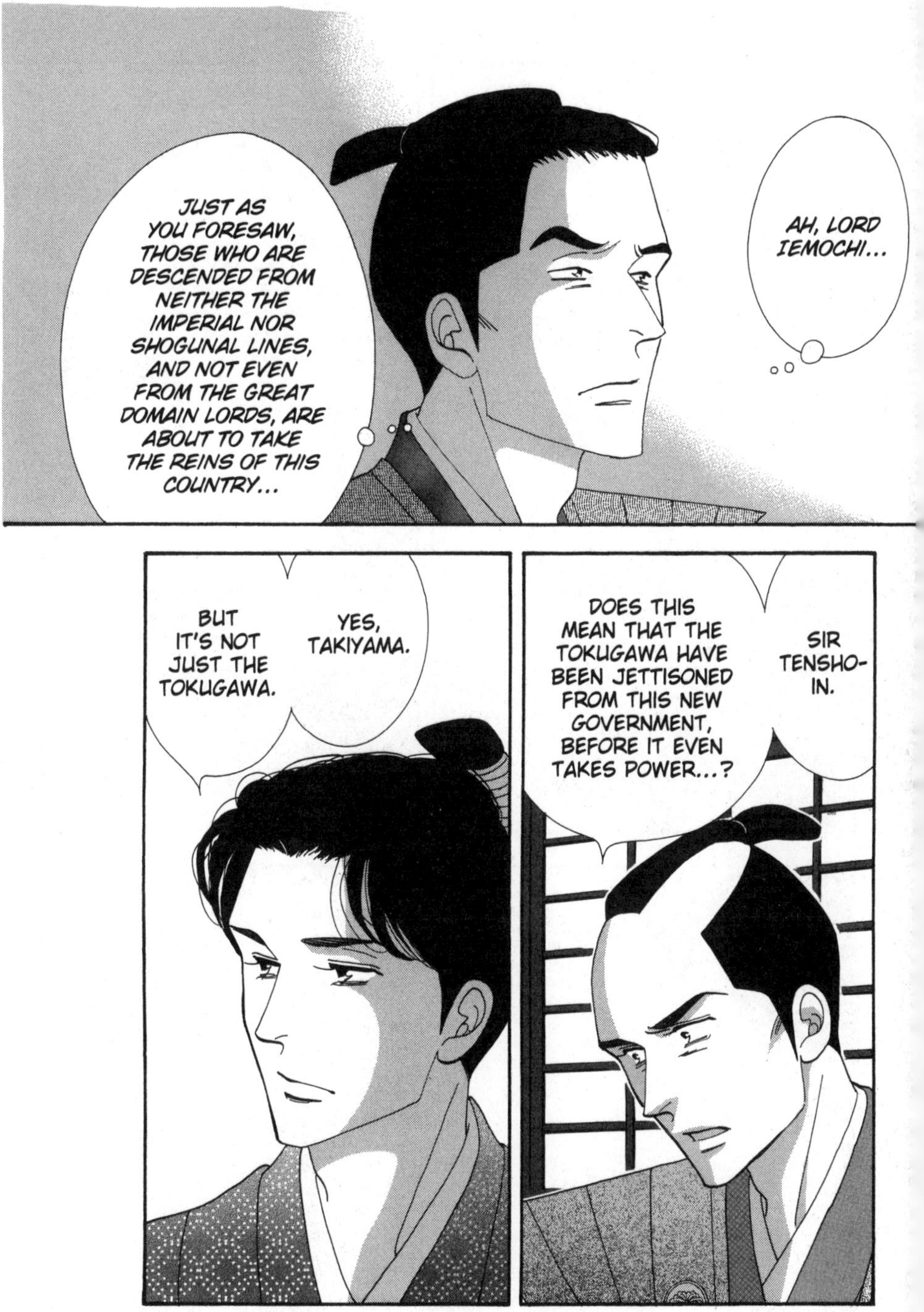
AH, LORD IEMOCHI...
JUST AS YOU FORESAW, THOSE WHO ARE DESCENDED FROM NEITHER THE IMPERIAL NOR SHOGUNAL LINES, AND NOT EVEN FROM THE GREAT DOMAIN LORDS, ARE ABOUT TO TAKE THE REINS OF THIS COUNTRY...
SIR TENSHO-IN.
DOES THIS MEAN THAT THE TOKUGAWA HAVE BEEN JETTISONED FROM THIS NEW GOVERNMENT, BEFORE IT EVEN TAKES POWER...?
YES, TAKIYAMA.
BUT IT'S NOT JUST THE TOKUGAWA.

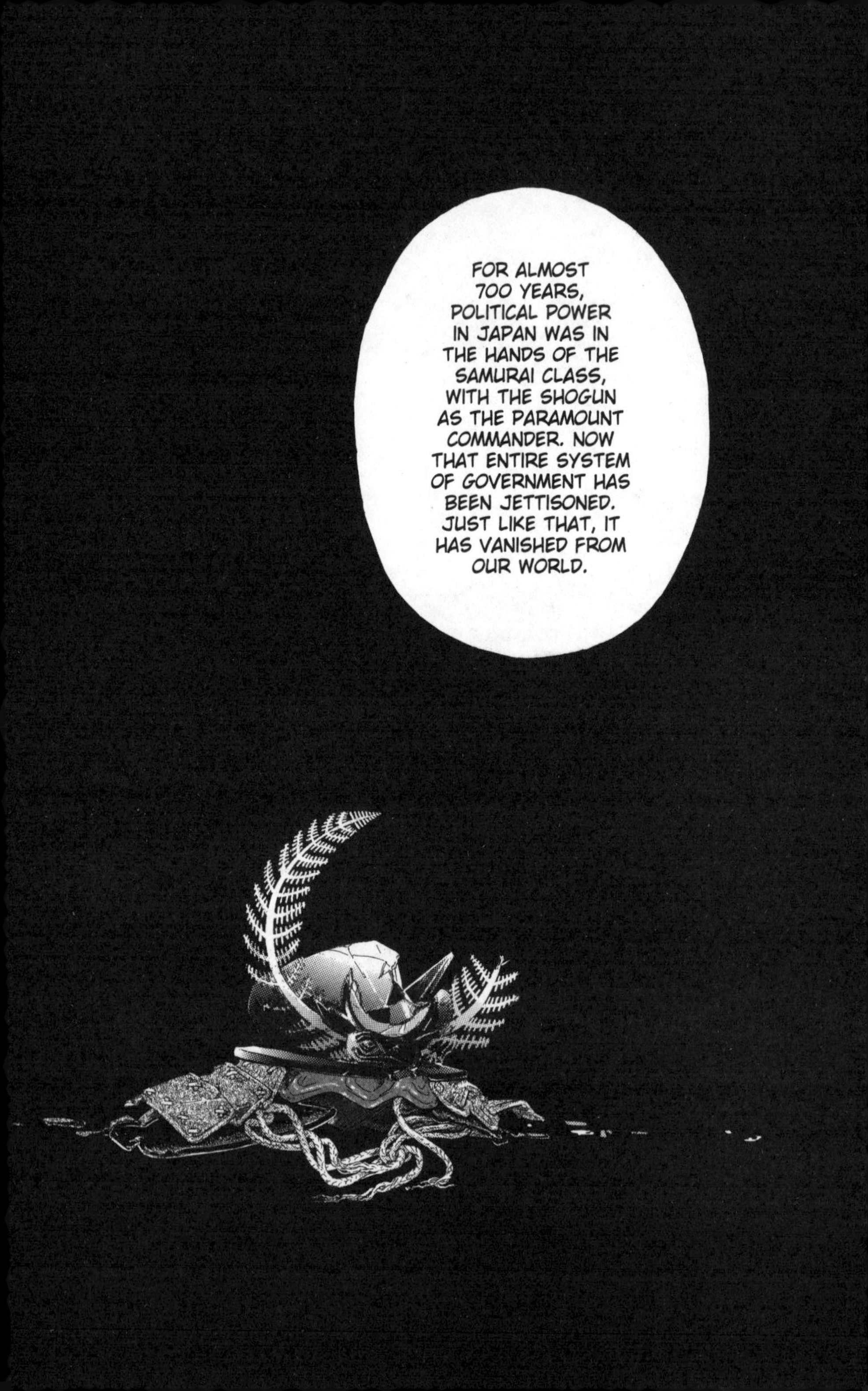
FOR ALMOST 700 YEARS, POLITICAL POWER IN JAPAN WAS IN THE HANDS OF THE SAMURAI CLASS, WITH THE SHOGUN AS THE PARAMOUNT COMMANDER. NOW THAT ENTIRE SYSTEM OF GOVERNMENT HAS BEEN JETTISONED. JUST LIKE THAT, IT HAS VANISHED FROM OUR WORLD.

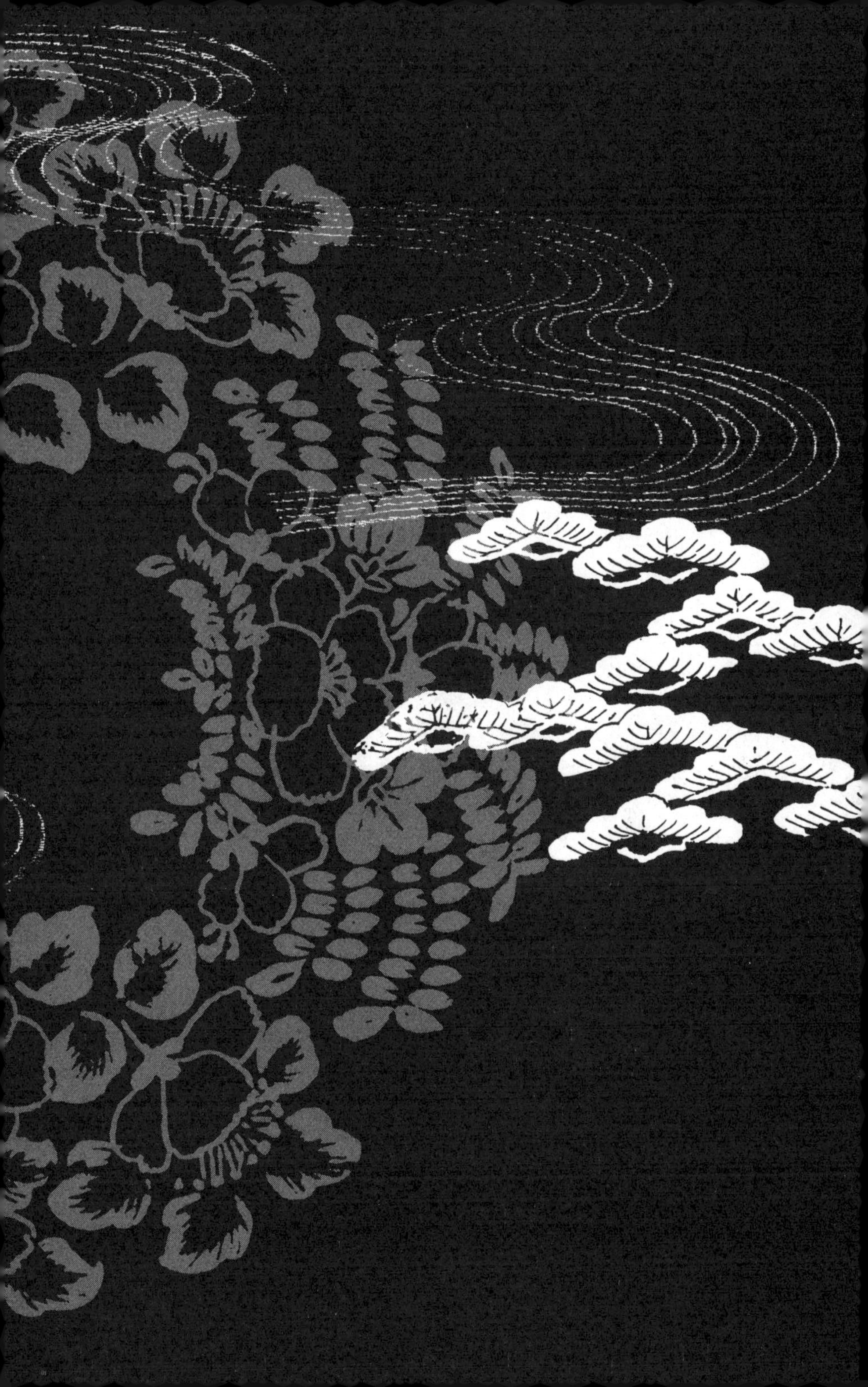

Ooku

✿ THE INNER CHAMBERS

Ōoku: The Inner Chambers

VOLUME 18 · END NOTES

by Akemi Wegmüller

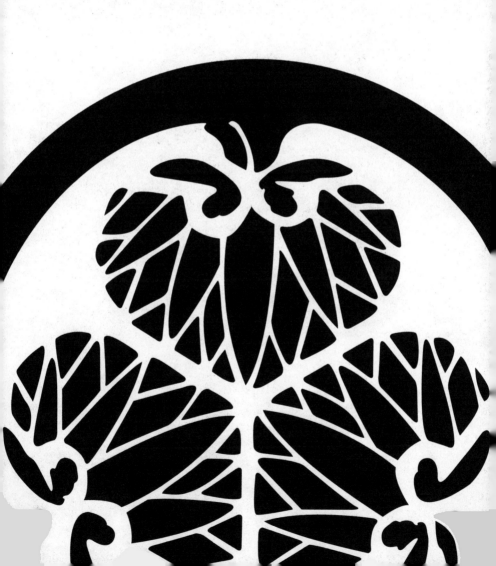

Page 12, panel 1 · SHINING PRINCE
This is a reference to the titular character of *The Tale of Genji* by Lady Murasaki.

Page 55, panel 4 · CINNABAR
A form of mercury ore, cinnabar was being used for embalming purposes here.

Page 63, panel 1 · AKI
Present-day Hiroshima Prefecture.

Page 100, panel 2 · HANABIRA-MOCHI
Gyuhi, colored a faint pink, is folded over a layer of sweet white miso paste and a piece of sweetened cooked burdock root. It's eaten at the New Year.

Page 107, panel 2 · GYUHI
A glutinous rice flour made into a soft dough and steamed, to which sugar or syrup is added. It is then heated and kneaded until it has the consistency of a very soft and pliable marzipan.

Page 116, panel 2 · KAGEMA
Young male prostitutes who served both male and female clients, and appeared in masculine or feminine attire.

Page 139, panel 1 · ECHIGO-JOFU
This high-quality, lightweight hemp fiber from Echigo is perfect for Japanese summers.

Page 139, panel 3 · KAMISHIMO
Formal attire. It literally means "upper and lower" and is an ensemble that goes over the kimono for formal occasions. The upper section is a sleeveless robe with wide starched

shoulders, and the lower section is an undivided *hakama*.

Page 166, panel 1 · THE 12TH MONTH OF KEIO 2
By the Gregorian calendar, January 30, 1867.

Page 171, panel 1 · EZO
Present-day Hokkaido, the northernmost island of the Japanese archipelago.

Page173, panel 3 · HAKAMA
The skirtlike pants that form the lower part of a *kamishimo* ensemble. *Nagabakama*, the long ones being abolished, drag on the floor.

Page 191, panel 3 · BOYS AGE EASILY, BUT LEARNING IS GAINED WITH DIFFICULTY
A Japanese proverb that is roughly equivalent to "Art is long, life is short."

CREATOR BIOGRAPHY
FUMI YOSHINAGA

Fumi Yoshinaga is a Tokyo-born manga creator who de-
buted in 1994 with *Tsuki to Sandaru* (*The Moon and the
Sandals*). Yoshinaga has won numerous awards, including the 2009 Osamu Tezuka Cultural Prize for *Ōoku*,
the 2002 Kodansha Manga Award for her series *Antique
Bakery* and the 2006 Japan Media Arts Festival Excel-
lence Award for *Ōoku*. She was also nominated for the
2008 Eisner Award for Best Writer/Artist.

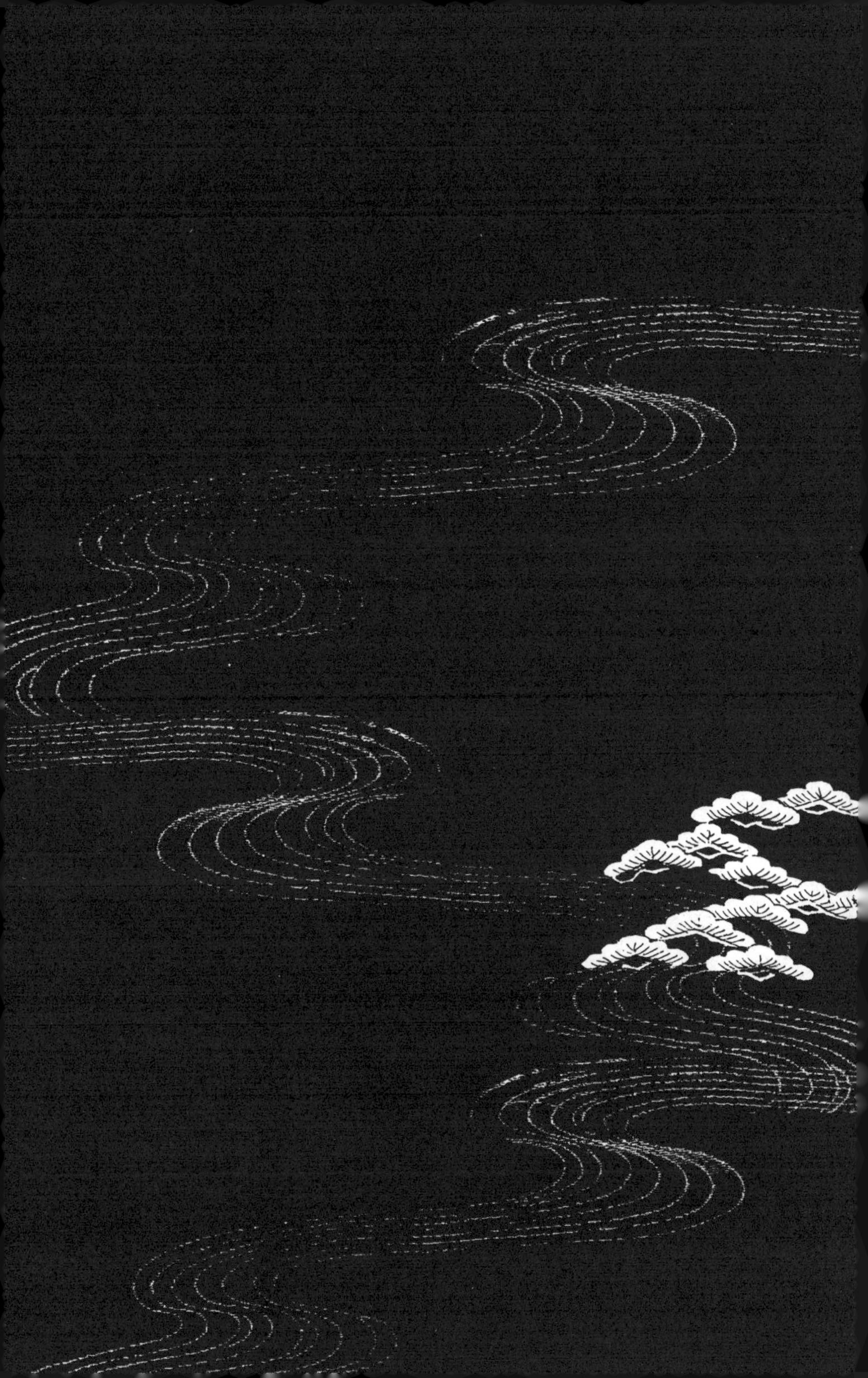

Ōoku

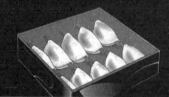

◉ THE INNER CHAMBERS

Ōoku: The Inner Chambers
Vol. 18

VIZ Signature Edition

Story and Art by Fumi Yoshinaga

Translation & Adaptation/Akemi Wegmüller
Touch-up Art & Lettering/Monaliza De Asis
Design/Yukiko Whitley
Editor/Pancha Diaz

Printed in Canada

Published by VIZ Media, LLC
P.O. Box 77010
San Francisco, CA 94107

10 9 8 7 6 5 4 3 2 1
First printing, June 2021

VIZ MEDIA
viz.com

VIZ SIGNATURE
vizsignature.com

THIS IS THE LAST PAGE.

Ōoku: The Inner Chambers has been printed in the original Japanese format in order to preserve the orientation of the original artwork.

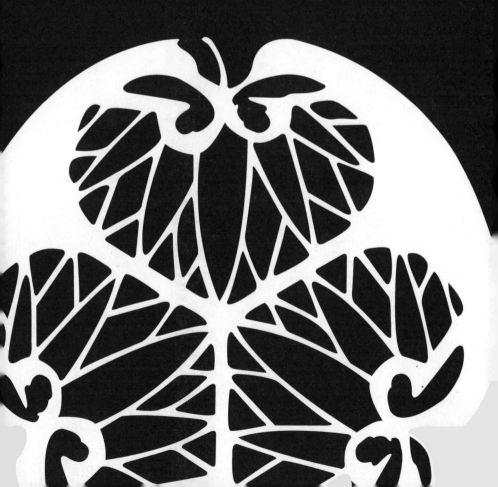